P9-DMU-327

DEALERS OF LIGHTNING

DEALERS

OF

LIGHTNING

Xerox PARC and
the Dawn of the Computer Age

Michael Hiltzik

HARPER

NEW YORK · LONDON · TORONTO · SYDNEY

HARPER

A hardcover edition of this book was published in 1999 by HarperBusiness,
an imprint of HarperCollins Publishers.

DEALERS OF LIGHTNING. Copyright © 1999 by Michael Hiltzik. All rights
reserved. Printed in the United States of America. No part of this book
may be used or reproduced in any manner whatsoever without written permission except in the case of brief quotations embodied in critical articles
and reviews. For information, address HarperCollins Publishers,
195 Broadway, New York, NY 10007.

HarperCollins books may be purchased for educational, business, or sales
promotional use. For information, please e-mail the Special Markets
Department at SPsales@harpercollins.com.

First paperback edition published 2000.

Designed by Jennie Malcolm

The Library of Congress has catalogued the hardcover edition as follows:
Hiltzik, Michael A.
    Dealers of lightning : Xerox PARC and the dawn of the computer age /
Michael Hiltzik. — 1st ed.
        p.   cm.
    Includes index.
    ISBN 0-88730-891-0
    1. Computer science—Research—California—Palo Alto—History.
    2. Xerox Corporation. Palo Alto Research Center—History.   I. Title.
    QA76.27.H55   1999
    004'.0720794'73—dc21   98-47043

ISBN 0-88730-989-5 (pbk.)

18 19 20 ❖/RRD 40 39 38 37 36 35 34 33 32 31

To Deborah, Andrew, and David

Contents

Cast of Characters

Xerox Corporation

Joseph C. Wilson, chief executive officer (1961–1967); chairman (1966–1971)

C. Peter McColough, chief executive officer (1968–1982); chairman (1971–1985)

David T. Kearns, chief executive officer (1982–1990); chairman (1985–1991)

Jacob E. Goldman, chief scientist; founder of PARC

George White, assistant to Goldman

Paul Strassmann, information technology supervisor

Shelby Carter, national sales director

Don Massaro, head of Office Products Division after 1979

The Palo Alto Research Center

ADMINISTRATION

George E. Pake, director (1970–1978); head of Xerox research (1978–1985)

Robert Spinrad, director (1978–1982)

William J. Spencer, director (1982–1985); head of Xerox research
  (1985–)

Richard E. Jones, chief administrative officer

M. Frank Squires, chief personnel officer

Gloria Warner, secretary to Pake

COMPUTER SCIENCE LABORATORY

Jerome I. Elkind, laboratory manager (1971–1978)

Robert W. Taylor, associate manager

Butler W. Lampson, key contributor to the Alto personal computer,
  Ethernet networking system, laser printer, Mesa
  programming language, Dorado computer, Dandelion
  processor

Charles P. Thacker, designer of MAXC time-sharing system and
  Alto and co-inventor of Ethernet

Bob Metcalfe, principal inventor of Ethernet

David Boggs, co-inventor of Ethernet

Dick Shoup, inventor of Superpaint, pioneering video graphic device

Charles Simonyi, developer of Bravo word processing program with
  "what you see is what you get" (WYSIWYG) capability

Peter Deutsch, expert programmer

Ed McCreight, hardware designer of MAXC time-sharing system
  and the Alto

Ed Fiala, co-designer of MAXC

Ron Rider, designer of the research character generator, adjunct to
  the laser printer

John Ellenby, head planner of Futures Day presentation (1977), at
  which PARC technology was introduced to Xerox senior
  management

Charles Geschke, co-developer of Mesa programming language and
  Interpress page description language

John Warnock, co-developer of Interpress and other printing and
  page description systems

Severo Ornstein, supervisor of the Dorado computer project

SYSTEMS SCIENCE LABORATORY

William F. Gunning, manager (1970–1973)

Harold H. Hall, manager (1973–1975), later the first manager of System Development Division, established to commercialize PARC technology

William R. (Bert) Sutherland, manager (1975–1981)

Alan C. Kay, head of the Learning Research Group (LRG), conceptualizer of the "Dynabook" personal computer and Smalltalk programming language

Daniel H. Ingalls, LRG member, developer of "BitBlt" graphic program and principal developer of Smalltalk

Adele Goldberg, LRG member, learning specialist and co-developer of Smalltalk

Ted Kaehler, LRG member, co-developer of Smalltalk and "Twang" music program

Diana Merry, LRG member and co-developer of Smalltalk

Larry Tesler, LRG member, co-designer of Gypsy user-friendly word processing program and first PARC principal scientist to be hired by Apple

John Shoch, LRG member, inventor of the Worm

Tim Mott, co-designer of Gypsy

Chris Jeffers, childhood friend of Kay's and "chief of staff" of LRG

Gary Starkweather, inventor of the laser printer

Lynn Conway, co-developer (with Carver Mead) of VLSI tools and technology allowing the design of highly complex integrated circuits on silicon chips

Douglas Fairbairn, hardware implementer of POLOS and co-designer (with Tesler) of the Notetaker portable computer

Bill English, head of POLOS (PARC On-Line Office System) group, early but unsuccessful multimedia office network

Bill Duvall, chief designer of POLOS

David Liddle, head of System Development Division after 1978, supervisor of the development of the Xerox Star, first fully realized commercial version of a PARC computer

GENERAL SCIENCE LABORATORY

Gerald Lucovsky, associate manager (reporting to Pake)
David Thornburg, scientist
David Biegelsen, scientist

OPTICAL SCIENCE LABORATORY (AFTER 1973):

John C. Urbach, manager

OTHERS:

Max Palevsky, founder of Scientific Data Systems (SDS), sold to
    Xerox in 1969
Rigdon Currie, chief of sales at SDS
Stewart Brand, founder of the *Whole Earth Catalog* and author of
    "Spacewar," 1972 article in *Rolling Stone* that introduced
    PARC to the general public
Carver Mead, California Institute of Technology professor and co-
    developer of VLSI tools and technology at PARC
James Clark, principal inventor of the "Geometry Engine" graphics
    chip at PARC, founder of Silicon Graphics Inc. and
    Netscape Communications Corp.
Wesley Clark, pioneering designer of digital computers and
    consultant to PARC
Steven Jobs, co-founder and chief executive of Apple Computer

Timeline

1969

May: Xerox purchases Scientific Data Systems for $920 million in stock; and its chief scientist, Jack Goldman, submits his proposal for an "Advanced Scientific & Systems Laboratory" to pursue research in computing and solid-state physics.

July: Alan C. Kay's doctoral dissertation, "The Reactive Engine," is accepted at the University of Utah; within it are found the seeds of his "Dynabook" personal computer.

October–December: The ARPANET, precursor to the Internet, becomes formally operational, with four "nodes" up and running.

1970

January: George Pake accepts the job of director of Xerox's new lab and persuades Goldman to locate it in Palo Alto, California, near Stanford University.

April: IBM brings out its first office copier, marking the end of Xerox's historic monopoly and introducing a period of painful retrenchment at Xerox.

July 1: Xerox Palo Alto Research Center officially opens its doors at 3180 Porter Drive. Pake hires Bob Taylor to help him staff the Computer Science Lab.

November 13: Berkeley Computer Company holds its last employee party and shuts its doors. Seven of its most influential engineers, including Butler Lampson, Chuck Thacker, and Peter Deutsch, will sign on to work at PARC.

1971

January: Gary Starkweather is transferred from Rochester to PARC, bringing with him the concept of the laser printer.

January: Journalist Don Hoefler, in a series of articles for the weekly newsletter *Electronics News*, popularizes the term "Silicon Valley."

February: Design work begins on PARC's cloned PDP–10 computer, known as MAXC.

June–August: Kay and a hand-picked team complete the first version of their revolutionary object-oriented programming language, Smalltalk, which will heavily influence such modern programming systems as C++ and Java.

November: Starkweather completes work on the world's first laser computer printer.

1972

June: Bob Metcalfe encounters a technical paper describing Hawaii's ALOHAnet, several principles of which he will incorporate into Ethernet.

September: MAXC having been completed, Thacker and Lampson invite Kay to join their project to build a small personal computer. The machine will be known as the Alto.

November 22: Thacker begins design work on the Alto.

December 7: *Rolling Stone* publishes Stewart Brand's article "Spacewar," sparking months of controversy by its depiction of computer research at PARC.

1973

April: The first Alto becomes operational, displaying an animated image of *Sesame Street*'s Cookie Monster.

April: Dick Shoup's "Superpaint" frame buffer records and stores its first video image, showing Shoup holding a sign reading, "It works, sort of."

May 22: Metcalfe writes a patent memo describing his networking system, using the term "Ethernet" for the first time.

August: Ground is broken for PARC's permanent headquarters at 3333 Coyote Hill Road, Palo Alto.

1974

September–November: Dan Ingalls invents "BitBlt," a display algorithm that will make possible the development of such features of the modern computer interface as overlapping screen windows and pop-up menus.

October: Charles Simonyi completes "Bravo"; Tim Mott and Larry Tesler begin work on "Gypsy." The two programs together represent the world's first user-friendly computer word processing system.

1975

January 1: Xerox establishes the System Development Division, its most comprehensive attempt to commercialize PARC technology. More than five years later, SDD will launch its masterwork, the Xerox Star.

January: The Altair 8800, a hobbyist's personal computer sold as a mail-order kit, is featured on the cover of *Popular Electronics*, enthralling a generation of youthful technology buffs—among them, Bill Gates—with the possibilities of personal computing.

February: PARC engineers demonstrate for their colleagues a graphical user interface for a personal computer, including icons and the first use of pop-up menus, that will develop into the Windows and Macintosh interfaces of today.

March 1: PARC's permanent headquarters at 3333 Coyote Hill Road are formally opened.

1977

January 3: Apple Computer is incorporated by Steve Jobs and Steve Wozniak.

August: Having perfected a new technology for designing high-density computer chips at PARC, Lynn Conway and Carver Mead begin drafting *Introduction to VLSI Systems*, a textbook on the technology that is written and typeset entirely on desktop publishing systems invented at the center.

August 18: Xerox shelves a plan to market the Alto as a commercial project, closing the door to any possibility that the company will be in the vanguard of personal computing.

November 10: "Futures Day" at the Xerox World Conference, Boca Raton, Florida, where personal computers, graphic user interfaces, and other PARC technologies are introduced to a dazzled sales force. Other than the laser printer, however, few will reach market under the Xerox name.

1978

June: The Dorado and Notetaker are completed—the former a high-performance personal computer described as "the best computer PARC ever made"; the latter a suitcase-sized machine that became the forerunner of a generation of portables.

1979

December: Using design principles formulated at PARC, Stanford University professor James Clark designs the "Geometry Engine," the first 3-D computer graphics chip and later the foundation of his company, Silicon Graphics, Inc.

December: Steve Jobs and a team of Apple Computer engineers visit PARC. After witnessing much of its hardware and software in action, they take steps to incorporate it in the design of the Apple Lisa and Macintosh.

1980

September 30: Xerox, Intel, and Digital Equipment jointly issue a formal specification for the Ethernet and make it publicly available for a nominal licensing fee— the first time a PARC invention is released to the world for commercialization. The move makes Ethernet the networking technology of choice.

1981

February: Charles Simonyi joins Microsoft, where he describes himself as "the messenger RNA of the PARC virus."

April 27: Xerox unveils the Star workstation, the commercial offspring of the Alto and other PARC technology, at a Chicago trade show to wide acclaim.

August 24: IBM unveils the Personal Computer, forever altering the commercial landscape of office computing and making the Star obsolete.

1983

May: Apple introduces the Lisa, a personal computer with a graphical interface based on principles developed at PARC.

September 19: Bob Taylor resigns from PARC under pressure. Within a few months many of the center's top computer engineers and scientists will resign in sympathy.

1984

January: Apple introduces the Macintosh, the popular successor to the Lisa and the most influential embodiment of the PARC personal computer, with a striking "1984"-style television commercial during the Super Bowl.

INTRODUCTION

The Time Machine

It was April in California's Santa Clara Valley, a fine time to be changing the world.

Very late one night in 1973 a small group assembled inside the office of an electronics engineer named Charles P. Thacker. The room was located on the ground floor of a low-slung building set upon the crest of a gentle ridge in the foothills of the Santa Cruz range. Pastureland and apricot orchards covered one side of the hill; a spreading growth of industrial laboratories and research facilities dotted the other, so that the ridge itself seemed to mark the divide between the region's agricultural past and its high-technology future. The building housing Thacker's lab, along with two others located in a dale about a half-mile away, encompassed Xerox Corporation's Palo Alto Research Center, known to its small but growing staff as Xerox PARC.

The visitors had come to attend the birth of a computer. Today such an event inevitably would be accompanied by crowds, banners, music, speeches, multimedia shows projected on three-story-high outdoor screens, press releases, media tours, and admiring cover pieces in all the important magazines. Not to mention the smell of money, the unambiguous signal of society's insatiable thirst for any technology promising a smarter, faster, and brighter destiny.

On this occasion there was no such fanfare—a shame, given that the machine Chuck Thacker was about to unveil to his colleagues would help plant the seed of that modern frenzy. There was no smell of money, only the barbed aroma of ozone and solder. None of those present had joined PARC with the thought of becoming rich, anyway. Xerox paid them well enough, a couple of notches over the standard for scientists and engineers possessing their considerable skills. But today's popular image of the computer nerd as incipient high-tech millionaire was nobody's fantasy then. Instead they had been attracted to PARC by the thrill of pioneering. One of them compared it many years later to the sheer joy of making the very first footprints in a field of virgin snow.

Thacker checked a few last electrical connections on his machine, his cigarette smoldering nearby. He was thirty and of medium height, with a squarish build and an unruly cowlick that seemed perpetually to overhang his wily eyes like an awning. Among this group of youthful Ph.D.s he was unusual in possessing merely a bachelor's degree in physics, but their deference to him on questions of engineering was unequivocal. Acknowledging the gifts that had already made him an indispensable participant in the design and construction of two trail-blazing large-scale computers, they paid him the ultimate accolade: Chuck Thacker, they said, was an "engineer's engineer."

Thacker's designs were simple and spare, devoid of the egotism that often spoiled the work of even the best of his fellow professionals. He was a master of parsimony and the sworn enemy of its opposite, which he called "biggerism." In a Thacker schematic one never found a logic gate or a ground wire out of place, and he policed the work of his colleagues so they would meet the same exacting standard. Any engineer who set forth a dubious or dishonest idea in PARC's Computer Science Laboratory, where Thacker worked, was likely to be stopped in his tracks by an explosive *"Bullshit!"* At PARC one found no shortage of big egos and stern judges, but one thing on which all agreed was that once Chuck Thacker pronounced your idea "bullshit," you had best shut up and start shoveling.

It was therefore not surprising that when in 1972 the scientists of PARC conceived a revolutionary kind of digital machine they relied on Thacker to convert the concept into circuitry. The machine he and his hand-picked team built in the course of an amazing few months conformed to specifications never before required of a working computer.

Its most arresting element was its human scale. Where the typical computer of this era was the size of two or three refrigerators standing back to back and wired to many more racks of special-purpose hardware, the "Alto" was to be self-contained and small enough to bark a shin on as you wheeled it under your desk.

The Alto was interactive, which meant instantly responsive to the user's demands. Contemporary computers communicated with their users indirectly, through punch cards or teletypes so slow and awkward that a single bleak exchange of query and response required days to complete. It was like trying to sustain an urgent conversation by Morse Code. But the Alto would communicate with its user via a full-sized TV screen that could display text and images mere nanoseconds after they were typed on a keyboard or drawn with an electronic device.

One more thing: Each Alto was to serve a single individual. This was a revolutionary concept to users whose experience consisted exclusively of sharing the precious resources of university mainframes with hundreds of other users. With the Alto there was to be no waiting in line for a turn to run one's own program. To use a term coined by Alan Kay, the PARC scientist who was one of the machine's principal conceptualizers, the Alto was to be a "personal computer."

Every one of these specifications violated the accepted wisdom of computer science. Computers were big because their hardware circuits took up room. They were slow because they were serving scores or hundreds of users at once. And they were shared because digital technology was so expensive its cost had to be diffused among many users per machine. It was the same rationale by which the airlines covered the cost of aircraft and fuel by transporting 300 passengers at a time in Boeing 747s. One computer per person? To contemporary designers this seemed an act of outrageous profligacy. The computer memory necessary to support a single user would cost nearly ten thousand dollars. Squandering so much money would be like giving every passenger from Boston to San Francisco an individual plane.

But to Thacker and his colleagues such objections missed the point. The Alto aimed to be not a machine of its time, but of the future. Computer memory was horrifically expensive at the moment, true, but it was getting cheaper every week. At the rate prices were falling, the same memory that cost ten grand in 1973 would be available in 1983 for thirty dollars. The governing principle of PARC was that the place existed to give their employer that ten-year head start on the future. They even contrived a shorthand phrase to explain the concept. The Alto, they said, was a time machine.

Thacker had spent much of the Alto design phase working out ways to make things smaller while retaining just enough memory and power to run complex software while simultaneously keeping the display active. In quest of efficiency he lifted tricks and shortcuts from every obscure corner of engineering science. Hardware added mass and slowed the system down, so wherever he could he replaced hard-wired circuits with miniature software programs called "microcode." This allowed him to wring bulk out of the design by jettisoning circuit boards like a balloonist dropping sandbags to gain a few more precious feet of lift. He knew his design was spare; he was just not sure it worked. Now the moment had come to find out.

The Alto's operating software had not yet been written, so its brains resided temporarily in a commercial minicomputer called a Nova, which was cabled to the Alto's back panel like a resuscitator to a comatose patient. A few members of the lab had crafted a sort of animated test pattern by converting several drawings of *Sesame Street*'s Cookie Monster into sequences of digital ones and zeros. Thacker flipped a switch or two and the bitstream flowed over the cables from the Nova into the Alto's own processor and memory. There it was reordered into machine instructions that governed which of the display screen's half-million dots, or "pixels," were to be turned on and which were to be left dark. If it worked properly, this process would produce the series of test images in black outline against a glowing white background.

Everyone's eyes focused on the screen as it flickered to life. Suddenly the pattern appeared. As the group watched, transfixed, Cookie Monster stared back at them, shaggy and bug-eyed, brandishing its goofy grin, flashing upon the screen while holding the letter "C" in one hand and a cookie in the other.

That the image itself stood in absurd counterpoint to the sheer power of the technology did not matter. The message was not in the content, any more than the world-altering significance of the telephone could have been found one century earlier within the literal meaning of the words, "Mr. Watson, come here. I want you."

They understood that just as Alexander Graham Bell's phrase had once been shot from one point to another by electrical impulses harnessed in a brand new way, so had the Cookie Monster been painted onto a phosphorescent screen by an entirely new power: Not drawn by hand, but created via a stream of electrical pulses mapped onto memory chips as digital bits and read out again as a moving image.

To Chuck Thacker the thrill was indescribable. He knew he had done more than create a novelty. He and his colleagues had reduced the computer to human scale and recast its destiny forever. The goofy figure munching its way across the display gave only a hint of what this technology would mean to people ten, twenty, even thirty years in the future. But its course was set. It was as though they had all stepped off a cliff into the void and alighted in a new world, bearing proof that time travel, after all, was real.

In 1973 the companies and individuals later to be identified with the advent of the personal computer were otherwise engaged. IBM was still turning out electric typewriters; Microsoft's Bill Gates was a freshman entering Harvard; and Steve Jobs, the future co-founder of Apple Computer, was a college dropout wandering around India in search of his Zen master.

But the Alto had arrived. Compact and powerful, small enough to fit under a desk and simple enough for children to use, it was truly the world's first personal computer. It was also nearly ten years ahead of its time, for the IBM PC and the Apple Macintosh, the first successful commercial expressions of the ideas PARC brought to fruition in 1973, did not appear until the 1980s were well under way.

Such was the operating standard in the lab where Alto was born. At Xerox PARC, the home of one of the most exceptional teams of inventing talent ever assembled in one place, prodigious feats of invention and engineering sprouted as commonly as daisies in an open field. Legendary names among the computer elite but almost entirely unknown to the general public, PARC's scientists pioneered the technology behind today's most exciting innovations. America and the world are today in the grip of an unprecedented technology craze; very few are aware that most of what drives the frenzy was invented, refined, or perfected at Xerox PARC.

At the moment of PARC's founding, computers were viewed much differently from the way they are now. They were exasperatingly difficult to use, the tools of a cult of professional engineers and designers who seemed to take a perverse pride in making them as obscure and intimidating as the oracles of ancient Greece. (This was, after all, exactly what gave those same engineers and designers their special status.)

The scientists of PARC changed all that. They took it as their credo that the computer must serve the user rather than the other way around. That it must be easy and intuitive to operate. That it must communicate with the user in human terms and on a human scale, even if at supernatural speeds. They were determined to tame the machine just as their ancestors tamed the wild dog and taught him to hunt and stand guard.

At a critical moment when the very science of computing stood at a crossroads, its future uncharted, they transformed the machine from a glorified calculator into the marvel of graphical communication it is today. Its role in modern life was far from preordained when PARC's scientists convened. They charted the course.

Every time you click a mouse on an icon or open overlapping windows on your computer screen today, you are using technology invented at PARC. Compose a document by word processor, and your words reach the display via software invented at PARC. Make the print larger or smaller, replace ordinary typewriter letters with a Braggadocio or Gothic typeface—that's also technology invented at PARC, as is the means by which a keystroke speeds the finished document by cable or infrared link to a laser printer. The laser printer, too, was invented at PARC.

Surf the Internet, send e-mail to a workmate, check your bank account at an ATM equipped with a touch screen, follow the route of a cold front across the Midwest on a TV weather forecaster's animated map: The pathway to the indispensable technology was blazed by PARC. There, too, originated the three-dimensional computer graphics that give life to the dinosaurs of *Jurassic Park* and the inspired playthings of *Toy Story*. How pervasive is PARC's technology in today's desktop computer world? When Apple sued Microsoft in 1988 for stealing the "look and feel" of its Macintosh graphical display to use in Windows, Bill Gates's defense was essentially that *both* companies had stolen it from Xerox.

One of the most unusual and prolific research facilities in history, PARC was originally conceived in much more modest terms—as a research lab for a computer subsidiary Xerox had recently acquired. How it burst those boundaries in the early 1970s to become something more closely resembling a national resource is part of its special mystique. Four factors contributed most to PARC's explosive creativity. One was Xerox's money, a seemingly limitless cascade of cash flowing from its near-monopoly on the office copier. The second was a buyer's market for high-caliber research talent. With the expenses and politics of the Vietnam War cutting into the government's research budget and a nationwide recession exerting the same effect on corporate research, Xerox was one of the rare enterprises in a position to bid for the best scientists and engineers around.

The third factor was the state of computer technology, which stood at a historic inflection point. The old architectures of mainframe computers and time-sharing systems were reaching the limits of traditional technologies, and new ones were just coming into play—semiconductor memories that offered huge gains in speed and economics, for example, and integrated circuits that allowed the science's most far-sighted visionaries to realize their dreams for the first time. Never before or since would computer science be poised to take such great leaps of understanding in so short a period. The intellectual hothouse of PARC was one of the few places on earth employing the creative brainpower to realize them.

The final factor was management. PARC was founded by men whose experience had taught them that the only way to get the best research was to hire the best researchers they could find and leave them unburdened by directives, instructions, or deadlines. For the most part, the computer engineers of PARC were exempt from corporate imperatives to improve Xerox's existing products. They had a different charge: to lead the company into new and uncharted territory.

That Xerox proved only sporadically willing to follow them is one of the ironies of this story. The best-publicized aspect of PARC's history is that its work was ignored by its parent company while earning billions for others. To a certain extent this is true. The scientists' unfettered creativity, not to mention their alien habits of mind and behavior, fomented unrelenting conflict with their stolid parent company. Determined in principle to move into the digital world but yoked in practice to the marketing of the copier machine (and unable to juggle two balls at once), Xerox management regarded PARC's achievements first with bemusement, then uneasiness, and finally hostility. Because Xerox never fully understood the potential value of PARC's technology, it stood frozen on the threshold of new markets while its rivals—including big, lumbering IBM—shot past into the computer age.

Yet this relationship is too easily, and too often, simplified. Legend becomes myth and myth becomes caricature—which soon enough gains a sort of liturgical certitude. PARC today remains a convenient cudgel with which to beat big business in general and Xerox in particular for their myriad sins, including imaginary ones, of corporate myopia and profligacy. Xerox was so indifferent to PARC that it "didn't even patent PARC's innovations," one leading business journal informed its readers not long before this writing—an assertion that would come as a surprise to the team of patent lawyers permanently assigned to PARC, not to mention the center's former scientists whose office walls are still decorated with complimentary plaques engraved with the cover pages of their patents. (As is the case with most corporate employees, the patent rights remained vested with their employer.) Another business journal writes authoritatively that the Alto "failed as a commercial product." In fact, the Alto was designed from the first strictly as a research prototype—no more destined for marketing as a commercial product than was, say, the Mercury space capsule.

Another great myth is that Xerox never earned any money from PARC. The truth is that its revenues from one invention alone, the laser printer, have come to billions of dollars—returning its investment in PARC many times over.

Xerox could certainly have better exploited the manifold new technologies issuing from PARC in its first fifteen years, the period covered in this book. The reasons it failed to do so will be examined in the chronicle ahead. But whether one company, no matter how wise and visionary, could ever have dominated, much less monopolized, technologies as amorphous and Protean as those of digital computing is a wide-open question. What is indisputable is that Xerox did bring together a group of superlatively creative minds at the very moment when they could exert maximal influence on a burgeoning technology, and financed their work with unexampled generosity.

This book is largely an oral history, drawn from the words and recollections of people who were there. Many have moved on to other work, some of it based on their discoveries at PARC and some of it spectacularly lucrative. Almost to a person, however, they remember their years at PARC as the most exciting and fulfilling of their lives.

It should be emphasized that PARC in this period was an exceptionally multifarious place, embracing not only computer technologies but solid-state physics and materials science. Most of the work accomplished at the research center in those latter disciplines lies outside the scope of this book for several reasons. For one thing, the more traditional physical sciences did not offer the same opportunities for extravagant and revolutionary results as computing, at least not at that moment. Nor did the physicists test Xerox's corporate strategy, internal politics, or, indeed, standards of employee behavior with quite the same zest as the computer people. This is not to say the physicists should be wholly deprived of their place in the limelight; in truth, some of the most exhilarating work of PARC's second fifteen years has occurred in the center's physics labs—another testament to its founders' patience and foresight. But because the intellectual ferment of PARC's formative years was concentrated so powerfully in the Computer and Systems Science Labs, I have chosen to focus on them.

In doing so I have strived to give the reader as close to a hallway-level view of PARC as could reasonably be attempted, starting with its birth pangs as a collection of youthful prodigies, through the rapturous years of exploration and discovery, and ending as the members of its first generation disperse to bring their discoveries to the rest of the world. It would be impossible for anyone who did not live through it to paint a truly comprehensive portrait of this period at PARC; even those who were there emerged with conflicting—sometimes wildly conflicting—recollections of the same events. My goal has been to assemble these recollections into a coherent history, and through it to shed light on how a unique convergence of events, personalities, and technologies happened to beget one of the most productive and inventive research centers ever known.

PART I
Prodigies

CHAPTER 1

The Impresario

The photograph shows a handsome man in a checked sport shirt, his boyish face half-obscured by a cloud of pipe smoke. Robert W. Taylor looks amused and slightly out of date, his sandy hair longer than one might wear it today but unfashionably short for the distant time period when the picture was taken by the famous photographer of a trendy magazine. His gaze is fixed on something beyond the camera as though contemplating the future, which would befit the man who brought together perhaps the greatest collection of computer engineering talent ever to work in one place.

On a sunny afternoon in July 1996 the same photograph looked down at a gathering of that same talent in the open-air restaurant of a Northern California winery. There were some changes from when it was first shot, however. This time the picture was blown up bigger than life, and the people celebrating under its amused gaze had aged a quarter-century.

They were there to mark the retirement of Bob Taylor, the unlikely impresario of computer science at Xerox PARC. Among the guests were several of his intellectual mentors, including a few who ranked as genuine Grand Old Men of a young and still-fluid discipline. This group included Wes Clark, an irascible genius of hardware design who started his career when even the smallest computers had to be operated from within their cavernous entrails; and seated not far away, the flinty Douglas C. Engelbart, the uncompromising prophet of multimedia interactivity whose principles of graphical user interfaces and mouse-click navigation were disdained in his own time but have become ubiquitous in ours.

Most of the company, however, consisted of Bob Taylor's chosen people. They were unabashed admirers whose careers he had launched by inviting them to sit beneath his commodious wing. Geniuses, prodigies, owners of doctorates from the leading halls of learning, they lived in the thrall of this psychologist from The University of Texas who stammered frightfully when trying to communicate an abstruse technical point, yet still managed to impart a vision of computing that reigns today on millions of desktops. Many moved on to more splendid achievements and some to astounding wealth. But none ever forgot how profoundly their professional lives were changed when Bob Taylor fixed them with his discerning eye and invited them to enlist in his tiny company of believers.

"As a leader of engineers and scientists he had no equal," said Chuck Thacker, who worked beside him longer than almost anyone else. "If you're looking for the magic, it was him."

Thacker served as the afternoon's master of ceremonies. Under his deft supervision the familiar old Bob Taylor stories got dusted off to be howled over anew. Bob arranging for Dr Pepper, the Texas state drink, to be imported into PARC "by the pallet load and stored in a special locked vault." Bob bombing through the streets of Washington in his Corvette Stingray as though saddled on a wild stallion. Or rigging his Alto to beep out "The Eyes of Texas Are Upon You" whenever he received an e-mail message on PARC's unique internal network. Taylor listened to it all in great good humor from the table of honor, way in the back, dressed in a short-sleeved striped shirt and resplendent cherry-red slacks. But then, nothing ever pleased him more than functioning as the lodestar of the proceedings while pretending to be nothing but an unassuming bystander.

Charles Simonyi, who was a naïve young Hungarian immigrant without a green card when Taylor brought him to PARC in 1972, flew down from Seattle in his own Learjet, one of the perquisites that accrue to a man who moved from PARC to become employee number forty of a small company named Microsoft.

"I remember Bob preparing me to deal with the three most powerful forces of the twentieth century," he said. "One of these was personal distributed computing. The second was the Internet. And the third very powerful force is football."

Appreciative laughter rippled across the floor. Everyone present understood football as an emblem of the darker currents driving Bob Taylor's personality and career. They knew that as a competitor he was an absolutely ruthless creature and that to protect and glorify the work of his group he would blindly trample anyone in the way like a fullback scenting the goal line—be they rivals, superiors, or members of his own circle judged to have fallen prey to heretical thoughts.

Over the years these habits left a trail of roasted relationships. Most of the guests at the retirement lunch were polite enough not to remark openly that the company giving Taylor the gold watch was Digital Equipment Corporation, not Xerox. Or that among the party's conspicuous absentees were George Pake, who had hired him to establish and oversee the computer science laboratory at PARC, and Pake's successor, Bill Spencer, who evicted Taylor from PARC more than a decade later. The common knowledge was that for every guest who owed a career to the guest of honor there existed not a few individuals who had felt the sting of Taylor's rivalry and damned him as one of the most arrogant, elitist, and unprincipled persons on the planet.

The allusions to this discomfiting truth were mostly indirect. At his touch football games, it was recalled, he was always the quarterback. The former PARC engineer Dick Shoup recalled how at softball Taylor would invariably wave all the other infielders off a pop-up. One day Shoup complained, "Bob, the other people came to play, too!"

"But they might miss it!" Taylor snapped. "Don't you want to win?"

Others dropped hints about Bob's genius at "managing down and in," meaning pampering and defending his own team, without explicitly stating the corollary: At managing up and out he was often a disaster. Finally one old colleague put into words what everyone always knew. "It's a lot better to work for Bob," he observed, "than to have Bob working for you."

Most of the pioneers of personal computing in attendance that day had worked for Bob, not the reverse. At PARC for thirteen years he managed a world-class collection of technical virtuosi with the same uncompromising passion as Diaghilev, that impresario of an earlier age, guiding his own troupe of temperamental artists—soothing ruffled feathers here, mediating egotistical outbursts there, sheltering them from enemies, and clearing a psychic space so their talents could reinforce each other to build a whole immeasurably greater than the dazzling parts. No doubt there were times when the task demanded all the reserves of psychological discernment Taylor owned. That is to be expected when one is surrounded by thirty prodigies who are all measurably smarter than oneself (and know it). Yet seldom would any of them think of challenging his ultimate authority. In Bob Taylor's lab you accepted his management, or you cleared out.

How and where Taylor acquired his gift for finding and cultivating the most talented researchers in his field no one ever quite figured out. Part of it was instinct. He might not be able to articulate or even understand all the technical details, but somehow he always knew when a researcher or a project would lead to something important, and how to prepare the ground for that person or project to ripen.

This mysterious quality of leadership was most aptly summed up by Butler Lampson, the only person on the floor who could match Thacker's record of playing time with Bob Taylor. Lampson's intellectual power was such a dominating feature of the Taylor lab that people joked about how it sometimes seemed that Bob Taylor worked for Butler Lampson rather than the other way around. Lampson disabused them of the notion by repeating the great old story about what occurred when he and Thacker were building the first PARC computer. This was a time-sharing machine called MAXC, which was cloned in the astoundingly short span of eighteen months from a leading minicomputer that had taken a major company years to develop (by coincidence, it was Digital Equipment). Taylor kept telling them they ought to be considering an alternative architecture without actually explaining just what alternative he had in mind. It was not until a couple of years later, when they completed work on the Alto, that they realized they had built what he meant them to from the very beginning.

"The master often speaks in somewhat inscrutable fashion," Lampson said to peals of knowing laughter, "with a deeper and more profound interpretation than his humble disciples are able to provide. In retrospect you can really see that the path has been plotted years in advance, and you've been following his footsteps all along."

Not long after that retirement party Taylor invited me to visit him at his home in Woodside, a bedroom community for high-tech executives and entrepreneurs that overlooks Silicon Valley from atop a thickly forested ridge. "Leave plenty of time," he said. "It'll take you a good hour to get here from where you are."

One reaches his home via a steep climb up a hillside to the west of Palo Alto, past the ridgetop thoroughfare known as Skyline Drive. It was terrifying to imagine him careening around those hairpins in his new BMW, the one with the license plate reading THE UDM (for "The Ultimate Driving Machine"). At the front door of a house densely hemmed in by oaks and Douglas firs, Taylor greeted me in slippers. Around us bounded his hyperactive giant poodle, Max. "Down, boy! Go lay down!" Taylor commanded. The dog humored his master for about five seconds before getting up to rampage again, about as tractable as Taylor must have been when confronted with a distasteful injunction from his own bosses.

From his comfortable living room one can peer down through the windows on either side of a pale stone fireplace toward the Hoover Tower of Stanford University, six miles away as the crow flies and eleven by road. PARC is invisible from this vantage point, except perhaps in Taylor's imagination. Divorced, his three sons grown and employed, he lives alone in this aerie and spends a certain amount of time fighting the last war. For him the world is easily divided between the geniuses he employed and those from whom he struggled to protect them.

I asked him to articulate the common theme lurking behind the great innovations achieved under his leadership. These included the ARPANET, the embryonic Internet he conceived and financed as a Pentagon *grantmeister* before joining PARC, and the idea of the personal computer, linked into a local network and equipped with a high-quality interactive display.

He settled back, slippers on the coffee table. "I was never interested in the computer as a mathematical device, but as a communications device," he said, then paused meaningfully, as if to suggest that I would almost have had to live within the military-industrial complex of the 1960s to understand how revolutionary a worldview that was. The history of the digital computer up to then was that of a glorified calculator. A mainframe taking up half the floor of a large office building could run a payroll, balance the books of a billion-dollar corporation, calculate in split seconds the optimum trajectory of an artillery shell or a manned spacecraft aimed at the moon. But it was a mute self-contained machine that received its questions via teletype or stacks of punch cards and delivered its answers in the same way.

"The notion of a human being having to punch holes in lots of cards, keep these cards straight, and then take this deck of what might be hundreds and hundreds of cards to a computer . . . You come back the next day and find out that your program executed up until card 433 and then stopped because you left out a comma. You fix that and this time the program gets to card 4006 and stops because you forgot to punch an O instead of a zero or some other stupid reason. It was bleak."

Taylor perceived the need for something entirely new. "I started talking functionally," he said. He asked himself: Which organ provides the greatest bandwidth in terms of its access to the human brain? Obviously, the eyeball. If one then contemplated how the computer could best communicate with its human operator, the answer suggested itself. "I thought the machine should concentrate its resources on the display."

The computer traditionalists goggled at him. Most were mathematicians or physicists and thus perfectly content to employ calculators the size of cement trucks in quest of the next prime number. In 1968, when he and his mentor, the eminent psychologist J.C.R. Licklider, published an article entitled "The Computer as a Communications Device," the kind of interactive display he was talking about would have consumed memory and processing power worth a million dollars even if limited to the size of a small television screen.

"It took me a couple of years to get them to come around. The designers said, the display? That's crazy, the display is peripheral! I said, No, the display is the entire point!"

The rest of his career would be devoted to making sure they never forgot it.

Bob Taylor was born in 1932. If one quarries his early life for keys to his temperament, two things stand out. One is his family's itinerant lifestyle. His father, the Reverend Raymond Taylor, was a Methodist minister in the West Texas of the Depression at a time when church policy was to relocate its ministers every couple of years. There would be two or three years in Uvalde a couple of hours north of the Mexican border, followed by a few in Victoria, Ozona, or Mercedes, none of these places notable for much except the wrenching poverty of field and ranch hands. Even today this is a region where one out of three residents lives below the poverty line.

This went on until almost the onset of war, when his father took a job teaching philosophy and religion at the Methodist University of San Antonio. The frequent relocations had already left their mark on the boy. "You've got to make a new set of friends and interact with a new set of prejudices every time," he recalled. Living under the spotlight that falls on the local minister's son scarcely made things any easier. "There's the usual number of fights you have to go through to find out where you stand in the pecking order." By the time he was ten Bob Taylor had mastered the skill of establishing his place in the local hierarchy and holding it against all comers.

The second element was something his mother, Audrey, revealed to him at a very early age. He had been adopted as a twenty-eight-day-old infant.

"The first bedtime story I remember being told was about how I had been chosen. Picked out by my mother and father. All the other parents had to take what they got, but I was chosen. That probably gave me an undeserved sense of confidence." He chuckled in a rare moment of self-deprecation. But throughout his adult life few things would be as sacred to Bob Taylor as the process of selection. For him it was almost an anointing. He would be the one doing the choosing, but he expected the select to feel invested with the same confidence he had felt, and the same profound gratitude.

After the war he was ready for college—or rather, not ready at all. There was a short stint at Southern Methodist University ("I majored in campusology") followed by a break for the Korean War, which he spent as a naval reserve officer landlocked at the Dallas Naval Air Station. The G.I. Bill paid for a berth at The University of Texas, where he followed an eccentric course of study for another two years. "One day in 1956 I realized I'd been in school an awfully long time. I walked into the Dean's office to find out what it would take to graduate. They checked and said, 'If you take these two courses you can graduate next semester. Your major will be psychology and you'll have minors in mathematics, English, philosophy, and religion.'" In truth it was not quite as haphazard as that. He stayed long enough to earn a master's in sensory psychology, the study of how the brain receives input from the senses.

The year 1961 found Bob Taylor in Washington, D.C., which he had reached by a circuitous route. After leaving UT he had briefly taught at an experimental boarding school run by a friend outside Orlando, Florida. But the arrival of his second and third children, twin boys, quickly put an end to life as a dormitory housemaster on $3,600 a year. He found a job at Martin Aircraft, which was building the mobile missile system known as Pershing at a nearby plant. A year later he jumped to a better-paying post with a Maryland company designing flight simulators for the military. What caught his attention here was the tremendous power of information delivered interactively. This was a principle everyone understood in the abstract, but got driven home only when they witnessed it in action: You could teach pilots from books and theory until your voice gave out, but find a way to place their hands on a joystick and their eyes on a simulated landscape and it was as though they were learning everything for the first time.

This job also led directly to his next stop. President Kennedy's exhortation to place a man on the moon by the end of the decade had the fledgling National Aeronautics and Space Administration scrounging for management talent wherever it might surface. Taylor, by lucky coincidence, had tried to sell NASA on a research program using one of his simulators to explore a wide variety of sensory inputs. NASA was intrigued by the idea, but even more by its proponent. The agency agreed to fund further work by his company, but only if he joined NASA as the project manager.

Not yet out of his twenties, the rural preacher's son was in the thick of the most important government crash program since the Manhattan Project. He met with the original seven Mercury astronauts, the era's reigning national heroes, and witnessed space shots first-hand. But such thrills soon paled. NASA and the Mercury program might appear the apogee of scientific glamour to a public devouring the polished hagiographies of the seven astronauts in *Life* Magazine, but the truth was less splendid.

"We said we were going to the moon, but we were a hell of a long way from getting there," Taylor recalled. "It was mostly engineering, and sometimes fairly pedestrian engineering. It wasn't science, and I was *much* more interested in science."

Deep down he was looking for a way out. He glimpsed it one day in 1962 when he received an unexpected invitation to an interagency meeting on computer technology. The summons came from the Pentagon, or more specifically from J.C.R. Licklider, an MIT behavioral psychologist who had taken charge of a new program at ARPA, the Defense Department's Advanced Research Projects Agency. Taylor knew Licklider only by his forbidding reputation, which had been forged in the same specialty, psychoacoustics—the study of the psychology of hearing—in which Taylor had done his master's thesis. What he did not anticipate was that Licklider would compliment him on his thesis during their first meeting. "I was thirty in 1962, and he was internationally known," Taylor said. "It floored me that he knew who I was."

In those days ARPA did science, not engineering. Founded in the nationwide panic that followed the Soviet Union's launch of Sputnik in 1957, the agency at first focused almost exclusively on missile physics—specifically, how to bring the United States quickly up to par with the Soviets in shooting projectiles into Earth orbit. By 1962, however, when Licklider was tapped to run a new Information Processing Techniques Office, or IPTO, the urgency had waned. Whatever military orientation ARPA still harbored was visible only as a sort of artifact, as when Licklider discovered by accident that one "cloak-and-dagger" project under his nominal jurisdiction was so highly classified even he was not cleared to know what it was. ("That made me nervous," he admitted later.)

ARPA had refocused itself on civilian research in broad scientific areas, some of them having only tenuous relevance to national security. "I did not feel much pressure to make a military case for anything," Licklider told an interviewer years later. Of course, the Pentagon did expect that the agency's work might serendipitously lead to solutions of some of its technical problems, such as the vexing issue of "command and control": how to employ effectively the immense volume of information generated on a battlefield to manage the armed forces' increasingly elaborate weapons systems.

For years the military had viewed this issue in terms of training the human beings with their fingers on the triggers. Licklider informed his bosses that the real solution lay in making the machine meet the human halfway. This was something he called "man-computer symbiosis," a subject on which he happened to have published a paper two years earlier. Traditionally, problems had to be written and presented to the computer very carefully so the machine would understand every step. One tiny error, and all computation would cease. Try planning a battle under these conditions—you would be obliterated before reaching the second step in the process. But what if the system were designed so the computer was no longer a mute data manipulator, but a participant in a dialogue—

something, he had written in that paper, like "a colleague whose competence supplements your own?"

Nothing like that was possible given the technology of the time, but it could be foreseen. "Every time I had the chance to talk, I said the mission is interactive computing," Licklider said. "I thought, this is going to revolutionize how people think, how things are done." He promptly allocated most of the money in his budget to its pursuit.

Licklider was a tall Midwesterner whose owlish glasses camouflaged a warm and pleasant personality. He loved nothing more than bringing people together and insisted that even new acquaintances address him as "Lick." A few months after joining ARPA he convened his summit of government agencies with computer research projects in their budgets. The group was an august one, encompassing not only ARPA and NASA but the research arms of the Navy, Army, and Air Force; the National Institutes of Health; and the National Science Foundation. When Lick opened the session by describing his own "very modest" program he left no doubt about who stood at the top of the computer funding pyramid. His $14 million budget, which already supported projects at MIT, Berkeley, and Carnegie-Mellon University, was larger than those of all the other agencies *combined*.

Licklider's program launched the golden age of government-funded computing research. Very soon he had established a full stable of academic scholars entitled to come back to his well whenever an appropriate new line of study struck their fancy. And Licklider defined "appropriate" broadly. He understood that computer research differed from traditional sciences like physics and chemistry, which lumbered incrementally from discovery to discovery, building on centuries of theory and experiment in a process that resembled geological accretion. Computing, by contrast, was young and explosive, driven forward as though by a series of pistol shots, every technological innovation inspiring a headlong leap ahead.

His Information Processing Techniques Office accordingly awarded its contracts without any of the bureaucratic paperwork other agencies required. Recalled Wes Clark, who had introduced Licklider to his first digital computer—the Clark-designed TX–2—when they shared an office floor at MIT: "I almost felt as though I was called up from time to time to see if I wouldn't be willing to take another quarter of a million dollars off their hands."

By the time he left IPTO in 1964 to return to MIT, Licklider had set in motion numerous trailblazing projects aimed at making the computer more accessible to the user. Studies in graphics pointed toward new ways of displaying computer-generated information. There were initiatives in computer networking and new programming languages. Systems to reorganize the computer's memory and processing cycles so it might serve many users simultaneously—which was known as time-sharing—brought the per-session cost of building and running these enormous contraptions down to a level that even midsized and small universities could afford.

Lick's successor seemed the perfect man to manage this expanding program. Ivan Sutherland was a brilliant MIT graduate who happened to be serving with the Army as a first lieutenant. Only twenty-six, he had already amassed an enviable research record, the crowning achievement of which had been the development of the first interactive computer graphics program. Known as Sketchpad, the system allowed a user to draw highly detailed and complex drawings directly on a computer's cathode-ray screen using a light pen and store them in memory. Among the bonds uniting Lick and Sutherland was that the latter had designed Sketchpad during a protracted series of half-hour sessions on that very same TX–2 computer.

Licklider left Sutherland with a $15 million budget, a workload that had grown far beyond what a single man could handle, and a suggested deputy: Bob Taylor. At first glance he was a strange choice. Taylor had never taken an advanced course in computing. He would never be able to design hardware or write a software program. But he displayed two qualities Licklider found appealing: an instinctive grasp of the promise of man-computer interaction, and an exceptionally high degree of "people skills." Next to this, Lick and Sutherland figured, his inability to get down among the bits and electrons was scarcely significant. They could not have known that within a few short years Bob Taylor would outshine them both in his influence over computer research in the United States. The humble job of serving as deputy to a first lieutenant with a Pentagon staff appointment was about to set Bob Taylor on the path to his, and the computer's, destiny.

Ivan Sutherland spent scarcely eighteen months at IPTO. Late in 1965 Harvard offered him a tenured position. He was officially gone by June 1966 but unofficially much earlier. By January or February that year Taylor was already running IPTO all by himself.

The apprenticeship had been short, but edifying enough. Taylor rapidly digested such important conventions of Pentagon life as the enormous significance of tiny gradations in rank. One day he learned that his own new assistant, a twenty-three-year-old MIT engineer named Barry Wessler, was to be assigned the humble civilian rank of GS–9. Too low: Taylor concluded the appropriate level would be GS–13. The difference was a trivial one in terms of pay, which was nearly the same for both grades. But Taylor reasoned that the higher rank would guarantee that Wessler got treated by the Pentagon's brass hats as a seasoned professional rather than a greenhorn. This was a distinction certain to return dividends day after day in terms of Wessler's interaction with military officialdom. (Plus there would be the satisfaction of having squeezed Pentagon rules until they squealed.)

As Wessler recalled, "Bob worked by finding out what he couldn't do, and then going for it. He could have gotten me a level or two higher without too much trouble, but GS–13? That was off the scale. But he got it done."

In contrast to the rigid protocol of the brass, ARPA's civilian chiefs left Taylor undisturbed to fashion his program as he chose. What he chose was distinctly an extension of Licklider's. Interactivity, time-sharing, graphics: All of Lick's pet preoccupations became Taylor's. He also shrewdly adjusted Licklider's management style to fit his own extroverted personality. He would visit his grant recipients several times a year, but not solely to hear the researchers' obligatory progress reports. He was engaged in something more like community outreach, developing new teams, nurturing up-and-coming young researchers, cultivating an entire new generation of virtuosi.

Taylor had spent enough time in academia to know that the most interesting intellectual ferment took place well below the stratum of full professor. "Who are your youngest faculty?" he would ask around. "What are their ambitions? Where are the most impressive graduate students?" He tracked down the young prodigies, captivating them with the peculiar charm of a leader who seemed inclined more to listen and encourage than to dictate. An impresario needs a company to put on stage; Taylor, in one sense, was holding auditions. In another, he was reproducing one of the most meaningful moments of his own past. The persons he surrounded himself with would get there not by chance or breeding. They would be chosen, selected . . . adopted.

In his first year as director Taylor organized one of what would become an annual series of nationwide IPTO research conferences. On the surface this filled a troublesome communications vacuum. Here were the top talents in the field of information processing, all working for ARPA on essentially the same problems. Yet most did not know each other except by reputation. He made the conference an annual affair, held each year at some different and gratifyingly "interesting" place. One year winter might find the group skiing at Park City, Utah; the following year would bring them to New Orleans in time for Mardi Gras.

Not that the purpose was chiefly to play. Rather, it was to build a network of people mirroring the one he would soon propose for computers. Lifelong professional and personal bonds were forged at these events. They would start the day with a communal breakfast, followed by several hours of discussion in the morning. They would eat lunch together, then were set free until dinner, another communal affair. The day ended with further colloquia.

The daily discussions unfolded in a pattern that remained peculiar to Taylor's management style for the rest of his career. Each participant got an hour or so to describe his work. Then he would be thrown to the mercy of the assembled court like a flank steak to a pack of ravenous wolves.

"I got them to argue with each other," Taylor recalled with unashamed glee. They went at the intellectual roughhouse with the scientist's unemotional candor, oblivious to everything but the substantiation of truth. "These were people who really cared about their work. They weren't interested in politics, they weren't interested in impressing any-body," Taylor said. "If they thought that something I was saying was dead wrong, they'd just as soon tell me as not. They'd just as soon tell one another as not if they thought *they* were wrong. And in the end these people, all of whom were pretty bright, got to know one another better."

Of course he had another motive in fomenting the intellectual free-for-all. It was the best way he knew of gleaning what they were up to. He could have asked any of his principal investigators to sit him down and explain their work, it was true, but he figured the chances were slim that he would even know the right questions to ask. Better to let his experts challenge each other while he watched, like a platoon leader subjecting his men to the rigors of field maneuvers to see whether they will break, and if so, where. "This way I would get insights about their strengths or weaknesses that otherwise might be hidden from me," he said. "If there were technical weak spots, they would almost always surface under these conditions. It was very, very healthy."

But it was not to be personal. Impugning a man's thinking was accept-able, but never his character. Taylor strived to create a democracy where everyone's ideas were impartially subject to the group's learned demoli-tion, regardless of the proponent's credentials or rank.

The same principle governed the once-a-year ARPA conferences Taylor established for graduate students. Faculty members and even Taylor himself were barred from these meetings. Barry Wessler, not long out of grad school himself, was delegated to supervise, receiving no instructions other than "to get people together and make something happen."

At the first session the group piled on an unfortunate wild man from that backwater, the University of Utah, named Alan Kay. Kay had stepped forth in a public session to pitch his vision of a computer you could hold in your hand. He had already coined a name for it: "Dynabook," a notebook-shaped machine with a display screen and a keyboard you could use to create, edit, and store a very personal sort of literature, music, and art.

"He was crazy," Wessler recalled. "People greeted the whole idea with disbelief and gave him a very tough time. He painted this picture of walking around with a computer under your arm, which we all thought was completely ridiculous."

Taylor, meanwhile, was fully occupied in finding ways to push forward the frontiers of interactive computing. At the time, this meant advancing the technology of time-sharing because there was simply no other way to pay for the enormous computing resources an interactive system demanded.

During his tenure Licklider had steered most ARPA funding to time-sharing projects of a certain majestic scale, such as MIT's vast Multics program, whose aim was to design a system capable of supporting 300 users at once. Taylor encouraged his contractors to embrace smaller-scale projects as well. One of these, an effort at the University of California at Berkeley called Project Genie, was based on the principle that not every university could afford the multimillion-dollar General Electric 645 mainframe Multics required. Instead Genie aimed to design a system for no more than ten or twenty users. If such a small machine could be widely distributed, Taylor reasoned, time-sharing might actually reach many more users than Multics could ever deliver.

Genie's host machine was the SDS 930, which was made by an entrepreneurial three-year-old company in Southern California named Scientific Data Systems and sold for only about $73,000. The 930 was a popular entry in the commercial market, where it was widely admired for its exceptional speed, excellent reliability, and large storage capacity. The Genie team demonstrated that with a nominal amount of new hardware and clever reprogramming the versatile 930 could be turned into a small-scale time-sharing machine. Then they proposed that Taylor arrange for Scientific Data Systems to bring out the modified 930 as a commercial product.

Taylor gave the idea his enthusiastic endorsement. He invited Max Palevsky, the founder and chairman of SDS, to the Pentagon for what ripened into a memorable encounter. Palevsky, offered a government-funded research prototype on a silver platter, turned him down flat.

The forty-two-year-old Palevsky was an executive whose heartfelt confidence in his own business acumen had been reinforced by his company's extraordinary success. (In 1965, the year of his encounter with Taylor, SDS had earned more than $5 million in pre-tax profits.) But Palevsky had no use for time-sharing. SDS made its money selling small- and medium-sized computer systems for a niche market of universities and aerospace firms. To Palevsky the technology of time-sharing appeared too elaborate by half and the commercial market a black hole— even IBM, the bellwether performer in the computer industry, had run aground trying to implement a time-sharing strategy of its own. "It was a very sophisticated scheme," Palevsky recalled, "and I just didn't think there were that many sophisticated customers around."

Equally strong-willed, Taylor and Palevsky conceived an instant mutual antipathy that had them at cross-purposes from the start. Taylor tried to draw Palevsky's attention to a terminal in his office linked directly to the reconfigured SDS 930 chugging away on the other side of the continent. Palevsky had not the slightest interest. Taylor judged Palevsky's knowledge of computing shallow and retrograde. Palevsky grew equally impatient with this government bureaucrat whose technical exuberance clearly outran his commercial sense. Beyond that, he announced that the work done by the vaunted Genie team was "full of holes."

"This thing'll never sell," he said.

Taylor was shaken to the core. For him interactivity was a sacred cause, and for Max Palevsky to stand in its way was intolerable. Taylor felt his old urge rising to establish his primacy in the pecking order. "You're wasting my time," he snarled. "Why don't you get the hell out of here?"

He would always cherish his memory of the day he threw Max Palevsky out of his office. But the issue they had so clumsily debated was not closed. A few minutes later Taylor heard someone knock on his door. It was Rigdon Currie, a courtly Georgian who served as Palevsky's director of sales and marketing. Currie had watched the recent showdown in mounting dismay. One of his responsibilities had been to keep an eye on the Genie team as they transformed the 930. In contrast to his boss, he was deeply impressed by the machine and its commercial potential.

"I think Max is wrong," he said.

"I know he is," Taylor replied. "What are you going to do about it?"

"I think we can turn him around as long as we get people lined up outside his door with money," Currie said. "Could I bring the customers up here to see your terminal?"

"You bet."

In the next few weeks Currie escorted scores of customers up to Taylor's Pentagon quarters and emerged with more than a dozen solid purchase orders. Palevsky had no choice but to capitulate. He authorized the marketing of the Genie machine as the SDS 940 with one stipulation: SDS was to recover all its development costs from the first three sold. As a result, the 940 was priced at $173,000, about $100,000 more than the base 930, although it carried no more than $5,000 in additional hardware.

The machine became one of the best-selling products SDS ever had, eventually accounting for nearly one-third of its sales. It helped turn time-sharing into a commercially viable business. But Palevsky never fully committed his company to the new venture. Right up until the end, the 940 was manufactured not on a dedicated assembly line, but by trucking conventional 930s to a special plant, where they were torn down and the new hardware installed by hand.

Taylor won that battle. But his encounters with Max Palevsky were not over, not by a long shot. A few short years later their destinies would converge again—this time in the aftermath of one of the costliest miscalculations any American corporation has ever made. The corporation was Xerox.

CHAPTER 2

McColough's Folly

New Year's Eve, 1968. From his office on the twenty-eighth floor of Xerox Corporation headquarters in Rochester, New York, Dr. Jacob E. Goldman stared testily out at the filthy weather. Like a prisoner marking off the term of his incarceration on the wall of a cell, he mentally toted up the days since he had seen any trace of the sun.

The number was thirty-one. Since arriving to take up the job of chief scientist at Xerox on the first of December, Jack Goldman had witnessed precipitation in Rochester every single day. He was thoroughly sick of it.

At that inauspicious moment C. Peter McColough, the company's chief executive, walked in to wish him a happy new year.

"Peter," Goldman blurted, "I think I've made a great mistake."

"What's the matter, Jack? Aren't you happy here?"

"Peter, look out the window."

Goldman reminded McColough that he had not even had time to move into a proper house. His car spent every night exposed to the elements outdoors, and every morning he wasted a half-hour scraping ice and snow off the windshield. Recently separated and living alone,

Goldman even found himself nervously pondering how future candidates for his hand might take to Rochester's dismal climate.

McColough had to be disconcerted by his chief scientist's misery, given the trouble he had taken to get Jack Goldman into the corporation. He believed fervently that Xerox, successful as it was, needed to absorb modern technology. The alternative was to risk sinking into oblivion as its products became supplanted by new developments. Hiring Jack Goldman, a visionary technologist and superb judge of research talent at Ford Motor Company, was a critical component of that strategy.

But to make way for the new appointee McColough had first had to dislodge the incumbent chief scientist. This was the aging John H. Dessauer, who had held the post for decades. "McColough thought it was time for Dessauer to step down as the chief technical officer of Xerox, make him emeritus, congratulate him and thank him for everything he's done, and get a hotshot technologist in there in his place," recalled one executive from that period. "Naturally Dessauer was very reluctant to go."

That placed McColough, then the Xerox president, in a delicate spot. Goldman refused to consider Xerox's offer until Dessauer's retirement was assured. As he bluntly told one corporate headhunter in 1966: "Come back when you're prepared to offer me his job." But Dessauer was close to a deity at Xerox. It was he who had inveigled his bosses at modest little Haloid Company into bankrolling the untested duplicating technology of an eccentric inventor named Chester Carlson and shepherded it toward commercialization. He had supervised the design and development of the celebrated Xerox 914 copier, which became the most successful industrial product in history. To put it bluntly, Dessauer was as responsible as any man alive for the fabulous prosperity of what had evolved into Xerox Corporation.

To overcome his recalcitrance McColough finally appealed to the lone individual at Xerox occupying an even higher level of divinity: the venerated chairman and chief executive, Joe Wilson. Wilson fully sympathized with McColough's desire to revitalize Xerox research. At length the two men came up with a plan to simultaneously announce Wilson's own retirement as chief executive (although not as chairman), McColough's promotion to CEO, and, as part of the changing of the guard, Dessauer's retirement as chief scientist. Almost no one personified an American corporation as Joe Wilson did Xerox, most of whose employees had never known another CEO. Dessauer could hardly resist such a self-sacrificing scenario. Grumbling to the end, he finally acquiesced.

After such maneuvering it would not do for Jack Goldman to get balky after a month on the job. On that snowy New Year's Eve McColough thought fast. He decided to mollify his new executive by tipping him to one of the two vital corporate secrets he was at that very moment holding close to his vest.

"Take heart, Jack," he said. "Things are in the offing. Soon you'll be thinking more kindly of the outside environment."

Goldman could not guess what exactly McColough had in mind, but the CEO's portentous manner told him it was something big. In fact, the company was finalizing plans to move its headquarters to Stamford, Connecticut. Given Xerox's stature as a native Rochester institution, this would be momentous news indeed. The relocation would drain the region's faltering economy of hundreds, maybe thousands, of jobs. Wary of a backlash, McColough had no intention of making the decision public until months more of subtle groundwork could be laid. Appeased by the hint that a favorable change was in the air, even if he could not know what it was, Goldman accepted his boss's holiday wishes in a much improved temper.

But it was the other secret, the one McColough failed even to hint at that evening, which would wind up exerting a much more powerful force on Xerox's future—and on Jack Goldman's. In a series of highly confidential talks, McColough had been negotiating for Xerox to acquire a computer company in Southern California. Less than six weeks into the new year he and its chairman would announce a deal worth nearly one billion dollars.

Not divulging this secret to his new chief scientist may have been one of the biggest mistakes of Peter McColough's career. Had he only opened up, Goldman mused later, "I could have led him to knowledgeable people in the computer field. People who would have advised against it."

Seen another way, however, it was fortunate he did not. For Xerox's purchase of Scientific Data Systems—a flagrant miscalculation when considered solely as an act of business strategy—would lead directly to the founding of PARC.

It was not that Goldman opposed the idea of Xerox getting into digital computing. After all, his responsibility as chief scientist was precisely to introduce novel technologies into a company grown narrow-minded and dull. What concerned him was the way it had been handled.

The urge to enter the computer business came from Joe Wilson, who had long expressed apprehension that new technologies might someday render Xerox's image-to-paper monopoly obsolete. "If we're going to be big ten or twenty years out," he once lectured McColough, "we've got to be able to handle information in digital form as well as graphic form."

McColough soon concluded that the best way to join the digital revolution was to buy a piece of it. This effort, however, turned into a long-running comedy. By the end of 1968 there were few computer companies in existence that Xerox had not approached with an acquisition offer. "Peter turned over every rock," recalled one executive who served on numerous corporate task forces over the course of the saga. "He looked at everybody." Honeywell, Burroughs, Sperry, Control Data—every leading manufacturer then competing with the redoubtable IBM rebuffed the overture. The one time Xerox found a company eager to sell, it developed cold feet. That happened when General Electric, which had uncharacteristically made a hash of its time-sharing business, offered the operation to Xerox at a bargain price. But GE appeared too desperate a seller. "They kept increasing the discount and making the terms more favorable," remembered the same executive. "They were trying to give McColough a deal he couldn't refuse. But it was a hopeless proposition. GE had neither technology nor a cutting-edge business, and we turned them down."

At other points there had been mixed signals and missed opportunities. Xerox made an offer to Ken Olsen, the founder and chairman of Digital Equipment Corporation, the young and aggressive company known as DEC. Olsen's answer was a flat refusal. Only years later did General

Georges Doriot, one of DEC's original financiers, inform Goldman that Xerox had approached the wrong person. "Peter was my student at Harvard," he complained. "He should have known you don't approach the president on a matter like this. You talk to the backers."

McColough's wish list eventually dwindled down to a single name: Max Palevsky's Scientific Data Systems, the same company for which Project Genie had built the SDS 940 a few years earlier.

Since bringing out the time-sharing machine SDS had continued to grow amazingly fast. In 1968, the year McColough came knocking, the company booked record profits of $10 million. Yet only someone with McColough's total lack of understanding of the computer industry could delude himself into viewing SDS as Xerox's entrée to a bright digital future. For the glittering numbers obscured some gloomy facts. SDS's success at mining a comfortable niche in scientific computing would not easily transfer to the high-volume business data processing market, the ferociously competitive sector dominated by IBM in which McColough now expected Xerox to play a major role. SDS's core market, meanwhile, was suffering from a serious economic downturn exacerbated by a drying up of government research funding. And there were nagging questions about the company's research capabilities and the depth of its management team.

A relentless salesman, Palevsky glided over such details. Privately considering Xerox management ponderous and unimaginative— textbook monopolists destined to be trampled in a competitive market —he gamely assured McColough that their two companies were "a perfect fit." The high-speed printing technology SDS owned, combined with Xerox's experience in making imaging systems (i.e., copiers) and marketing them to large corporations, would create unique new business products to beard IBM in its own lair, he proclaimed. McColough allowed himself to be persuaded that if Xerox wanted in, it had to move fast. SDS, as he later put it, was "the only ballgame left in town."

Had he inquired within his own organization before straying into Palevsky's lair, he might have been better armed to deal with this master pitchman. Xerox headquarters was equipped with a corps of talented financial experts trained to analyze every major industry. It was a corporate rule that no acquisition could ever be considered until a task force placed the target's books and markets under a microscope and delivered a thoroughly reasoned recommendation to the board.

This time, however, McColough unwisely left the experts at home. It may have been out of an excess of caution: A run Xerox had made at SDS five years earlier had collapsed amid rumors that a Xerox executive had illicitly bought SDS stock in anticipation of the takeover. For whatever reason, under conditions of extreme secrecy and with virtually no backup he met with Palevsky in El Segundo, the industrial hamlet where the modern SDS complex nestled against the boundary line of Los Angeles International Airport, to "dicker about price." Which side had the upper hand was, in retrospect, crystal clear. McColough, Palevsky recalled later, "was determined to make a deal." The meetings, he said, "were very, very short. Two half-days were all it took."

On Monday, February 10, 1969, the two of them announced that Xerox, in the largest transaction it had ever undertaken and one of the largest in American corporate history up to that time, would buy Scientific Data Systems for more than $920 million. McColough's one-man initiative stunned the investment community. For one thing, he proposed to pay Palevsky in Xerox shares. It was true that the stock was a high-flying favorite on Wall Street—trading at $269 a share, it was cheap currency indeed to spend on an acquisition. But that did not mean it could not be squandered. Xerox would have to issue nearly 3.5 million new shares to pay for the deal. Max Palevsky would be transformed into Xerox's single largest stockholder in one giant step. Plus he was to be awarded seats on the board of directors for himself, his venture banker Arthur Rock, and two trusted lieutenants.

This for a company that had never made more than $10 million in a single year. IBM itself traded for less than half the purchase premium McColough had agreed to pay for a company with one-hundredth of its market share. If things did not pick up at SDS, Xerox's investment would not be paid off for 92 years.

Concerns surfaced immediately that Xerox was buying an empty shell in its desperation to get into the computer business. Top managers were already leaving SDS in droves, many of them retiring on what they had made from the rise in its stock price over the previous few years. Palevsky himself had openly announced his intention to withdraw from day-to-day management as soon as possible. On the job he was prone to distraction, a dabbler in politics, movies, the peace movement. There was reason to question whether anyone would be left to mind the store.

Back at headquarters Jack Goldman was as shocked by the SDS deal as everybody else. "I was the head of research for the company," he said, "but I wasn't consulted. At all."

He was willing to forgive the slight as the price of being a newcomer, but only up to a point. For his opinion to be overlooked on a major technology venture tasted disagreeably of Xerox's traditional conception of research: fine in its place, but irrelevant to anything as important as strategic planning.

From what Goldman could tell, this attitude pervaded the company, to its misfortune. It affected even the kind of research being done at Xerox's main technical laboratory, a vast installation spread over the Rochester suburb of Webster. At Ford, Goldman's biggest budgetary headache had been finding money for all the computers the engineers and scientists demanded for their labs, not to mention the outside experts imported by the platoon to help them exploit the new technology in designing cars.

Nothing of the kind ever occurred at Xerox research. The Webster engineering and research staff treated the new science of computer-aided design with utter indifference. Webster's classically educated chemists, physicists, and metallurgists devoted their attention to narrow, product-oriented tasks, trying to develop better toners and photoreceptors to drop into copiers designed the same old way. As far as that went they were talented enough, but they had no incentive to keep up with new research techniques. As for applying imagination to an entirely new science, concept, or machine, Webster was hopeless. It was not research as Jack Goldman understood the word; it was product development, which was something very different.

"Real research people tend to interact with the world at large," he observed. "They know what's happening on the university campuses and get invited back and forth, so they become an avenue through which you can attract new ideas into the company. Research is a funnel through which you can bring in people who normally won't talk to the guys down in the trenches designing equipment," he said. Xerox had not been getting new ideas, and it showed. By allowing its researchers to isolate themselves the company had become as musty as a sealed tomb.

Goldman had only agreed to join Xerox because he saw a glimmer of hope in McColough's forward-looking determination. The gentlemanly Canadian-born executive had lured Goldman away from Ford by pledging to place corporate research on an entirely new footing. Goldman may have felt somewhat out of place at headquarters—short, rotund, and profane, quick-witted and sharp-tongued, and educated at Yeshiva University, he certainly made a contrast to the patrician, Ivy-Leaguish executives that commercial success had attracted the Xerox management cadre. But McColough had promised that as chief scientist he would have the authority to conduct research from the bottom up, following wherever science led him, rather than top-down, which only served the interests of the company's old guard. That made the offer hard to resist.

Now Goldman found his confidence shaken. Acquiring a computer manufacturer could have helped inject a new attitude into a Xerox that had devolved from a nimble, innovative risk-taker into a creaking giant. But SDS was not that kind of acquisition. He was appalled at its intellectual conservatism. SDS computers were good enough in their own market, he confided to his colleague George White, but their day had passed. No one would mistake them any longer for leading-edge. "He felt those guys down there in El Segundo were just a bunch of dumbbell copycats as far as technology was concerned," White recalled. "They were never going to be first on anything that mattered."

Yet they might serve a subtler purpose. As the SDS purchase moved toward a shareholder vote at the corporate annual meeting in June, Jack Goldman contemplated how to snatch a new opportunity for Xerox from what was already being labeled "Peter McColough's Folly."

McColough fought Wall Street's doubts about SDS with all the rhetoric a corporate chief executive could muster. His waning prestige made it an uphill battle. A year or so earlier he had disgruntled the investment community with an equally headstrong—and unsuccessful—takeover bid for the financial services company CIT. This new transaction revived complaints about his "golf-course" deal-making, a label he detested. SDS was a successful company with its best years still ahead, he asserted. "It had been making profits every year. The growth record was great. The profitability record was great. So we made a deal."

His arguments only incited more skepticism. The growth prospects in SDS's main lines of business were meager, not great, according to industry analysts whose ardor for the transaction continued to cool. Finally, at a luncheon meeting of New York securities analysts, McColough laid out a grandiloquent vision. It was wrong to look at SDS and Xerox as separate companies, he said. His idea was for SDS to help Xerox expand its rule over the office copier market into the domination of a greater universe— "the office of the future." The Xerox to come, he declared emphatically, would control "the architecture of information."

The phrase was classic CEO-speak, grave, tendentious, and nebulous enough to be perfectly consistent with any strategy Xerox chose to pursue. McColough later attributed the wording to his speechwriter. Yet for the next decade it would hang in the air like an persistent echo. The architecture of information: The phrase might as well have been chiseled over the doors of the hilltop palace Xerox would soon build to house a group of employees quite unlike any others the company had ever placed on its payroll.

"It was a great phrase," one PARC engineer said later, "because nobody knew exactly what it meant. So there were quite a few interesting things you could do and simply cite that as the justification."

In May the shareholders, accepting on faith McColough's hazy vision of the future, approved the acquisition of SDS for a final price of $918 million in stock. Xerox owned its computer company. Now it needed to figure out what to do with it.

That is where Jack Goldman stepped in. Six weeks after the annual meeting he delivered to McColough a twenty-one-page proposal, complete with staffing charts and pro-forma budgets looking ahead five years, for a dynamic new scientific facility.

The SDS purchase had given him a peg on which to hang the proposal. On the surface the rationale for the so-called "Xerox Advanced Scientific & Systems Laboratory" was to fortify the new subsidiary's weak research capability. But from that foundation Goldman was intent on building a much larger edifice. Cannily recognizing that Xerox yearned to be ranked alongside such paragons of industrial muscle as IBM and AT&T, he sketched out a corporate research center engaged in basic science independent of any existing product group, exactly like IBM's fabled Yorktown Heights research center and AT&T's Bell Laboratories. About half the staff would be devoted to advanced physics and materials research, and the rest to the new sciences of systems and computing.

"He was talking about a first-class research facility," one Webster staff executive of the time recalled later. "Something that would become known worldwide by attracting top scientists doing fundamental research, and maybe winning a Nobel Prize or two."

Goldman therefore associated the lab not only with the immediate needs of SDS but more vaguely with "Xerox's long-range interests." The staff would be assigned "to establish scientific preeminence in those disciplines that appear relevant or likely to become relevant." Even if computer science demanded the lion's share of attention, Goldman warned that Xerox must learn to expect the unexpected. "The use of computers has developed at least as fast as anticipated, but not in the manner anticipated by most prognosticators." Overall, while encouraging his superiors to believe the new lab sprang logically from Xerox's existing business strategy, he subtly built a case for using basic research to identify new, unanticipated opportunities.

Goldman had often been reproached at Ford for lacking a refined sense of business or commerce. (He never tired of telling the story of how Henry Ford II, witnessing a demonstration of some remarkable but impractical new technology, remarked: "Not much of your stuff gets on a car, does it, Jack?") He would later face the same criticism at Xerox. Yet his memo glimpsed where computing might lead the company. Among other things, Goldman recognized—significantly ahead of many others in the field—that software would soon outstrip hardware as the driving force of innovation. More important, he saw that it would be the key to Xerox's ability to profit from the computer's ability to drive a high-tech printer.

"Xerox should be the one to revolutionize certain printing functions with a machine which is half xerographic printer and half computing machine," he wrote, thus anticipating by more than ten years the product with which Xerox would most profitably commercialize the work of PARC: the laser printer. He also accurately forecast burgeoning opportunities in education and graphics long before the hardware existed to run anything even faintly resembling a commercial system.

Yet it is also evident that Goldman did not fully appreciate the hazards of creating a laboratory almost entirely divorced from the needs of Xerox's existing businesses. Who could have foreseen the abyss that would alienate one tiny group of sequestered and privileged theoreticians from the thousands of ordinary engineers who faced relentless deadlines to get product out the door? Or perhaps he was merely being disingenuous when he wrote of a systems science laboratory that would "develop rapport with the entire company."

Goldman proposed an ambitious growth plan for the corporate lab. It would open with twenty-five to thirty researchers and a budget of less than $1 million, but equal Webster's size within about four years with a staff of 300 housed in a seven-million-dollar facility. The operating budget, he forecast, would plateau at about $6 million a year in 1969 dollars. (The figure turned out to be short by a factor of five.)

As for the new lab's location, he recommended New Haven, which offered Yale University's "intellectual night life" as a lure for prospective recruits as well as proximity to the new corporate seat in Stamford. "If the new research center is too isolated from Xerox environment and Xerox thinking, the chances of relevant coupling to Xerox's needs and practices will be severely diminished," he wrote prophetically. "On the other hand, a site near corporate headquarters has very much to offer in terms of coupling to the full range of future as well as present business interests of Xerox."

The liberal and enterprising Peter McColough was thoroughly enchanted by the notion of a corporate research hermitage. His enthusiasm, however, was not unanimously shared in the top reaches of the company. At the board meeting at which Goldman presented his plans for the new lab, strident opposition arose from an unexpected source: the new board members from SDS.

Max Palevsky balked violently at the idea of dissipating five or six million dollars a year on pie-in-the-sky research. He thought McColough and Goldman were approaching a serious financial commitment like dilettantes and that their motives were irrelevant to real corporate goals. "The memory I carried away was the number of times IBM came up in the discussions about the research center," he recalled later. "It was corporate conspicuous consumption. I never got the feeling that the people at Xerox understood that something like this didn't pay unless you really did basic research like IBM—treat it as a big undertaking that would need years to give you any return." If Xerox was serious about computer research, he groused, why not simply give the money to SDS? Then the computer division would be able to develop a new version of its Sigma series computer, which had been brought out to supplant the aging 930.

Goldman was disgusted. He replied that the best way to serve SDS interests was to mount an independent, far-reaching effort in basic research, not by financing incremental upgrades for an aging product. "They were the people who could best profit from the research lab, and they were completely disinterested," he said later.

In any event, McColough had the necessary authority to green-light the new lab on his own. He had brought Goldman into the meeting as a courtesy to the board, not as a bid for votes. As for the SDS faction, "Peter didn't pay too much attention to their objections, bless his soul," Goldman recalled. "But as a matter of record he did not require nor did he ask for board approval."

To Goldman he gave his blessing to establish Xerox's second full-scale research laboratory on a site to be determined, with the understanding that it was not to outshine in manpower or budget the proud Webster research park outside Rochester. Goldman shrugged at this solitary caveat. According to his master plan, the two labs would be pointed in entirely different directions. Still, there was no question with which one his heart lay. With seed money in his pocket, he set off to build Xerox a shrine to a new science.

CHAPTER 3

The House on Porter Drive

In May 1969, about the time Xerox shareholders voted to approve the purchase of SDS, the provost of Washington University in St. Louis was reaching the end of his rope.

The academic year just ending had been the most trying of George E. Pake's career. The 1960s were not easy on anyone in a college administration, but Pake felt that unrest on his own normally placid liberal arts campus had reached a high-water mark during the previous semester. A group of protesting students had occupied the chancellor's office. Someone tossed a Molotov cocktail into the ROTC Quonset hut and burned it to the ground. Pake spent the year contending with all sorts of reactionary trustees and alumni who, he recalled, "wondered why we didn't just fire the students and keep the faculty." As spring drew to a close, he said, "I was a case of battle fatigue."

In a more peaceful era Pake would have seemed the ideal college administrator. Narrow-shouldered and retiring, he possessed a clipped and slightly distracted manner of speaking that reinforced his donnish air. But this diffidence was deceptive. When the faculty got fractious he could dig in his heels and hold his ground, especially when called upon to uphold his standards of academic propriety. Fairness, he insisted, was the key. No administrator of a large academic institution could possibly know enough to mediate every issue purely on academic or scholastic grounds. The trick in refereeing among powerful faculty with their overdeveloped intellects and underdeveloped social graces was to remain unyieldingly impartial. When all else fails, split everything down the middle.

This was a skill he had tried to hone in the years since he had come to St. Louis from Stanford, where he had held a physics professorship. Washington University had installed a dynamic new chancellor determined to enhance its reputation as a first-class academic institution, and Pake had accepted his call to join the crusade as a senior administrator. At first the change fed his idealism. He imagined himself promoting the social benefits of higher education in ways that would be closed to him if he remained merely a teacher and laboratory researcher. But by the spring of 1969, when he was next in line to succeed that chancellor, he had also become profoundly disillusioned.

"I hadn't visualized myself as running a command post in a military operation," he said. "I knew I did not want to be a candidate for chancellor, not to lead that goldfish-bowl kind of life. My wife would have hated it."

So that fall he returned to teaching. On Thanksgiving weekend, just as he was finally reacclimating to the milieu of classroom and chalkboard, he got a phone call from his old friend Jack Goldman.

"George," Goldman said, "I got a proposition for you."

Jack Goldman's relationship with George Pake dated back twenty-five years to when they had worked together on wartime projects at Westinghouse Research Laboratory, Goldman as a senior fellow and Pake as a Westinghouse undergraduate scholar.

After the war Goldman remained in industry while Pake moved on to Harvard for his doctorate. But they kept track of each other's careers within the insular community of working physicists. Just as he was starting his search for a director for his new research center, Goldman heard that Ford had offered his former job to Pake, and that Pake had turned it down.

Goldman guessed Pake's reasoning had something to do with Ford's erratic commitment to basic research. "I figured I could make a better case for Xerox than Ford could make for Ford," he recalled. After a speaking engagement in Chicago he swung down to St. Louis in Xerox's new Sabreliner corporate jet (his favorite mode of transportation). "I met Pake at the airport, invited him aboard the company plane, gave him a couple of drinks and proposed that he join up."

In truth, Goldman's pitch was more focused than this breezy description suggests. From the airport the two of them repaired to a nearby hotel, where Goldman spent the better part of a day spinning a seductive vision of computer research conducted in a pristine setting with Xerox's copious cash. "We're talking real money, George," he said, showing him the growth plan for a lab that would employ 300 professionals within four years.

Pake hesitated, wondering about Xerox's resolve over the long haul. "I had a lot of friends at other industrial research establishments and the usual thing they were worried about was the feast-or-famine effect," he said later. "You know, in the good business years the company invests in research, but in the bad years they want to pull out." That was a recipe for wasting millions of dollars. "Research is a steady-state thing. You can't just turn it on and off."

Goldman tried his best to be reassuring. He reminded Pake that in 1944 the Haloid Company had offered Chester Carlson research support when no other corporation would. Carlson had scarcely anything to demonstrate the potential of his invention other than a tiny scrap of paper on which he had duplicated his own scrawled "10–22–38 Astoria"—the date and place of his first successful xerographic copy. The company that was now Xerox had invested in that improbable invention for fifteen years before the first Model 914 came off the production line in 1959 and made its fortune. Long-range research? Was there an enterprise anywhere in the land that understood it better than Xerox?

"Yes, but it seems to me the corporation has got it backwards," Pake replied. "If you're going into the computer business, you should have got the researchers first to help you identify the right corporation to buy."

"Unfortunately," Goldman said, "it's too late for that."

Pake ended the meeting insisting how deeply he enjoyed the life of a college professor in St. Louis, but he was beginning to crack. Before

Jack Goldman reboarded his plane he extracted Pake's agreement to visit Rochester and Stamford to meet Peter McColough and the chairman, Joe Wilson. If anyone could charm his wavering quarry into joining the company, they could.

"When I went back I asked Peter McColough why he wanted to start a new research center," Pake recalled later. "I said, 'You've got a research center here that has developed xerography. To build a new one you'll have to have a new research library and new research machine shop and all the other things. Lot of fixed costs you have to duplicate. Wouldn't it be easier to expand the laboratory in Rochester?'

"McColough turned to me—and I remember this conversation very well, it's indelible in my memory. He said, 'George, I think these people here in Rochester have had a heady success with xerography. But I'm not sure they're adaptable enough to take on new and different technologies. If we're going to bring new technologies into Xerox it would be better to do it in a whole new setting.'"

McColough's reply might have come directly from the Jack Goldman playbook. Despite himself, Pake was utterly taken with McColough and Wilson and deeply flattered by their apparent willingness to place him in charge of a multimillion-dollar corporate asset after only one interview, especially since he told them he would expect to be held to a liberal standard of success.

"I said if you hire me you will get nothing of business value in five years," he recalled. "But if you don't have something of value in ten years, then you'll know you've hired the wrong guy."

Pake understood that managing a research center devoted to finding a common ground between his first love, physics, and the intriguing new field of digital computing was a once-in-a-lifetime opportunity. In comparison, the charm of closing out one's teaching career in the Midwest seemed meager indeed. Just after New Year's Day 1970, he telephoned Jack Goldman to accept the job.

The first order of business was to find a site.

Goldman's plan to locate the lab in New Haven had collapsed even before Pake came aboard. Yale, as it turned out, was afflicted by a strain of that old malady known as the town-gown syndrome more virulent than Goldman had suspected. The university, it was true, was famous for the snobbery of its faculty, but he was still shocked at its unfriendliness to enterprises located outside the grimy stone campus walls. Faced with the prospect of being shut off from the very resources for which he sought an academic setting in the first place, Goldman decided to look elsewhere.

Several other possibilities were culled early. These included Webster, where Goldman feared his new lab would come under the intellectual domination of the copier bureaucracy still entrenched in Rochester. Also rejected were Princeton; Stony Brook on Long Island, where the State University of New York was building a new campus; and several other East Coast sites that were either too far from an established Xerox facility or lacked the cachet Goldman craved for his would-be Bell Labs.

Pake directed Goldman's attention westward. Teaching at Stanford in the early 1960s had given him a glimpse of the phenomenon that would shortly make the Santa Clara peninsula famous as "Silicon Valley." A few weeks after signing on, he proposed that Goldman charter the company plane for a California excursion. Ardent corporate wayfarer that he was, Goldman agreed with alacrity. Soon he and Pake were working their way south from Berkeley to San Diego, stopping at every major university campus in search of the ideal spot.

But at Berkeley there was no available real estate to support a corporate research facility. At Santa Barbara, where a new state university campus was sprouting on the dazzling coastline, there was real estate but no major airport. "Oxnard . . . dismal," Pake recalled. "Pasadena . . . Smog was terrible. Xerox had a division called Electro-Optical Systems there with a fairly big site but it was not something that could interact with Caltech—too industrial. So we didn't see anything very encouraging."

That suited his purposes fine. For the whirlwind tour on which he led Goldman was mostly window dressing. Pake's primary objective was Stanford and its vibrant home town, Palo Alto. Goldman had initially ruled out the site for lack of any nearby Xerox facility, but Pake goaded him to reconsider. He knew from experience that the university was anxious to develop strong relationships with the industrial enterprises springing up like anthills all over the valley. Then there was the salubrious physical and cultural climate—not a trivial consideration if one hoped to attract gifted researchers to an embryonic lab.

As for Goldman's objection that Palo Alto was too far from any Xerox property, Pake countered with a neat equivocation: Let proximity mean being close enough to reach a Xerox facility in time for lunch. SDS was in Los Angeles, an hour's flight from the Bay Area. Anyone could leave Palo Alto in the morning, lunch at SDS, and get home in time for dinner. And was not the original rationale for the lab to be SDS's research support?

"That's a very interesting thought," Goldman said, bowing to the inevitable.° In early March, Pake invested his first two staff members, a pair of administrative officials from the Webster research division named Richard E. Jones and M. Frank Squires, with the task of flying to Palo Alto and finding a building suitable to rent.

"Nobody at Webster wanted the job," Rick Jones chuckled, remembering how he became PARC's first official employee. "I was the administrative manager at research and development in Webster. Everyone else had kids in school in Rochester and I only had a nine-month-old son. I had married a Rochester girl in 1966, but when I said, 'How about leaving Rochester and moving to California?' she said, 'Sure.'" Squires was similarly unencumbered by a growing family, having only recently mustered out of the service, so Jones tapped him as personnel manager.

On their first reconnaissance trip they found that cutbacks in government and military research spending had left plenty of vacant research facilities to choose from. In a couple of days they visited thirteen empty locations before settling on one in a development known as Stanford Industrial Park. This was a compound of one- and two-story buildings occupying a parcel of land the cash-strapped university had decided to

---

°He also acceded to Pake's repudiation of the designation "Advanced Scientific and Systems Lab," the name the lab bore in Goldman's original proposal, in favor of the bucolic-sounding "PARC." As Goldman acknowledged later, "The acronym of the former would have invited ridicule."

lease out to small businesses. It was located just beyond the campus boundary, in a dale surrounded by orchards and horse pastures where the grass had turned brown in the dry peninsular spring. Its main street, Porter Drive, meandered in gentle curves among the squat industrial buildings before disappearing over a low hill.

About halfway down Porter stood a two-building complex that had been vacant since the Encyclopedia Britannica moved out a couple of years before. Facing the street was a cinderblock building windowless on two sides and with a concrete floor sturdy enough to support heavy lab equipment. Behind it was a somewhat larger structure that presented an exterior of floor-to-ceiling plate glass to the bright California sun. Trailing behind the rental agent, they stepped inside, disturbing a layer of dust and filth that seemed to have remained untrammeled since the beginning of time. A musty stench pervaded the air. The floor, littered with pieces of crumbled ceiling tile, traced a large square around an interior courtyard adorned with one lonely olive tree. Squires and Jones contemplated the squalor, which was illuminated by a few dim rays of sunlight straggling in through streaks in the windows. The place needed work. But every other site they inspected would have needed more. And at a total of 25,000 square feet, the two buildings together were the roomiest they had seen. They gave the real estate agent a handshake deal and flew home to Rochester to pack up.

In mid-May Jones returned with his wife and infant son as Pake's advance guard. He temporarily parked his family a mile or two from the site at Rickey's Hyatt House, a motel on El Camino Real that would serve as a transitional home for scores of PARC recruits over the next dozen years. After picking up the keys to his new workplace from the rental agent, he headed over to the property. As he coasted up the long driveway he could make out a stranger peering through one of the big windows.

"Can I help you?" Jones asked.

"I must be lost," the man replied. "Do you know where there's a Xerox research facility around here?"

"You're at it," Jones said.

"Really?" An expression of grave doubt passed over the stranger's face. He introduced himself as Frank Galeener, a newly graduated Ph.D. from Purdue who had been hired as a materials scientist in the new physics lab.

"Oh, right, I recognize your name," Jones said. "But you're not supposed to start for a couple of weeks."

"No . . . I was in the area and thought I'd stop by and see what it looked like." He cast another anxious look through the window at the debris-strewn interior.

"We're not set up just yet," Jones hastily reassured him. "But don't worry. It's going to be great."

"Thank goodness," Galeener said. "For a minute there I thought I'd made a terrible mistake."

Jones, Squires, and Gloria Warner, a senior secretary who relocated from Webster to work for Pake, spent the next week working like charwomen. With brooms, buckets, and mops purchased from the nearest K Mart, they swept up the accumulated filth themselves and installed a rickety table and chairs in the clearing. A day or two later a man showed up from Pacific Bell to install the first telephone and a van arrived from Webster with a load of surplus oscilloscopes and other castoff equipment that Jones had redeemed from the Webster storage sheds. By the time Pake arrived on June 30 a local contractor had been in to fashion a few office cubicles and a large library space out of the bare interior. The next day Xerox's Palo Alto Research Center officially opened for business at 3180 Porter Drive.

Pake had also been busy. While closing out his final semester's teaching obligations at Washington, he wrestled with the challenge of getting up to speed on the science of digital computing. He felt like an old dog trying to learn new tricks. "I was starting from scratch," he said. "I had to ask around to find out who are the good people, what are the big issues and so on. But I did worry because I was not a computer scientist."

He did, however, know one person who boasted a first-rate familiarity with the Young Turks of the new discipline: Bob Taylor.

Pake had met Taylor in 1964, back when Washington University undertook an unusual rescue operation for Wes Clark, the MIT computer pioneer. Among Clark's idiosyncrasies was a visceral antipathy to the concept of time-sharing. ("I'm one of the oldest continuing floating objectors in the business," he once told an interviewer.) Time-sharing, he believed, encouraged institutions like universities to lust after grander and costlier machines that were by their nature inefficient for the small-scale work students and professors typically did. Their only virtue was that they could be paid off by overcharging every user for his or her time-slice of the entire behemoth, no matter how much of it the user actually employed. Thus was computing rendered more remote and intimidating than ever—a backwards trend exemplified in Clark's view by the archetypal system at MIT: "That of a very large International Business Machine in a tightly sealed Computation Center: The computer not as *tool*, but as *demigod*." What Clark found even more troubling was that subdividing the main processor, as time-sharing did, rendered impossible the sort of display-based research that Ivan Sutherland had achieved so spectacularly on the TX–2. No user of a time-shared computer could ever monopolize the processor long enough to drive a coherent visual display as Sutherland had. (Clark allowed the TX–2 to be shared, but only serially—you signed up for a block of time on it, but during that period the entire machine was yours.) Time-sharers were limited to communicating with their machines via teletype, because the sluggish rate at which people typed was what gave the system the necessary opportunities to shift its attention from one customer to another between keystrokes.

Clark thought computer science would be better served by jumping directly to single-user machines, even if that meant temporarily making do with underpowered computers. "He would talk about how it was not going to be too many years before we would have a computer you could hold in your hand," recalled Severo Ornstein, a PARC engineer who was one of Clark's longtime associates. "At that time computers were filling buildings larger than this one—a single computer. But he said, 'Yeah, you'll just paint 'em on your desk, just like that.' So a lot of us felt that time-sharing was an enormous waste."

Starting in 1962 Clark underscored his conviction by designing and building the legendary "LINC." (Its name stood for "Laboratory Instrument Computer" but echoed the name of its birthplace, MIT's Lincoln Lab.) The LINC was unique for its time in that it could be operated by a single user from a desk-sized console, although its processor and memory were housed in a wardrobe-sized unit typically concealed in a nearby closet. Designed specifically to serve biomedical research rather than as a general-purpose machine—which helped keep it compact—the LINC "was the first machine that you could take apart and put in the back of your car, carry somewhere else, put back together again, and it would run," Ornstein recalled. "That idea had never previously seemed conceivable."

But the machine was almost too fascinating. It attracted the interest of the National Institutes of Health, which in 1964 offered MIT the unprecedented sum of $37 million to establish around the LINC an inter-university program of computer-aided biomedical research. The scent of money attracted MIT's academic mandarins to a project they had previously relegated to the fringes of the research departments, which Clark preferred anyway. He did not relish seeing his own program coming under the academic establishment's thumb. Obstreperous to the last, he flatly refused to cooperate, forcing the exasperated university to abruptly withdraw its support for the entire venture.

For the next few weeks Clark frantically canvassed the country to find a new home for the machine and the dozen junior researchers whose livelihoods and careers depended on it. Washington University, which was trying to build both a medical school and a digital computing program, saw opportunity in MIT's pique, not to mention the chance to turn the tables on a big East Coast institution by raiding *it* for a change. A few days before his scheduled eviction from Lincoln Lab, Clark looked up from his desk. A stranger in spectacles was standing in the office, stammering out a transparent story about "just happening" to be passing through Cambridge en route to an engagement in Woods Hole. It was George Pake, come to check Clark out on the recommendation of a mutual friend. Before returning to St. Louis a few days later, he agreed to give Clark's project a permanent home at Washington University, where it was to obtain further funding through one Bob Taylor, at ARPA.

Pake and Taylor each came away from this initial interaction favorably disposed toward the other. Pake was impressed by Taylor's excellent contacts within the computing fraternity and his apparent authority to disburse millions of dollars with a minimum of fuss. (Formally speaking, Taylor was still Ivan Sutherland's deputy at the time.) Taylor saw Pake as a pragmatic administrator capable of cutting through red tape to assist a program and a researcher he valued highly. They obviously could have had no inkling of how, within a few short years, their lives would intertwine as colleagues and adversaries.

Before the two would have a chance to meet again Taylor's capacious net would come to embrace areas of computer research that barely existed when ARPA delivered its lifesaving shot to Wes Clark's project. At ARPA he funded the country's first full-fledged graduate degree programs in computer science at Stanford, Carnegie-Mellon, and MIT. Some fields of study virtually owed their existence to his largesse. Among them was computer graphics, which came to life at the University of Utah when Dave Evans, a devout Mormon who had led the Genie team building the time-sharing SDS 940 at UC Berkeley, called Taylor to say his alma mater had invited him to return to Salt Lake to start a computer program. How about an ARPA project, he asked, to get it going?

Computer graphics was then attracting almost no one's attention, for the simple reason that most computers lacked visual displays of any kind. If Evans was willing to start such a program in the backwater of Utah, where it could develop in pristine isolation from the traditionalist thinking elsewhere, Taylor was all for it. The venture turned out better than anyone could have expected. The program Taylor funded partially as a personal experiment and partially as a favor to an old friend evolved into a world leader in computer graphics research.

His most enduring legacy, however, was not a university program but a leap of intuition that tied together everything else he had done. This was the ARPANET, the precursor of today's Internet.

Taylor's original model of a nationwide computer network grew out of his observation that time-sharing was starting to promote the formation of a sort of nationwide computing brotherhood (at this time very few members were women). Whether they were at MIT, Stanford, or UCLA, researchers were all looking for answers to the same general questions. "These people began to know one another, share a lot of information, and ask of one another, 'How do I use this? Where do I find that?'" Taylor recalled. "It was really phenomenal to see this computer become a medium that stimulated the formation of a human community."

There was still a long way to go before reaching that ideal, however. The community was less like a nation than a swarm of tribal hamlets, often mutually unintelligible or even mutually hostile. Design differences among their machines kept many groups digitally isolated from the others. The risk was that each institution would develop its own unique and insular culture, like related species of birds evolving independently on islands in a vast uncharted sea. Pondering how to bind them into a larger whole, Taylor sought a way for all groups to interact via their computers, each island community enjoying constant access to the others' machines as though they all lived on one contiguous virtual continent.

This concept would develop into the ARPANET. The idea owed something to Licklider, who had earlier proposed what he dryly called an "intergalactic network" of mainframes. During his time at ARPA the notion remained theoretical, however; it was hard enough to get small-scale time-sharing systems to run individually, much less in concert with one another. But Taylor judged that the technology had now progressed far enough to make the concept practical. He did not deceive himself: Building such a system meant overcoming prodigious obstacles. On the other hand, ARPA's generous umbrella sheltered hundreds of scientists and engineers whose prodigious talents, he reasoned, were fully up to the challenge.

One day in February 1966 Taylor knocked at the office of ARPA's director, the Austrian-born physicist Charles Herzfeld, armed with little more than this vague notion of a digital web connecting bands of time-sharers around the country. At any other agency he would have been expected to produce reams of documentation rationalizing the program and projecting its costs out to the next millennium; not ARPA. "I had no formal proposals for the ARPANET," he recounted later. "I just decided that we were going to build a network that would connect these interactive communities into a larger community in such a way that a user of one community could connect to a distant community as though that user were on his own local system."

After listening politely for a short time, Herzfeld interrupted Taylor's rambling presentation. He had followed his young associate's theoretical research closely enough to know already the gist of his ideas. All he had was a question.

"How much money do you need to get it off the ground?"

"I'd say about a million dollars or so, just to start getting organized."

"You've got it," Herzfeld said.

"That," Taylor remembered years later of the meeting at which the Internet was born, "was literally a twenty-minute conversation."

Actually getting the program underway required some further maneuvering, Taylor-style. His candidate for program manager, a twenty-nine-year-old MIT researcher named Lawrence G. Roberts, refused to leave his secure and intellectually rewarding post at Lincoln Lab despite Taylor's relentless wheedling. After seven or eight months, Taylor was desperate to resolve the standoff.

"Do we still support fifty-one percent of Lincoln Lab?" he asked Herzfeld, who confirmed the figure. Taylor asked Herzfeld to put in a call to Lincoln's director. "Tell him that it's in Lincoln Lab's and ARPA's best interests to tell Larry Roberts to come down and do this." Within two weeks, Roberts accepted a job that would eventually secure him a permanent place in the computing Pantheon, as the Internet's founding engineer. As Taylor later crowed: "I blackmailed Larry Roberts into fame!"

But by 1969 Bob Taylor was feeling burned out. He had spent more than four years at ARPA's Information Processing Technologies Office, nearly three of those as director. His annual research budget of $30 million had become the single most important force in U.S. computer research. But the research agency was changing around him. The inescapable catalyst was Vietnam.

In 1967 the war had reached into the comfortable civilian enclosure of ARPA and touched Taylor personally. The Johnson White House had appealed for help with a logistical nightmare that had nothing to do with materiel or troop deployment. The issue was information. The Vietnam military command, it seemed, had got itself bogged down in a statistical quagmire. "There were discrepancies in the reporting coming back from Vietnam to the White House about enemy killed, supplies captured, bullets on hand, logistics reports of various kinds," Taylor recalled. "The Army had one reporting system; the Navy had another; the Marine Corps had another."

Unsurprisingly, this system produced ludicrous results. Estimates of enemy casualties exceeded the known population of North Vietnam, while the reported quantities of captured sugar reached levels equivalent to three-quarters of the world supply. "It was ridiculous. Out of frustration the White House turned to the Secretary of Defense to clean this mess up. The Secretary of Defense turned to ARPA, because ARPA was a quick-response kind of agency. The director of ARPA asked me to go out to Vietnam and see whether or not any kind of computer technology could bring at least some semblance of agreement, if not sanity, to this whole process."

Joined by his assistant, Barry Wessler, and three Pentagon-based representatives from the Army, Navy, and Air Force, Taylor made several trips to the war zone. The situation was even worse than he expected. The military was literally drowning in information. Data flowed into depots and never flowed out. Pilots returning from missions would get debriefed their reports entered on punch cards; then their co-pilots would get debriefed and *their* reports recorded. But no one did anything with the information, which piled up without anyone bothering to figure out how or even why these reports should be collated and organized.

Taylor assigned technical teams to the trouble spots to straighten out the chaos, although not without meeting resistance. Occasionally some base commander would refuse to grant ARPA's civilian analysts access to his precious cache of useless data, at which point Taylor, who traveled on government business as a one-star general, would be forced to step in and pull rank.

Taylor and his group solved the military's problem, after a fashion. They installed a master computer at the U.S. military command headquarters at Ton Son Nhut Air Base and made it the lone repository of all data. "After that the White House got a single report rather than several," Taylor remarked. "Whether the data were any more correct or not I don't know, but at least it was more consistent."

But the experience left him feeling increasingly uneasy about his role at the Pentagon. "My first trip out to Vietnam I was thinking, 'Well, we're doing a good thing for these oppressed people. We're out here to clean this mess up.' But by the second or third trip I realized this is a civil war and I didn't want to have much to do with it. Nor did I think my country should have anything to do with it."°

Adding to his frustration was the war's increasing toll on ARPA. For most of the decade the agency's civilian character had insulated it from the deepening rifts within the military establishment. But as the war encroached more and more, the agency had to fight for resources. By the close of the 1960s the Pentagon had slashed ARPA's budget to half of what it had been at mid-decade.

The agency faced mounting political troubles, too. The notion that any arm of the Pentagon could engage in wholly innocent and purely civilian research incited mistrust across the country. As a defensive measure, ARPA started to shed its civilian entanglements and consciously remake itself into what the nation thought it was anyway—an arm of the war machine. When the Caltech engineer Eberhardt Rechtin succeeded Herzfeld as director in 1967, he assured his congressional overseers he would nudge ARPA toward "mission-oriented" objectives—programs aimed at satisfying chiefly military goals. The 1969 Mansfield Amend-

---

°Perhaps he was also put off by the effect American morals and money were having on the bucolic country. Wessler recalled an incident one evening when he and Taylor were being relentlessly importuned by two Vietnamese prostitutes at the bar of their Saigon hotel. One pressed herself with particular vigor on Taylor, who kept turning her away with the excuse that as a mere government employee he could never meet her price. As the two men were leaving, the second prostitute stopped Wessler. "My friend would like to sleep with your friend," she said. "Would you please arrange it?" Wessler solemnly shook his head. "I do a lot of things for Bob Taylor," he replied. "But I *don't* do that."

ment to the military appropriations bill would formalize the trend, directing the Pentagon henceforth to fund only projects of obvious military relevance. As if to underscore the point, the amendment changed ARPA's name to DARPA, the *Defense* Advanced Research Projects Agency.

Taylor beheld the emasculation of government research with frank alarm. "Most of the time I was there ARPA was going for projects with an order-of-magnitude impact on the state of the science," he reflected. "We had made a decision that we would not go for incremental things. But as soon as you get mission orientation you're focusing on very narrow objectives."

He felt it was the right time to leave. He had held his job longer than both his predecessors combined. The ARPANET was securely launched under Larry Roberts's unwavering eye. In September the network's first four nodes—at UCLA, Stanford Research Institute, the University of California at Santa Barbara, and the University of Utah—went operational. Taylor accepted an invitation from Dave Evans to help Utah undertake a research coordination effort of conveniently vague scope. In late 1969 he left Washington for good and headed for Salt Lake City. He was still there a year later when George Pake tracked him down.

"I heard through the grapevine that he wasn't altogether happy at Utah," Pake recalled. This was certainly the prevailing opinion among Taylor's friends, who found it hard to imagine him careening through the stolid precincts of Salt Lake in his blue Corvette. On campus his recommendations to cancel some programs and merge others together caused, he freely admitted, "some dissatisfaction." Clearly Dave Evans had done him a favor by facilitating his departure from Washington. But beyond that, Bob Taylor was marking time.

Pake's purpose in inviting Taylor to Palo Alto was to pick his brains rather than offer him a job (although he did not rule out the latter possibility). He had been unable to solve his most pressing administrative problem: identifying the best researchers in the computing field. It was one thing to compile a list of the country's best computer science programs—the same few names kept coming up, including Berkeley, MIT, Carnegie-Mellon, and Stanford—but quite another to appraise the individual talents within, or to know which projects pointed toward progress and which were intellectual cul-de-sacs. Pake recognized that Taylor's job for five productive years had involved making exactly those sorts of judgments.

A few days later Taylor was ushered into Pake's office on Porter Drive. There were two men in the room other than his host—Frank Squires, the personnel chief, and Bill Gunning, a pleasant and unassuming engineer with twenty years' experience in analog and digital electronics who had been appointed manager of PARC's Systems Science Lab.

"They sat me down and Pake said, 'We bought a computer company,'" Taylor recalled. "I said, 'Yeah, that's too bad. You bought the wrong one.' I told them that SDS wasn't interested in interactive computing, and that's what I'd be doing." Without humility he proceeded to summarize how he believed SDS and Max Palevsky had gone astray, the memory of his bitter encounter with the computer magnate (then still a Xerox director) apparently still fresh. As his hosts listened patiently, he outlined his vision of a future in which interactive computers harnessed to nationwide networks enhanced the communication of human to human.

Pake, for one, took his caustic critique of SDS in stride. He had already encountered the people in El Segundo and largely agreed with Taylor's assessment. The lecture on distributed personal computing was a different matter. No one in the room valued Bob Taylor as an important theoretician and his digression elicited only their mental shrugs. "We were interested in him not because of any vision he had of distributed computing," recalled Squires, "but because of the people he knew—and that meant every significant computer scientist in the United States."

When the meeting ended they were sure they needed him on board. He was equally certain his plain talk had ensured he would never hear from them again. "I left thinking, 'I don't want them and they don't want me,'" he said. Therefore he was all the more surprised when Pake called him a few days later in Salt Lake.

"I want you to come help build the computer lab," he said.

Pake's offer sounded straightforward enough, but there were oddly ambivalent feelings on both sides. Taylor understood that the titular head of the PARC computer lab would have to spend most of his time "attending to matters with corporate types and educating Pake," rather than directly supervising research. This was a job he considered out of his competence and disinclined to learn. Fortunately enough, it was not exactly what Pake had in mind, either.

The job, he told Taylor, would involve recruiting an entire laboratory staff—including his own boss. Taylor would be hired in an associate management position, but Pake took pains to warn him that on paper he was underqualified even for that and would have to prove himself before advancing.

"I didn't exactly say to him, 'You don't have the right research credentials for the job I'm about to offer you,'" Pake recalled. "What I did say was: 'Bob, it seems to me that what you need to do is to develop real research credentials if you want to go on. Why don't you come into this laboratory as associate manager and help me recruit its manager, your boss, and undertake a research program that would develop these credentials for you?'"

What he meant, of course, was chiefly that Taylor lacked a respectable Ph.D. In Pake's hard science universe, where researchers laid their bricks upon foundations that had been built as long as three centuries earlier, a doctorate was a certificate of genuine originality and achievement. That was not true in the fledgling science of computing, which was erecting its own academic foundation as it went along. Nor did Pake's viewpoint apply very well to Taylor's unique abilities as a master motivator of top research talent, which could never be encompassed within the rubric of any advanced university degree. In the coming years this absurd yet unspoken issue of Taylor's nonexistent Ph.D. would help poison the two men's relationship. It would never cease to color Pake's assessment of Taylor's abilities, which only added to Taylor's belligerence toward the Ph.D.-laden physicists who he viewed as sucking down half of the PARC budget as members of the "General Science Lab." He was determined to prove that his ragtag bunch of engineering gunslingers could out-research any credentialed physicist in town, and he would never let an opportunity pass without reiterating the challenge.

For the moment, however, enraptured by the chance to finally realize his own vision of computing with a hand-picked team, he tried to ignore Pake's condescension. He and his protégés had encountered these quaint prejudices of "hard science" bureaucrats on every university campus. All he asked to be spelled out was Pake's understanding that Xerox's cherished "office of the future" would embrace networking and interactive computers. Pake agreed without devoting much thought to what those terms implied.

Shortly after arriving in Palo Alto to take up his new responsibilities, Taylor found a more direct way to explain himself. Walking down the hall one day he noticed Pake's secretary, Gloria Warner, showing off her new IBM Selectric typewriter. With its distinctive golf ball-shaped striking mechanism, this machine was the most elegant and popular piece of office equipment of the time. Taylor stepped up and tapped it with his finger.

"You know," he said, "we're going to make this thing obsolete."

CHAPTER 4

Utopia

D avid Biegelsen's first impression of PARC almost made him sick to his stomach.

A freshly minted physics Ph.D. from Washington University, Biegelsen had been personally recruited by George Pake in March 1970, when the Porter Drive building was still a littered and empty shell. It had been cleaned up but not filled up by September, when he and his wife arrived to lay eyes on California for the first time. The remodelers had been in, partitioning off the space in the big building so that both sides of the square corridor were lined with (mostly vacant) offices, but the first thing Biegelsen noticed when he walked into the building was its sunlit interior courtyard.

"The atrium had an olive tree in it and not much else," he remembered. "But the ground underneath was just covered with olives. I thought, 'Wow, this is California, the food is just lying there on the ground!' I picked one up and put it in my mouth and just about died from the acidity in it. Later I spent hours in the library trying to find out how to cure the things."

That was a fair enough introduction to the virtues and challenges of this mysterious place, so new that everyone's first task was deciding what to do with their freedom. For Biegelsen there was a bittersweet and slightly frightening aspect to the empty offices and the clean slate. It was the trepidation sensed by any pioneer in the split second before he takes his very first step into the unknown.

"Here I was fresh out of graduate school and I didn't have the vaguest idea of what I was to do. I was groping through the insecurity of trying to find something really worthy of this job. But the area was so beautiful, so lush and green, and there was this mixture of wonderful good luck of this really great job and the need to make something happen."

Over the next few months the arrival of more young scientists like himself lent the glass-walled building on Porter a deceptively bustling air. In fact, the staffing proceeded slowly, by design. Although the announcement of PARC's founding had brought in more than 900 resumes in the first few weeks, Pake and Squires took their time making offers. Government funding cuts and the dire economics of the aerospace and defense industries, they figured, were sure to produce a robust supply of gifted candidates. Pake was especially cautious, his ambitions fixed on assembling a cadre of exceptional scientists capable of winning Xerox a Nobel Prize, as Bell Labs had already won two for AT&T.* At its six-month anniversary on New Year's Day 1971, PARC's staff, including administrators and secretaries, still numbered only twenty-three.

The languid pace of recruitment left plenty of time for the ceremonies that often accompany the launch of new corporate ventures. PARC was formally dedicated at a dinner in October by none other than Peter McColough, who happened to be in California peddling an issue of Xerox bonds to West Coast investors.

Pake was delighted to show off his fledgling research center and its minuscule staff. Jack Goldman flew in for the occasion and invitations were dispatched to such Silicon Valley luminaries as Bill Hewlett, the cofounder of Hewlett-Packard, and Stanford President Richard Lyman. Rick Jones ordered a catered dinner and rented extra tables and chairs.

---

*As of 1970. In the subsequent decade Bell Labs scientists won two more.

Then a freak heat wave struck and the temperature settled at a humid 95 degrees.

This meant trouble. The one system not yet operational on Porter Drive was the air conditioning. Envisioning a hundred guests dozing through the ritual speeches and keeling over into their fancy hors d'oeuvres, Jones hastily equipped a couple of workmen with ladders and water hoses and instructed them to cool off the roof while he sped down to San Jose to rent a few big floor fans.

By the time the guests arrived that evening, the building was cool enough for Silicon Valley's founding generation of high-tech entrepreneurs to mingle comfortably with the freshman class of PARC scientists in the harmony of shared knowledge and ambition. But as the guests moved to the buffet, something made Jones glance up at the ceiling, where a dark stain was spreading among the tiles directly over the buffet table. "My God," he said to himself, "they forgot to turn off the hoses!" He bolted upstairs to stanch the flow of water while several intrepid guests bore the tables, laden with expensive delicacies, to safety—just before the compromised ceiling started to drip.

Finally the groaning boards were relocated under a dry area and, disaster averted, Goldman and Pake made their welcoming speeches. A beaming Peter McColough basked in his newfound reputation as an enlightened technological leader. For the rest of his administration he would think fondly of PARC as one of his finest achievements and Xerox's crown jewel. It was not an opinion all his successors would share.

By the end of 1970, long before PARC reached its full complement of staff, Pake established its long-term organizational structure by subdividing the center into three distinct units. The Computer Science Laboratory had Taylor as acting manager over five scientists, including Jim Curry and Robert Flegal, a pair of graphics specialists he brought along from Utah. The Systems Science Laboratory (SSL), also with five professionals, had been placed temporarily under the management of a reluctant Bill Gunning, who had accepted the job as a stopgap but was anxious to return to hands-on research (a more willing research manager would not be recruited for another two years). The third leg of the structure was the General Science Lab (GSL), the solid-state physics branch nominally headed by Pake. GSL employed four scientists, one of whom, an ex-Webster physicist named Gerald Lucovsky, served under Pake as GSL's associate manager.

This structure mirrored Pake's determination to set the new science of computing and the classical science of physics on equal footings, which he believed would encourage the two sides to intermingle. Even if this dream would never be realized, the optimistic structure endured through the next decade with only minor changes, as when Pake severed the Optical Science Lab from SSL to give its work on laser printing and optical memory technology greater status.

Pake also established by the close of 1970 a full research agenda. In a corporate memo dated January 4, 1971, he outlined an ambitious program for his group of twenty-three, augmented by another eight or ten professionals due to start work over the following few months. The Systems Science Lab was to take over development of a laser-driven computer printer whose inventor, a Webster engineer, had come west after failing to interest his bosses in its potential. SSL researchers would also investigate optical memories, a technology that would eventually give rise to today's compact disc and CD-ROM, and speech recognition by computer. Taylor's Computer Science Lab was to pursue his pet interest in graphics while developing specifications for a basic center-wide computer system. And GSL was assigned studies in solid-state technologies, including the electrical and optical qualities of crystals.

Pake warned his superiors that under the projected growth curve the Porter Drive complex, which at the time housed everyone comfortably, would certainly burst its seams by the close of 1971. He was too upbeat. In the first weeks of the year Xerox headquarters knocked the staffing projections flat by imposing a company-wide hiring freeze.

Xerox at that moment was a company in siege mode. Its pattern of consistently rising earnings, virtually unbroken since the introduction of the 914, was cracking. The year just ended had brought a general economic slowdown and, consequently, cutbacks in capital spending by its biggest customers. More troubling, 1970 had also marked the end of Xerox's monopoly over the copier market. In April IBM had brought out its first office copier. It was a slow, clunky machine that could scarcely match the Xerox line for speed and reliability. But with one of the great names of American industrial muscle behind it, the new entry cast a very menacing shadow.

Meanwhile, Xerox's patent was about to expire on its selenium-alloy photoreceptor, the material that lined a revolving drum inside every copier. The selenium was a critical element of xerography. Its electrostatic charge was neutralized by light and preserved by shadow in a way that mirrored the image of a page to be copied. Particles of toner stuck to the charged regions of the drum, which corresponded to dark marks on the original, and could then be transferred to a fresh page to reproduce the image. Although numerous other parts of the process—notably the composition of the toner itself—were still protected by patents or by corporate secrecy, the expiration of the selenium patent demolished one key barrier preventing interlopers from playing in Xerox's private preserve. IBM used a different process, but others were sure to take advantage of this technological bonus. Eastman Kodak, the company's Rochester-based big brother, was already known to be working on a rival machine. More ominously, halfway around the world, teams of American, German, and Japanese engineers were developing a small tabletop copier, ultimately to be marketed in the United States as the Savin 750. By offering high-speed office duplication to the millions of mid-sized and small customers Xerox had always ignored, the Savin would threaten the company's very survival.

These events kicked off what corporate historians dubbed Xerox's "lost decade." The 1970s, a period of conspicuous creativity at PARC, would be better remembered at headquarters as an era of shriveling market share, financial stagnation, and unceasing litigation over patent and antitrust claims. Presaging the coming storm, the company had missed its revenue and profit targets for November and December 1970. The panicked Stamford headquarters, no longer under the control of the engineers and sales executives of Joe Wilson's era but of accountants and financial engineers, moved rapidly to rein in spending.

The danger to PARC in this period was even graver than a simple hold on new hiring. Few of its tiny staff ever knew how close the research center came to being exterminated before it even reached puberty. For among the cost-cutting steps the finance-minded executives proposed to the board of directors was the closure or sale of the new Palo Alto facility. There did not seem to be anything to lose or much point in carrying on: The fixed investment was still negligible; the buildings leased; the value to Xerox still conjectural. (Had not Pake warned them not to expect a return for at least five years?)

But at the last minute one director stood up to interpose his incontestable authority before the hangman. John Bardeen was a towering figure of scientific research, perhaps the most accomplished engineer of his time. In 1971 he already had one Nobel Prize under his belt, for co-inventing the transistor at Bell Labs with William Brittain and William Schockley. (Another would follow in 1972, for his contributions to the theory of superconductivity.)

Bardeen crisply informed his fellow directors of his opinion that divesting PARC would be an irresponsibly shortsighted act. Its budget was $1.7 million, barely a flyspeck on the bottom line. By contrast, its potential was limitless. "This is the most promising thing you've got," he said (as Jack Goldman, also a board member, nodded silent and relieved assent). "Keep it!" The center was saved.

While that small drama played itself out in Stamford, PARC's first few recruits got to know each other amid rented furniture and vacant offices. In time the administrative divisions Pake established would congeal into battle lines of contentious perspectives and personalities, but that was still far in the future. "We were all intermingled with each other, so it wasn't as if one group was in one part of a building and the systems people were in another part and the computer people were in another part," recalled David Thornburg, who slid in just under the wire of the hiring freeze and arrived for work shortly after New Year's Day as employee number twenty-five. "We were a small enough group so everyone knew everyone else."

For a glittering instant it seemed as though PARC might fulfill Pake's dream of a utopia where physicists and computer scientists communed in quest of a common science. They mixed freely in PARC's small yet somehow all-encompassing world, a place full of possibilities and mysterious conjunctions. Thornburg was still unpacking his things on his very first day when Biegelsen, who on the strength of his three months' tenure already ranked as a seasoned PARC veteran, showed up at his office door.

"I just came to introduce you to your next-door neighbor," Biegelsen said, leading Thornburg into the adjoining warren. "This is George. I thought you guys should get together because you shared a similar research interest in grad school."

Thornburg was perplexed. He understood George to be working on speech recognition and he had come in as a thin-film metallurgist.

"Really?" the neighbor asked. "What did you do your work in?"

That was all the voluble Thornburg needed to set off on a thorough explication of his doctoral career, not excepting the time he had to change themes in midcourse thanks to the preemptive publication of a thesis on the same subject by a guy from Oregon named George White.

"I'm pleased to meet you," his neighbor said, smiling. "I'm George White."

What particularly delighted the new staff was the atmosphere of determined informality and lack of pretension. That PARC seemed more like a university department than a corporate research facility was unsurprising, given that most of the staff were being exposed to the nonacademic world virtually for the first time in their lives. Since all but two of the principal scientists (John Urbach, an optical expert from Webster, and Lucovsky) were newcomers to Xerox, Pake and Jones took to sending them on field trips to Rochester, Webster, El Segundo, and the Electro-Optical Systems division in Pasadena, just to give them some feeling for the corporate culture. But the center of their existence remained the two buildings on Porter Drive.

"We would get together once a week and just sort of share what was going on in the lab," Thornburg recalled. "It became almost a quasi-social event." PARC was so new that no one had been issued security badges or company identification. With scant equipment of any value on the premises, the building stayed unlocked and hospitable to outsiders. "We were physically adjacent to Stanford University, so there were visitors dropping in and out of the lab all the time. A lot of us even came to feel we were sort of like university instructors who got to spend all our time doing research without having to teach classes. So we operated as though this were an open environment where we were free to share what we were doing with anyone we wanted to."

Or occasionally *too* free. One morning in early 1971 the weekly meeting was addressed by Jack Goldman, who was in the habit of paying frequent visits to his new incubator. Goldman's talk—perhaps inspired by PARC's recent close call—had to do with the need to start generating formal reports and white papers to reassure Stamford that the money being spent out west was buying genuine intellectual achievement.

Someone Thornburg did not recognize interrupted Goldman with a suggestion. "He said, 'Well, if you ask me, Jack'—the rest of us never called him anything but 'Dr. Goldman'—'If you ask me, Jack, what we should do is build a computer-based query system where we can tag the different levels of the report, so somebody who just wants an executive summary could get that and someone who wants more could get the full report.' He was basically talking about a hypertext-like environment. We were all sitting there thinking this is pretty good stuff, and Goldman was up front, chomping on his cigar, saying 'Yeah, that's a good idea.'"

The moment the meeting broke up Thornburg saw his friend Bob Bauer shoot out into the hallway. Curious, he followed, and finally found Bauer leaned up against a wall, laughing so hard he could hardly catch his breath.

"What's so funny?" Thornburg asked.

"You know that guy who said, 'Well, if you ask me, Jack?'"

"Yeah, who is he?"

"He doesn't work here," Bauer said. "He just came over from Stanford to have lunch with somebody in computer science. They said, 'We got a meeting, stick around,' so he followed them in. Goldman is probably going to want to give him a bonus or something, and the guy doesn't even work for Xerox!"

But the paradise of collegiality was more mythical than real, or at least it was destined to be short-lived. Jack Goldman had not acceded to Pake's desire to have physicists and other traditional scientists on the premises because he subscribed to any notion of marrying the old science to the new. Instead he saw it as a way to rapidly ramp up PARC's head count by kidnapping available talent from Webster while recruiting the computer and systems experts he was counting on to make PARC's reputation.

"The idea was that when you brought new people in you wanted them to have someone to talk to," Goldman said. "So we sort of seeded the two scientific departments"—that is, physics and optics—"with people from the company, a few of the shining lights from Rochester who were desirous of moving. They were very good guys and I suffered a certain amount of criticism for taking them away from Webster and essentially lowering the average IQ of the Webster group." But he sensed that the physicists and computer scientists would end up in a profound philosophical and scientific tug of war. If Pake believed he could paper over such an elemental conflict, Goldman thought, he was mistaken.

The hiring freeze ended after a couple of months. In that period the downsizing in the research industries had sharply intensified, in part because the Mansfield Amendment restricting Pentagon spending to specifically military research had begun to bite nationwide. Pake and Squires resumed recruiting with the same cautious deliberation as before.

In a superb buyers' market for research and engineering talent, PARC's lavish budget and open-ended charter stood alone among corporate entities. Other industrial research centers might enjoy generous funding or comparably liberal charters, but none had both the open checkbook and apparent immunity from product development pressures enjoyed by PARC. From the point of view of the nation's outstanding computer research scientists, Xerox—outside of a handful of top universities—was the only game in town. "All the super-bright guys who had swell ideas were tickled pink to go work for George Pake and Jack Goldman," recalled George M. White, the research executive on Goldman's staff.[*] "Nobody was going to float money and start a company for them, like

_____
[*]No relation to George White, the PARC researcher.

they would today. At PARC they could get a good budget and a good lab and independence, all of which Pake and Goldman provided."

Adding to PARC's charm was its premium pay scale. This was partially the result of shrewd entreaties to corporate management by Pake, who feared that Xerox policy requiring PARC's salary scale to match Webster's, dollar for dollar, would allow the most prestigious universities to outbid PARC for the best talent.

Pake urged Jack Goldman to secure PARC a dispensation on the grounds that computer scientists were a different breed from the physicists and chemists of Webster. For one thing they were comparatively scarce. In 1970 a mere handful of academic institutions offered graduate programs in computer science. The congressional restrictions on ARPA grants foretold that the number would stay small and the inventory of first-class graduates thin. At length Goldman secured a differential for computer science Ph.D.s of 15 to 20 percent over Webster scale. That helped PARC secure the best recruits, but had the predictable side effect of generating resentment among the General Science Lab's physicists and optical scientists, who were excluded.

Henceforth PARC could offer people with advanced computer science degrees or working experience in the field starting salaries between $30,000 and $35,000—excellent pay for Ph.D.s at the time, although the range remained wide and often depended on a recruit's worldliness and bargaining skills. Some from Stanford University, which was known for its stinginess with salaried professionals, got low-balled. One recalled accepting a full-time PARC salary of $24,000, which was at the low end of pay for principal researchers in the computer lab but a big step up from the $16,000 he had earned at the Stanford Artificial Intelligence Lab.

As though to foreshadow the shoals ahead, it was Taylor's pay that caused Pake the biggest headache. Despite his lack of formal credentials Pake had rostered him on the payroll as associate manager of the Computer Science Lab and, more formally, as area manager of computer graphics within CSL. The starting salary for an area manager in PARC's order of battle was $44,000, off the scale for a non-Ph.D. anywhere at Xerox. "I had to fight with Goldman and he had to fight with headquarters to get that, because Taylor had only a master's degree in psychology and it didn't look right," Pake said. "Of course, I could understand the bureaucratic problems with that myself."

It was not only Taylor's lack of credentials that made his salary a sore point. Within months of his arrival at PARC his personality started to grate on the other lab managers, who understandably took exception to his attitude that PARC's sole *raison d'être* was to pursue computer research and that anything spent on the hard sciences was by definition money down a rathole.

A man who would never tolerate personal attacks at his ARPA conferences, Taylor seemed to tack treacherously close to the *ad hominem* at PARC management meetings. The other lab managers were particularly appalled by his treatment of Gunning, a warm and charming individual who had spent almost as many years in the electronics industry as Taylor had spent on Earth. "He treated Gunning with the utmost condescension," Jones recalled. "It really created a lot of strife. Bill would say something and Bob would come out with, 'That's stupid!' or, 'I'm just wasting my time in here!' It was very unprofessional, and not at all the general atmosphere everyone was used to."

Before the year was out a delegation of several middle managers marched into Pake's office to demand Taylor be fired for his behavior. On this occasion, Pake demurred. He was no more charmed by Taylor than they, but he was more acutely aware of the man's uncommon value to the organization. The Taylor who had spun a web of carefully nurtured loyalties among the nation's best young computer researchers seemed an entirely different character from the one who so charmlessly provoked his peers and superiors. The bottom line was that no one could match his ability to lure research talent to PARC; virtually everyone hired thus far into the Computer Science Lab was someone who knew and respected him personally. Pake felt there were many more gifted scientists yet to be snagged.

He was right about that. Toward the end of 1970 Taylor called in some of his old chits to stage a pair of dazzling heists.

The first was a raid on the only laboratory on the West Coast—possibly the country—whose work on interactive computing met his stern standards. The lab belonged to the legendary engineer Douglas C. Engelbart, an adamantine visionary who held court out of a small think tank called SRI, or the Stanford Research Institute, a couple of miles north of Palo Alto in the community of Menlo Park.

There Engelbart had established his "Augmentation Research Center." The name derived from his conviction that the computer was not only capable of assisting the human thought process, but reinventing it on a higher plane. The "augmentation of human intellect," as he defined it, meant that the computer's ability to store, classify, and retrieve information would someday alter the very way people thought, wrote, and figured.

Engelbart's vision refined and expanded a concept memorably set forth by Dr. Vannevar Bush, an MIT engineering dean and wartime science advisor to Franklin D. Roosevelt. In 1945 Bush had turned his attention to the scientific advances produced in the name of war and to how they might serve the peace. The result was a small masterpiece of scientific augury entitled "As We May Think," which appeared in the July 1945 issue of *The Atlantic Monthly*.

"As We May Think" remains one of the few genuinely seminal documents of the computer age. Even today it stands out as a work of meticulous scientific and social analysis. The contemporary reader is struck by its pragmatism and farsightedness, expressed without a hint of platitude or utopianism, those common afflictions of writing about the future. Bush was not interested in drawing magical pictures in the air; he was busy scrutinizing the new technologies of the postwar world to see how they might relieve society's pressing burdens.

His essay dealt chiefly with technology's ability to manage information. Bush discerned the birth of what would come to be called the "information glut" and projected it forward to a cacophonous posterity. "Publication has been extended far beyond our present ability to make real use of the record," he wrote. "The summation of human experience is being expanded at a prodigious rate, and the means we use for threading through the consequent maze to the momentarily important item is the same as was used in the days of square-rigged ships."

Himself the inventor of a successful analog computer, Bush understood that computer technology might help society draw sense out of the chaos. He sketched out something called the "memex," which he described as "a device in which an individual stores all his books, records, and communications, and which is mechanized so that it may be consulted with exceeding speed and flexibility." The mechanism of consultation would be "associative indexing . . . whereby any item may be caused at will to select immediately and automatically another. This is the essential feature of the memex."

Doug Engelbart first encountered Bush's memex in a magazine article he found in an a Red Cross library in Manila, where he was awaiting transport home from his World War II service. He succumbed to the author's vision of a world of interlinked data as though to a sorcerer's spell. By the time he left Berkeley a few years later with a Ph.D. in engineering, he had decided that his mission in life would be, in effect, to turn the memex into reality.

In the event, he went far beyond anything Bush himself had imagined. At SRI he propagated from Bush's rough blueprint a full-blown system of interactive hardware and software aimed at managing, manipulating, and communicating text and video images. The achievement was all the more remarkable given that it involved an uphill battle against nearly universal skepticism. More than once Engelbart's thinly financed project narrowly eluded extermination. Gradually, however, he acquired a sizable coterie of young engineers and scientists who felt their lives altered by their first meetings with the charismatic Doug Engelbart and who regarded his vision with an almost religious awe. "He not only made sense," recalled Bill Duvall, one of the early disciples. "It was like someone turning on a light. Love at first sight is perhaps the wrong term to use, but it was as close to that as you can get."

One other individual entranced by Engelbart's work was Bob Taylor. At NASA in 1963 Taylor had saved Engelbart's lab by scrounging enough money to overcome a budget crisis. After moving on to ARPA he turned the trickle of funding into a flood. By the end of the decade the Augmentation Research Center, fueled by ARPA's half-million-dollar annual grant and occupying one entire wing of SRI's Menlo Park headquarters, reigned as the think tank's dominant research program.

What it produced was nothing short of astonishing. Obsessed with developing new ways for man and computer to interact, Engelbart linked video terminals to mainframes by cable and communicated with the machines via televised images. To allow the user to move the insertion point, or cursor, from place to place in a block of text instantaneously, he outfitted a hollowed-out block of wood with two small wheels fixed at right angles so it could be rolled smoothly over a flat surface. The wheels communicated their motion to potentiometers whose signals in turn were translated by the computer into the placement of the cursor on the screen. From this crude device would spring an entire culture. "No one is quite sure why it got named a 'mouse,'" Engelbart said years later. "None of us thought that the name would have stayed with it, out in the world." The entire interactive system—mouse, screen, computer, software, and underlying philosophy—was known by the acronym "NLS," for "oNLine System."

Until 1968 Engelbart and his aides labored in relative obscurity, their work known only within the insular fraternity of government grant-makers and computer theorists. That year he requested ninety minutes to demonstrate NLS at the Fall Joint Computer Conference of two leading engineering societies, scheduled for San Francisco in December. The result was one of the most famous events in computing history.

The mouse, making its first public appearance, was the least of it. Engelbart and his sixteen assistants stretched existing electronic technology nearly to the breaking point. He recalled later: "We built special electronics that picked up the control inputs from my mouse, keyset, and keyboard and piped them down to SRI [that is, Stanford Research Institute] over a telephone hookup. We leased two microwave lines up from our laboratory, roughly thirty miles. It took two additional antennas on the roof at SRI, four more on a truck on Skyline Boulevard, and two on the roof of the conference center. It cost money . . . The nice people at ARPA and NASA, who were funding us, effectively had to say, 'Don't tell me!'"

The effort was worth every penny. The audience was riveted, as Engelbart in his subdued drone described and demonstrated a fully operational system of interactive video conferencing, multimedia displays, and split-screen technology.

At one point half of a twenty-foot-tall projection screen was occupied by a live video image of Engelbart on stage, the other half by text transmitted live from Menlo Park (it was a shopping list including apples, oranges, bean soup, and French bread). Minutes later the screen carried a live video image of a hand rolling the unusual "mouse" around a desktop while a superimposed computer display showed how the cursor simultaneously and obediently followed its path.

The *piece de resistance* was Engelbart's implementation of the memex. The screen showed how a user could select a single word in a text document and be instantly transported to the relevant portion of a second document—the essence of hypertext, found today, some thirty years later, on every World Wide Web page and countless word-processed documents. At the conclusion of the bravura performance Doug Engelbart, previously a prophet without honor, was rewarded with a standing ovation.

In 1971 Taylor, whose ARPA funds had helped pay for that demo, was intent on somehow importing Engelbart's interactive vision into PARC. The only question was how to do it without also importing Doug Engelbart. The problem was that the master's inspirational dreams were inseparable from his inflexible and self-righteous disposition. One admirer called him "a prophet of biblical dimensions," a role he fit down to his physical appearance. Tall and craggy, with deepset eyes and a hawklike nose, he might have been carved from a slab of antediluvian granite. Softspoken but intransigent, his years of battling unbelievers had convinced him that he was fated to remain the solitary leader of a devoted cadre.

By the time Taylor was poised to strike, that cadre was showing signs of serious discontent. As the novelty of his ideas wore off (to be fair, this was a process that could take several years), some disciples started to discern the drawbacks of working for so uncompromising a boss—particularly one whose tendency to oracular pronouncements required a stratum of top assistants to periodically sit the rest of the staff down and explain what Doug had in mind.

Engelbart's self-defined mission was not to produce a product, or even a prototype; it was an open-ended search for knowledge. Consequently, no project in his lab ever seemed to come to an end. Whenever one approached a milestone he would abruptly redefine it, condemning the lab to months or years of further work. The finish line was constantly receding, like the oasis in a desert mirage. Said one long-term member of his lab: "We were like rats running in his maze."

The first to defect was William K. English, a brilliant engineer who had been with Engelbart almost from the start, joining him in 1962 as his hardware ace and all-around major-domo. Wiry and deliberative, Bill English had been the invisible guiding hand behind the 1968 demo. He was ferociously loyal to his boss but bridled at the lab's perpetual lack of closure. Some also believed he was fed up with Engelbart's way of monopolizing credit for the lab's accomplishments.

Taylor offered English a solution to both complaints: reproduce NLS, or something like it, at PARC. English could thus fulfill his treasured goal of bringing the system to commercial fruition *and* be in charge of his own lab, out from under the shadow of the implacable Engelbart. Whether English hesitated leaving the leader he had followed for nearly a decade is hard to say, but he continued the raid where Taylor left off, eventually recruiting a dozen of Engelbart's most important followers.

As a team they infused Engelbart's principles into PARC like apostles spreading religion. Thanks to them, the Augmentation Research Center left its indelible stamp on almost every major innovation to emerge from PARC in the next decade. Yet this triumph was not without its painful ironies. English's reworked version of NLS, the direct descendant of Vannevar Bush's vision and Engelbart's work, would be remembered chiefly as PARC's biggest failure.

The agents of its ruin, as it happened, came to PARC via Bob Taylor's second great heist. Taylor knew that up in Berkeley a handful of extraordinarily talented engineers were about to lose their jobs. In his view PARC could scarcely exist without them. Toward the end of 1970, with George Pake's approval, he took the necessary steps to reel them in.

CHAPTER 5

Berkeley's Second System

The year 1968 was not a tranquil one for Berkeley, California. It was the time of riots on Telegraph Avenue, the battle over People's Park, and the calling out of the National Guard by Governor Ronald Reagan. Buildings on the University of California campus were occupied, barricaded, firebombed. The police oscillated between paralysis and overreaction. Turmoil and radicalism were in the air, along with tear gas and a mysterious white powder dropped from helicopters that made demonstrators' skin itch and burn as though attacked by hornets.

The owners of Berkeley Computer Corporation thought it wise to lay low. Radical groups of the time manifested a distinctly Luddite streak, and computer facilities were prominent targets—witness the bombing by one anti-government group of the Army Mathematics Research Center at the University of Wisconsin, which cost a young physicist his life. UC Berkeley seemed a good bet for much of the same.

Berkeley Computer therefore inconspicuously spread itself out over the city in three separate locations. One building housed the programmers. Then there was what Chuck Thacker remembered as "a somewhat more shoddy place where the hardware people lived, essentially a walkup above a warehouse on Sixth Street." The third was a nondescript edifice a few blocks further along Sixth, a few miles from the campus and not far from the waterfront, in which they were actually building the machine they thought would make their fortune. Thacker recalled: "We found a concrete building that was the fur storage vault for a warehouse, except the warehouse had burned down around the vault. So here was this block structure, two stories, about fifty feet on a side, just a big concrete tube really. When we first saw the place it was filled with two million plastic champagne corks." After they cleared out the corks and fitted out the building to be even more nondescript, he said, "You'd drive by on the street and never know what it was."

Inside this prosaic structure worked some of the most creative computer designers alive.

The team had taken several years to coalesce. Although incorporated in 1968, BCC's roots reached back to Project Genie, the ARPA time-sharing scheme that designed the 940 computer for Max Palevsky's SDS. One could even date the company's spiritual birth to a day in 1964 when a graduate student named Butler Lampson passed through an unmarked door on the Berkeley campus and found Peter Deutsch on the other side.

The son of foreign service parents, Lampson had come to study physics at Berkeley with a first-class undergraduate pedigree from Harvard and a reputation for being preternaturally smart. He was rail-thin and stood a little over six feet, with a loping gait that made him seem taller. His manner of speaking was fleet but cogent, unless he was in the grip of some particularly compelling idea, in which case his thought system would rush ahead of his speech processes and he would stumble over his words until his mouth caught up to his brain. When all the inputs and outputs were synchronized, it often seemed as if his mind worked about a thousand times faster than anyone else's. ("We can now appreciate that in spoken discourse the theoretical speed limit is the *Lampson*," Wes Clark famously cracked at a professional conference a few years later following one of his customarily breakneck presentations.)

Sharp as he was, however, even Butler Lampson was a little daunted by the challenge of physics at Berkeley. Later he claimed that he transferred into computer science because it was "not as hard" as physics, but he scarcely meant it the way normal persons do. He meant he found the task of advancing a science that history's greatest intellects had been mining for 300 years fundamentally uninteresting. Especially when a brand-new field beckoned in which every new discovery represented a terrific leap forward in human enlightenment. So he was primed for the challenge when a friend he ran into at a computer conference in San Francisco asked how things were going across the bay with Project Genie.

Lampson returned a blank look. "I've never heard of it," he admitted. He left the party with a description of an intriguing study of computer architectures, along with directions to a building located at the far northeast corner of the Berkeley campus. A few days later he found himself standing on the ground floor of Cory Hall, facing an unmarked door.

Even in 1964 one could hardly fault the Genie people for their circumspection; the project was funded by the Defense Department. On the other hand there was a limit to paranoia, even at Berkeley. The unmarked door was unlocked. Lampson pushed it open and walked in.

He might have stepped into the lair of the White Rabbit. It was a big room, mostly empty. On one side stood a Bendix LGP30 computer, a massive and obsolete digital machine serving no purpose he could discern. Facing the Bendix was a much smaller Scientific Data Systems 930, a rugged computer of fairly recent vintage. In a swivel chair parked by the 930 sat a short, pudgy, barefooted human being with a mane of black hair and a dense beard, serenely feeding a paper tape into a computer input. The paper tape was not very long and Lampson watched as the stranger fed it in all the way and then, oddly, took it out and fed it back in again.

Lampson could no longer stifle his curiosity. "That's weird," he said. "Why did you just do that?"

"It's a two-pass relocatable loader!" the man said without looking up.

"But that's ridiculous!"

"I know! I know!" was the impatient reply. "I'm rewriting it!"

To an outsider the conversation might have sounded like something out of the Theatre of the Absurd. But as speakers of a shared technical language, the two men understood each other as clearly as fellow initiates to the Masonic mysteries. The two-pass relocatable loader did exist and it was a kludge: an inefficient, overelaborated piece of machinery that had been poorly designed by the machine's manufacturer. And it did require the programmer to input a paper tape twice in succession because on each sequence the computer could only glean half the information it needed to function.

Lampson recognized the system as a waste of time and energy and appreciated at a glance that the man at the console possessed the inborn skill to redesign it so the damn machine would actually learn something new, like how to absorb all the necessary data on a single pass of the tape. His name was Peter Deutsch. He and Lampson would work side by side for the better part of the next twenty years.

They were an unlikely pair, one of many that would later give PARC its unique character. Lampson's patrician bearing left people with the impression that he was contemplating science from a great metaphorical height. Deutsch was a white tornado, impatient, perpetually chafing to get his hands on the next arcane programming task. As fast as Lampson's mind grasped concepts and principles, it worked faster when interacting with the people around him (usually attempting to convince them he was right). Deutsch seemed to prefer unraveling the riddles of computer programming in communion with himself.

The emblematic image of the gifted Deutsch was a photograph taken of him as a preadolescent. It showed him writing a program for the world's first minicomputer, a Digital Equipment Corporation PDP-1, perched on a chair padded with a cushion or phone book so he could reach the keyboard. By then he was already a master of the occult art of computer programming, which he began to learn at the age of twelve when his father, an MIT physicist, brought home a manual for the campus Univac 1.

The manual covered the Univac's assembly code, a system of symbolic statements which engineers used as building blocks to write programs for the machine. "Somehow it struck a spark," Deutsch remembered. "I said I wanted to meet the person who wrote that manual and my father arranged it. He was a person named Lanza, and he actually found a small computational program that needed coding and asked if I wanted to do it. I said sure. I still don't know what the program computed, whether he trusted the answers he got out of it, or anything else about it."

But it started him hanging around the Univac, as well as other mainframe computers to which his father's connections got him access. The grad student programmers in the computer center became accustomed to (if not necessarily patient with) this diminutive soul peppering them with impertinent questions about their work. The wiser among them may even have realized that it would not be long before *they* were asking *him* questions.

Soon he was cadging stray time in half-hour segments from the supervisors with the understanding that if anyone came along with serious work, he would get bumped. By the time the university acquired its PDP-1, he had matured into an adept and dexterous programmer with the instincts of an artist. After he moved to Berkeley for his undergraduate education, he would still drop in at MIT now and then during vacations to visit his father and dash off a few lines of code. Students would literally ransack the wastebaskets to read what he had discarded with the hope of absorbing a trace of his inventive technique.

Still a Berkeley freshman, Deutsch had been involved with Genie only a few months when he was encountered by Butler Lampson. He explained that Genie's goal was to refashion the SDS 930 into a small-scale time-sharing machine and that it was run out of the electrical engineering department by David Evans and Mel Pirtle—the first an unassuming computer science professor who limited himself as much as possible to such tasks as raising grant money from the government, the second a garrulous Californian graduate student who designed the hardware.

Lampson felt irresistibly drawn to this remote corner of the university campus. "I found out from Peter what was going on, then I started to hang around there a lot," he recalled. "After a while it became clear that this was going to be a lot more interesting than physics."

With Lampson on board, Genie picked up momentum. The group tore apart the SDS 930, tacked on new hardware, and wrote an entirely new operating system. "There weren't any spectacularly new ideas in the project," Lampson said later. "The point was to try to take ideas that other people had, some of which had been implemented on other machines, and show you could make it all work in a much less grandiose environment." Genie accomplished its goal, which was to bring time-sharing to the masses by implementing it on the small machine that Taylor and Currie eventually beguiled Palevsky into marketing as the SDS 940.

The Genie team then turned to the eternal question of what to do for an encore. They were a powerful group of talents, especially after Deutsch and Lampson, as good at designing and debugging operating systems as anyone in the field, were joined by Chuck Thacker, whose hardware skills represented the third side, so to speak, of a very sturdy triangle.

Growing up poor and fatherless in a suburb of Los Angeles, Thacker had paid his way through school with a succession of jobs at small local engineering shops, including one that made the devices Civil Defense would use to measure ground radiation after the Bomb dropped. (This was the 1950s, after all.) He had always been an electronics nut—he could still remember the day he acquired his very first transistor as a schoolboy—but it was from these shirt-sleeved shop men that he learned to pare a decent design into a manufacturable one by stripping it down to its frugal essence. "They were the real engineer's engineers," he said.

At Caltech, where he made a short and unsuccessful first run at obtaining a bachelor's degree, physics was divided into two distinct parts. There was the theory side, which involved a lot of math and cosmological speculation, and what Thacker called "the giant tinker toy side," which involved building immense, elaborately engineered structures like synchrotrons and cyclotrons. That was the part he loved.

In fact, Thacker was animated by the same love of gadgetry that lured countless other physicists like himself into computing. When he moved north to Berkeley to get away from the L.A. smog and give his faltering academic career a fresh start, he fell in among the computing crowd, a course that led him inexorably to the same unmarked door Lampson had discovered a few months earlier.

Now it was 1968. Work on the 940 had ended and Dave Evans had relocated to the University of Utah, leaving Pirtle and the others to think about working on a much larger canvas than the 940—a time-sharing system, for example, that would serve not a dozen but 500 users at a time. They imagined a machine with several processors, each assigned a specific task and all interconnected, like the tentacles of mating octopuses. It was huge, exciting, innovative, and envisioned not as an academic or government-funded venture, but strictly as a commercial one. Thus was Berkeley Computer Corporation born.

Although BCC was based on speculative technology, its financial structure appeared at first glance to be made of sterner stuff. Pirtle had arranged through his Wall Street connections to secure $2 million in financing from a company called Data Processing Financial and General, underwritten by the white-shoe investment firm of White, Weld & Co. That sounded like plenty, but it was only seed money. The team figured that bringing the Berkeley 1 computer to market would consume that sum many times over, which meant they would have to become very familiar with the demands of bankers and the intricacies of high finance.

"This was definitely not your two-guys-in-a-garage startup," said Lampson, who by now held a faculty appointment at Berkeley and set his own name down as a co-founder. It was, however, something infinitely more risky. The BCC pioneers were about to become victims of the "second-system effect."

The theory of second systems was formulated by an IBM executive named Frederick Brooks, whose career supervising large-scale software teams taught him that designers of computer systems tend to build into their second projects all the pet features that tight finances or short deadlines forced them to leave out of their first. The result is an overgrown, inefficient monstrosity that rarely works as expected. As he put it in his pithy masterpiece, *The Mythical Man-Month*: "The second is the most dangerous system a man ever designs."

The BCC machine could have sprung full-blown from the pages of Brooks's text. As Lampson recalled, the designers of the economical and practical SDS 940 regarded their next machine as an opportunity to "look at all the things you could make much more wonderful, and plan to make them all more wonderful by creating a system that could handle a lot more users and much larger programs and was much faster and used computing resources much more efficiently and was better and more wonderful in every possible way.

"It was not a very realistic enterprise," he acknowledged. "But at the time it seemed great, the proper next step, as second systems often do."

Their exuberance made Berkeley Computer, by all accounts, a jolly place to work, its scientists and engineers propelled by pure hubris into working the kind of inhuman hours that would become a Silicon Valley cliché—when Silicon Valley came into its own fifteen years later. They believed they were breaking new ground in computer design, and they were right. Among other things, their machine incorporated "virtual memory," a system for swapping jobs from disk to memory and back again that enabled it to accommodate much more activity than its physical specifications otherwise would, like a house with the exterior dimensions of a bungalow but the interior floor plan of a regal palace.

In hardware terms, however, the machine was a beast. "The machine consisted of a number of specialized processors, one to handle the disk and drum input/output system, one to handle communications, and one to handle job scheduling," recalled Thacker, who designed them. "And these things cooperated with two processors which were somewhat larger, which were the central processors for the machine which actually ran the user jobs." The processors all had to be physically connected to each other and also to the memory, which required a couple of miles of cable snaking among eight six-foot-tall cabinets full of equipment, and then out to peripherals such as teletypes and line printers.

Some of the workers, including Thacker, could tell early on that the project was getting out of hand. The engineer's engineer possessed the unique trait of aiming for less, not more, in his systems. "This was so unusual for an engineer," recalled Charles Simonyi, a young immigrant from communist Hungary who assisted Thacker, watching as he chain-smoked through the night designing the machine's logic. "He had this word for what was happening. He called it 'biggerism.' I heard this word from him and my English was not that good and I always thought it sounded slightly obscene, because he'd say, you know, 'This project has been biggered.'"

Adding to the challenge, the hardware comprised an unwieldy mix of ancient and modern components. The processors were built using a brand-new, and far from bug-free, technology known as TTL (for "transistor-transistor logic"). But the read-only memory, which carried the machine's basic operating code, was an array of diodes soldered onto some 20 circuit boards—hundreds of thousands of tiny diodes each representing a digital bit. Editing the operating code during the debugging phase, Simonyi recalled, meant finding the errant diode on a foot-square circuit board, clipping it by hand with a die cutter, then drilling new holes and soldering a fresh diode in place. It was like editing text with a hammer and chisel.

More problems cropped up in designing the operating system. In computing, economies of scale often work in reverse: As a system grows larger it becomes exponentially more complicated. A computer designed to serve fifty users is not ten times more complicated than a machine for five users, but one hundred times, or a thousand. Berkeley's 500-user machine proved more complex than even this exquisitely talented team could handle. As Frederick Brooks would have predicted, when they finally got it working it did not work perfectly—and never well enough for the rated capacity of 500 users.

The full-bore crash of expectations, however, came late in the company's life cycle. For the first year or two BCC's fortunes resembled the rising curve of an arc. The company ramped up employment to more than 100 hardware and software engineers. The prototype's name got upgraded from the Berkeley 1 to the Berkeley 500, the better to express their confidence in its capacity (and, as Lampson said, "for marketing purposes").

Pirtle had an artful way of squelching any doubts that might arise about the program. One recruit, an engineer named Ed Fiala who came from the Boston engineering firm of Bolt, Beranek & Newman, had taken the precaution of ordering a Dun & Bradstreet credit report on BCC before deciding whether to accept the job. "It said, 'Well, they're paying their bills but we don't exactly know how,'" Fiala recalled. He stifled his misgivings and moved to Berkeley anyway, arriving on a night when BCC was having a big party.

"Everybody was all smiles and enthusiasm, and I asked Mel Pirtle how the company was doing," Fiala recalled. "He said, 'We're doing great!' I was a little concerned. I asked, 'What sort of financing do you have?' He said, 'Oh, we have lots. We just got three hundred thousand dollars.' And I asked how long that would last and he said, 'Six weeks.'

"Now, three hundred thousand dollars sounded like a lot of money to me but the six weeks didn't seem all that long. So I said, 'Isn't that a lot less time than it's going to take you to complete your project?' He said, 'Well, yes . . . but we can always get more money.'"

For a while that was true. Backers touring the BCC quarters invariably came away convinced by the staff's high spirits that everything was on track. ("I know I tried to look enthusiastic," Fiala said.) But in 1970 the well ran dry. Not only had the recession dug in, but the technological risks confronted so cavalierly by BCC and other time-sharing companies turned out to be tougher than anyone expected. There were new questions about whether the machine would ever get done, and who would buy it if it did. Pirtle started to pare staff. Early in the year he placed those who were left on half salary and advised everyone to look for work.

Around then Bob Taylor made his first appearance on the premises. To the younger programmers he cut quite the intriguing figure, a natty, self-assured individual to whom Pirtle and Lampson seemed to pay an unusual degree of respect—even deference. "I didn't know what to make of him," said Simonyi, still a cultural innocent living hand-to-mouth as a Berkeley undergraduate while working part-time at BCC. "I had this impression of a laid-back Playboy type, a Hugh Hefner type, good looking, good dresser, athletic, with the pipe of course, always with the pipe. Taylor never had the airs of the false technical B.S. artist. It was a plus that he didn't, but at the same time I had to ask myself: 'If he's not technical, not a technical B.S.'er, then what the hell is he?'"

The answer was: A man energetically pursuing a deal. Having alerted Pake to BCC's financial problems and the likelihood of a rare cache of first-rank talent hitting the market, his initial idea was for Xerox to buy BCC outright and fold it whole into PARC, like a fresh egg into raw batter. That way PARC would acquire an advanced time-sharing prototype along with at least twenty top people and a sizable complement of junior staff. Negotiations with Pirtle along those lines proceeded into the fall.

But whether because Pirtle quoted too high a price or BCC failed too rapidly, the wholesale deal collapsed in favor of a sort of *à la carte* arrangement. Just as BCC filed for bankruptcy (one final drunken party on Friday, November 13, 1970, drained the last of its petty cash), PARC hired six of its best people—Lampson, Thacker, Deutsch, Fiala, a hardware designer named Richard Shoup, and a software programmer named Jim Mitchell. Pirtle was not interested in coming along. Instead he took over the management of a colossal government project to build the world's first parallel-architecture supercomputer, the Illiac IV, at NASA's Ames Research Center in neighboring Mountain View (although some thought that the real reason was that he knew he would never get along with Taylor). Simonyi went with him, for the moment.

The Berkeley 500, the only machine of its kind ever built, was purchased by ARPA on Taylor's recommendation and shipped to the University of Hawaii to allow that institution to join the ARPANET. The last employees of Berkeley Computer got it up and running in the cavernous building on Sixth Street, then watched with bittersweet emotions as it got crated up. "It was a very complex and interesting project," Fiala mused later. "It would have been fun to work on it for five years."

Virtually at a single stroke, Taylor had completed his team—almost. He had the best hardware man (Thacker), the best designer of operating systems (Lampson), and an entire cell of other computer science prodigies. PARC was missing only one thing: a philosopher.

For there was still the obstacle that among the leading computer experts in the country, including those now on his payroll, very few agreed with him that the goal of computer design was to create a personal machine that interacted with the user via a high-powered display. The BCC group, deeply rooted in the culture of time-sharing, was still intent on getting as many users hooked into a single machine as technologically possible. That goal, as Wes Clark contended, remained incompatible with giving the individual the kind of speed and responsiveness that interactivity required. When Taylor tried to explicate his notion of a display-based user interface, they tuned him out. They would not come around to his point of view for nearly two years.

But one man was way ahead of them all. That one had written a doctoral thesis at Utah in 1969 describing an idealized interactive computer called the FLEX machine. He had experimented with powerful displays and with computers networked in intricate configurations. On page after page of his dissertation he lamented the inability of the world's existing hardware to realize his dream of an interactive personal computer. He set before science the challenge to build the machine he imagined, one with "enough power to outrace your senses of sight and hearing, enough capacity to store thousands of pages, poems, letters, recipes, records, drawings, animations, musical scores, and anything else you would like to remember and change."

To Taylor he was a soulmate and a profound thinker, capable of seeing a computing future far beyond anything even he could imagine. Among the computer scientists familiar with his ideas, half thought he was a crackpot and the other half a visionary. His name was Alan Kay.

CHAPTER 6

"Not Your Normal Person"

The hallmark mop of shaggy black hair is shot with gray, but as he nears a quite implausible sixty years of age, little else has changed. Certainly not the energy level, or the sneakers, so characteristic of his working uniform, or the unceasing effulgence from his mind of historical observation, moral instruction, and technological vision.

"Conversations with Alan Kay aren't about any particular thing," says Carver Mead, a Caltech professor who developed the technology of complex integrated circuits at PARC. "They're more a ramble through Ideaspace."

Ideaspace Central today is divided between two Southern California locations about ten miles apart. One is Kay's home in an affluent part of Los Angeles. It is unassuming from the outside except for a towering V-roofed addition. This curious annex was custom-built to shelter a two-story pipe organ professionally hand-crafted of exquisite blond spruce, on which Kay can be heard almost any morning practicing his favorite music by Buxtehude and J. S. Bach. ("Alan believed his role was to make it possible to build the organ, after which he would be the happy caretaker," remarked its architect, Greg Harrold.)

The second location is a warehouse-like building in Glendale, a smoggy precinct of the San Gabriel Valley just north of L.A. Artfully arranged partitions and bookcases provide Kay with a spacious work area open to the floor through a doorless passage on one side—not too private, for he likes to spend the workday in constant stir, eliciting and dispensing ideas among his co-workers with equal generosity. He greets you wearing an oval name tag reading "Alan" and bearing a picture of Mickey Mouse. It should look ludicrous and it does, until you remember that this is the man whose playful digitized image of Cookie Monster launched the age of the personal computer. Or that he is now employed—as are two other members of the extraordinary team he assembled at PARC—by the Walt Disney Company, which has entrusted him with helping to develop new ways to transmit story and idea from creator to audience.

Alan Kay might have been the role model for the modern computer nerd, a Chuck Yeager for the generation that got engaged by the new technology in the 1970s. If you lived within that era's insular community of students and electronics nuts you knew his name, perhaps because you had read his lucid explications of microelectronics and software in *Scientific American*, or read an article featuring him in (of all places) *Rolling Stone*. You had been socially conditioned to feel ungainly and isolated by your devotion to machines and math; Alan Kay positively reveled in it, swaggered with it, declared in the pages of the counterculture bible itself that you and your awkward pals in all your nebbishy glory were the prophets of a new world in which computers and their unparalleled power would belong to the masses.

The Computer Bum, as he enlightened *Rolling Stone*'s readers, was someone who looked "about as straight as you'd expect hot-rodders to look. It's that kind of fanaticism. He's a person who loves to stay up all night, he and the machine in a love-hate relationship." The hacker as rebel: Not an undernourished weirdo, merely someone "not very interested in conventional goals."

"Alan had been thrown out of every university in the country," recalled John Warnock, a mathematician who knew him first as a fellow graduate student at the University of Utah and later as a colleague at PARC. "He's not your normal person. He's a child prodigy who doesn't quite fit in with your normal academics."

His wife, Bonnie MacBird, would transfer his personality to a character (distribute it among several, actually) in her original screenplay for the first computer-animated high-tech thriller, a Disney film entitled *Tron* in which his boldness, his confidence, his exhilarating kinesthesia somehow survived the merciless dilution of Hollywood script doctoring. Alan Kay today is still the kind of person who communicates an impression of pure motion even when he is sitting down. As Carver Mead suggests, a conversation with him is an exhausting scaled-up affair. Once you get him talking he performs what he calls a "brain dump" on you, years of accumulated knowledge and synthesis pouring forth in a flood of narrative in which the protagonists are Alan Kay and the startling and visionary ideas he holds dear (many of them still deplorably unrealized), and their adversaries are managers, executives, bean-counters, corporate boards, schoolteachers, and all others who regard the unshackled imagination as a menace rather than a gift.

Visible within the flood of ideas is the Alan Kay who made computing cool. He declared publicly that it was all right to use three-million-dollar machines to play games and "screw around." If that meant grad students were blasting digital rocket ships off their computer screens in a game called "Spacewar," it was all part of the weaving of new technology into the cultural fabric. His unashamed view of the computer as very much a toy liberated many others to explore its genius for procedures other than the parsing of numbers and the sequencing of databases—to see it, in other words, as a creative tool.

This notion of technology as a means to an end still distinguishes Kay from most other practitioners of the art and science of technology. One factor in his powerful kinship with Bob Taylor was their shared curiosity about *what* this machine could be made to do, more than *how*. Notwithstanding his incessant harangues, most of the inspired engineers Taylor recruited to CSL, the Lampsons and Thackers, started out too blindly focused on the issue of what was within their power to actually build. They would ask: What is the next stop on the road? Kay turned the question inside out: Let's figure out where we want to go, and that will show us how to get there. He never lost sight of the computer's appropriate station in the world: to conform to the user's desires, not the other way around.

"It's almost impossible for most people to see technology as the tool rather than the end," he was saying one day in his cubicle at Disney Imagineering's Glendale warehouse. He was about to embark on another excursion through what Carver Mead called Ideaspace, where hyperbole and metaphor are equivalent coins of the realm (or obverse sides of the same coin). "People get trapped in thinking that anything in the environment is to be taken as a given. It's part of the way our nervous system works. But it's dangerous to take it as a given because then it controls you, rather than the other way around. That's McLuhan's insight, one of the bigger ones in the twentieth century. Zen in the twentieth century is about taking things that have been rendered invisible by this process and trying to make them visible again.

"Parents ask me what they should do to help their kids with science. I say, on a walk always take a magnifying glass along. Be a miniature exploratorium. . . ."

You would have to know something about his life to recognize this as a scene from his childhood. Kay's father was a scientist, a physiologist engaged in designing prostheses for arms and legs. "I can certainly remember going on walks with him," Kay recalled. "And when you go on a walk with a parent who's interested in science, it's usually about all the things that you can't readily see."

This sort of unleashed curiosity would allow him to recognize new ways of placing computing power in everyone's hands. But he had to travel a fair distance before discovering that his destiny lay in the arcane science of systems programming. That might never have happened at all had circumstances not left him becalmed on an Air Force base in Waco, Texas, in the suspended state of existence known as "Figmo."

The term is a military acronym for "Fuck it, got my orders." As always with service slang, one can hardly think of a better way to describe the condition. It was 1961 and Kay was marking off the last two years of his enlistment. At this moment he was working in the pathology lab at James Conway AFB, on the verge of being transferred on.

"I was in figmo, when you're at your old base but everybody knows you're about to go somewhere else. You're not for real anymore on this old base. You sit around and play cards and read books, one of the best things in the military. I was trying to get a little better at poker with a figmo who was a professional poker player, the trick being to see if I could make it a learning experience instead of just getting fleeced."

But if Kay could not be ordered to do a damn thing pending his transfer, his state of enforced idleness left him wide open to being enticed. In this case the enticement was the scheduling of an aptitude test for computer programmers. No one from Conway had ever passed this test. To a prodigy, however, any standardized test is like a carnival midway. Kay, whose mind was as nimble as it was underemployed, viewed it as a lark. "No way I'd ever pass up a test," he said. Naturally, he passed handily.

As luck would have it, the Air Force did not view programmer training quite so casually. Undergoing a full-scale conversion from primitive punch card tabulators to the IBM 1401, the world's first popular general business computer, the service was pulling linguists out of Europe to turn them into programmers and scouring the ranks for anyone showing the slightest ability.

"They figured that since you'd taken this test, IBM could teach you to program the 1401 from scratch in one week," Kay recalled. "It wasn't computer science, just training, but it was the best training I've ever had. You worked your ass off and at the end of the week you could program a computer."

On the surface Kay seemed an unlikely candidate to take to the rigors of instructing a machine how to operate, for by habit he responded poorly to rules and regulations not his own. The explanation, however, lies in how a computer's stern and unyielding logical rules can lead to infinitely creative results.

Computers look smart, but their intelligence is a fraud, a sleight-of-hand stunt abetted by blinding speed and a capacity for infinite reiteration. They must be instructed how to perform every tiny step of a problem of ratiocination, and in what sequence. That is why nothing that ever happens inside a computer is entirely unexpected (unless it is going wrong). The machine has been shown the way by its programmer, like a child taken for a stroll along a garden path. Both partners know the rules of the journey. Let the programmer stray one step off the path—let's say by coding a command that violates the machine's logic—and the computer will refuse to follow. Let the computer break the rules—refusing to take the next step along the mandated path—and the programmer will know it is sick and must be cured before they can take even one more stride together.

Obviously, then, programmers must conform to a system. They instruct the machine to follow a series of conditions (*if* such-and-such a condition is met, do *this*; otherwise do *that*. . . . *If* you have done *that*, and such-and-such a state also exists, do *this*; else *that*). But the conditions must themselves conform to logic that has been burned into the machine's circuits by the designer, or it will not comprehend. Computer programming is the process of telling a computer in its own language how to read and follow this cascade of "ifs." The programmer establishes a set of rules that happen to conform in a very fundamental way to the machine's own. It is the ultimate recursive endeavor, the joint discovery of rules and regulations leading to the invention of more rules and regulations that allow the machine to extend and expand its abilities and, consequently, those of its programmer and user. Alan Kay would become an expert in this partnership (and in a related field, the programming of programmers; but that lay far in the future).

But there is a marvelous catch: These logical rules and regulations can apply to any abstract conditions the programmer chooses to define. As Kay put it years later: "Computers' use of symbols, like the use of symbols in language and mathematics, is sufficiently disconnected from the real world to enable them to create splendid nonsense . . . Although the hardware of the computer is subject to natural laws (electrons can move through the circuits only in certain physically defined ways), the range of simulations the computer can perform is bounded only by the limits of human imagination. In a computer, spacecraft can be made to travel faster than the speed of light, time to travel in reverse."

His enchantment with a system so rigidly structured yet infinitely malleable may have had to do with his childhood in the bosom of a close but itinerant family. One year after his birth in 1940 in Spring-field, Massachusetts, the family had moved to Australia, his father's native land. Only four years later they were on the move again, fleeing a Japanese fleet that had already reached New Guinea and seemed prepared to continue its way south without resistance. Back in the United States the Kays took up residence in the Hadley, Massachu-setts, farmhouse of Alan's maternal grandfather. He was Clifton John-son, a writer, musician, and pioneering documentary photographer early in the century. In this farmhouse Kay's education began.

Clifton Johnson had died the year of Alan's birth, inspiring a family fancy that the old man's inquisitive and creative temperament had been infused into the grandson's. More prosaically, Johnson had filled the house with books, five thousand of them, addressing every topic under the sun. Alan reached first grade as a five-year-old autodidact. "By the time I got to school, I had already read a couple hundred books. I knew in the first grade that they were lying to me because I had already been exposed to other points of view. They didn't like the idea of having different points of view, so it was a battle."

There were some respites from the combat. One was music, taught to him by his mother, who had received her own musical training from Johnson himself. But otherwise the contest continued through his entire school career. This ranged, thanks to his father's career as a uni-versity scientist and a physiologist, from the elite Brooklyn Technical High School to public school in Port Washington on suburban Long Island. There were sickly periods leading to further self-education, including a bad bout of rheumatic fever in his senior year of high school, and further contentiousness (a dismissal for insubordination in Brooklyn).

Port Washington in Kay's recollection was a community suffused with music. "This was a place where football players played in the band and orchestra for status. It was the thing. The Congregational Church had five choirs, each with 100 voices. I'll never forget Easter, when they'd combine the choirs for sunrise services. Full orchestra. Five hundred voices. The best, best stuff." There he also met Chris Jeffers, who would introduce him to his first computer. Jeffers was a junior, a year behind Kay (although since Kay's illness lost him a year of school, they graduated together). He was also a superb pianist with perfect pitch and a thriving jazz band. Kay joined up on guitar. The band played Dixieland jazz from Jeffers's effortless arrangements, an interesting choice if one is looking for a form that imposes strict formal rules on players who are encouraged to break them according to another set of strict formal rules.

They split for college, Jeffers to the University of Colorado and Kay to Bethany College, a small West Virginia school with a decent program in biology. Academic disaster reunited them. As Kay tells the story, Bethany took umbrage at his charge that the administration imposed a Jewish quota to control the number of New Yorkers in its pre-medical program. The dean instructed him not to return to campus after Easter recess. Kay called Jeffers, unaware that his friend had himself been suspended for spending all his time on a student musical production instead of classwork.

"Guess what, Chris," Kay said. "I just got thrown out of school!"

"Great, me too! When you coming out?"

Jeffers had decided to stay in Denver, taking a job at the national reservations office of United Airlines, a vast computer depot located near Stapleton International Airport, until he could resume his education. The two friends took up residence in the basement of a condemned building not far from the end of the runway. Kay found work in a music store, where he could wait for lightning to jolt him into the next stage of his life.

One day Jeffers invited him to visit United. Kay understood computers in the abstract, the way curious kids understood them in the days when the most modest machine represented a ten-million-dollar capital investment. United's IBM 305 RAMAC was the first one he ever touched. It was huge, specifically designed to manage colossal databases like the fifty-two weeks' worth of reservations and seating records consigned to Denver's safekeeping. But what really struck Kay was the primitiveness of its operational routine. The system was serviced by platoons of attendants, full-time menials doing nothing more refined than taking stacks of punch cards from one machine and loading them in the next. To his amazement, digital electronics turned out to be as mindless and labor-intensive as laying a sewer line. As Kay's eyes followed the drones traversing the workhouse floor, the germ of an idea took hold. There was an exorbitant discrepancy between the purpose of the machine—which was to simplify human endeavor—and the effort required to realize it. Kay banked the insight. He would not begin to understand it until much later, well after the lark of taking an Air Force aptitude test metamorphosed into a serious career choice.

The two-week IBM course he received courtesy of Conway AFB was effective, but rudimentary. "Programming is in two parts," he said later. "The bricklaying part, which IBM taught, and the architecture part, which can take two or three years."

In those days every computer was different. There was nothing like today's standardized architectures, according to which all IBM-compatible machines, for instance, respond to the same set of operating instructions even though they may be manufactured by different companies according to widely variant specifications of memory, data storage, and even microprocessor design. Standardization has helped make computers a mass-market phenomenon. It allows users to be reasonably confident that a program bought off the shelf will work properly regardless of who manufactured their computer, just as they know they will find the accelerator and brake pedal in the same location regardless of whether their car is a Ford or a Chevrolet.

Nothing of the kind existed in the computer world in the 1960s. Machines differed in shape, size, and architecture down to the circuitry inside their cabinets and the sequences of digital ones and zeros delivering instructions to the central processing unit. The same eight-bit sequence, say "11110000," might tell a Burroughs computer to add two numbers together and a Control Data 6600 to divide one by the other. Each machine had its unique method for everything from storing files on disk or drum to performing basic mathematical functions. The differences were entirely arbitrary, no more consistent than if the pedal by the right foot operated the accelerator on a Ford but the headlights on a Chevy.

Nor did the manufacturers see any advantage to marketing machines even remotely like their competitors'. Once IBM sold a system to United Airlines it could rest assured that the frightful effort of rewriting software, retraining staff, and moving tons of iron and steel cabinets around would make United think very long and hard before replacing its IBM system by one made by, say, Honeywell.

Therefore Kay, who had programmed everything from a Burroughs 5000 at the Air Force Air Training Command to a Control Data 6600 at NCAR, the National Center for Atmospheric Research, was compelled to become a student of computer architectures. Subconsciously his mind was absorbing the principles of programming that would grow a few years hence at PARC into an extraordinary advance in software design. As he recalled later, however, at the moment "I barely saw it."

So too did he assimilate only subconsciously an article in a technical magazine he came upon while debugging NCAR's giant CDC 6600 in Chippewa Falls, Wisconsin, in 1965. The magazine was *Electronics*. For its thirty-fifth anniversary issue it had invited a few industry leaders to plot a technology curve for the next ten years. The research director at Fairchild Semiconductor Co., a brilliant engineer named Gordon Moore, contributed a four-page piece insouciantly entitled "Cramming More Components onto Integrated Circuits." The essay forecast that as circuits became more densely packed with microscopic transistors, computing power would exponentially increase in performance and diminish in cost over the years. Moore contended that this trend could be predicted mathematically, so that memory costing $500,000 in 1965 would come all the way down to $3,000 by 1985—an insight so basic to the subsequent growth and expansion of the computer industry that ever since then it has been known as "Moore's Law."

That day in 1965, however, Alan Kay skimmed Moore's article and laid it aside, unmoved. The dream of a computer scaled down to serve a single human being would not come to him for another couple of years. As he toiled in Chippewa Falls on a room-sized, freon-cooled CDC 6600,

Gordon Moore's astonishing prediction that electronics had embarked on a journey of unceasing miniaturization seemed to have no relevance to his life at all.

"I was in an embryonic state. I didn't want to work and get a real job, but go to graduate school. The only criterion was that it had to be above four thousand feet in altitude."

In 1966 Kay finally secured his bachelor's degree from the University of Colorado, a double major in mathematics and molecular biology. The only doctoral program he could find to fit his exacting specification was the one Dave Evans had established at Utah with a $5 million grant from Bob Taylor at ARPA. To his own amazement he got accepted as the seventh graduate student in the school's tiny department of computer science.

"I discovered later that Evans never looked at my grades," Kay said. "He didn't believe in it. You had to send him a resume, which was all he ever looked at. He was like Al Davis of the Oakland Raiders; his theory was to let everybody into training camp and give them a really decent chance, then be incredibly savage cutting the roster. I was completely thrilled that this guy seemed to think so much of my abilities. One thing I resolved was that he'd never find out the truth."

Taylor's ARPA money had turned Utah into a hotbed of computer graphics. Kay discovered that the day he walked into Evans's office to meet his new mentor. Evans, an introverted gentleman of few words, reached over to a foot-high stack of documents bound in brown paper piled on his desk. He handed one to Kay and said, "Take this and read it."

The title read, "Sketchpad: A Man-Machine Graphical Communications System." The 1963 MIT doctoral thesis of Ivan Sutherland, Taylor's predecessor at IPTO, the paper described a program that had become the cornerstone of the young science of interactive computer graphics. Sketchpad worked on only one machine in the world, Wes Clark's TX–2 at Lincoln Lab. But its precepts were infinitely applicable to a whole range of increasingly nimble and powerful computers then coming into existence. Sketchpad was also, by Evans's mandate, the cardinal intro-duction to computing in his doctoral program. "Basically," Kay said, "you had to understand that before you were a real person at Utah."

Sutherland's system could create graphic objects of dazzling complex-ity, all the more amazing given the severe limitations of the contempo-rary hardware. With Sketchpad the user could skew straight lines into curves ("rubber-banding"), make engineering-precise lines and angles (the system straightened out the draftsman's rough sketches), and zoom the display resolution in and out. The program pioneered the "virtual desktop," in which the user sketched on the visible portion of a theoret-ical drawing space about one-third of a mile square (the invisible por-tions were held in the computer's memory and could be scrolled into view). Contemplating the power of Sketchpad was "like seeing a glimpse of heaven," Kay said later. "It had all of the kinds of things that the com-puter seemed to promise. You could think of it as a light that was sort of showing us the way."

That graphics could be a directly manipulable—and minutely per-sonalized—element of the computer interface was one of dozens of new concepts that bombarded Kay in his first few weeks at Utah. His mind on fire, he spent hours in the library stacks photocopying every-thing that grabbed his interest in the computing literature. He emerged with hundreds of articles, virtually a living history of comput-ing for his parched intellect to absorb.

He soon came under other powerful influences. At one conference he heard the oracular Marvin Minsky speak. Minsky was an MIT psycholo-gist and a computing pioneer, a disciple of the child psychologist Jean Piaget and a founder of the new science of artificial intelligence, which aimed to reproduce human psychology in the computer. His speech was a "terrific diatribe" about how traditional education destroys the learn-ing aptitude of children, a subject that must have resounded to the pre-cocious Kay's very soul. Minsky did not specifically prescribe computers as the answer. But he made intriguing mention of the work a colleague had done in designing a computer language to help children learn pro-gramming.

Early the next year Kay got to meet this colleague. Seymour Papert was a burly, bushy-bearded South African, a Cambridge-trained mathematician who managed to combine a single-minded absorption with the learning skills of children with a profound absent-mindedness about everything else. Papert had devised a simple programming language known as "LOGO," the aim of which was to teach children about computers by giving them a tool to see the machine instantaneously respond to their commands. LOGO literally turned the computer into a toy. Its most conspicuous feature was a turtle-shaped robot the size of a dinner plate. This device would crawl about on a schoolroom floor according to simple commands children could type onto a computer screen: "forward 100" directed it in a straight line 100 turtle steps, "right 90" dictated a 90-degree right turn, and so on. A pen protruding from the turtle's belly would trace its path on the floor, allowing the more adept of its young programmers to create patterns of almost limitless intricacy.

LOGO's genius was its ability to turn the abstract (one can command a computer to do something) into the concrete (one can direct the turtle to draw a parallelogram). To Kay it was a revelation to watch Papert's ten-, eleven-, and twelve-year-old subjects use a simple computer to create designs one would otherwise assume could only be achieved by mainframe systems loaded with complex algorithms. Papert showed the way toward reducing the machine from demigod to tool (in Wes Clark's phrase) by subjecting it to the unforgiving scrutiny of children. Kay never forgot the lesson. As he wrote later, "The best outputs that time-sharing can provide are crude green-tinted line drawings and square-wave musical tones. Children, however, are used to finger paints, color television and stereophonic records, and they usually find the things that can be accomplished with a low-capacity time-sharing system insufficiently stimulating to maintain their interest." Or as Kay and his colleague Adele Goldberg wrote later: "If 'the medium is the message,' then the message of low-bandwidth time-sharing is 'blah.'"

When his turn came to design a programming language at PARC, he would invest it with several unmistakable elements of Papert's system: its visual feedback, its accessibility to novices, and its orientation to the wonder and creativity of childhood. Partially in deference to this last factor, he would call it "Smalltalk."

While Kay was taking these first mind-blowing excursions into Ideaspace, the caliber of graphics research at Utah was exploding. Ivan Sutherland had joined the faculty to work with his friend Dave Evans (they would eventually form a partnership to manufacture interactive military simulators). Kay's fellow grad student John Warnock achieved a graphics milestone by solving the famous "hidden-line problem," which applied to how computers could draw the outline of a form when it is partially hidden behind another—the sides of a triangle hidden behind a ball, for example—so all the visible sides and angles convincingly line up. (Warnock's solution is a *tour de force* of such compactness that his doctoral thesis, in which it is described, runs to only 32 pages.)

Kay's own 1969 thesis incorporated these ideas and others into what must be one of the oddest dissertations ever submitted for a doctorate in a scientific discipline, featuring as it did epigraphs from, among others, W. H. Auden, J. S. Bach, and Kahlil Gibran ("You would touch with your fingers the naked body of your dreams"). The hand-drawn illustrations included not only complex diagrams of functions and logical trees but line drawings of fanciful single-user machines. These had screen, keyboard, and mouse unified into a desktop console, a big brother to the portable all-purpose computer that had provoked such controversy when he described it at the ARPA grad students' conference two years earlier.

Kay's thesis outlined an interactive computer called the FLEX machine which he had designed in partnership with an unsung hardware genius named Ed Cheadle, who was an important engineer for a Salt Lake aerospace company. The FLEX incorporated many of the ideas Kay would develop in the coming years at PARC, including compactness, object-oriented programming, and the use of a display screen. But it was not quite the personal computer he envisioned, in part because it was not powerful enough to perform all the functions required by his ideal and in part because it utilized a complicated and stilted language which, as Kay recalled, "users found repellent to learn."

Despite its idiosyncrasies (or because of them), Kay's thesis readily passed the muster of a five-man committee that included Sutherland and Evans. But he was tormented by a sense of things half-done. Parts of his FLEX machine could be implemented on existing hardware, but a truly suitable technology seemed to be tantalizingly just out of reach. "The big whammy for me came during a conference tour of the University of Illinois, where I saw a one-inch-square lump of glass and neon gas in which individual spots would light up on command—it was the first flat-panel display. I spent the rest of the conference calculating just when the silicon of the FLEX could be put on the back of the display." The answer, according to Moore's Law, seemed to be at least ten years off.

If contemporary machines were inadequate, Kay's goals had not changed. The quest was still for something simple enough for a child to use yet powerful enough to slake the human thirst for creativity. Kay imagined an invention called the "KiddiComp" or "Dynabook." To make the abstraction tangible, he built himself a model box about nine inches by twelve and a half inches deep, with a flat screen and keyboard drawn on the top surface, and filled it with lead pellets as a way of divining its optimum weight (about two pounds, he judged).

He was at loose ends, depressed over having failed to make his great idea materialize in more than cardboard form. While holding a temporary appointment at the Stanford artificial intelligence lab he underwent a year of gestalt therapy ("a very California thing to do"). He was on the verge of accepting a post at Carnegie-Mellon when Bob Taylor called him with the electrifying news that Lampson, Thacker, and several of their BCC colleagues were joining Xerox PARC *en masse*. Kay reconsidered his plans. Butler Lampson was one of his intellectual heroes. Through the ARPA grad student conferences he knew the others as first-class talents. If all these people were to converge at PARC under Bob Taylor, there was no telling what they could accomplish— even build his Dynabook.

One night he and Taylor stayed up nearly until dawn, batting around the possibilities implicit in a conjuncture of Xerox's money, Kay's ideas, and the engineering of Lampson and Thacker. A computer simple enough to be worked by children! Small enough to be carried under your arm! Powerful enough to drive a display in full color! There was only one thing, Taylor informed him at some point. Kay would not be assigned with the others to his lab, but to the competing Systems Science Lab under Bill Gunning.

Much has been made of Taylor's motives in keeping Kay out of his own lab. Some believe Taylor wished to place a "ringer" in the rival SSL—a "colonization," Kay said, "so two of the four labs at PARC would have ex-ARPA people" to more effectively propagate his ideas throughout the organization. It is just as likely that Taylor's BCC coup had filled CSL's allotted head count for the moment. Since he was advising Gunning on recruitment anyway, there was nothing untoward in offering him Alan Kay.

It is also certain that landing in Gunning's SSL was Kay's lucky break. He tended to work as a loner—either by himself or as leader of a small team. Could he have maintained his intellectual autonomy in CSL, where the only group was Taylor's and the intellectual engine was Butler Lampson? Working out of SSL allowed Kay to work as a full participant in CSL's program without ceding his independent spirit. He could interact with CSL as a privileged equal, outside Taylor's direct supervision and Lampson's intellectual domination.

As events unfolded, Kay and Taylor apart proved more powerful a force than they would have been together. Where Taylor could be vague and inarticulate in describing computing's future, Kay was never less than crystal-clear. The day he came to PARC for his job interview, Rick Jones invited him into his office and asked him a stock question.

"What do you think your greatest achievement will be at PARC?" he asked.

"It'll be a personal computer," Kay replied.

"What's *that*?"

Spying a flat portfolio on Jones's desk the size of a student's notebook, Kay seized it and flipped it open. "This will be a flat-panel display," he said, indicating the cover, which he held upright. "There'll be a keyboard here on the bottom, and enough power to store your mail, files, music, artwork, and books. All in a package about this size and weighing a couple of pounds. That's what I'm talking about.".

He walked out, leaving Jones scratching his head and saying to himself, "Yeah, *right*."

With Kay's arrival the computer research team at PARC achieved critical mass. They had the people and the leadership, a seemingly unlimited amount of money, and Xerox's liberal commission to pursue whatever course of inquiry they wished.

All they needed now to start work was a computer. Pake gave them a month or so to study the available alternatives before recommending a system to be used by the entire research center. But in making their choice they provoked the first great donnybrook of PARC's young existence.

CHAPTER 7

The Clone

Perhaps Taylor and his hand-picked team should have known by sheer intuition that when you are about to spend a half-million dollars of your employer's money, you do not go spending it on a competitor's product. After all, Ford employees do not drive Toyotas, and the soda machines at Pepsi headquarters do not get stocked with Coke.

Or perhaps, having almost all come from academia and government service, they were simply too green at working for an industrial enterprise to understand why Xerox's computer company, SDS, would take amiss Taylor's proposal that PARC purchase as its main computer a machine manufactured by its commercial archenemy. Especially when the choice seemed to them a no-brainer.

Yet that is what happened. As Taylor put it later, "We upset the apple cart and didn't realize how badly." Badly enough: PARC's opening blunder would not be forgotten at Xerox headquarters for many years.

The Computer System Lab's inaugural task of selecting the main computing hardware for all the PARC labs seemed straightforward enough from the standpoint of pure engineering. When the lab drew up the specifications there was no need to hold a colloquium to weigh their options. There was only one: The PDP-10, manufactured by Digital Equipment Corporation.

Over the previous year the PDP-10 had taken the computing world by storm. One of DEC's series of commercially successful units that had grown out of the artificial intelligence programs at MIT and Stanford, the PDP-10 was exceptional: A relatively compact computer (though it still took up a good-sized room) with time-sharing hardware that rapidly replaced the aging SDS 940s in scores of college computer centers and corporate back offices. The PDP-10 was so well designed that it is still treated with a cliquish reverence by computer jocks today, more than a decade after the last unit rolled off the factory line.

The PDP-10 was also becoming the computer of choice—a *de facto* standard—for research departments linked to the burgeoning ARPANET. It possessed the special virtue of having been specifically tailored to run Lisp, a popular programming language in which ARPANET researchers turned out software by the ream. Moreover, its operating system, Tenex, had been developed on an ARPA contract with government funds, and was thus available for anyone to use, free of charge.

By the mid-1970s, thanks to these features and others, computer science in the United States would cease to be a Babel of dozens of mutually incompatible machines. Instead, the prototypical computer research group would be a university department using PDP-10s equipped with the Tenex operating system and linked to the ARPANET.° Even as early as 1971, it was hard to imagine a better description of CSL's self-image. After all, Taylor was the ARPANET's patriarch and they were almost all ARPANET "brats," as they labeled themselves. To the Computer Science Lab it was almost an article of faith that PARC should be the PDP-10 node *par excellence*.

But the lab was about to discover that purchasing capital equipment for a corporate facility could never be as straightforward a question of engineering as it might be for a faculty department at, say, MIT. For

---

°In 1979, ARPANET officials reported that of 202 host computers connected to the network, 104 were PDP-10s or their corporate relatives, PDP-11s.

when word got out that Bob Taylor was planning to install a DEC computer at PARC, the executives at SDS went off like Roman candles. This was understandable. In 1971 SDS was fighting for its life, and DEC was its principal foe.

Not long after completing its purchase of SDS Xerox had discerned that all was not well at its new computer division. Max Palevsky, who had personally pocketed some $100 million from the billion-dollar transaction, was happier spending his money on Democratic campaigns and movie and magazine ventures ("I must be on every sucker list in town," he said cheerily) than burying himself in the day-to-day problems of his old firm. Suspicion was rife that his real business talent resided in his knowing how to get out while the getting was good; popular rumor even had him confiding to aides about the SDS deal: "We sold them a dead horse before it hit the ground." He denied the epigram, but acknowledged knowing that at the time of the sale SDS had entered a rocky stretch of the business cycle.

As though to confirm everyone's worst suspicions, SDS profits peaked in May 1969, at almost the very moment that ownership formally changed hands. That calendar year SDS recorded about $12 million in net income. The following year was its best ever in terms of sales—but for every dollar it recorded in revenue, it lost two. The division never again showed a profit. Over the following three years the losses would add up to nearly $120 million.

No later than early 1970, Rigdon Currie recalled, "the handwriting was on the wall." At that time Currie, as head of sales, was instructed to prepare a detailed presentation on SDS prospects for a management meeting to be chaired by the choleric ex-West Pointer Dan McGurk, a former Palevsky lieutenant who had become the division's president following the sale.

Currie was a Georgia Tech-trained engineer whose southern courtliness masked a wicked sense of humor. He was determined to make sure his presentation would not easily be forgotten. On the appointed day he greeted the assembled executives while standing by a flip chart three feet tall. From the outset it was clear the news was not good. The condition of every one of the company's leading customers was dire, he said. Government agencies like NASA and the National Science Foundation were sharply cutting their budgets. Time-sharing companies like Tymshare, which ran its nationwide network on SDS 940s, were encountering sales resistance at all levels. With the education, government, and aerospace industries all slumping simultaneously, nearly every market SDS served was on the rocks.

Moreover, thanks to the PDP-10, SDS no longer found itself on the cutting edge of the time-sharing market, where it had been placed by the work of Project Genie. Even long-term customers turned in their leases on the SDS 940 once they got a look at the new DEC machine. That was an ominous trend. The old SDS leases were a fiscal time bomb: They permitted the customers to return their machines prior to expiration for a full pro-rata credit on the unexpired period. Unfortunately, SDS had long since recorded the full-term lease payments as revenue. This meant that as computers came back from failed or defecting clients SDS would have to recalculate the profits it had already reported for earlier quarters and quite possibly restate them—as losses.

"Now, taking all these factors together, where are we?" Currie asked out loud. He turned over the top card on his flip chart. The next one was blank except for two words in huge block letters: "DEEP SHIT."

"McGurk almost killed me," he remembered.

Adding to the predicament of shrinking markets was Peter McColough's determination to push SDS into a new one: the business data processing business ruled by IBM.

Although McColough has been roundly chastised for this strategy, it may actually have originated with Max Palevsky. The SDS founder had always weighed his company against IBM as a benchmark. To outsiders this resembled weighing a puppy against a horse; no matter how big it grows, it can never play in the same league. Yet in the weeks following the Xerox sale Palevsky had openly fantasized about placing Xerox's capital base behind the engineering skills of SDS and marching jointly into war against Big Blue. (Much later he hinted he was only telling McColough what the Xerox CEO wanted to hear.)

To the rest of the industry the act of stepping into IBM's den seemed a fool's errand. Big Blue did not always offer the most technologically advanced products in the market and frequently charged the highest prices, but the ruthlessness of its sales and marketing more than made up for these shortcomings (and fomented an epic battle with federal antitrust authorities). Companies that tried to dislodge IBM from its perch generally got butchered in the attempt. That had been the fate even of the industrial powerhouses General Electric and RCA, which had given up after losing a combined $600 million in ten years of trying.

The only major competitors left in the market were five large computer makers known familiarly as the "Bunch." The term was an acronym of their names—Burroughs, (Sperry) Univac, NCR, Control Data, and Honeywell—but it was also descriptive. The Bunch trailed IBM in a distant cluster, like a field of thoroughbreds struggling to keep up with Secretariat. From 1960 through 1970 the five competitors lost a combined $167 million while IBM racked up profits of more than $3.5 *billion*.

Into this valley of death Peter McColough now proposed to ride SDS. The very notion all but proclaimed his ignorance of the computer industry in general and his own subsidiary in particular, for there could scarcely exist a company less qualified to take on this particular fight.

"We did not have the tools to do it," Robert Spinrad recalled.

Bob Spinrad was an experienced scientist and engineer, unassertive but rigorously analytical. He was a gregarious gentleman of the old school, with a round face marked by eyebrows as dark and emphatic as exclamation points. Spinrad had joined SDS in 1968 to run its software group after several years at Brookhaven National Laboratory, where the computer of choice was an SDS machine. Now he found himself swept unwillingly into McColough's foolhardy crusade. Shortly after the chief executive's decree, Spinrad met with a couple of Xerox officials sent belatedly from Stamford to El Segundo to appraise the division's competitive ability in the new market.

"How good is your COBOL compiler?" they asked. COBOL was the tedious programming language used for repetitive and uncomplicated business programs such as payrolls and budgets. On hearing the question, Bob Spinrad recognized as though for the first time the enormity of the task confronting the company. Scientific and research programmers, like those who worked for SDS and its traditional customers, would not be caught dead working in COBOL, which they considered a lame language suitable only for clerks and drones. He shifted uneasily in his chair.

"It's not a question of how good our COBOL compiler is," he told the visitors.

"Why not?"

"Because we don't have one."

Xerox had thoroughly misunderstood the difference between scientific computing, in which SDS might with great effort manage to hold its own, and business computing, in which it was a non-starter. The company could not offer a fraction of the product line any business client would expect as a matter of course, whether high-speed line printers or robust database programs. As Spinrad recalled, "A lot of things that were ho-hum standard operating procedure for companies that served a commercial environment just weren't in our lexicon or armament."

The harvest was a profound morale crisis in El Segundo, where every employee understood what the company's limitations were, how hard it would be to change course, and how determined Xerox was to do it anyway.

One weekend McGurk summoned his department heads to a weekend "retreat" in a hotel near Los Angeles International Airport to iron out the difficulties. They broke into study groups, turned over the issues late into the night, and reconvened around a very long conference table on Sunday afternoon.

"All right," McGurk said. "One by one, let's have your reaction to whether we can make this change."

"I said, 'No, I've got a problem,'" Spinrad recalled. "McGurk went around the table and, one by one, everyone else said the same thing. 'I've got this problem,' 'I've got that problem.'"

McGurk fell silent for a moment, then slammed his fist on the table. "Okay," he said, "we'll do it!"

In this cheerless atmosphere PARC's request for a PDP–10 detonated like a grenade. It had been only a few months earlier that SDS had launched its latest scientific computer, the Sigma 7—designed specifically to compete head to head with the PDP–10. Having been ordered to stage a frontal assault on IBM's market, SDS now felt tripped up by the rearguard action launched by its own corporate brethren.

SDS executives wasted no time in starting a campaign at headquarters to kill the proposal. "I was for anything that would keep them from buying that computer," recalled Currie, who outlined for the Stamford brass a scenario in which a computing trade magazine like *Datamation* splashed a photograph across its front cover of a DEC truck pulled up to the loading dock of Xerox PARC. Try selling a Sigma machine to another customer after that!

Taylor maintained that his group considered the PDP–10 so self-evidently superior to the Sigma they never gave a moment's thought to how their request would resonate in El Segundo. Yet they could not have been entirely blind to the fact that the Stamford bosses regarded big computers as fungible commodities, one very much like another. After all, these were the people who had bought the wrong computer company to begin with, then compounded the gaffe by urging it to compete in a manifestly inappropriate market. No one should have been surprised that they would regard PARC's insistence on buying a rival company's machine as an act of sheer perversity.

The task of formally vetoing the request fell to the company's new chief information officer, a systems expert named Paul Strassmann. Strassmann's primary job was to install an SDS computer wherever Xerox currently ran an IBM machine. He came with sterling qualifications, since his greatest accomplishment as the computing czar at his previous company, Kraft Foods, was to junk its system of underperforming IBM 360 data processing computers and replace them with Honeywells.

IBM's failed attempt to get him fired for this rare affront had left Strassmann with no shortage of self-confidence in his own judgment. A severe character whose Teutonic accent soon won him the nickname "the Prussian" at PARC, he imagined his greater role to be that of Xerox's technological policeman. He harbored no illusions about the stupidity of forcing SDS to compete with IBM, a move he regarded as "just a spastic afterthought" by management. But he also believed his responsibility was to ride herd on the proliferation of incompatible computers at Xerox offices around the globe. He was not about to rubber-stamp a half-million-dollar purchase order for a DEC computer to please anyone, research hotshots included. He boomeranged the PDP–10 order back to PARC with instructions to produce a point-by-point technical justification, in writing.

This turned out to be the start of fifteen years of miscommunication and hostility between Xerox's east coast and west. "I told them to show me what the PDP–10 would do that the Sigma 7 wouldn't," Strassmann recalled. "This is what hardass corporate information officers do. They say, 'Show me a competitive analysis.' But PARC never sent one. They thought it was beneath them to show a technical analysis to the headquarters guys. They didn't know how to act like corporate citizens. They just said, 'Don't ask questions.'"

The battle raged for weeks. The official SDS line was that the PDP's popularity over the Sigma among researchers was purely an accident of timing and would soon correct itself. As Currie, a savvy enough computer man but one whose judgment was colored by his position at SDS, recalled, "The PDP had come out a little earlier than the Sigma and they were ahead of us mostly in software." He thought the issue boiled down to "a question of religion," and the least PARC could do as a new Xerox facility was try a new theology on for size. In Stamford the battle was viewed even more simple-mindedly. Headquarters executives thought of software as the gobbledygook that made a machine run, like the hamster driving the wheel. They could not understand why the decision between the PDP–10 and the Sigma needed to be any more complicated than, say, choosing an albino rodent over a brown one.

But from a technical point of view, the issue was hardly that casual. Software was the factor that defined the fundamental incompatibility between the Sigma and PDP machines and the superiority, for PARC's purposes, of the latter. The architectures of the two computers were so radically different that software written for the PDP would not properly fit into the memory space the Sigma allocated for data. Even if the program could be made to run—a doubtful prospect—it would require nearly twice as much memory to run as fast on the Sigma as it did on the PDP–10. Given the high price of memory at the time, this was a major shortcoming.

Although it was theoretically possible to simply "port" all the PDP software over to the Sigma, the CSL engineers calculated that such a job would mean rewriting every single line of every PDP program, a task that would take three years and cost $4 million.

"The only lie in the analysis we did," Lampson later remarked, "was that we never could actually have done it because you couldn't have motivated people to do such a pointless thing."

This was, indeed, the very technical analysis Strassmann had demanded. He received it, too, as part of the lab's capital request—but because it focused on software costs it was not the sort of analysis he expected, which would have been a hardware-by-hardware comparison of the two machines.

"In a way we were cooking the books," Lampson stated later, "but actually this was a pretty accurate way of turning the facts about doing computing research into dollar numbers that Strassmann could understand."

Meanwhile, Taylor invited a group of El Segundo designers to Palo Alto for a two-day "discourse" on the technical issues. His goal was to persuade them that the Sigma and PDP–10 were not really competing in the same market, and they should therefore back off. Instead of engaging in the civil dialogue he had hoped for, however, his cocksure engineers pitilessly dissected the Sigma's shortcomings in front of its designers and Pake, who was sitting in.

Taylor had to admit that the affair was a complete frost. "It ended up like a trial," he said. "Butler and Chuck Thacker knew the Sigma system very well, and they just demolished the Sigma 7. They gave the SDS people fits." When the inquisition finally concluded, Pake took Taylor aside. "You sure know a bunch of smart people," he said. "Butler Lampson seems to understand those guys' machines better than they do."

Neither side seemed able to budge, despite Pake's efforts to find grounds for a truce. He recalled "I asked my guys, 'Is there any way we can reconfigure that Sigma machine and make it work?' The answer kept coming back no from everybody. Meanwhile we talked to SDS to see if they were interested in making any changes. They weren't. They wanted to sell us whatever they had."

Pake's desperation communicated itself to the computer scientists. The choices indeed looked bleak. They could accept the Sigma, which meant suffering with an inadequate machine *and* knuckling under to the corporate suits the very first time their interests conflicted. Or they could stand their ground and browbeat Xerox into buying them the PDP. "But that would cost us so many brownie points we figured it was not a good idea," Lampson recalled. Not a few times in the heat of discussion was the suggestion heard that they should all just quit.

Yet a different impulse, one much more powerful, was beginning to assert itself. This was the engineer's equivalent to the "fight or flight" syndrome, the instinct when confronted by an obstacle not to back off, but to barrel through it.

"We started having these long discussions," Alan Kay remembered. "I was saying, 'Let's not chuck our badges in just yet. Let's think it through.'" Someone else suggested that perhaps they were looking at the question from the wrong end. They had made an issue out of hardware—what machine to buy—when their real concern was software—what programs they could run. What if they simply built their own machine to run the programs they needed?

Asking the question was the same as answering it. "The talk," Kay said, "turned to how long it would take us to *build* our own PDP–10." The answer was about one year and less than $1 million. The truth was that Xerox had only forbidden the lab to buy a PDP–10. Nobody had said anything about cloning one.

"We were fearless," Lampson recalled. "We had built this BCC machine which was a substantially more complicated and elaborate machine than a PDP–10. And furthermore the underlying technology was evolving very rapidly, so we actually had much better physical resources at our disposal. We had great confidence that we could build this thing with a fairly modest investment of effort, and very little risk. Which turned out to be absolutely correct." The machine, he said, "was not built because Xerox refused to let us buy a PDP–10, but because we thought it was the path of least resistance."

Work on the clone began in February. Thacker assumed the role of project manager as well as the bedrock task of designing the internal logic. The other jobs got apportioned out to the lab members willy-nilly, as among townspeople at a community barn-raising, often with little relation to the work in which they were most expert—but then, anyone who could make it through Taylor's selection process was assumed to be smart enough to learn anything. Lampson was an operating systems designer *nonpareil*, for example, but with Tenex they already had their operating system. So he was dragooned into designing the central processor, a hardware task unlike anything he had ever undertaken in his life.

Another who got swept into the project was Ed McCreight, an ex-Boeing engineer of unshakably sunny disposition who was still in his first week or two on the job, "rummaging around for something to do." No one could remain in that state for long at PARC. Thacker lassoed him into designing the disk controller, a hardware unit that would supervise the way the machine moved data to and from a spinning magnetic hard disk. McCreight recalled, "I told him, 'I don't know squat about disk controllers but, hey, I'm game. If you promise to answer all of my questions I'll do it.'"

They all were game because they viewed the task as the construction of their own laboratory. One principle Taylor imparted to his people was that the things they built had to be designed for daily use. Too many research labs turned out playthings and prototypes designed to go on a shelf, as though merely for display.

"They show wonderful things and nothing much ever comes of them," he complained. That would not happen on his watch. They would build nothing that could not be put to work, because that was the only way to find out in the end if the stuff was any good.

This rule would become one of the hallmarks of PARC's creative method. Undoubtedly it held special meaning for the CSL members who had lived through the painful saga of Berkeley Computer, whose machine relied too much on idealistic designs and not enough on working pragmatism. As Kay recalled, "Within a couple of weeks after the BCC people showed up Butler got up at a meeting. BCC had failed and he was still venting. He said he was sick and tired of the sixties, when your stuff 'sort of' worked and you could usually get it to work long enough for a demo, but that was about it. He said we should decide never to make something at PARC that isn't engineered for a hundred users. If we were building a time-sharing computer, it should support a hundred people, a network should take a hundred connections, and so on. Our initial reaction to that was, 'Gee, it's really going to cramp our style.' But in fact the extra thought we had to put into everything in order to support it for a hundred users made things work so much better that it probably sped us up by a factor of three."

The idea that they were building their own computing environment galvanized them into working at breakneck speed, like settlers hastening to erect a rudimentary shelter before the onset of a hard winter. An almost alchemical change overtook the lab, infusing it with the pure excitement of discovery that a research manager may be lucky to witness once in a lifetime. People would contend later that being forced to clone the PDP–10 was the best thing that ever happened to CSL—even Strassmann eventually bragged, "I made everyone a hero." This is the period they were referring to, when a bunch of disparate talents came together in appreciation of the virtues of working together on challenges that had virtually no precedent and the air filled with new ideas. Then there was the added satisfaction of testing their mastery of a new technology. "It was fun," Lampson said later, "to see how easy it was."

The fundamental problem was that to the extent the PDP–10's physical design belonged to Digital Equipment Corporation it could not simply be copied, at least not legally. In any case, no one at PARC had spent enough time inside that machine to reproduce it circuit for circuit. The trick was to turn this limitation into an advantage. Since the task at hand was not really to build a PDP–10, only a machine that would follow the same instructions as a PDP–10, there was no reason not to find a shortcut. The best shortcut, as they all knew, was to substitute their own microcode for the PDP–10's wiring.

DEC's machine, as it happened, was the epitome of the "hard-wired" computer. Its operation depended on the physical configuration of its transistors; these were arranged into intricately linked "gates"—the building blocks of traditional digital computers that received electrical impulses at one end and passed, propagated, blocked, or modified them according to the rules of binary mathematics and nineteenth-century Boolean logic.

From thousands of these devices, artfully arranged, could be constructed a machine able to add, subtract, multiply, and divide; read a character from a teletype and output it to a cathode-ray screen; or forecast the trajectory of a launched missile. But it was no longer necessary to fashion the gates out of wires and transistors. In place of much of the PDP–10's intricate circuitry the CSL engineers planned to substitute a class of software known as microcode.

One can think of microcode as a way of allowing digital signals to replicate the twists and turns of a hard-wired machine's circuits without actually traversing the physical pathways. Microcode examines a programmed instruction, determines where it would end up if it primly followed all the wiring, and deposits it in the right place without making the arduous overland trek.

Microcode's great advantage over hard-wiring is that, as Lampson notes, "it's much easier to express something complicated in program instructions, or micro-instructions, than directly in gates." Detect a bug in a hard-wired machine and you have to rip out the errant circuits and solder in new ones. With microcode you just rewrite the program. It is as though in traversing the United States from Boston to San Francisco you find that the paved highway through Cincinnati leads not to San Francisco but San Diego. Microcode would be the equivalent of getting on an airplane and changing the flight path rather than ripping up and relocating the highway.

Translating hardware into software in quest of this simplicity is, as processes go, fiendishly complex—the digital signals take a lot more twists and turns in microcode than in a hard-wired machine; but to Taylor's group its mysteries were an open book. The BCC 500 was microcoded, as was the FLEX machine Kay designed for his Utah doctorate.

"We knew a lot about microcode," recalled the latter, who contributed some conceptual ideas while observing CSL's actual design and construction of the machine from the sidelines. "One of the world's great microcoders, Ed Fiala, was with us, so that was a big plus. One of the great hardware designers, Thacker, was there, that was a big plus. The minus was that there were only about ten people to do it all. And it had to be done quickly."

Once they settled on the new course of action, a whole world of possibilities suddenly opened to them. They could not only clone the PDP-10; they could *improve* on it. The first place to do so was the memory. PDP machines used ferrite core memory, the standard in the industry since its invention in 1951 by Jay Forrester at MIT. Core memories were made of tiny rings (or "cores") woven into a mat of copper filaments that allowed each ring to be magnetically polarized. The cores held, or "remembered," their charge until deliberately overridden, leaving a pattern to be read back and interpreted as data bits in storage.

Core's great virtue was its reliability. But it had to be manufactured by hand and suffered from the defects of great bulkiness and slow speed. The 300-kilobyte core memory of Wes Clark's TX-2, for instance, was a handmade block of about a cubic yard, or the size of a large file cabinet, costing roughly half a million dollars. This volume of memory was large for its time but trivial by today's standards, when a desktop computer's semiconductor memory can hold about one hundred times as much information in the physical volume of a couple of credit cards, at a cost of about forty dollars.

By 1971 core memories were about to be supplanted by a brand-new technology based on silicon semiconductors. The previous October a one-kilobit memory chip (that is, 1,024 bits of memory per chip) had been introduced by Intel, a young engineering company co-founded by Gordon Moore of "Moore's law" fame.

Intel's 1103 chip was struggling for acceptance in the computer industry, largely because its peculiarities gave system designers migraines. The 1103 memories were "volatile," meaning that all the stored data were wiped out whenever the chip's charge was lost. Because the 1103's charge had a tendency to gradually leak away, the chip had to be recharged, or refreshed, by zapping it with an electrical impulse several thousand times a *second* to keep data from evaporating. (Cores, by contrast, were "non-volatile," meaning they held their stored data indefinitely, charged or not.) The 1103 required users to supply it with all sorts of "weird voltages," as Lampson later put it, and looked like it might be prone to a host of data errors arising from the density at which designers crammed it with microscopic transistors.

Such flaws made the 1103 a spectacularly stubborn and perverse contrivance. Its patriarch, Gordon Moore, termed it "the most difficult-to-use semiconductor ever created by man." It was also hard to manufacture. Intel had so much difficulty turning out an economical volume of working chips that it had to assign entire teams of engineers and technicians to the drudgery of picking good chips out from the river of useless silicon coming off the fabrication line, a job so fervently detested it was labeled "turd polishing."

To the CSL team, however, the 1103's shortcomings were obstacles to be overcome. "It seemed pretty clear to us that the memory should be semiconductor, although we didn't really know whether those chips worked—and it turned out later that they don't," Lampson recalled. "We certainly would have preferred a more robust chip. But we were very confident that by putting in error correction we could make up a very satisfactory system that *would* work." That was an understatement. As CSL well knew, if they could only overcome the 1103's manifold obstinacies, their machine would boast the speediest and most reliable memory on Earth.

CSL's resolution of the PDP-Sigma imbroglio failed to quell entirely SDS's discontent with the outcome. From El Segundo was heard continuous carping that PARC had caused the division insupportable embarrassment by spurning its top-of-the-line product. This provoked Pake into an outburst that settled the matter once and for all. In a blistering memo he reminded headquarters that his best new engineers had voluntarily agreed to suspend bona fide research projects for the year or more it would take them to satisfy SDS's querulous concerns. "It is unthinkable to me that Xerox sets me the task of hiring creative, imaginative, top-rank researchers and then expects me to insist that they handcuff themselves with inappropriate equipment," he wrote. "I will do my best to provide them with the kind of first-rate technical support it is reasonable to expect in Xerox research laboratories. If that is the wrong way to build a first-rate corporate research center for Xerox, then I am the wrong man for the job."

Meanwhile, the CSL rank and file's lingering resentment at their Southern California in-laws was manifested when the time came to give their clone a name. One afternoon a group of engineers gathered at someone's house to mark an intermediate milestone on the project.

"A moderate amount of beer had been consumed and we were trying to figure out what to name this thing and there was considerable hilarity," Thacker recalled of the day they came up with the formal moniker of "Multiple Access Xerox Computer." It sounded conventional, but everyone on the scene got the joke. In honor of the man who had sold his lousy computer company to Xerox, the first major project undertaken by PARC would be known for all time by the acronym "MAXC." No member of the lab ever forgot to remind outsiders, "The 'C' is silent."

MAXC's christening was more than an opportunity to tweak Max Palevsky.* It crystallized their awareness that what was coming together in the Computer Science Lab was no longer a DEC machine, but their own.

"We did everything, from soup to nuts," McCreight said. Liberated from slavish adherence to the PDP–10 design, they were able to get dozens of functions running faster or cheaper. McCreight performed one such feat with his disk controller. Conventional disk controllers were generally equipped with their own separate processing units, like Stegosauruses with their second brains, which added significantly to their cost and complexity. Poring over the system schematics in his office one day, he was struck by the realization that there would occur certain periods when, having executed one instruction and not yet received the next, MAXC's central processor would be idle but available, like a car left running unattended in the driveway.

---

*The point was probably lost on the target. As Pake said later, "I doubt that Max Palevsky ever cared, or even knew about it."

"I learned enough about the processor to realize I could use some of those spare cycles," he recounted. "In effect I could kidnap the processor to do some arithmetic for the disk controller. I wouldn't have to put so many gates into the disk controller"—saving another few thousand dollars in hardware—"if I could periodically borrow the processor to compute some of the things I needed to compute." McCreight's realization was their first embrace of the concept of "multitasking"—giving the processor numerous jobs to juggle at once. Implemented on this modest scale in MAXC, it was destined to pay enormous dividends later.

Meanwhile, they continued to inject refinements into the PDP–10 design. If along the way they discovered some flaw, an inelegance or vulgarity committed by the original designers, they had no compunction about fixing it. At least once this resulted in making MAXC *too* good. This was the episode of Fiala's floating-point bug.

Floating point operations allow computers to handle huge numbers by breaking them into two pieces: the mantissa, which comprises the significant digits, and the exponent, which is a power of ten. Thus the number 632,100,000 would be split into a mantissa of 6.321 and an exponent of eight (i.e., 10 to the 8th power). To multiply two numbers in a floating-point operation, the computer simply multiplies the mantissas and sums the exponents.

Floating point functions are critical to the efficient use of a computer's resources. But they are among the most difficult to properly implement in hardware. Sure enough, while coding the floating point microcode Fiala discovered a number of bugs in the PDP hardware, or at least places where he could improve on it. Without thinking twice, he did so. As McCreight recalled, "He figured it's his floating point, and it was up to him to make it more accurate than the PDP's."

One of the classic frustrations of systems design is that fixing a bug in one place often creates others elsewhere, the way squeezing a balloon at one end makes it bulge out at the other. Something like that happened in this case.

When the MAXC team tried to launch a program called Interlisp that had been written for the original PDP–10, "for some reason we couldn't bring it up," McCreight said. "We couldn't even find *nil*, which is the first thing you look for in Lisp—if you can't find *nil*, you're in trouble." The problem, as they discovered after hours of tedious investigation, was that Interlisp utilized the PDP's inefficient floating-point algorithms to execute its own code. Fiala's fixes left the program hopelessly confused, as though someone had rearranged its furniture in the dark. Unfortunately, one reason they were building MAXC was to run Lisp. So with a great show of reluctance, Fiala acceded to pressure from the rest of the lab— and programmed the bugs back in.

As they anticipated, Intel's 1103 memory chips proved to be a major nuisance. The reputedly serviceable chips that survived the "turd polishing" stage still arrived at PARC with their deeply flawed design intact. Among the headaches was their so-called pattern sensitivity: Certain combinations of bits would cause an intermediate bit to "flip," so that a sequence of 1001 might read out incorrectly as 1101 or 1011.

Thacker overcame the fault with an error correction system that could identify and reflip erroneous bits. This worked as long as they only occurred one at a time. Eventually, however, a second bit would fail. "Then," Thacker recalled, "you'd get an honest error and the system would crash and we'd have to change the chip." That was not as rare an occurrence as it might seem. For a time MAXC boasted the largest semiconductor memory of any computer in the world, an achievement that temporarily made PARC Intel's single biggest customer. Approximately 25,000 of the 1103s got packed into four cabinets standing six feet high, each one containing four card cages with sixteen circuit boards that in turn were each about the height and width of a standard sheet of typewriter paper and held ninety-six chips apiece.

The memory boards were the only part of MAXC the lab sent outside for fabrication. "There were so many of them—two hundred and fifty-six, not including spares—that it was economical to make a printed circuit board for the memory, which was not an inconsiderable task in those days," Thacker recalled.

At one point the need for a dependable board-maker threatened to set Thacker on a life of crime. Intel had sublicensed the manufacture of 1103s to a Canadian company called Microsystems International Ltd., or MIL, a subsidiary of the Canadian telephone company. "They offered to make boards at a substantially lower price than we were paying," Thacker said. "I remember going to Ottawa one time carrying a sample memory board with me, at that time a one-thousand-dollar object."

As he breezed through Canadian Customs, he was stopped by an officer who asked what he was carrying.

"It's a printed circuit board," Thacker replied.

"You'll have to pay duty on that."

"But it's just a prototype. I'm bringing it in today and bringing it back out tomorrow."

"In that case you'll have to pay duty both ways. What's it worth?"

Thacker thought quickly. "About fifteen dollars."

"Oh," the officer said, waving him through. "If that's all, don't worry about it."

Notwithstanding the stubborn 1103s, MAXC proved a superbly robust machine thanks to Thacker's inspired design and the lab's resourceful craftsmanship. Because Thacker had designed in more physical memory than was needed for all its logical operations, whole memory boards could be pulled out for repair without taking the system down for even a nanosecond. Once fully debugged, the machine set records for uninterrupted availability on the ARPANET, handily outperforming computers that had taken squadrons of engineers years to design. In contrast, the Computer Science Lab at PARC implemented MAXC in scarcely more than eighteen months. The cost to Xerox was about $750,000, of which roughly a third went for the memory.

All this was accomplished under intense deadline pressure. "Everybody was waiting for MAXC to exist," recalled McCreight, whose office at Porter Drive was so crammed with equipment—six-foot-high racks holding twenty-four spinning disks on two spindles, arranged one on top and one below like pizza ovens—there was barely room for human beings. "Every day guys would show up in my office and say, 'How soon, is it coming now?' So we knew it was a very much desired thing. I mean, the point of the lab was to program and we couldn't program until we had the computer system."

As Taylor anticipated, moreover, the seemingly make-work project paid exponential dividends in group dynamics. At first glance, devoting so much time and money to reproducing a computer available on the open market seemed sheer profligacy. But from Taylor's point of view, the assignment to produce a real machine had given his engineers a unique opportunity to parse out their own strengths and weaknesses in ways Taylor could never have devised himself. What emerged at the end of the program was a seamless, remarkably powerful unit.

"In a small group the dynamics are like those on a good basketball team," Kay observed. "Everybody has to be able to play the whole game. Each person should have certain things they're better at than the others, but everyone should be pretty good at everything." MAXC proved they were all pretty good at everything that mattered: hardware, software, microcoding, programming. "They made having to do MAXC into a virtue. No matter how you slice it, the job was amazing. It was not trivial. Not even close to trivial."

It was, however, merely the first step in a long journey. MAXC was barely finished before they started thinking about what to do next.

CHAPTER 8

The Future Invented

While his lab staff occupied themselves with implementing MAXC in the spring of 1971, Taylor got around to one of the keystone tasks Pake had set down for him: He recruited his own boss.

This did not happen a moment too soon. Taylor was in critical need of a buffer between himself and the rest of the organization. He and Pake were still on speaking terms, but there was little more to say about their relationship. "It was like a bad marriage where two people stay together because of the kids," remarked Rick Jones.

No one would dispute that "the kids" were worth the effort. CSL's work on MAXC provided just a hint of what they might be capable of once they hit their stride. But accepting Taylor's crew at this level involved a sort of Manichean bargain: Perhaps the intellectual tension the Computer Science Lab generated on Porter Drive helped goad the other labs into matching their energy and creativity, but they also made things harder than was necessary. Pake, who had literally put his job on the line for MAXC, observed privately that his efforts to build a bridge between PARC and SDS might actually have borne fruit if only the CSL engineers had not taken every opportunity to belittle El Segundo's work. Pake's proclivity for solving conflicts by splitting them down the middle and Taylor's for establishing and holding his position in the local pecking order stood in direct opposition to each other. This situation was not destined to improve.

At least Taylor had the wisdom to see that his buffer to the outside world should in training and experience resemble Pake more than himself. The man in question was yet another charter member of the ARPANET clan. In the late 1960s Jerome I. Elkind had been in charge of computer research at Bolt, Beranek & Newman (BBN), a firm of Boston engineering consultants known familiarly as BBN. There he had supervised the firm's successful bid to build a critical piece of Taylor's cherished nationwide network. This was the system of "IMPs," or Interface Message Processors. The IMPs formed a subnetwork of standardized computers (they were remodeled Honeywell minicomputers) that stood as a gateway between each host's mainframe and the central network. In effect they functioned as universal translators, allowing the network to interconnect dozens of incompatible computers without turning into a cacophonous Babel. (The concept, which solved one of the fundamental technical problems bedeviling the ARPANET's designers, was the brainchild of Wes Clark.)

Thanks mostly to its extensive work on the ARPANET, Bolt, Beranek & Newman became one of ARPA's largest private contractors. This circumstance had forged an amicable relationship between Elkind and Taylor. Elkind also had bonds with several other PARC people, including Butler Lampson, who he had met when his BBN division bought one of the first SDS 940s, and Peter Deutsch, who had worked at BBN as a high school student and during summer vacations from Berkeley.

Elkind was an empirical-minded scientist with a conspicuous streak of skepticism. This temperament elicited sharply divergent reactions from his peers. Some appreciated his discretion—a trait which, after all, would not be such a drawback for the manager of a lab venturing to the edge of the unknown. Others found him an insufferable pessimist whose disposition was certain to clash sooner or later with Taylor's enthusiastic cajolery. Even at BBN, observed Severo Ornstein, "Jerry was not universally liked as a technical supervisor. I think he didn't have the right touch."

Taylor reassured the lab, however, that his and Elkind's personalities would be complementary, not contentious. He saw Elkind as playing "Mr. Outside" to his own "Mr. Inside"—as a sort of human IMP providing a painless interface between CSL and PARC. Elkind could handle the bureaucratic rubbish for which Taylor had no patience, leaving him free to keep to his role of evangelist, guru, and all-around father figure. Presented so abstractly, the arrangement almost seemed rational.

Taylor laid the groundwork carefully for Elkind's recruitment. He asked Wes Clark, an Elkind admirer from his MIT days, to pass on a glowing recommendation to Pake, and called Elkind himself to sell him on his Outside/Inside plan before he met with Pake. Elkind listened, intrigued, but his understanding of the arrangement never fully matched Taylor's. "I always thought Bob's role was to be there as a very strong associate director," he said later. "My role was that I was going to be managing the lab."

It was not that Elkind was intent on micromanaging his researchers. On the contrary, as a research chief he had always believed in granting his best people a large measure of independence. "The style of research that I had been used to at BBN was certainly one of very strong principal investigators ordinarily doing work on their own," he recollected. But he also viewed it as the manager's responsibility to impose a group philosophy—"a vector in certain areas" so they would not be "proceeding off at random." As for the proper vector of research at PARC, "the fact that we were a part of Xerox meant that one would spend a great amount of time and effort doing things that were useful to the corporation." If upon hearing these words Taylor felt any impulse to tell Elkind to leave the vectoring to him, he stifled it—for the moment.

One glorious spring day George Pake made his way to Elkind's house in a quiet suburb west of Boston to take his measure. They had never met, but everything Pake had heard about Elkind, including Wes Clark's fulsome praise, predisposed him to like the man. Over the course of a few gratifying hours under the crisp New England sun he satisfied himself that Elkind was everything Taylor was not: a sober scientist with indisputably sober credentials, among them an MIT engineering doctorate (achieved under Licklider, no less). Elkind's research experience was unassailable, as was his experience managing large research teams in a corporate setting. His gravity did not for a minute faze Pake, who interpreted it as seriousness of purpose. Jerry Elkind was exactly the sort of high-caliber manager he had dreamed about placing in charge of the labs ever since PARC had opened its doors. (Instead he had gotten the reluctant and distracted Bill Gunning and the academically suspect Bob Taylor.)

Yet Elkind must have sensed something vaguely eccentric about the position he was being offered. "Why not just let Bob manage the lab?" he asked.

"I need someone with more scientific training than just in the computer field," Pake replied smoothly. "The computer side is only twenty people now, but it will grow. Once the Computer Science Lab gets to thirty or forty scientists we'll need managers who can meld it with the physical and information sciences." Elkind, he implied, was just that sort of manager. Melding the labs? Bob Taylor's agenda seemed to lay entirely in *obliterating* the other labs.

"George made it sound very exciting," Elkind recalled. "Here was a lab that was going to be supported well and the motivation was solid. It seemed like a very, very talented group of people had already come there."

He came west to indulge CSL in its ritual of subjecting prospective new members to serial interviews with the entire staff. Taylor had originally established this system of vetting recruits to the team, along with the rule that a candidate was required to win approval by a near-unanimous vote.

"The system meant Joe Blow would have a huge advantage coming in," he explained, "because a whole bunch of people would have committed themselves to his success." Subjecting their future boss to the same all-day process was a bit on the bizarre side, but since they were already in place and Elkind was not, they went through with it. By all accounts Elkind acquitted himself well. "He certainly had good paper credentials from BBN," recalled Jim Mitchell. "But I didn't know him so I went on the basis of the interview, and he gave good interview."

Pake was cheered, if a bit surprised, to see that Elkind and Taylor "seemed to interact pretty well. I would suspect that Taylor, who never had a low opinion of himself, felt that he really didn't need this other guy. But there was no problem about that, not at first."

In any event with construction of MAXC well under way, CSL's "vector" needed no fine-tuning. If Elkind cared, or even noticed, that most of his new staff bypassed his office and did their brainstorming next door with Bob Taylor, he did not show it. He did, however, recruit a cadre of his own, raiding BBN for Daniel Bobrow and Warren Teitelman, two talented Lisp programmers he encouraged to continue their work on artificial intelligence. Bobrow, who would remain deeply loyal to Elkind throughout the strife to come, almost immediately detected something unsettling about CSL's ambiance. One day he confronted Taylor about it.

"I asked him why he recruited somebody to be his own boss," he recalled. Taylor repeated his mantra about needing someone with better credentials to head CSL so he could be more free to exert his influence over both computer labs, SSL included. Bobrow was not completely satisfied. "I thought he felt that, just as at ARPA he was the power behind a lot of thrones, he could be the power behind a lot of thrones here, too," he observed. The unanswered question, however, was what might happen if he ever got a hankering to sit on the throne himself.

If PARC's computer engineers thought the design and construction of MAXC would place the PDP–10 controversy behind them, they were mistaken. At Xerox headquarters the contretemps earned PARC a reputation for insolence it would never entirely shake. Reinforced by a thousand further affronts over time, this would evolve into a major handicap in its relations with headquarters in Stamford. At first, however, it simply gave Xerox a pretext to pay closer attention to what the research center was up to. The agent of this unwritten policy was a man named Don Pendery.

A Xerox corporate planning executive, Pendery chaired a headquarters task force—one of innumerable such bodies—devoted to monitoring technological changes that might affect the company's business plan. In pursuit of the answers, he made frequent contact with the people at PARC, who tended to regard his concerns as shortsighted and parochial. Alan Kay, the center's self-defined futurist-in-residence, took particular umbrage at Pendery's approach, which treated the future largely as a Pandora's Box of threats to the bottom line. Kay and his colleagues preferred to consider it more as a harbinger of limitless opportunity. To scan the horizon only for hints of Xerox's future, they thought, forced the company to ask the wrong questions and ensured that whatever answers came would be misinterpreted or ignored.

Pendery "really didn't understand what we were talking about," Kay recalled. Instead he was "interested in 'trends' and 'what was the future going to be like' and how Xerox could 'defend against it.'"

In the course of one frustrating encounter Kay blurted out the line destined to become his (and PARC's) unofficial credo. "Look," he said, "the best way to predict the future is to *invent* it!"

But PARC had come face to face with a force of nature, the corporate instinct for self-preservation. While Kay urged upon Xerox the virtues of patience and trust in scientific serendipity, Pendery pressed for a definition of its vision that could be reduced to paper and presented in a boardroom. Finally he got it. In mid–1971 George Pake sent up to headquarters a half-inch-thick folder containing seven documents, each written by an individual PARC scientist—scarcely sixty pages altogether. Someone had cheekily labeled it "PARC Papers for Pendery and Planning Purposes." In lab shorthand they were henceforth known as the "Pendery Papers."

Not since Vannevar Bush had forecast how we might think in his essay for *The Atlantic* had such a comprehensive vision of technology and the future been set down in writing. The Pendery Papers were at once a survey of the most promising technologies on the horizon and a road map for PARC's ten-year exploratory journey. Some of the forecasts overshot their marks. Kay, for instance, anticipated (perhaps wishfully) portable flat-screen displays at nominal cost by 1980. Jim Mitchell, writing on future office systems, envisioned error-free and infinitely customizable software, transmitted from vender to buyer over network connections, running flawlessly on a full spectrum of incompatible machines (as of this writing still a hazy dream). But on the whole the package stands with Bush's as a remarkable feat of scientific prognostication.

Mitchell's office of the future was one in which uncompleted memos, letters, and reports would exist solely on computer, to be printed out only when a final hard copy was needed. ("Much of the current 'paper pushing' in today's offices will be replaced by people spending a large portion of their time using a computer via some personal terminal.") He forecast the propagation of electronic mail and divined its unique ability to allow people to "communicate and manipulate information simultaneously, without the necessity of physical proximity." The floppy disk would replace the file cabinet as the principal repository of documents and information.

Dick Shoup, reporting on integrated circuit technology, anticipated the development of "smart" appliances such as toasters and alarm clocks equipped with simple but powerful chips. John Urbach's paper on "archival memory" described digital photo-optical media resembling today's CD-ROMs and compact audio discs. "There seems little reason to store sound in analog form," he wrote, observing that acoustical information is easily reduced to bursts of digital bits—thus consigning the LP record to the dustbin more than fifteen years before it actually met such a fate.

To be fair, many of the startling innovations posited by the Pendery authors were ringers: They were only modest extrapolations from technologies well-known throughout the research community, if not among the broad public. Mitchell's description of tomorrow's text-editing and office systems drew heavily from Doug Engelbart's 1968 demonstration. Shoup's survey of integrated circuitry scarcely ventured much beyond devices that were already on the market or known to be under active development. Still, futurists have no obligation to venture solely into the realm of magic and crystal balls; sometimes a clear vision of what lies around the next bend will do. As things stood, the Pendery Papers were important for PARC and Xerox in three ways.

The first was that they implicitly embraced the immense but still widely unappreciated power of Moore's Law. The term appeared nowhere in the Pendery Papers, but its significance permeated every page. The implication of Moore's article had been that technologies impractical in 1965 would be commonplace within a decade or two. In the Pendery Papers PARC informed Xerox that the devices on the drawing board today would be marketable in ten years, so it was time to get ready.

"This was their version of the old hunter's saying, 'Never aim at the ass end of a duck,'" remarked George White, Jack Goldman's assistant, who served on Pendery's task force. "PARC was telling us that if you want to invest in research at Palo Alto you've got to get way ahead. Otherwise, by the time the ripening and maturing process from your research comes through events will have overtaken you."

PARC further understood that Moore's Law would pack its greatest wattage in the visual interaction between computer and man. Virtually every paper touched on this topic and some dwelled on it at length (Kay's was devoted entirely to display technology). It was as though the lab had finally absorbed the lesson Bob Taylor had been pressing on it for more than a year: The computer is a communications device in which the display is *the whole point*.

The third benefit of the Pendery Papers inured to PARC alone. "It was a matter of setting the primary focus for the lab," recalled Peter Deutsch. "Even though in our guts nobody believed that you would be able to put a portable computer on every desk ten years from now, that was what was said by the industry trend and the curves of various things. You'd be able to put something equivalent to MAXC on everybody's desk in ten years."

One might argue that the Pendery Papers were another example, like Strassmann's veto of the PDP-10, of how a hectoring from headquarters proved itself to be a blessing in disguise. They named their file of white papers after their tormentor from the home office, but they wrote it for themselves. With dazzling audacity Mitchell, Kay, Urbach, and the others had fixed on their destination. Now it was up to all of them, working together, to blaze the path that would take them there.

PART II

Inventors

CHAPTER 9

The Refugee

I f anyone symbolized the gulf separating the inventors of the future in Palo Alto from the Xerox development drones back East, that person was Gary Starkweather.

Starkweather was highly trained in an arcane subspecialty of physics, but he did not look like anyone's idea of a master physicist. With his stocky frame and friendly, guileless features, he more resembled your neighborhood phone lineman. But to his colleagues at PARC he was a special catch. He was the scientist outcast, the man who got branded a renegade by his bosses at Webster simply for proving that the novel technology of lasers could be used to "paint" an image onto a xerographic drum with greater speed and precision than ordinary white light.

Instead of garnering praise and encouragement he was ordered to abandon his research and threatened with the loss of his lab assistants. His bosses hinted that his future at Xerox would be bleak if he failed to redirect his energies back to the pressing issues of lenses and white light. "We had almost reached the point of maximum disconnect," he recalled, when it was finally recognized that the only place for him was that madhouse out in Palo Alto.

And there at PARC he invented the laser printer, the success of which contradicts the canard that Xerox never earned a dime from the Palo Alto Research Center. It is one of the ironies of the story that despite Jack Goldman's tireless efforts to keep PARC insulated from Webster's copier-duplicator mentality, the most profitable product PARC ever produced sprang from the mind of a Webster man.

Not that they ever thought of him that way at PARC. "Gary Starkweather had been thrown out of Webster," Alan Kay remarked with manifest approval. "We considered him one of us."

For all his considerable skills at manipulating light, Gary Starkweather's career in optics began more or less on a whim. In 1960, having just received his bachelor's degree in physics from Michigan State University, he faced a limited spectrum of career options. "The choices were I could go into nuclear power, which was a hot thing in 1960, or I could go into optics. And I looked at nuclear and said, I don't think so. I wasn't sure how people would live with the problems, because when nuclear fails, it fails big. So I went into optics." It was a lucky choice. Just a year or so into his master's studies at the University of Rochester, the entire field blew wide open.

At Hughes Research Laboratory in Malibu, Theodore Maiman had coiled an electronic tube around a cylinder of pink ruby polished at either end to a mirrored sheen. He touched off a flash of electrons within the coil, exciting the ruby into firing an instantaneous burst of single-wavelength red light from one end. The science of optics was never the same.

Before the laser's appearance, light was a crude implement. Optical scientists could knock it about with lenses and mirrors and sort it into its constituent wavelengths with prisms. But these processes bore all the delicacy of surgery performed with a jackhammer. By contrast, the laser cut like a scalpel.

White light generated thermally—by bulbs and electric arcs—comprises all the colors of the spectrum, oscillating at different wavelengths and consisting of photons generated out of phase with one another. Under such conditions light inevitably scatters and diffuses over distance, like ocean waves spending themselves on the beach. Maiman's ruby device, however, emitted a beam immune to the scattering effect. It had spatial coherence (all the light in the beam was the same wavelength) and temporal coherence, meaning that its photons were in phase. The laser could be "tuned," like a radio antenna, to be so bright and fine that a beam shined from the Earth could visibly illuminate a spot on the moon.

Optical scientists welcomed the new technology as a tool for making the theoretical concrete. Hypotheses of the existence of certain photoelectric effects and other phenomena could now be tested in the lab. At the University of Rochester Gary Starkweather abandoned his original master's topic in classical optics, refocused his attention on lasers, and received his degree for a thesis exploring holography, the laser-aided creation of three-dimensional images. With great anticipation he brought his knowledge back to Xerox's Webster lab, where he had worked his way through school, only to be instructed to stop talking like a madman.

For a company whose vast corporate fortune depended on the manipulation of light, Xerox remained resolutely behind the curve in exploiting Ted Maiman's discovery. Everywhere Starkweather turned at Webster he saw projects coming to naught because they employed light sources too feeble. Whenever he pointed out that the laser packed 10,000 times the brightness of a conventional light source he encountered sneers, especially when he suggested that the new devices might play a role in xerographic imaging. Lasers were difficult to handle and burned out faster than a rick of dry timber, his colleagues responded. Bristling with electrodes and emitting bursts of blinding light, they seemed about as safe to put into an office machine as nuclear warheads. And they were expensive—$2,500 to $25,000 for a single unit.

For the next few years Starkweather had no choice but to experiment on his own. His instincts told him that a beam so precise could be modulated—that is, altered in intensity—to carry information, just like radio waves or the pulses on a phone line. Suppose one could educate a light beam to reliably transmit digital bits: These could then be translated into marks on a blank sheet, a feat that would allow one to consign to paper the thoughts and images created inside a machine.

Enlisting the help of a couple of lab assistants, he built a clumsy prototype, hitching a laser apparatus to an old seven-page-a-minute copier no one used anymore. Whenever he could steal an hour or two early in the morning or late at night he would run some equally clumsy tests by bombarding an unused xerographic drum with laser beams. Eventually he learned how to scan an original image and turn out a duplicate. True, his first samples were crude and pale, not at all ready for prime time. Still, they were scarcely any worse than the faded, scrawled "10–22–38 Astoria" Chester Carlson had reproduced on a coarse apparatus in his kitchen. From Carlson's crude and pale sample, Starkweather kept reminding himself, an awesome new industry had sprung. Who was to say that his might not do the same?

Nevertheless, Starkweather got scarcely more respect than Carlson had at the start of his own researches. "The theoreticians gave me every excuse," he recalled. "All hogwash. They told me the beam would be moving so rapidly the photoreceptor would never see it. They talked about 'photoconductor fatigue' and asked, How will you modulate? They thought there was no practical value in it. 'We got copiers we need to ship, you need to work on the lenses for that . . . Painting laser beams, these things are expensive, they never last very long and they look like a ham radio set. It's a completely useless application. If you paint at 200 dots per inch that's a million bits of data, where will you ever get a million bits of information?' In 1968 that was probably a valid question. But it wasn't a valid question if you looked at where the technology might go."

Over months and years of trying, fueled by the inner conviction that drives natural inventors, he fashioned experiments that answered every objection. He could modulate the beam by varying the power input and scan it by the clever application of a set of mirrors. He was proudest of disproving the old bugaboo about "photoconductor fatigue." This referred to a hypothetical property of the selenium coating of the copier's xerographic drum, the electrostatic charge of which must be neutralized by light in order for the duplicating process to work.

Laboratory dogma maintained that excessively bright light would drive the neutralization effect deep into the selenium layer, like a hammer driving a nail through soft wood. Once the photoconductor thus became too "fatigued" to consistently snap back to a blank, quiescent state, one would see persistent "ghosts" of earlier copies, all transferred together to the blank paper. The objection, being strictly theoretical, was hard to discount. "It was only an inkling," Starkweather explained, "because no one had ever tried to expose things in a few billionths of a second before."

Starkweather's experiments proved the inkling false. He showed that bathing a photoreceptor with the laser's extraordinarily potent beam for a fraction of a second had the same effect as applying conventional light for the much longer period employed in ordinary xerography. The brevity of the exposure canceled out the strength of the beam, and the selenium survived just fine.

As for the complaints about the devices' cost, Starkweather figured lasers were bound to come down in price. What, after all, was the laser? A neon tube with mirrors on the ends. A sign that says "Eat at Joe's," unfurled into a straight line. "There's a feeling down in your stomach where you're sure the thing has potential," he recalled of those solitary days and nights. "You have to believe against all odds that the thing will work."

He also realized he might have an answer to a problem computer science had not yet solved satisfactorily: how to transform a stream of digital bits into something intelligible on paper. A laser could address a photosensitive drum with enough speed to print microscopic dots as fine as 500 to the inch, each one corresponding to a bit of digital data. "I said, what if instead of scanning the image in, as is done in office xerography, I actually just created the data on the computer? If I could modulate the beam to match the digital bits, I could actually print with this thing. I did some test experiments in Rochester, which my immediate management felt was probably the most lunatic project they'd ever seen in their lives. That's when my section manager said, 'Stop, or I'm going to take your people away.'"

One day in 1970 Starkweather poured out his heart to George White in White's office high atop Rochester's Xerox Square office tower. Starkweather complained that he had been caught in a vise. He felt as though his talents had been wasted and, worse, that they had led his career at Xerox to a dead end.

He was convinced he could learn to safely manipulate the laser beam in a way that would give Xerox the opportunity to market an entirely new kind of imaging machine. Yet no one in the company seemed willing to pay him the slightest heed. He had run out of places to turn.

There had been one glimmer of hope, he told White. During the summer he had seen an item in the employee newsletter about the new lab being built out in Palo Alto.

"I think I did the hundred-yard dash to the nearest phone and called out there," he recounted. "They said, 'Well, we won't really transfer people, we're going to hire from the West Coast.' I said, 'Can I come out and tell you what I'm working on?'"

His persistence won him an interview in California with George Pake, but he came home feeling like the victim of a Catch–22. The lab was fascinated with his work, but refused to put in for his transfer. Webster was already aggravated that too many of its top people had been relocated to PARC, Pake explained. "We won't ask for you," he said. "We don't want to start an avalanche. But we'd take you, if you could happen to get a transfer on your own."

His immediate boss at Webster had not only turned down his transfer but seemed infuriated at the very idea. "Forget it, Gary," he said, "you're never going to be moved to the West Coast. And you're to stop playing around with that laser stuff."

White was Starkweather's superior a couple of levels removed, but had heard nothing of this before. He listened to the saga with mounting frustration. There was no question that the lab's treatment of Starkweather had been asinine, exactly the sort of parochialism his own boss, Jack Goldman, was determined to eradicate. White tried to reassure Starkweather that there was an answer.

"Sit tight," he said. "I'll need some time."

"How much time? This guy's threatening to take all my people away."

"Just hang in there," White replied. "If he throws rocks at you, try to duck."

By lucky chance, George White was one of the few people at Xerox who shared Starkweather's appreciation for the laser. Having earned his Ph.D. in nuclear physics from the University of Iowa, he had experimented with the new technology himself as a young lab employee at Sperry Rand in 1962. On the strength of that work he had been recruited by a small Pasadena company called Electro-Optical Systems (EOS), which was subsequently sold to Xerox Corporation.

White also empathized with Starkweather because he had personally experienced the same narrow-mindedness as his younger colleague, at its source. "At EOS we understood lasers and we'd just been acquired by Xerox, so we hitched the two together and showed how you could take a laser beam and expose a xerographic drum," he recalled. The man to whom White demonstrated this first raw achievement of laser xerography was John Dessauer. "He didn't have the orientation or the context to understand the hottest new scientific breakthrough of the age," White recalled. "He just let it drop."

White now perceived that fate had granted Xerox another crack at the gold ring. Dessauer was gone. His successor, Jack Goldman, had appointed White head of advanced product development. As one of Goldman's shock troops, White figured there were two components to his job: refining existing copier technology to reproduce conventional images sharper and faster; and perfecting new forms of document imaging that the old technology could not handle.

But these two goals demanded completely different mentalities. "Webster could spend an infinite amount of money doing their prissy little chemistry and fine-tuning second-order effects in copiers," he said. "But they would never find their way to the new world."

There was no point in forcing Gary Starkweather, a creature of that new world, to live in the old. Like anyone who tried to pursue a radical new vector at Webster, he was almost certain to get squashed. "Gary's project at best would have limped along without enough power to allow his full productivity," White concluded. "At worst it would have got canceled, and if he wasn't willing to just design lenses and illuminators for classical copiers he'd have had to look for another job."

So White went up the ladder to Goldman. "Starkweather's doing some amazing things," he told his boss. "But he can't thrive at Webster. Nobody will listen to him, and even if they did they'll never do anything that far advanced."

With scarcely a second thought Goldman lifted the hold on Starkweather's transfer. Webster be damned. If they could not use the man's talents, he was not going to stand by and see them go to waste.

Starkweather arrived in January 1971 as PARC employee number 26, assigned to the optical science lab under his old Webster colleague John Urbach. Having scratched and clawed for the assignment he was appalled, as many of his fellow newcomers had been in their turn, by the sheer barrenness of the facility.

His quarters turned out to be four bare walls and a plug outlet in the lab building fronting on Porter Drive. Say what you would about Webster, every project there started out with a gleaming, fully equipped laboratory. By contrast, this place was nothing but vacant spaces partitioned off by cinder block walls. Starkweather's glance fell on a strange feature of the walls—they all had some sort of curious rectangular opening down by where they met the floor. "What are those for?" he asked someone.

The answer was not exactly cheering. The building, it turned out, formerly had been an animal behavior lab. The openings gave its four-legged inhabitants the freedom to move from room to room. Each room was known by the name of its former inhabitants; there was a dog room, a cat room. "You've been assigned the rat room," they told him.

At least everyone else also seemed to be starting from scratch. When Starkweather asked one of his co-workers how to get his hands on a few tools, the man flipped him a dog-eared catalog from a scientific supply house.

"Just order what you need."

That night he was tormented by the thought of having given up his secure, comfortable existence in Webster in favor of . . . the rat room! Would going back to copier work really have been that bad?

"I was thinking, 'You gave it all up so you could sit alone in this cement block building. You must be an idiot!'"

Yet PARC's magic did not take long to assert itself. Within a few days he discovered the upside of its ascetic bareness: Money to furnish the rat room seemed to flow in a limitless cascade. At Webster the lab management had pissed and moaned about the purchase of a single $2,500 laser. Here no one so much as blinked at his order for a $15,000 half-watt behemoth (or for the water lines and pump that had to be specially constructed to keep it cooled). Rather than make do with an old surplus copier for his experiments, Starkweather ordered up a Model 7000 capable of turning out sixty pages a minute. This duly arrived, attended by a Xerox field technician perplexed at his assignment to set up a top-of-the-line office copier on the bare concrete floor of an unfurnished lab.

He would have been even more surprised to see what Starkweather was planning to do to it.

Computer printers had existed for years, yet none had ever been endowed with enough brainpower to take full advantage of the digital bit. They were huge, awkward affairs, messy mechanical systems of solenoids driving hammers into carbon strips, rather like electric typewriters as imagined by a Soviet design team—the epitome of the sort of contraption engineers dismissed as a "kludge" (pronounced "klooge"). From a functional standpoint they were slow, clumsy, and lacked any graphic flexibility. Most were limited to printing the 128 characters comprising the so-called ASCII character set (the acronym stood for "American Standard Code for Information Interchange").

ASCII encoded every numeral and English-language letter, along with a handful of line-setting characters, as a sequence of seven digital bits—hence the constraint to 128 characters, the maximum number that can be expressed in seven binary digits. If you wanted something unusual, like a German *ü* or French *ç*, much less lettering of an unconventional size and a fancy typeface, you were out of luck. Computer designers were happy enough that the seven-bit code at least allowed them to have upper- *and* lower-case letters.

Starkweather's assignment was to build a machine that could print on paper almost any image a computer could create. The first problem he needed to solve was how to build a machine that could make, as he put it, "intelligent marks on the sheet at a page a second" to match the 7000's capacity. This was essentially a speeded-up version of the task he had been working on at Webster all those long years. Solving it at PARC took another eleven months, or until November 1971.

His design was deceptively uncomplicated. At its heart was a spinning disk about the size and shape of a hockey puck. Milled around the rim were twenty-four flat mirrored facets, which gave it the appearance of a cross-sectional slice of a discotheque ball. As the disk spun, each mirror picked up the beam of the laser and redirected it onto the photoreceptor as a sweeping line of modulated light. (Think of a lighthouse beam sweeping horizontally across a wall—thousands of times per second.) The process produced an image that looked clean and solid to the naked eye, but was in fact comprised of millions of minute dots etched on the photoreceptor (and transferred in turn to a blank page) at a resolution of five hundred horizontal lines to the inch.

Considerable fine-tuning was necessary to keep this complicated system humming along. Assembling the hardware and synchronizing the components was like getting a herd of cats to sing in unison. Since the polygonal disk spun at 10,000 revolutions per minute (the original glass prototype was soon replaced by aluminum), even the way the facet edges "paddled" the air produced measurable resistance. The laser itself had to be modulated up to fifty million times a second by a "shutter" fashioned from a polarizing filter driven by a $10,000 piezoelectric cell. And because it had to conform to the speed of the copier, Starkweather's laser apparatus had to mark more than 20 million dots on a page every second.

Still, the most troublesome problem was not electronic. Instead it fell squarely within the domain of traditional optics. Starkweather knew that if the mirrored facets were even microscopically out of alignment, the scan lines would be out of place and the resultant image distorted or unintelligible, for the same reason a wobbly tape deck makes an audio-cassette warble as though recorded under water. To produce clean images, he calculated, the facets could not be out of vertical alignment by more than an arc-second—a microscopic variance. In visual terms, the mirrors could not be off by more than the diameter of a dime as viewed from a mile away.

Disks fabricated to such an exacting standard would cost at least $10,000 each—assuming this were technically possible, which Starkweather doubted. It was true that there existed servo-mechanical and optical devices that could quite effectively redirect an errant scan back in place. But they were even more expensive and, as a further drawback, meant adding another complicated and failure-prone component to his printer. Starkweather understood that the tolerance issue was critical. If he could not solve it, he would have designed a machine that could not be cost-effectively manufactured.

For more than two months he wrestled with the puzzle. "I would sit and write out a list of all the problems that were difficult. One by one they would all drop away, but the mirrors would still be left."

One day he was sitting glumly in his optical lab. The walls were painted matte black and the lights dimmed in deference to a photoreceptor drum mounted nearby, as sensitive to overexposure as a photographic plate. Starkweather doodled on a pad, revisiting the rudimentary principles of optics he had learned as a first-year student at Michigan State. What was the conventional means for refracting light? The prism, of course. He sketched out a pyramid of prisms, one on top of another, each one smaller than the one below to accommodate the sharper angle of necessary deflection. He held the page at arm's length and realized the prisms reminded him of something out of the old textbooks: an ordinary cylindrical lens, wide in the middle and narrowed at the top and bottom. "I remember saying to myself, 'Be careful, this may not work. It's way too easy.' I showed it to one of my lab assistants and *he* said, 'Isn't that a little too simple?'"

It *was* simple. But it was also dazzlingly effective. Starkweather's brainstorm was that a cylindrical lens interposed at the proper distance between the disk and the photoreceptor drum would catch a beam coming in too high or low and automatically deflect it back to the proper point on the drum, exactly as an eyeglass lens refocuses the image of a landscape onto a person's misaligned retina.

"I ran to the phone and called Edmund Scientific, my supply house, gave them my credit card, and bought ten bucks' worth of war surplus lenses," he recalled. "I could hardly sleep the two days before they arrived. But then they came, I put them in, and sure enough they worked." The lens scheme was foolproof. It involved a simple physical relationship, so it could never fail. It had no moving parts, so it could never malfunction. And it permitted the polygonal disks to be stamped out like doughnuts—not at $10,000 apiece, but $100.

"The mirrors no longer had to conform by the diameter of a dime at a mile's distance," Starkweather recalled. "They could be off by the diameter of a tabletop, which was a standard anyone could meet. I made a lot of discoveries building that machine, but it was the cylindrical lens that made me say 'Eureka!'"

Starkweather's finished printer was a large, bulky machine. His open arrangement of plump black-tubed lasers, mirrors, and wires sat atop the clean but stolid Model 7000 copier like a ridiculous hat on a dowager aunt. He christened the machine SLOT, for "scanning laser output terminal."

"I would have called it the scanning laser output printer," he said, "but that wouldn't have made a very good acronym."

Building the SLOT solved only half the riddle of how to convert digital images to marks on paper—the back end, so to speak, of how to apply toner once the image was delivered to the laser beam. The front end involved translating the computer's images into something the laser could actually read.

That half was solved by the invention of the so-called Research Character Generator (RCG), another healthy piece of iron and silicon, by Lampson and a newly hired engineer named Ron Rider. The RCG, which stood several feet high and nineteen inches wide, and housed 33 wire-wrapped memory cards holding nearly 3,000 integrated circuits, was a sort of super memory buffer, spacious enough to accept a digital file from a computer, evaluate it scan line by scan line, and tell the printer which dots to print at which point. This generated on paper an image created by pure electronics.

Today this procedure is trivial. Memory is so cheap that the computer and printer both come with enough to hold several pages at a time. As a page comes in from a word-processor program, it is fitted into a print buffer the way craftsmen of the old printing trades clamped lines and columns of leaded type into rectangular frames. Once in memory, the page image can be manipulated in an almost infinite number of ways. It can be fed to the printer narrow or wide end first, backwards, upside-down, or wrapped around a geometrical design. The most unassuming desktop computer can store character sets in dozens of font styles and sizes, any of which can be summoned at will and applied to a document as a paintbrush swipes color at a wall.

Nothing like this was simple in 1972 because of the cost of memory. Nor was it enough for Rider's machine to generate only the bland standardized ASCII text of conventional line printers. The RCG had to incorporate a large number of custom typefaces that were to be drawn by hand, converted into digital bits, and stored somewhere in memory until needed, as if on an electronic shelf.

This meant an exponential increase in the complexity of the task. ASCII characters were all the same size and each fit into the same squared-off shape. The only formatting a conventional document normally required was a command instructing the printer when to move to the next line. By contrast, the custom-designed characters PARC desired to print would be proportionately spaced: some fat, some thin, some reaching above the print line, some dangling below; some roman, some *italic*, some **BOLD**.

Finally, the character generator had to adapt to the Model 7000's system of feeding in pages wide-edge-first, which moved paper through the machine at a faster rate. For copiers this posed no problem—one simply aligned the originals along the same axis. For a printer, however, it was a horror. The image coming from the computer would somehow have to be rotated before it could be printed out. Instead of printing a page in prim linear order like a typewriter, SLOT would have to reproduce the characters in vertical slices, somehow keeping its place on twenty or thirty lines of print per page.

Rider ultimately came to see the proliferation of complications as a blessing in disguise. "It forced you to think about the problem of printing in a much more generalized fashion, so the solution turned out to be much more robust." Despite its name, the research character generator was less about delivering images character-by-character than about transmitting digitized images in whatever form the computer dictated. Like so much PARC developed in those first few years, this turned out to be the answer to a multitude of questions no one was yet even asking.

Starkweather and Rider worked together on coordinating the SLOT and character generator until early 1972, when they were stymied not by a technical obstacle but one entirely man-made. This was the relocation of more than twenty of PARC's seventy scientists up the hill to a building newly rented from the Singer Company and known as Building 34 (because its address was 3406 Hillview). The Computer Science Lab, including Rider, got bundled off to the new quarters while everyone else, including Starkweather, temporarily stayed behind on Porter. The move separated the two by a kilometer of real estate—too far to string an overhead line and, with the four-lane Foothill Highway in the way, impossible to link via a ground cable.

"The administrators said, 'Don't worry. You'll be back together in another year,'" Starkweather recalled. "I said, 'Great, what are we supposed to do in the meantime?'"

But one Sunday afternoon shortly after the move Starkweather got a brainstorm while sitting at home. He immediately jumped in his car, drove to Porter Drive, and mounted a stairwell to the roof. Just as he had thought, he could take line-of-sight aim from where he stood to the rooftop of Building 34. He might not be able to span the distance by cable or wire—but he could do it by laser beam.

The next day he ordered four telescopes from Edmund's for about $300 apiece. He and Rider replaced the eyepieces of two with low-power lasers and the others with sensitive photodetectors. They bolted one laser scope and one detector on each roof, aiming each at its complement across the way, to create a visible light data link. The circuit worked flawlessly in almost any weather, even fog, although minor adjustments were often necessary after a rainstorm, when the weight of accumulated water made the roofs sag slightly.

"When SLOT was running I'd send a pulse of light up the hill to signal the character generator to send a line of data down to the detector on my roof, which would send it down to this laser and then to the printer,"

Starkweather recalled. "After all, we were only encoding ones and zeros. It was like sending binary data on a long wire made out of light, instead of copper."

The only real problem arose from the arrangement's elemental spookiness. One morning after a foggy night Rick Jones was summoned from his office to field a complaint from a peeved Palo Alto police officer. It seemed that a local motorist startled by a ghostly red beam crossing overhead had run herself off Foothill Highway into a ditch the night before. Whatever PARC was up to, it had created a traffic hazard and would have to stop.

Jones placated the officer and brought the issue to Starkweather, who averted further mishaps by coarsening the focus just a bit. From then on the beam would be too broad to be seen even in the fog, but not so much that it could not be refocused to adequate tolerance at the receptor end.

"That way we were able to keep the experiment going for a year, until we could move everybody up the hill," Starkweather recalled. "Outside of that and a couple of birds that got hit with a bright red flash, we never had a single problem."

Starkweather's SLOT and Rider's character generator were two of the four legs of the complete interactive office environment PARC was creating on the fly. In the same period Thacker, McCreight, and Lampson were building the Alto; Alan Kay and his Learning Research Group were designing a graphical user interface aimed at making computers intuitively simple to use; and Bob Metcalfe and David Boggs were designing a network—the Ethernet—to tie all the other components together. "We had in mind that you ought to be able to create a file on the Alto and ship it via the Ethernet to a print server [that is, a communal computer managing everyone's print orders], which would convert it to a raster and print it out," Rider recalled. When it was finally implemented, the whole array would be known by the rather inelegant acronym EARS, which stood for "Ethernet-Alto-RCG-SLOT."

Of the four, the laser printer was closest to being marketable, representing as it did a fairly straightforward modification of a standard Xerox copier. Yet its road to commercialization would be a long and "gory" one, as Jack Goldman later remarked—presaging other battles to come in the war to bring PARC's inventions to market.

The first stumble occurred in 1972, even before EARS's other components were operational. That year the Lawrence Livermore National Laboratory, an institution always primed to promote new technologies, publicly requested bids for five laser printers. Only on the surface was this a public solicitation, for Livermore knew that PARC alone had developed the applicable technology.

Jack Goldman was eager to fill the bid, figuring that the Livermore contract would guarantee instant celebrity for PARC's first marketable product. Unexpectedly, he was overruled by James O'Neill, a former Ford Motor Company finance man who was in charge of Xerox's engineering and manufacturing group.

Goldman was furious. "I raised a fuss with him," he recalled. "I said, 'Why are you turning it down?' He said, 'I'm turning it down because we'll lose money. The reliability of the Xerox 7000 can't stand the copy volume Livermore will be turning out. We'll be sending so many repairmen out there we'll lose $150,000 over the life of the contract.'"

O'Neill had it all wrong, Goldman argued. PARC had shown that the machine's reliability improved by more than tenfold when it operated in laser mode, because laser printing circumvented the moving parts most prone to failure. "We had a lot of experience in the reliability of this thing," he said. "We had turned out millions of copies already in the lab, where everyone was using it."

Yet the two executives' disagreement was more than a technical misunderstanding. It reflected a fundamental clash of marketing values. O'Neill saw little point in committing Xerox to selling a machine for which there was no immediate prospect of high-volume production or marketing backup. The company would not sell Livermore a prototype copier; why sell it a prototype laser printer?

Goldman's rejoinder was that there was a world of difference between introducing a new version of an old copier and launching an entirely new technology; the only way to accomplish the latter was to feed the appetite of "early adopters"—clients willing to take a chance on unfamiliar products just to see what they might do. But he lost the argument.

"You have to take certain chances if you're going to introduce a new product," he said later. "O'Neill refused to let us fill that order, and look what he sacrificed. That machine would have had the world by the tail."

Instead the laser printer spent another two years in product planning limbo, at which point Goldman had to intercede again—this time more successfully—to save it from extinction.

That happened in 1974 when Xerox's product review committee, on which corporate staff planners were overrepresented and engineers almost nonexistent, debated which kind of computer printer Xerox should bring to market. At the eleventh hour Goldman discovered that the committee planned to recommend a Webster-designed machine known as the "Superprinter," which used CRTs, or cathode ray tubes— thousands of times dimmer than a laser—to project an image onto a photoreceptor.

"A bunch of horse's asses who didn't know anything about technology were making the decision," Goldman recollected. The Superprinter, he contended, was hopelessly unequal to the demands of high-speed printing. "Here laser printing had already been developed by Starkweather, and the guys back in Rochester were thinking in terms of CRTs, which was absolutely a backward way of doing it."

This time Goldman did more than argue. Commandeering a company plane, he hustled two key committee members onto it—Don Pendery, the planning vice president, and his boss, a staff vice president named Bill Souders—for a hastily arranged demo of laser printing at PARC.

"It was Monday night. I said, 'We're going out tonight and coming back tomorrow night in time for Wednesday morning's meeting.' And we made believers out of them. The guys at Palo Alto did a masterful job of presenting it. Everything worked without a hitch. These two guys looked at it and said, 'Hey, this is really the way to go.' And we were able to override the proposal from Webster."

Still, it was a Xerox-style victory, Pyrrhic at best. Although the committee accepted laser technology, it rejected Goldman's appeal to build laser-adapted Model 7000 copiers, as Starkweather had done. This would have allowed the company to market a laser printer within a year. The panel decided instead to wait until the launch of Xerox's next generation of high-speed copiers, the 9000 series—which was not scheduled for another three years.

It was a perilous delay. The plan to commercialize the laser printer would be killed and resurrected three times in that period, saved only by the obstinacy of an executive named Jack Lewis, who ran the company's printing division and ignored the orders from higher-ups to deep-six the project. Finally launched in 1977 as the 9700 printer, Gary Starkweather's laser device fulfilled its inventor's faith by becoming one of Xerox's best-selling products of all time.

Even so, for the white-light copier engineers of Webster the laser printer never shed the frightening aspect of an alien technology.

"Years afterwards I went back there," Starkweather said. "I ran into my old boss, the one who had tried to keep me from leaving. His last words to me were, 'Are you still playing around with that laser stuff?'

"By then the laser printer was a $2 billion-a-year business."

CHAPTER 10

Beating the Dealer

Chris Jeffers took a deep breath before walking into the big corner conference room on Porter Drive. Alan Kay, who had recruited his childhood friend to join PARC as a sort of amanuensis and chief of staff, had guided him through the rigorous interview process and as far as this last hurdle, the delivering of a technical presentation to his future colleagues sitting in a sort of plenary session. Waiting for Jeffers inside the room were about twenty scientists and engineers, all lounging improbably on beanbag chairs upholstered in a ghastly mustard-yellow fabric. The weekly meeting about to convene had come to be known simply as "Dealer." It was already a PARC institution.

Bob Taylor liked to tell people that his style of managing CSL combined the best features of all the research labs he had ever known. But its structure sprouted largely from a small kernel: the management principles developed at ARPA. Taylor's predecessors had bequeathed him the axiom that the best way to manage research was to select the best people in a given field and set them loose. Scientists with the lofty skills ARPA demanded, Ivan Sutherland said, "are people who have ideas you can either back or not, but they are quite difficult to influence. You can maybe convince them that something's of interest and importance, but you cannot tell them what to do."

On the other hand, you can find a way for them to tell each other. The uncompromising give-and-take of Taylor's ARPA contractor meetings lent itself to reproduction at PARC in the form of "Dealer."

The name derived from the book *Beat the Dealer*, by Edward O. Thorp, an MIT math professor who had developed a surefire system for winning at blackjack—"beating the dealer"—by counting the high- and low-value cards dealt out in hands. (This truly effective system would make the unassuming Ed Thorp the godfather of professional blackjack card-counting.)

Taylor was not much of a blackjack buff. What interested him about *Beat the Dealer* was its compelling metaphor of a doughty individual fielding the challenge of a group of trained and determined adversaries. In casino blackjack the dealer plays against everyone at the table. In Taylor's variant a single researcher would propose an idea or project, then stand alone to defend it against dissection by his peers.

Dealer was soon institutionalized as the beating heart of CSL's professional organism, a time when the entire lab would gather in a room furnished with the beanbag chairs that Peter Deutsch and his wife, Barbara, had discovered at a friend's shop in Berkeley. The meetings, which were usually on a Tuesday (although the designated day changed from time to time), were scheduled more or less at lunchtime and generally lasted an hour. Attendance was mandatory for all of Taylor's subordinates, the only lab rule he rigidly enforced, and the other labs were welcome to attend, at least at first. Later, as PARC expanded and the crowd at Dealer threatened to become unmanageable, non-CSL personnel became welcome only upon invitation or special dispensation. (Kay, though an SSL member, owned a permanent pass.)

Taylor would open each session with ten to fifteen minutes of housekeeping items before yielding the floor to that week's designated dealer. At that point the game transmuted into something more like poker. It was the dealer's prerogative to set not only the topic of discussion, but the rules of debate.

"I wanted to have conditions where someone could get up to the table and set rules as czar," Taylor recalled. "You could say, no interruptions; or interrupt whenever you want. Or I'll only debate x, y, or z; or only right-handers can argue." The discussion topics were similarly unconstrained. Certainly they tended toward issues of importance to the lab, but that category was broadly defined. Bob Flegal, a CSL graphics expert, once demonstrated for his colleagues how to take a bicycle apart and lubricate the parts, and Ed Fiala was famous for a memorable presentation on how programming algorithms resemble kitchen recipes.

Outsiders arriving with influential backing got extra latitude, as happened when Kay surprised Jeffers with the news that he would be making a speech at the next Dealer. Jeffers, the farthest thing from a trained computer scientist, had spent the previous few years first as a Peace Corps volunteer in Nepal and then as an official in the agency's Washington office. He told Kay there was no way he could cook up an appropriate presentation to the digital elect of PARC.

Kay advised, "Just talk about something you know."

"So I gave a speech about the sociolinguistics of Nepalese language and culture, and we had a good time with that," Jeffers recalled with relief. "Actually, I felt quite at home."

This was also part of Taylor's scheme. Once accepted into the lab, you were immune to the petty harassments common to university departments. "You were part of the extended family," related John Shoch, a member of Kay's lab. "No one ever asked, 'Who the hell are you and what are you doing here?'" The alternative, Taylor believed, was for one-upmanship to hobble the unfettered exchange of ideas. "If someone tried to push their personality rather than their argument, they'd find that it wouldn't work."

But the argument had best be carefully thought out. Anyone trying to slip an unsound concept past this group was sure to be stopped short by an explosive *"Bullshit!"* from Thacker or *"Nonsense!"* from the beetle-browed ARPANET veteran Severo Ornstein. Then would follow a cascade of angry denunciations: "You don't know what you're talking about!" "That'll never work!" "That's the stupidest idea I've ever heard!" Lampson might add a warp-speed chapter-and-verse deconstruction of the speaker's sorry reasoning. If the chastened dealer was lucky (and still standing), the discussion might finally turn to how he might improve on his poor first effort.

The criticisms could be particularly ruthless when Dealer turned to the qualifications of a job candidate. Scientific prodigies who had spent half their lives defending abstruse research before hostile faculty committees were easily unnerved by this small group slouched in their beanbags, rudely firing off comments of annihilating incisiveness. Newcomers almost always came away from Dealer profoundly unsettled.

But even the most experienced lecturers could get themselves manhandled. The featured speaker at one memorable Dealer was Alan Newell, a distinguished professor at Carnegie-Mellon University, or CMU, who was not only friend but mentor to a good half-dozen of the engineers in the room. Newell literally had written the textbook on computer architectures. On this occasion the agenda called for him to solve a tricky programming problem in front of a video camera so his students back in Pittsburgh would be able to study his thought process step by step, as though debugging lines of code. Within the first few steps, however, he unwittingly committed a rudimentary mistake. What the students got on tape instead was a roomful of smartassed engineers peppering the increasingly flustered Newell with bluntly phrased suggestions about how to recover from his blunder.

Only once could anyone recall the group's being specifically ordered to go easy on a guest. In early 1973 Pake decided to hire Harold Hall, an avuncular research executive who had worked at ARPA and Ford, to be the long-awaited replacement for Bill Gunning as SSL chief. Hall was not exempt from the ritual of the mass interview, but Pake did not want him roughhoused, either.

"Taylor obviously had been told that he had to make sure Harold got a nice respectful reception," recalled the CSL engineer Chuck Geschke. "So rather than have him come in right at the beginning of Dealer, Bob first gave us a little lecture on appropriate modes of behavior and how most executives in the Xerox Corporation wouldn't be accustomed to what normally went on in Dealer." Jim Morris, an acid-tongued transplant from CMU, was sitting in the back. "Suddenly," Geschke recalled,

"Morris said, 'Wait a minute! I get it! You're trying to tell us that you're just about to send a piece of china into the bull shop!' "

But such special handling was rare. The pitiless judgments dispensed at Dealer derived from the ethos of the engineer, who is taught that an answer can be right or wrong, "one" or "zero," but not anything in between. It was felt that if you were wrong you were done no favor in being told you were right, or half-right, or had made a decent try. "There was nothing personal about it," said Ornstein. "We didn't want to be coddled or have our time wasted."

That is not to say that the system was entirely objective. One who thought the lab occasionally used the brutish spirit of Dealer to enforce its own prejudgments was Bob Metcalfe, who arrived at CSL in 1972 with the reassuring credentials of a Harvard and MIT education. Metcalfe was acerbic and free-speaking, a man who never met an ego he couldn't pierce. At Dealer his radar often detected the unmistakable "ping" of people pulling rank.

"I'm being cynical now, but if you were from Berkeley or MIT or, especially, CMU, you'd give your talk, you'd get some questions, you'd get congratulated, and you'd get a job offer," he said. "But if you were some poor schmuck from the University of Arizona, they'd grill you and it was all over. In other words, if the department head at CMU said you were cool, that was good enough for them."

Others did not overlook the converse of Taylor's effort to promote a group sensibility at CSL. If there were no walls within the lab, there were certainly barriers erected against the outside. "It was almost a cult-like thing," remembered Lynn Conway, an SSL engineer whose background included work on an IBM supercomputer. "I'm not easily attracted to cults and it always made me a little uncomfortable. Taylor's a very powerful personality. Here he was in the background with these gunslingers out front and the groupies in back."

Taylor's chief gunslinger was Butler Lampson. His combination of a razor-sharp intellect with peerless debating skills raised the bar for new ideas to an intimidating height. It was not impossible to win an argument with Lampson, but it was not at all rare for him to win one even when he was wrong. Even as practiced a navigator of Ideaspace as Alan Kay could be backed to the wall when one of his flights of fancy came up against Lampson's rigorous command of pragmatic engineering. Routed in the battles, Kay sometimes had to retreat and regroup for another run at the fence. "I can't ever remember winning an argument with Butler on the same day," he said later. "I could win quite a few on the second day. His mind worked about twice as fast as anyone else's."

Lampson was fiercely intellectual, an inveterate kibitzer whose finely realized insights and designs, often recorded on the run on scraps of yellow paper, became indispensable ingredients of more PARC inventions than anyone has bothered to count. He could also be ferociously temperamental, a fearsome screamer and tantrum-thrower when thwarted or contradicted. Once Warren Teitelman managed to goad Lampson into firing a glass ashtray at him. "Butler tended to intimidate people," recalled the outspoken Teitelman. "He made it very difficult for those who didn't think quite as fast as he did or weren't quite as smart."

On this occasion "Butler was doing one of these 'That's ridiculous!' things, and I just replied, 'Why? Because you say it's ridiculous?' and he heaved the ashtray at me," Teitelman recalled. The ashtray shattered harmlessly on the wall behind him, but Teitelman understood the lesson. "He was the 400-pound gorilla in that lab. You had to be real careful." Teitelman's friends suggested he attend future Dealers wearing a hard hat.

Outside Dealer with its deliberate intellectual gunplay, PARC in this period was a model of casual collegiality. The place retained the ambiance of a college campus, which was unsurprising. Most of the staff, after all, were fresh out of grad school (some were still working toward their advanced degrees while working full-time at PARC). Unmarried or with young families, their social spheres would not extend much beyond their laboratory colleagues until much later, when those families began to grow and exercised their own gravitational pull. For now, driven by the thrill of pursuing a common vision, they would work together all day and late into the night.

To let off steam there were family picnics and a softball team Rick Jones organized to play in a Palo Alto community league. In the spacious open yard behind Building 34, to which the computer and systems science labs relocated in early 1972, was strung a volleyball net for daily lunchtime matches.

For the extended family of the Computer Science Lab, Bob Taylor served as a sort of social director. On weekends there might be touch football (quarterback: Bob Taylor) or marathon sessions of "Diplomacy," a board game whose framework of negotiation, alliance, and betrayal fed the host's appetite for intrigue, at his Palo Alto house. "That was great fun, when you had nothing to do for a whole eight or ten hours on a Saturday or Sunday," one participant recalled.

This was the sunny side of Taylor's personality. When he was playing the role of *paterfamilias*, as opposed to sneering at the physicists or disputing a football ref's call with an opponent's shirt grasped in his fist, one could appreciate the 95 percent of the time he could be "an absolutely charming person," as Jones recalled, without thinking of the other 5 percent when he was a rude and arrogant beast. Even his beleaguered superiors could laugh at his foibles and persnickety habits, as they did one Halloween when half of CSL came dressed as Bob Taylor, in nearly identical plaid slacks, blue blazers, and white turtleneck sweaters, then sat together at a table in the cafeteria with pipes in one hand and Dr Peppers in the other.

"There isn't an organization newly begun where you don't find those honeymoon years where there's a special bond among people," reflected Jeffers, who recognized the phenomenon from the Peace Corps. "It was true there, it was true in PARC. It's true in anything that's new. It's a great period. Everyone should be a part of something at the beginning."

This atmosphere of professional and personal fellowship was a powerful factor behind some of the center's earliest projects, including MAXC. They called the process of informal collaboration by the name "Tom Sawyering." Like Tom with his paintbrush and whitewash, someone would set forth his idea or project—whether it was in a formal meeting or a hallway bull session was unimportant—to mobilize a few intrigued colleagues in an attempt to make it happen. If you saw a glimmer of how to implement a new operation in microcode, you would gather a few expert coders in a room and have at the problem until every whiteboard in the place was filled with boxes and arrows and symbols as arcane as Nordic runes. If you had a big project with a lot of soldering to be done, everyone who knew how to wield a soldering gun strapped on his holster.

If an idea worked, the team stuck together for the next three or six months to complete the job; if not, everyone simply dispersed like free electrons in search of a new creative valence. Thacker viewed this system as "a continuous form of peer review. Projects that were exciting and challenging received something much more important than financial and administrative support. They received help and participation . . . As a result, quality work flourished, less interesting work tended to wither."

In this spirit Systems Science Lab engineers wrote code for Computer Science Lab hardware, CSL designers helped SSL build prototypes, and the General Science Lab's physicists chipped in with valuable insights into material properties and electrical behavior (as when Dave Biegelsen told Starkweather how to use sound waves to modulate a light beam and got his offhand suggestion incorporated into the world's first laser printer).

At one point Tom Sawyering even begot an audacious extracurricular project. This was the so-called "Bose Conspiracy," which was hatched at a poker game at Rick Jones's house. Jones, Kay, Thacker, Dick Shoup, Chuck Geschke, and a couple of others had fallen into a discussion of the merits of stereo speakers. Kay was a particular fan of the state-of-the-art Bose 901s, which came with their own electronic equalizer and cost $1,100 the set (in the pre-oil shock dollars of the early 1970s). He was also the only one in the group who owned a pair, having acquired them on his PARC budget as part of a real-time music synthesizer his group was developing.

"You know," someone said as cards riffled in the background, "there's no reason why we couldn't make the electronics work just as well. And for a lot less money, too."

Appropriating a basement room in Building 34, the group took apart

Kay's speakers and painstakingly analyzed the design. They bought cone speakers from the same Kentucky factory that supplied them to Bose, and on a shrieking diamond-toothed radial saw in Jones's garage they cut and shaped the sound baffles out of high-density particle board. (The marathon session left Kay covered with an inch-thick coating of sawdust and Jones with a lifelong case of tinnitus.) Then they apportioned the assembly tasks—one conspirator handled the soldering, another installed the speaker cones, and so on—the same way they had distributed the tasks on MAXC, which happened to be running contentedly in its own air-conditioned room a few doors away. All told, they manufactured more than forty pairs at $125 each. The buyers among their PARC colleagues could customize the units with their choice of grille cloth but were otherwise challenged to tell the knockoffs apart from the real thing. No one could.

"It was so typical of PARC," Kay recalled. "If you didn't know how something was done, you just rolled your own."

The realization that something extraordinary was germinating on a Palo Alto hillside soon started permeating the world of computer science, thanks in part to the researchers' eagerness to give demos to friends visiting from Stanford, Berkeley, or Carnegie-Mellon. The names on the employee roster added further luster. Gathering Lampson, Kay, and Deutsch under one roof would have been enough on its own to make PARC a byword; but the center employed a dozen others with reputations nearly as luminous. Kay was fond of proclaiming that of the top hundred computer scientists in the country, fifty-six worked at PARC.

Or sometimes he was quoted saying fifty-eight, or seventy-eight. Kay's formulation has appeared in a hundred different versions, none of which is correct in a mathematical sense (PARC never employed as many as seventy-eight computer scientists). But all are accurate metaphorically. PARC had become the premier draw for the country's best computer scientists, like Disneyland for seven-year-olds. Under the circumstances it was easy to imagine that almost every talented young scientist or engineer in the land was already inside.

"People were accusing us of monopolizing the field," recalled Jack Goldman. One day at a formal luncheon he was cornered by Jerome Wiesner, the president of MIT. "Wiesner accused me of destroying the ability of universities to teach computing because we were grabbing all the good people."

Delighted as he was by the complaint, Goldman recognized that the key to PARC's success was not the head count of researchers but their exceptional gifts. He found it hard to keep away from his pampered child. Arriving in Palo Alto in the evening on a company plane, sometimes with his wife along ("My only inhibition to her coming along was it stifled my ability to play poker with the guys"), he would drive directly to the lab to drink in the atmosphere.

"The lights would all be lit and dozens of people around, even it if was nine or ten at night," he recalled. "Often they were playing computer games. Now, just remember, in those days computer games were not what they are today. This was a new thing. These guys were literally inventing computer games and learning how to use the machine."

Yet there was a downside to the cheery insularity and game-playing that Goldman so enjoyed witnessing at PARC. For one thing, the center's attitude problem was growing worse. Xerox headquarters discovered this to its dismay the day that attitude got laid out for public view in the pages of a rather unsavory magazine.

CHAPTER 11

Spacewar

One day early in December 1972, Rick Jones and Gloria Warner drove to the San Francisco airport to meet George Pake's plane from New York. Normally they would not have made the effort. The established routine whenever Pake returned from a visit to Xerox headquarters was for Warner to send a car for him. This time she canceled the arrangement. The moment Pake saw his two assistants waiting at the gate, he got a bad feeling.

"What's the matter?" he asked.

"George, you better have a look at this," Jones said. He handed over a tabloid-sized biweekly magazine he had bought that morning at a newsstand across from the Stanford campus. Pake's glance took in the cover and its unfamiliar banner: *Rolling Stone*.

"What is this?" Pake asked.

"Start on page fifty," Jones replied.

Pake opened the magazine to a feature article entitled "Spacewar: Fanatic Life and Symbolic Death among the Computer Bums." Its language was loose and profane, its attitude toward computer science individualistic and anti-corporate, and among its leading characters were the not particularly presentable scientists of Xerox Palo Alto Research Center, shown lounging about in their sandals and T-shirts. The date on the cover was December the seventh. If Pake happened to notice it was Pearl Harbor Day he would have thought it grimly appropriate.

"As we were driving back from the airport," Jones remembered, "all I could hear was George sitting in the back seat, leafing through the article and going, 'Oh, no . . . Oh, no . . . Oh, *no!*'"

The piece that was to cause Xerox and PARC so much distress over the following few weeks had in a sense been underwritten by Xerox money. *Rolling Stone* was then five years old. Its founder, a Berkeley dropout named Jann Wenner who had started the magazine on a shoestring, had recently turned up backing from a decidedly mainstream source: Max Palevsky, who had left the Xerox board that May. Always in search of entrée to the snazzier milieus of countercultural life, Palevsky had placed some of his gains from the sale of SDS at Wenner's disposal and taken for himself the title of *Rolling Stone's* chairman of the board.

By this time, *Rolling Stone* had matured well beyond its origins as a fresh voice in rock journalism and had turned into a purveyor of offbeat but incisive reporting on a wide range of issues, including presidential politics and economic policy. But its audience was still essentially a college age crowd, as tuned in to the music of Hendrix, Joplin, and the Grateful Dead as to the writing of Hunter S. Thompson.

Rick Jones had never heard of it before that morning, when Gloria Warner knocked on his door to report that a friend had just called her from San Francisco to say PARC had been written up.

"What the hell is *Rolling Stone?*" he asked.

"It's some druggie magazine," she reported.

Jones swallowed hard. "We'd better get a look at it."

Together they drove to an off-campus newsstand where they found the magazine prominently displayed. Before they had read to the end of "Spacewar" they knew they had a major crisis on their hands.

With Bob Taylor's apparent permission, but to the complete ignorance of anyone else in PARC management, the writer Stewart Brand
had apparently been ranging freely through the Computer Science
Lab for weeks. Brand was a technology fancier whose recent sale of
the *Whole Earth Catalog*, his popular offbeat guidebook, had left him
with the money and time to conduct a personal grand tour of the Bay
Area's leading computer research facilities. (A few years later he would
resurface as a founder of The Well, a pioneering on-line computer service.) At the outset, he said later, some old friends at Doug Engelbart's
lab put him in touch with Bill English at PARC. But it was Taylor, he
recalled, who actually arranged for him to walk into the lab past the
lone receptionist who counted, for the moment, as PARC's entire security force.

"Spacewar" was Brand's travel report. From its dramatic opening
scene, an imaginary battle among players of the eponymous interactive
spaceship-and-torpedo computer game invented at MIT in 1962, the
article captured the adolescent ferment at the heart of the computer culture. Echoing the phantasmagoric tone of hacker favorite E. E. "Doc"
Smith's cosmic swashbucklers ("Beams, rods, and lances of energy
flamed and flared . . ."), "Spacewar" painted its subjects as dashing young
figures engaged in dynamic battle with a sinister state.

Conspicuous among those heroes was Alan Kay, who Brand introduced as something of a hacker eminence offering his own definition
of "the standard Computer Bum": "He's someone about as straight as
you'd expect hot-rodders to look. It's that kind of fanaticism. A true
hacker is not a group person. He's a person who loves to stay up all
night, he and the machine in a love-hate relationship. . . . They're kids
who tended to be brilliant but not very interested in conventional
goals." Kay's assessment of the computer scientist's professional mores
could not have been better designed to raise hackles in the Stamford
executive suite. "People are willing to pay you if you're any good at all,"
he observed, "and you have plenty of time for screwing around."

There was much in what he said, and much of himself. The hackers
he evoked were the kind of independent souls more easily found on

the university campuses where he had spent much of his life than in traditional corporate headquarters, which did not figure in "Spacewar" except as the enemy lair.

Kay's idiosyncratic techno-romanticism colored Brand's entire piece. His heartfelt view of the computer as a tool for at once simplifying and enriching human life came through unambiguously in his breezy apotheosis of the hacker as gamester-king.

In terms of PARC's internal and external politics, however, Taylor's depiction in the article was bound to reverberate even more. He and his happy band of ex-ARPA warriors came across as if they owned the place, or at least as though there was nothing much more to PARC than their work. They talked as if they had won the battle for the computer's future and were already writing its history.

Brand described PARC's scientists as aggies in a game of marbles and Taylor as the center's "chief marble collector" (which was accurate enough, for the moment). Asked about his job title, Taylor got cagey: "It's not very sharply defined. You could call me a research planner."

But there was no need for him to be more specific. When Brand described the lab's "general bent of research" as "soft, away from hugeness and centrality, toward the small and the personal, toward putting maximum computer power in the hands of every individual who wants it," there was no mistaking whose philosophy was being articulated. As for the duly appointed director of CSL, Jerry Elkind merited not a single mention in "Spacewar," an ominous token of his tenuous authority.

"Spacewar" delighted PARC's computer scientists, particularly the younger set fresh out of graduate school. And why not? They had welcomed Brand, fed his notebook with their ambitions, and sat docilely for *Rolling Stone*'s glamorous photographer Annie Leibovitz, who was taking a sort of sabbatical from her usual fare of movie and rock stars to get the architects of the future down on film.

But their attitude came as a disagreeable shock to the company. Xerox's enormous bureaucracy served a customer base that was the very definition of huge, centralized, and impersonal. It manufactured big machines whose output got measured by the millions of pages. Stamford's planners no more anticipated placing computing power in individual hands than they would think of installing a copier at every secretary's desk.

If the computer scientists of PARC had intended to throw down a challenge to those who paid their salaries, they could scarcely have chosen a more provocative way to do so. Xerox had once been a small, scrappy, risk-taking company, but the long years of monopoly had driven that sort of passion clear out of the corridors of power. What had replaced it by 1972 was the sober mentality of professional finance and sales management. There was no room for the unexpected, especially where the corporate image was concerned. Headquarters employed platoons of professional image-polishers to protect the corporation against exactly this sort of ambush. The rules were explicit: No employee, from the chief executive down to the lowliest mailroom clerk, could talk to the press without a PR minder in tow. The communications department ruthlessly monitored all press coverage, issuing stern correctives to newspapers or magazines that erred on so much as an executive title.

Yet here was its new multi-million-dollar research center spread out for unsupervised public view in a ratty rock music magazine, with actual Xerox scientists photographed in their T-shirts and jeans, barefooted, lounging self-indulgently in beanbag chairs. In the light of the times and in the context of *Rolling Stone*'s usual fare, corporate executives could only conclude from their insular perch in Stamford that PARC was reeling out of control, shamelessly squandering the research facility's budget on adolescent techno-fantasy trips rather than solid, marketable scientific pursuits. This was symbolized by Pake's (inaccurate) recollection years later that the *Rolling Stone* article "flat out stat[ed] that a lot of these guys were brilliant druggies. [That] wasn't the kind of publicity the corporation wanted."

In fact, the article neither stated nor even remotely implied anything about drug use at PARC. Brand was no Ken Kesey chronicling the escapades of a merry band of stoned-out party guys but a self-styled social theorist interpreting the new technologies against the era's political backdrop. Nevertheless, for the stolid traditionalists who inhabited

Xerox headquarters "Spacewar's" text and pictures inescapably evoked lax morals and California hippiedom.

Pake was anguished about "Spacewar" because more than almost anyone else at the research center, he was intensely aware of PARC's shaky standing at headquarters. It had been scarcely a year since John Bardeen had saved the center from extinction. PARC had yet to turn out a product of indisputable value; nor had it garnered the Bell Labs–like renown that would have been proof against further attack. (The notoriety of an article in *Rolling Stone* would hardly fill that void.) But at least he was insulated by distance from the worst of the shock waves. The same could not be said about Jack Goldman, who was stuck on the East Coast to weather the storm. Murmurs of reproach lurked around every corner on the executive floor: For *these* slobs you cadged a 20 percent pay differential? More ominously, he was getting blamed for a serious breach of security.

At first Goldman tried to deflect the criticism by arguing that on balance the portrait of PARC was a positive one and that *Rolling Stone*, alien as it was to the indignant mandarins of Stamford, had an undeniable appeal to the population from which PARC drew its best recruits. "It's probably indicative of the culture that was prevalent at PARC that they looked up to *Rolling Stone* as a proper vehicle for their community," he said later. "It was their peer group who would read about what's going on there." But this argument, he acknowledged, unsurprisingly failed to sway "the white-shoe legal types, who looked at *Rolling Stone* as something to be disdained." There was no use arguing that more than half of "Spacewar" dealt with Bay Area labs other than PARC (where "Spacewar" the game was in fact seldom played). The piece would be forever remembered as the one that introduced PARC to the world in an entirely undignified light.

In the end Goldman had no choice but to make a show of reining in PARC's free spirits. Accompanied by a corporate lawyer, he flew out to read the riot act to his pet researchers, paying special attention to those unwise enough to have allowed themselves to be directly quoted, Taylor and Kay.

"I recall almost a sadness on Jack Goldman's part," recalled David

Thornburg. "Here we were operating in a very free environment, and somehow there was a sense that a trust had been violated. It was made crystal clear to us that this was *not* all right. If it happened again, the lab *was* going to be shut down."

Within weeks the consequences became concrete. The inmates-running-the-asylum democracy that had prevailed since the founding, particularly on the computer science side, was ended. All employees were issued identification badges and instructed to keep them displayed at all times. The building entrances were outfitted with security stations, where visitors were stopped and handed a nondisclosure pledge to sign. (Quirkily enough, the pledge attested that the visitor would not "import" any of his or her ideas *into* PARC, a departure from customary agreements, which bar visitors from carrying proprietary information *out* of the lab. In any case, the goal was to protect Xerox from a claim that PARC had misappropriated someone else's ideas, and it was still in use as of this writing.)

Xerox also clamped down hard on PARC's contacts with the media, especially the popular press. Although publication in peer-reviewed technical journals was allowed to continue, the articles were closely vetted by corporate examiners newly aware that there might be developments at PARC worth safeguarding.

A few people tried to make light of the new arrangements. Badges got blown up into T-shirt imprints, so they could be more fashionably worn. One employee turned his into a belt buckle. If the guards and receptionists noted that the ID photographs on others had been artfully pasted over with the heads of Mickey Mouse or the face of George Washington cut from a dollar bill, they never said so.

But the atmosphere at CSL and SSL subtly and permanently changed. In a sense the *Rolling Stone* flap catalyzed a process that was bound to take place anyway. With MAXC behind them and the computer labs' head counts approaching critical mass, it was time to recognize that their work was too innovative and important to be any longer the grist of carefree gossip. It was time for them to abandon the childishness of prodigies. They were engaged in a greater quest.

At the same time, however, "Spacewar" carried the seed of the

PARC mystique farther beyond its boundaries than ever before. Before its publication the center's fame extended only to the limits of an insular circle of computer pros. Then came Alan Kay, sharing with Stewart Brand's hip and impressionable readers his assessment of his colleagues as "really a frightening group, by far the best I know of as far as talent and creativity. The people here all are used to dealing lightning with both hands."

These were bold words when Kay uttered them to Brand in the fall of 1972. Once PARC unveiled its newest machine a few short months later, they would sound like an understatement.

CHAPTER 12

Thacker's Bet

The race to build the Alto began one beautiful day in September when Chuck Thacker and Butler Lampson showed up at Alan Kay's office door.

"Alan," they said, "do you have any money?"

"Sure," he replied. "I've got about $230,000 in my budget. Why?"

"How would you like us to use it to build your little machine?"

"I'd like it fine," Kay replied. "But what's the hurry?"

"Well, we were going to do it anyway," Lampson replied. "But Chuck's just made a bet that he can design a whole machine in just three months."

For Kay, the appearance of his two colleagues from down the hall marked the end of a long, difficult summer.

The year had started with a glimmer of optimism. Kay had the feeling he might finally be within striking distance of turning some of his great ideas into reality. He had reworked his Dynabook concept into something he called "miniCom," a keyboard, screen, and processor bundled into a portable, suitcase-sized package. Meanwhile, the software aces he had brought together as PARC's Learning Research

Group had turned his outline for a simplified programming language into real code, to which he gave the characteristically puckish name "Smalltalk." (Most programming systems "were named Zeus, Odin, and Thor and hardly did anything," he explained. "I figured that 'Smalltalk' was so innocuous a label that if it ever did anything nice people would be pleasantly surprised.")

Kay's team had already demonstrated Smalltalk's implicit power by running rudimentary but dazzling programs of computer-generated graphics and animation on a video display system built by Bill English's design group. Kay himself was a compulsive promoter, producing a steady stream of articles and conference abstracts, often illustrated with his own hand drawings of children in bucolic settings playing with their Dynabook, to proclaim the death of the mainframe and the advent of the "personal computer."

By the spring of 1972 he was ready for the next step. Having drawn on Seymour Papert's LOGO for some of Smalltalk's basic ideas (although the two languages worked much differently under the surface), Kay was anxious to give it a Papert-style test run. That meant giving children, its idealized subjects, a shot at performing simple programming tasks on miniComs. He figured he would need about thirty of the small machines, to be built by the Computer Science Lab's crack hardware engineers.

The only thing left to do was persuade CSL to take the job.

That May at a CSL lab meeting, Kay made his pitch. As the lab staff lounged in front of him in their beanbag chairs, he laid out the argument for building the world's first personal computer. He understood this would mean pushing the envelope on display technology—the smallest screens used at PARC were still the size of household television sets, although systems in which digital bits controlled "pixels," or dots on the display screen, had been tested by numerous researchers in the building. They would have to spend thousands of dollars on semiconductor memory to drive the miniCom's high-performance graphical display, but they all knew the price was destined to fall sharply. In fact, there was hardly anything in the blueprint that would not be commercially accessible to the average user within ten years. And wasn't that why they were here—

to build the most capable system they could imagine, so far ahead of the curve that they could figure out what to do with it by the time the rest of the world caught up?

"We know everything," he told his audience. "We know exactly how big the pixels are, we know how many pixels we can get by with, we know how much computing power we need. The uses for a personal gadget as an editor, reader, take-home context, and intelligent terminal are fairly obvious. Now let's build thirty of these things so we can get on with it." He regained his seat, confident as always of having made an incontestable case.

Then Jerry Elkind took the floor.

At CSL Elkind held the purse strings. No large-scale hardware project like Kay's could be undertaken without his say-so. But Jerry Elkind and Alan Kay were like creatures from different planets, one an austere by-the-numbers engineer and the other a brash philosophical freebooter. Let others have stars in their eyes—Elkind was not the type to be beguiled by Kay's romantic glow. As a manager he responded to rationales on paper and rigorous questions asked and answered, not hazy visions of children toying with computers on grassy meadows. He was a tough customer, demanding and abrasive. He asked too many questions and, more's the pity, they were often good ones. As Jim Mitchell once remarked, "Jerry Elkind knows enough to be dangerous."

At this moment he pronounced the words that most CSL engineers had learned to dread as his kiss of death.

"Let me play devil's advocate," he said.

He proceeded to pick apart Kay's proposal in pitiless detail. The technology was speculative and untested, he pointed out. To the extent that the miniCom was geared toward child's play, it fell outside PARC's mandate to create the office system of the future. To the extent that it fell within that mandate, it was on entirely the wrong vector.

Perhaps Kay had not noticed, but PARC had not yet finished exhausting the possibilities of time-sharing. That was the whole point of building MAXC, which was after all a time-sharing minicomputer. As Kay recalled later, the sting still fresh: "He essentially said that we had used too many Green Stamps getting Xerox to fund the time-shared MAXC, and this use of resources for personal machines would confuse them."

And what about the issue of PARC's overall deployment of resources, Elkind asked. A major office computer program was already well under way in Kay's own lab. Had Kay given any thought to how his project might fit in with that one?

Elkind was referring to POLOS, the so-called "PARC On-line Office System," which was Bill English's attempt to reproduce the Engelbart system on a large network of commercial minicomputers known as Nova 800s. He was correct in stating that POLOS ranked as PARC's official entry in the architecture-of-information race. This was so in part because English had cannily put a stake in the ground with a round of purchase orders for the Novas, which committed Xerox to following through. The small, versatile machines were already proliferating at SSL like refrigerator-sized *Star Wars* droids.

But Kay considered POLOS irrelevant to his project. POLOS was explicitly a big-system prototype, an expensive luxury model as far removed from the homey, individualistic package Kay had in mind as a Lincoln Town Car is from a two-seat runabout. But under Elkind's condescending assault Kay's customary fluency deserted him. He sat mute while Elkind patronizingly dismissed his life's work as a quixotic dream.

"I was shocked," he said later. "I crawled away." Once outside the room and beyond the hearing of his audience, he succumbed to his ordeal and broke down in tears.

A few days later, back in the Systems Science Lab, Kay sought out Bill English. To the extent Elkind thought of English and Kay as rivals for PARC resources, he was mistaken. In truth, English had become something of a father figure for Kay, whose academic training at Utah had left him with the impression that one acquired research funds simply by calling up ARPA and asking for money. Shortly after they both arrived at PARC, English had taken it upon himself to introduce Kay to such elementary corporate concepts as research budgets. ("I'm afraid I really did ask Bill, 'What's a budget?'" Kay recalled of the first lesson English ever gave him.)

Now English volunteered some further advice to his wounded young colleague. Among the PARC brass, Kay lacked credibility. All the way up to George Pake he was regarded tolerantly as a sort of precocious child, engaging enough in his place but profoundly in need of adult supervision. His reputation as a dreamer only made it easier for bureaucratic types like Jerry Elkind to dismiss his ideas without affording them serious scrutiny. English informed Kay, in essence, that his barefooted treks through Ideaspace would no longer do. He had to learn to develop written research plans, compile budgets, and keep notes—in short, to look and act like a serious researcher.

Kay took the advice to heart. Over the next few months he drafted a detailed plan for a music, drawing, and animation system to teach kids creative programming on Novas. He did not abandon his cherished miniCom, but recognized that he would have to reach the grail via a series of smaller steps and commit himself to a program of several years. The effort bore fruit. By summer's end he had acquired a $230,000 appropriation to equip a bank of Novas with character generators that produced text and simple graphics for display on a high-quality screen. His small group of learning software specialists had been about to begin developing the programming environment for this jury-rigged system when Lampson and Thacker knocked at his door with a different idea.

Elkind, not for the last time, had been following a different vector from that of his principal research scientists. As it happened, many CSL engineers were convinced that time-sharing's potential *was* thoroughly exhausted. Lampson and Thacker had thought hard about how to redistribute computer power so no one would have to share processing cycles with anyone else. They agreed with Kay that this meant building dozens of individual machines, not just one. This would take money. Not that funds were scarce at PARC; but they were scattered too widely for any single group to have enough to finance the massive engineering program they envisioned. What was required was a fiscal version of "Tom Sawyering," in which they would collect contributions from every interested researcher and rake them together in one great pile.

Thacker and Lampson regarded Kay as a prime donor. For one thing, the architecture of his cherished Dynabook, or miniCom, or

Kiddicomp—whatever he was calling the thing in its latest incarnation—corresponded neatly with their own visions of the ideal personal computer—for Lampson a suitcase-sized MAXC with a component cost of about $500; and for Thacker a computer with the Nova 800's capabilities and ten times its speed.

The notions of all three intersected at one common goal: a fast, compact machine with a high-resolution display. "The thing had to fit in a reasonable sized box and it couldn't cost too much," said Lampson. "Small and simple was critical, because the whole point of it was to have one for everybody." By combining the latest electronic components coming into the market with their own powerful intellects, they might just pull it off. Not the Dynabook in all its interactive glory, perhaps, but a giant leap in the right direction—in Kay's words, an "interim Dynabook."

Hearing their offer, Kay could barely contain his excitement—until he realized they might still face one important obstacle.

"What are you going to do about Jerry?" he asked glumly. Elkind still controlled the CSL budget. Lampson and Thacker had both been present the day he shot down the miniCom. Was there really any hope that he would see this new project any differently?

"Jerry's out of the office for a few months on a corporate task force," Lampson replied. "Maybe we can sneak it in before he gets back."

"Can you get it done that quickly?"

"We'll have to. Anyway, there's another reason to move fast."

"What is it?"

That was when they told him about Thacker's bet.

"Bill Vitek was a vice president at SDS," Thacker recalled later. "I had been down in El Segundo visiting SDS for some reason I don't remember. We didn't make a lot of friends there when we built MAXC, and the fact it took only eighteen months led them to think that somehow we had cheated, although they couldn't quite figure out how.

"So I was arguing about that with Bill Vitek, and being a cocky and fairly arrogant guy I said, 'You know, you can build a computer in three months if it's small enough.' And Vitek said, 'Aw, bullshit!' And I said,

'Not bullshit at all!' And we ended up betting a bottle of wine or a dinner, I don't even remember which.

"But I do remember that I won that bet."

Chuck Thacker started designing the Alto on November 22, 1972. He enlisted Ed McCreight to help with the engineering and completed the design before the end of February, beating Vitek's deadline.

The original plan was to manufacture up to thirty Altos for distribution to the engineers in the Computer Science Lab and to Kay's Learning Research Group (his seed money was allocated to finance the first ten). But from the moment of its birth the Alto created a sensation. As Taylor had long anticipated, the power of the interactive display spoke for itself. The Alto's screen, whose dimensions and alignment replicated that of an 8½-by-11-inch sheet of paper, produced such a vivid impression that the lab's modest construction plan was soon expanded. In the end Xerox would build not thirty Altos, but nearly two thousand.

The Alto was by no means the fastest or most powerful computer of its time. MAXC could blow it away on any performance measure in existence and for a considerable time remained the machine of choice at PARC for heavy-duty computation. Even without the burden of illuminating the full-screen display, the Alto ran relatively slowly, with a processor rate of less than 6 megahertz (the ordinary desktop personal computer as of this writing runs at a rate of 400 MHz or faster); the display slowed it further by a factor of three.

But the Alto's great popularity derived from other characteristics. To computer scientists who had spent too much of their lives working between midnight and dawn to avoid the sluggishness of mainframes burdened by prime-time crowds, the Alto's principal virtue was not its speed but its predictability. No one said it better than the CSL engineer Jim Morris: "The great thing about the Alto is that it doesn't run faster at night."

Then there was the marvelous sleekness of its engineering. To some extent this was an artifact of Thacker's haste, for his tight deadline erased any impulse he might have felt to create a second system variation on MAXC. There was simply no opportunity for biggerism.

Instead, to save time and money Thacker and his team went entirely the other way. Alto was like a fine timepiece somehow assembled from pieces of stray hardware lying around the lab. Rather than design new memory components, they ingeniously reused boards that had already been built for MAXC. Ed McCreight revisited his own design of the MAXC disk controller and managed to strip out a few more circuits for the Alto. Even the display monitors were appropriated from POLOS, which had fallen so far behind schedule that its specially ordered video display terminals were still sitting around in boxes.

In almost every respect the Alto design was so compact and uncomplicated that during the first months, while prototypes were still scarce, engineers desperate to get their hands on one were invited to come into the lab and assemble their own. Ron Rider, who had joined PARC only a few months earlier upon graduating from Washington University, "had an Alto when Altos were impossible to get," recalled one of the lab managers. "When I asked him how he got one, he told me that he went around to the various laboratories, collected parts that people owed him, and put it together himself."

Of course Thacker did not really design the Alto from scratch in three short months. His wager with Bill Vitek was something of a sucker bet. Several basic elements of Alto's design had been known to computer science for years, and others had been kicking around CSL ever since the completion of MAXC. During the summer of 1972 Thacker had even outlined for CSL the design points for a small machine in a ten-page memo entitled "A Personal Computer with Microparallel Processing."

The philosophical core of the design came from Bob Taylor, who also supplied the machine's name (Alan Kay never entirely ceased calling it the "interim Dynabook"). As Taylor constantly informed his top engineers, time-sharing's success in making computing more accessible to the user quantitatively was only part of the equation: Nothing had yet been accomplished in terms of improving "the *quality* of man-machine interaction." Finishing the job involved three steps: placing computing power in individual hands, delivering information directly to the eyeball via a high-performance display, and linking the computers together on a high-speed network.

As late as 1971, all three steps still seemed technically unfeasible. Computing power and memory were plainly too expensive to hand out in individual parcels, especially since they were consumed insatiably by the so-called "calligraphic" display tubes then in use with graphics-oriented computers. Moreover, because these displays laboriously constructed their images stroke by stroke, rather than by scanning a phosphor beam across a luminous surface thousands of times a second like television tubes, they were prone to annoying flicker. These were not qualities that would lend themselves to relaxed communication between man and machine. As for existing network technologies, they were either complex and slow or, like the ARPANET, required the installation of hundreds of thousands of dollars in specialized hardware.

Then there was Taylor's habit of speaking in parables when he could not articulate his ideas in the precise argot of engineering. "When we were building MAXC, Taylor told Chuck and me a bunch of stuff we couldn't understand at all at the time," Lampson recalled in amusement. "We dismissed it as the ravings of a technically illiterate manager. But looking back on it two years later, it was crystal clear what he was trying to tell us to do: *Build the Alto*."

What had changed by mid–1972 was their recognition of how quickly memory and computing power were sliding down the cost curve. "It was only when we realized that memory would get really cheap, when we understood Moore's Law and internalized it," recalled Thacker, "that it became clear that this is what Bob had been saying all along. All of a sudden it was perfectly sensible to build a computer that used two-thirds of its processor cycles and three-fourths of its memory to run the display. From then on it was all downhill. The engineering was easy. But getting that basic idea required understanding that eventually you'd have so much power in a machine that running the display wouldn't require anywhere near two-thirds of it."

Thacker still had to solve numerous problems in designing a serviceable personal computer that would be fast and compact without sacrificing versatility and power, and that would also have a display clear, sharp, and nimble enough to keep up with the processor without driving the user blind. In the end he found the crucial answers inside PARC itself.

His first inspiration was the concept of "microparallel processing." The basic idea came from a singular aspect of MAXC's operation—what Ed McCreight had described as "hijacking" the central processing unit. Thanks to a common bottleneck in computer architectures, the processor, or brain, of a typical machine shared access to the computer's main memory with all the machine's peripheral devices. Because only one device could be serviced at a time, the processor was often left idle while some other component temporarily monopolized the memory. "While the disk was accessing the memory, for instance," Thacker said, "the processor essentially stopped because it was waiting its turn."

Thacker's inspiration was to shift the bottleneck from the memory to the processor itself. In his design, only the CPU, which after all was the most important component of the machine, would be permitted to address the main memory at any time. The CPU would take over the computing functions of all the peripherals—disk drive, keyboard, and display—deciding on its own when they needed servicing and for how long.

Thacker reasoned that if each of the computer's routine tasks could somehow be ranked by urgency and funneled through the processor in appropriate order, he could keep the processor occupied almost fulltime. If the ranking was correct, every task would be handled when it needed to be, no sooner and no later. Low-priority tasks could be interrupted for brief periods to make way for more urgent ones, then resumed later, when nothing more pressing was in the way. The gain in efficiency, speed, and hardware was potentially huge. Whole circuit boards that served as the ancillary brains of disk drives and other units could be dispensed with. The Alto's CPU would be drafted into doing the thinking for all of them.

Thacker's second crucial inspiration involved the question of how to power a high-performance display without busting the budget on memory. This was not trivial: He understood that the quality of the display would make or break his new computer.

Up until then, computer designers wishing to provide an interactive display faced two equally unappetizing choices: They could give the display little memory support, which led to flickering and slow performance, or they could provide backup memory through a character generator, which meant burdening the system with another and bug-prone peripheral the size of a washing machine.

Thacker struggled at length with the riddle of how to direct a suitable volume of information to the screen without adding excess hardware. The answer came to him one day while he was watching a demonstration of one of Kay's graphics programs in the Systems Science Lab.

The demo utilized a character generator designed by a former Engelbart engineer named Roger Bates (with Lampson's assistance). This unit, which had thousands of dollars' worth of memory inside, was a distant relative of the one Ron Rider would later build for the SLOT. It was designed to store custom fonts by allowing each character to occupy a small rectangular patch of memory until summoned to the screen. Most of the PARC engineers considered it a disappointment, largely because the designers' ambition to reproduce book-quality pages on the POLOS screen turned out to be a tougher programming challenge than they anticipated.

Kay's group was an exception. Bored with the idea of painting text on the screen but fascinated with the possibility of displaying images, they had appropriated the system—"perverted it," in Lampson's unpejorative phrase—to use for their graphics and animation programs by loading its memory not with print characters, but graphical designs. The result was a rudimentary black-and-white "bitmap"—a block of memory in which each bit corresponded to a dot on a display screen. Flip a given memory bit "on" and the corresponding dot lit up on the display; turn on these bits in a given pattern and you could map the same image to the screen.

As Lampson explained, "In the normal deal there would be a little bitmap for the character 'A' in the font memory and a bitmap for 'B' and 'C' and so on, and then the character memory would say display an 'A,' an 'h,' and an 'a,' and aha, you have 'Aha.' Alan said, 'We'll have a whole bunch of artificial characters numbered 1 through 500, and the character memory will say display 1, then 2, then 3.' The result was to take the font memory and turn it into a bitmap"—that is, well before the lab had the resources to build a full-scale bitmap.

Kay's group had only begun to investigate the potential of this new way of displaying information (although they had done enough to help persuade Thacker and Lampson of the need to equip the Alto with a high-resolution display). Among their first simple programs was one that could embed "icons," or thumbnail-sized pictures, within blocks of text. Another was a painting system in which users wielded square "brushes" up to four pixels wide to draw or erase lines and curves on the screen.

Impressed as he was by these applications, Thacker was struck more by the underlying principle by which Kay's system used the memory blocks. He realized that just as Kay's team had turned the character generator into a simple bitmap, he could convert idle blocks of the Alto's main memory into a bitmap for the display screen. Forcing the memory to perform this double duty would eliminate the need for a separate character generator. This required cutting a few corners, because the display would now have to compete with all of the machine's other functions for memory blocks. When the Alto placed a text document on its screen, for example, it would economize by omitting from the bitmap any part of the page that lacked text, such as the white spaces between lines and at all four margins. Also, whenever there were competing demands for memory from data and display, the display lost. Users had to be alerted to expect a strange phenomenon: During a work session the image of the document they were writing or editing would gradually shrink, like a window shade rolling up from the bottom. The reason was that as the increasing volume and complexity of the data claimed more memory, less remained for the bitmap. The same phenomenon accounted for what happened whenever the Alto displayed a full-screen graphical image. On those occasions it tended to run agonizingly slowly, in part because so many processor cycles were consumed in painting the screen, but also because the display consumed so much memory there was barely enough left to keep the program percolating along.

Without this sort of artfulness the Alto display would not have been possible at all. Even within its limits it made severe demands on the machine; its resolution of 606 by 808 pixels meant that nearly a half-million bits needed to be refreshed thirty times per second. (Kay envisioned a one-million-pixel display for his Dynabook, but had to be satisfied with what he got.)

Once it was running, however, it made believers out of skeptics. Not the least important of these was Jerry Elkind.

Elkind had returned to PARC from his task force assignment in the late fall. Already uneasy at the necessity of reasserting his authority following a nearly six-month absence, he was even more put out to find that a full-scale skunk works had been launched behind his back to pursue a project whose value he questioned.

One peek into the basement workshop of Building 34 told him it might be too late to do much about it. Clearly the Alto had taken on a life of its own. But he also thought the important issues he had raised with Lampson, Thacker, and Kay remained unaddressed.

"Are we going to invest a major hunk of the lab's resources and a lot of money in developing five or six prototypes of something we're not sure will work?" he asked. For all that Thacker and Lampson assured him the finished product would be the epitome of cool, a glance at the schematics failed to ease his concerns—especially after he noticed the huge proportion of memory that would be devoted to maintaining the display.

"I don't think I had the skills to appreciate what could be done with it without seeing it work," he said later. "I certainly had questions about what the end result was going to cost and how many we could afford." He instructed Lampson to give him some answers, in writing.

Lampson's response was a December 19 memo entitled simply "Why Alto." In three and a half sharply reasoned pages he furnished the project all the technical and philosophical justification it would ever need. While acknowledging that some of the "original motivation" for the Alto came from Alan Kay, an SSL engineer, he also portrayed it as a machine of tantalizing potential for everyone in the Computer Science Lab. The Alto would be capable of performing almost any computation a PDP–10 (that is, MAXC) could do. It would be more powerful than the video terminal system Bill English was designing for

POLOS, with better graphics. It would run all the office system software being written in various labs at PARC with power to spare. And it would render the costly Novas obsolete.

Lampson pointed out that at $10,500 per machine the Altos would cost barely half what PARC had spent per CSL member in building MAXC. (With a full complement of memory, as it turned out, the first few Altos cost closer to $18,000. After the original design was reengineered for efficiency and a high-volume manufacturing program was put in place, however, that dropped down to about $12,000.) Lampson considered himself on firm ground in stating that the machine would be cheap enough to enable PARC to afford one for every member of the lab.

"If our theories about the utility of cheap, powerful personal computers are correct," he concluded, "we should be able to demonstrate them convincingly on Alto. If they are wrong, we can find out why."

By early April the first prototype was ready to start computing. Thacker and McCreight together had worked out the priority by which sixteen essential computing tasks would contend for the processor's attention. This basically involved determining how quickly each task had to be completed before it failed, and how important it was for the rest of the machine. Transferring data between the disk and the memory was particularly critical, for instance, because without data in memory nothing else would work. Therefore disk operations earned the highest priority. Next came the display (actually three tasks—one to refresh the horizontal scan, one for the vertical, and a third to transfer display data into and out of memory). Any untoward delay here would mean rendering the screen unintelligible. Farther down the list came monitoring the local network (the Ethernet, being invented concurrently down the hall by Bob Metcalfe and David Boggs) and running the Alto's basic program, a variant of the Nova's.

Thacker and McCreight were so pleased with their task-switching scheme they started preparing a patent application, at which point they discovered to their great embarrassment that someone had got there first. The bearer of this jarring news was Wes Clark, who was the pioneer in question. Trim and lantern-jawed as ever, Clark served as senior consultant to the Computer Science Lab. During one of his regular consulting visits he had learned of the patent proposal. One day thereafter he showed up in the Alto workshop.

"This Alto stuff is pretty interesting," he observed, deadpan. "I wonder if, in a few words, you could say what the relationship is to the TX–2 and in particular to the task structure of the TX–2?"

Neither Thacker nor McCreight knew much about Clark's trailblazing thirteen-year-old machine. They looked at each other, perplexed.

"Well, ah, well, ah," McCreight stammered out, "not very well."

"Well, as it happens I have some copies of the TX–2 documentation here I could leave with you," Clark said. "Why don't I just come back and ask the question later?"

That night they pored over the papers in a state of shock. Clark's TX–2, they recognized, had used almost exactly the same task-priority scheme as the Alto.

The next day Clark returned to find the two engineers profoundly ashamed at not having read the literature earlier.

"Wes," said McCreight, "my only excuse is I was in the eighth grade at the time."

The first two prototype Altos took shape in the basement workshop of Building 34. They came into the world naked and blind, as helpless as hatchlings, for the hardware had been built so quickly that the software to run it was still months from completion and its essential programs had to be bootstrapped in from the nearest Nova.

Any semblance of helplessness dissolved, however, the moment the screen lit up. The sight of black letters, figures, and symbols displayed in sharp relief against its glowing white background burned itself instantly into one's consciousness. No one doubted that the Alto marked the omega to every thread of computer science that had come before and the alpha of a dazzling new world; and no one ever forgot the pure euphoria they felt the first time they saw an Alto running.

"It was like watching a baby waving its arms," recalled John Shoch. "Waving its arms as if to say, 'I'm alive! I'm alive!'"

CHAPTER 13

The Bobbsey Twins Build a Network

David Boggs was in his usual haunt—the basement workshop where he uncrated, assembled, and tested POLOS's newly ordered Novas—when he first laid eyes on the red-bearded stranger.

Burly and athletic, the man came down into the shop carrying a yellow reel of coaxial television cable like a fireman toting a length of hose. He sidestepped the piles of wood and particle board the Bose Conspiracy had piled up in a corner to build their fake 901s; and manhandled the thousand-foot reel up to a workbench, on which he deposited an oscilloscope and a pulse generator. Then he started fumbling around with a soldering iron.

Boggs watched with curiosity. "I knew what he was doing," he said later. "He was going to be firing pulses down the cable and looking at the output through the scope." He also recognized, the way a horseman does a greenhorn who has never been in a saddle before, that this individual was no artist with a soldering iron.

Boggs, in contrast, had cut his teeth wiring ham radios while growing up in Washington, D.C., then had spent his college breaks wielding all manner of electrical implement to keep the local NBC television transmitter on the air. He padded over in his moccasins, his blond ponytail swinging to and fro, to offer the stranger a helping hand. It was the first time he and Bob Metcalfe would work together, but not the last. Over the next two years they would be so inseparable they would become known throughout PARC as the Bobbsey Twins.

Few would have cast them as plausible partners. Metcalfe hailed, as though at the top of his lungs, from Brooklyn and Long Island. He had graduated from Harvard and MIT—bitching every step of the way, to hear him tell it—with degrees in electrical engineering, business, and applied mathematics. Boggs was the quintessential introvert, an ascetic radiohead with an undergraduate degree from Princeton. Metcalfe was all sharp elbows, opinionated and confrontational, not above giving the caldron a stir if he did not sniff enough conflict in the air. Boggs kept to himself—in a conversation he spoke slowly and carefully, his eyes focused on the ground or off into space, as though scrupulously weighing every word.

Their aspirations appeared to be at odds, too. Metcalfe was embarked on a determined search for the main chance. (He would eventually leave PARC to start a multimillion-dollar networking company.) "The first time I ever heard the term 'venture capital,'" one colleague remembered, "I heard it from Bob Metcalfe." But Boggs always talked as though he would be content doing pure research all his life.

In sum, they seemed to have little in common beyond the Brooks Brothers button-down shirts they both favored (though Boggs preferred yellow and Metcalfe blue). They were the most eccentric partnership PARC ever knew, and the most productive. Working together in mysterious harmony they invented a new way for computers to talk to each other, the great digital party line known as Ethernet.

Brash and outspoken by nature, Metcalfe arrived in Palo Alto in June 1972 bearing a humiliating burden: Harvard had rejected his doctoral thesis.

This affront had capped a long and difficult relationship. Metcalfe had earned his dual bachelor's degrees (electrical engineering and business) down the road at MIT. As a graduate school, he believed, Harvard could never measure up to Tech. "It's probably an idiosyncratic thing," he related acerbically years later. "But I hated Harvard. At MIT students got to do stuff and at Harvard they didn't. At MIT you learn by doing because you're an engineer. At Harvard they want you to be a scientist, and scientists would *never* soil themselves by *doing* things."

The difference had been driven home to him shortly after he started working part-time on the ARPANET. As an eager new grad student he offered to help Harvard get on the system by building the necessary interface between its PDP–10 and the IMP, one of the stand-alone machines that was every node's portal to the main network. This was not rocket science; he planned simply to duplicate the unit he had already built for MIT. But Harvard turned him down.

"They said, 'You're just a grad student, and we're going to have it done by a company named Bolt, Beranek & Newman,'" he recalled. "And BBN assigned the job to a part-time employee on their staff named Ben Barker, who turned out to be a grad student at Harvard, just like me."

But if the snub helped sour him on Harvard, it had no effect on his burgeoning enchantment with the ARPANET. Metcalfe was every bit as preoccupied as Bob Taylor with the idea of placing computers in direct digital conjunction. But he engaged in it at a level closer to the machine—he was less interested in what could be accomplished by linking computers than in how to actually move the bits from node to node. Finding new ways to make that happen would become his life's work.

While completing his studies at Harvard, he continued to work part-time on the ARPANET link at MIT. By 1972, when he was ready to take his doctorate, he was so securely bound into the ARPANET bureaucracy that he was chosen as a so-called "facilitator"—a sort of technical nursemaid who escorted IMPs to their new homes around the country to make sure they got properly hooked in and booted up. His connections made him a valuable property on the outside. "I was hot stuff because the ARPANET was hot stuff and ARPA was a major source of funding," he recalled. He spent that spring getting wined and dined by prospective employers, eventually landing nine job offers from supplicants that included BBN, Doug Engelbart, and a number of leading universities. The best offer—no surprise—came from Jerry Elkind and Bob Taylor at PARC. Not only was it the most money ($19,000, beating everyone else by several thousand dollars), "but it was the cleanest, most straightforward deal in the world, a high-paying job in a beautiful place with no teaching responsibilities. There was no tenure bullshit and no students, and you got to work with Butler Lampson and Alan Kay and Chuck Thacker."

Metcalfe returned to Cambridge to pack with his wife and suffer through his one remaining academic obligation, the defense of his doctoral thesis before a faculty committee. He expected it to be a breeze, insofar as his thesis was a study of how networks transmitted data in discrete digital packets and he had just spent two years with his head buried in IMP circuitry. The committee, as it happened, was waiting for him with a sock filled with wet sand. He went into the committee room for his oral defense and received his answer on the spot: His thesis was "insufficiently theoretical," the committee ruled. All his laborious discussion of physical systems? Good enough for MIT engineering, but this was Harvard science. In other words, he should add some formulas with Greek symbols, and try again later.

Metcalfe was stunned by the rejection. He thought he knew what the real problem was: Not that his work was "insufficiently theoretical," but that he had spent all those years hanging around the MIT campus instead of carrying water for some Harvard professor who happened to be on his thesis committee. Bob Metcalfe had thumbed his nose at Harvard, and it was payback time. "My thesis advisor should never have let that happen," he said later. "But I wasn't playing ball with him, so he didn't play ball with me."

In any case no amount of fulmination would solve his immediate dilemma. He had accepted a job from PARC with the understanding that he would arrive properly garlanded with a Harvard Ph.D. Apprehensively he called Taylor from home to deliver the bad news.

"He didn't even hesitate," Metcalfe recalled. "He said, 'Just come on out and finish your thesis here.' That felt very, very good."

Bob Metcalfe's personality added a tart new ingredient to the CSL stew. He was a one-man deflation brigade, ever poised to puncture the bravado of his talented peers. Let someone boast at Dealer of having implemented some cool program in just two or three hours of stringently applied brainpower and Metcalfe was likely to remark, "Really? Then what were you doing sitting next to me in the lab for ten hours last night?"

"And by the way," he recalled some twenty-five years later. "I didn't do it nicely. I was not a nice person."

His favorite target was Chuck Thacker.

It is hard to gauge what produced the bad chemistry between Metcalfe and Thacker. Some thought it a clash of like egos—except that a similarly elevated self-esteem characterized pretty much everyone else in the lab and not everyone paired off like raging mastodons. "It was just random interpersonal chemistry," Metcalfe said later. "I have a Ph.D.; he doesn't. He's a world-class processor designer; I'm not. And I'm not an easy-to-get-along-with person and neither was he, so I was on his case all the time and he was on my case all the time. It's not that he's not a good guy. He *is* a good guy. But we just didn't get along."

Some even believed the animus might reside mostly in Metcalfe's imagination, for Thacker never made as much of it as he did. Indeed, some of their colleagues were unaware that there was any bad blood between them at all. Yet even Taylor recognized that Metcalfe/Thacker was the yang to the yin of Metcalfe/Boggs, a relationship whose iciness would resonate for years. Thacker and Metcalfe, he said later, were locked in what he called a Class One disagreement.

"That's when two people disagree and neither can explain to the other person's satisfaction that other person's point of view," he said. "A Class Two disagreement is when each *can* explain to the other's satisfaction the other's point of view. Class Two disagreements enable people to work together even when they disagree. Class One is destructive. Most disturbances and international crises and most of the pain and suffering and difficulty in the world are based on Class One disagreements. Thacker and Metcalfe could never reach a Class Two disagreement, and they've been enemies ever since."

Metcalfe believed he had earned Thacker's undying enmity within days of his joining PARC by identifying a memory fault in MAXC long after Thacker had declared the machine finished. This was the incident of the so-called "Munger." Metcalfe's inaugural assignment was to connect MAXC to the ARPANET. This should not have been a hard job for someone of his experience. But for some reason MAXC was giving him a hell of a time. Every time he tried to launch the connection, the damn machine crashed. He checked and rechecked his work until he finally became convinced that the problem was MAXC itself. The machine, he decided, was suffering from a memory bug.

As MAXC's principal designer, Thacker would not hear of it. Not with the fail-safe system of error correction and memory diagnostics he had implemented. Summoned down to the basement room where MAXC hummed away under the powerful draft of high-capacity air conditioning, he conducted his own tests for the newcomer from Harvard and MIT. As far as he could tell, everything ran flawlessly.

"The machine is reliable," he declared.

"So Chuck left," Metcalfe said. "He insisted MAXC was absolutely fine and chalked up the problems to me, a guy he didn't think much of in the first place."

Therefore Metcalfe devised his own test. Calling it "Munger" was his way of enjoying a private joke at Thacker's expense. The word derived from "mung," MIT hacker slang that meant "Mash Until No Good" and signified the making of large, permanent, and (generally) malicious changes to a computer file. Metcalfe's nondestructive Munger simply fed a random stream of bits into MAXC's memory and read them out again. If the sequence mutated along the way by so much as a single bit, the program would clang a bell on a teletype nearby and log the discrepancy. Metcalfe fired Munger up and waited to see what would happen. He did not have to wait long. Literally within seconds the teletype went off like a fire alarm.

That proved it. There *was* a memory flaw in MAXC—only not where everyone (including Thacker) had been searching for it. What they had overlooked was that MAXC actually had two ports into memory, one via the central processor and the other through the disk controller. Because Thacker's test program ran from inside the machine, it surveyed only the processor port, which worked fine. But Munger, like the ARPANET link that had stymied Metcalfe, ran as an external program from the disk—where the memory port was indeed broken. "My fucking program found the bug," Metcalfe recalled, "and Chuck never forgave me."

"I believe firmly to this day that Metcalfe misread Chuck," Taylor said later. "Thacker liked to have bugs pointed out, because he loved to fix them." On the other hand, not many of Thacker's colleagues displayed Metcalfe's pure delight in rubbing it in. He even had a rubber stamp made up echoing a catchphrase from the movie *Love Story*. It read, "Reliability is never having to say you're sorry."

"I used to stamp that on all the memos I was writing," Metcalfe said many years later, still grinning at the thought. "Chuck hated it. Poor Thacker!"

After finally getting MAXC hooked up to the ARPANET, Metcalfe moved on to the challenge that was to bring him and Boggs together. This involved finding a simple and reliable way to connect PARC's Altos to each other. The local network was the *sine qua non* of interactive distributed computing, Taylor believed: He was after more than the symbiosis of one man and one machine, but rather the unique energy sure to issue from joining together a multitude of people and machines all as one.

Unfortunately, none of the network architectures then in use suited PARC's specifications. The ARPANET was too large-scale and required too much extra hardware to link computers together in discrete local networks at a reasonable cost. IBM and several other computer manufacturers had developed their own proprietary systems, but they were specifically tailored to their own machines and difficult to adapt to others. They also tended to break down when the local loop got too large. The POLOS group's adaptation of a network technology provided by Data General for its Nova minicomputers underscored these shortcomings.

The network's maximum capacity was fifteen computers. POLOS's attempt to double the number had produced a multi-tentacled horror of cable and hardware. "We were able to network up to 29 Novas, but that was the limit," Metcalfe recalled. "The ultimate 29-Nova daisy chain had twenty-eight 40-conductor cables, sixty 40-conductor connectors, and the nasty habit of crashing if any one of these fragile devices was disturbed." The basement room at PARC where all these cables came together was aptly labeled the "rat's nest."

Obviously this would not do for Taylor, who envisioned a system linking hundreds of Altos. His other specifications were similarly stringent. The network had to be cheap—no more than 5 percent of the cost of the computers it was connecting. It had to be simple, without any fussy new hardware, in order to promote long-term reliability. It had to be easily expandable—unlike POLOS, where adding a Nova meant taking down the network and splicing a new line into the rat's nest. And it had to be fast, because it would be feeding files to Gary Starkweather's swift laser printer and would need to keep up.

When Metcalfe first got to PARC he found several networking schemes already percolating on CSL's back burner, none of them to his liking. One was a local version of the ARPANET (but 1,000 times faster) devised by Charles Simonyi, who had finally rejoined his old Berkeley Computer colleagues at PARC. Simonyi's design was nicknamed SIGnet, which stood for "Simonyi's Infinitely Glorious Network." Metcalfe studied the specifications for about a week before rejecting it for having "too many moving parts for a local network."

He started to look elsewhere while a deadline loomed. Thacker's Alto schematics, which were coming together around the end of 1972, left a blank space where the network controller was supposed to fit. If Metcalfe could not come up with something to fill the blank, the matter would be taken out of his hands—which would be not only a challenge to his intellectual authority as the network guy, but a blow to his pride.

That dismal outcome was averted when he suddenly recalled a concept he had first encountered months earlier. Back in June, while visiting Washington on ARPANET business, he had lodged on the guest room sofa-bed of his friend Steve Crocker, an ARPA program manager. Late that night he pulled down from a handy bookshelf a heavy volume of papers from an obscure technical conference, "a sure cure for jet-lag sleeplessness," and lumbered his way through one written by a University of Hawaii professor named Norman Abramson.

Abramson's paper described ALOHAnet, a radio network designed to allow computers to communicate with one another along the Hawaiian archipelago. ALOHAnet was loosely derived from the ARPANET, as could be seen from the nickname of its central control computer: Menehune, a mythical Hawaiian "imp." Metcalfe was annoyed by the pun but intrigued by the scheme. ALOHAnet messages were transmitted in discrete digital packets through the atmosphere. Because air is a passive medium (in contrast to, say, an electrically charged phone line), that feature made the system fetchingly simple. Abramson further described the network's clever means of handling the interference that occurred whenever two or more stations tried to transmit simultaneously. If they failed to hear an acknowledgment from the receiving station indicating that their messages had arrived safely, they retransmitted after waiting a random interval so the messages would not collide a second time. This, Metcalfe perceived, would be a highly useful feature in a local network where scores of computers might be trying to send messages on the same line.

The main limitation of ALOHAnet appeared to be its tendency toward gridlock. The paper suggested that the channel could be loaded up to only 17 percent of its capacity before breaking down into a incoherent jabber of retransmitted and recolliding messages.

"That can't be right," Metcalfe said to himself, propped up on Crocker's sofa-bed. It had not escaped his notice that Abramson's figures were not based on experience—the existing ALOHAnet linked only seven computers—but on theory, and misapplied theory at that. He realized Abramson had made two impossible assumptions: That the number of users was infinite, and that each one kept mindlessly typing even after the acknowledgments stopped coming. No wonder the model filled up with messages and retransmissions until it crashed like an overloaded blimp. "Totally unacceptable," Metcalfe thought.

But suppose one imposed a couple of real-life assumptions on Abramson's model? Such as that the system had a finite number of terminals—thirty, forty, even a hundred—and that users stopped transmitting if the system stopped responding. In that case, Metcalfe calculated, the system should remain stable even at 90 percent of capacity.

Cheap, simple, and capacious: Back at PARC, he realized that ALO-HAnet possessed most of the qualities the lab sought in a local network. Over the next few months Metcalfe worked to adapt it to the center's high-volume, high-performance specifications. He junked the central control computer, Menehune, because each Alto would control its own transmission rate. He designed a scheme by which each station would listen to the line and stop transmitting the instant it heard any interference, instead of continuing to chatter. And rather than transmit via radio, he proposed joining the Altos by some sort of physical line.

The key element was that the medium had to be inert. Metcalfe understood that if the line had to carry an electrical current to aid transmission, like a phone line, Murphy's Law would take over. The line voltage would become the component most vulnerable to failure. But if there was no power on the line, Murphy would be defeated. It was possible and much better, he reasoned, to send messages into a passive medium, like the "'luminiferous aether' once thought to pervade the universe as the medium for the propagation of light."

On May 22, 1973, he drafted his first memo describing the concept for PARC's patent attorneys. Subject: "The ETHER Network." Soon after that, he met David Boggs for the first time.

Meanwhile, Boggs had found his own separate way to PARC—escorted, as had been so many others, by Alan Kay.

Like all of Stanford's grad students in electrical engineering, Boggs had been sentenced to snooze through a weekly one-hour seminar in the department's largest lecture hall featuring a talk from some person prominent in industry. The point was to inoculate the ripening "double-E's" with the excitement of engineering in the real world. For the most part, however, the sessions merged into a single soporific ten-week drone.

That is, until Kay showed up shortly before Christmas 1972. He started speaking in general terms about the interesting work taking place at the research center Xerox had opened up across the street from the campus. Then he put up a series of slides of a machine he and his colleagues had built to mimic the PDP–10. Boggs shook off his torpor and sat upright. High-performance computing was his field. He understood that any group that could build a PDP–10 from scratch was something special. When the seminar ended at five and everyone was free to leave, he bolted down front and subjected Kay to close questioning.

The latter, who was always on the lookout for potential recruits with what he called "special stars in their eyes," noticed the telltale stellar glow in Boggs's. Knowing that Novas were starting to arrive at the rate of two or three a week for the POLOS team and that they needed someone to assemble them to make sure nothing was dead on arrival, he forwarded Boggs's resume to Bill English, who hired him to work part-time through the end of the Stanford school year. Boggs was duly anointed keeper of the test stand, which was a steel rack erected in the basement of Building 34. It held a perfectly functional Nova, the cover removed and the parts arranged to be easily accessible in case they needed to be swapped with those of a balky machine to determine which piece was causing the glitch. To the rest of the lab Boggs seemed rather a solitary figure in his basement lair. But he was available for kibitzing the day Bob Metcalfe stumbled by, hauling his bale of yellow co-ax.

Metcalfe had sketched Ethernet out in a series of memos with a fair amount of input from Thacker and Lampson—"inventing the network in real time, working out bits and pieces of the idea," as Boggs later recalled. But until then he had made no effort to determine if the parts would work together in the real world as well as they did on paper. The most critical question concerned the cable—the passive ether itself. An electrical pulse, Metcalfe understood, becomes attenuated, or stretched, as it travels along a wire. The longer the distance, the worse the resulting dilution and the more difficult for a receiver to recapture the original data. As he and Boggs soldered the test apparatus together, he explained that this was the reason he needed to fire pulses down the cable and read what came out at the other end.

"I have to know how bad it is," he said.

After that day they did not encounter each other for a couple of months, until Metcalfe reappeared in the basement one afternoon, this time holding a small piece of hardware he had designed to connect the POLOS Novas to the ARPANET.

"Can I smoke test this on your rack?" he asked Boggs. (The allusion was to a procedure that works exactly as it sounds: You shoot a voltage surge through a circuit to test whether some hidden fault will make it burst into flame.)

They spent a week or two testing the circuit together for a few hours each day. Debugging a complex electronic device being almost as powerful a bonding experience as, say, serving on a submarine in wartime, Metcalfe learned a lot about his partner: That he was a digital whiz, accomplished at wielding the oscilloscope, and, most interesting, underemployed in his POLOS work. Presently the pair showed up at Bill English's office door, figuratively holding paintbrushes and a bucket of whitewash. "Metcalfe wants me to work on something with him for a while," Boggs said. "Is that okay with you?"

Having secured English's acquiescence they walked on down the hall to Metcalfe's office, where Metcalfe raked together a thick wad of memos comprising the Ethernet invention record he had assembled for Xerox's patent department. "Go read this," he said.

"That," Boggs recalled, "was pretty much the last time SSL got any work out of me. For the next twelve months at least I spent every working day with Metcalfe."

They slept when they were exhausted and the rest of the time they worked, as unconscious of alarm clocks or the sun as casino players on a roll. "There was no chip on the Ethernet board that both of us didn't know about," Metcalfe recalled. "There was no line of my microcode that Boggs did not understand. We worked on the whole thing together, every minute, every piece of it." Boggs was placed on the payroll full-time for the summer and stayed even after the school year resumed, placing his Stanford Ph.D. studies on hold. He did not finish his doctorate for another nine years.

Metcalfe, by contrast, resubmitted his doctoral dissertation to Harvard, fattened up with a properly theoretical digression covering the ALO-HAnet. In June 1973 his thesis, entitled "Packet Communication," was finally accepted ("without enthusiasm," he later groused).

As a working system Ethernet differed from other PARC inventions in one crucial detail: It was explicitly designed to be imperfect. Metcalfe labeled the network a "best efforts" system—that is, the computers were instructed not to rely on everything working perfectly. This ensured that the system would not crash in the event of a single minor glitch (or even a torrent), of the sort certain to crop up in a network of bug-prone experimental computers. "I loved it," said Kay, one of its earliest fans. "It was one of the great finesses of all time, an object lesson in how to make something work when you don't know how to make it work well."

Ethernet's basic procedure resembled getting somebody's attention in a crowded library by the most efficient, if crude, method: by shouting. The ether—that is, the coaxial cable connecting the Altos—was usually silent. When a machine was ready to transmit a message, it shot a wakeup bit onto the ether, alerting every other machine that something was about to happen. Then it sent a packet comprising, consecutively, an eight-bit destination address (the digital tag of the Alto for which the message was intended); its own address; the message itself; and a string of verification bits known as a "checksum." Receiving stations would check the destination address to see if the message was intended for them. If so, they would copy the whole packet into memory; if not, back to sleep.

Meanwhile, the transmitting station would listen for any sign that its packet had collided with another machine's. If it detected interference, it would instantly stop sending, count off a random delay (as would the transmitter of the conflicting message), and send again. The listen-and-retransmit process could be repeated as many as fifteen times before the machines would give up.

As much an enemy of "biggerism" as Thacker, Metcalfe implemented these complicated electronics on the single circuit board the Alto design allotted to Ethernet by stripping the system down to its bare essentials. The original Ethernet board did not even have a timer of its own, relying instead on the Alto's internal clock for the critical duty of synchronizing transmissions.

Toward the end of the design phase, however, Boggs insisted on adding one feature he deemed crucial. This was the "checksum," a bit sequence that would enable the receiving station to verify that a message had not been subtly garbled in transmission.

"Sure, David," Metcalfe said. "If you can find room on the board to fit the checksum logic, you can add it."

This struck Boggs as a little cynical. A checksum system would require at least eight integrated circuits, or chips. Of the sixty chip positions on the boards they were using, fifty-nine were already occupied. Then he noticed that just enough space remained around the margins to wedge in a few more chips. By the time he was done there was scarcely a millimeter of unused room. Some chips literally hung off the edge of the board, like refugees clinging to a packed lifeboat. But Ethernet got its checksum.

With that, Metcalfe and Boggs's invention proved as facile and forgiving as they had hoped. Adding new machines, or "nodes," to the system without interrupting service for even a split second was a cinch: One punched a tiny hole in the main co-ax and, using a simple piece of cable TV hardware called a "Jerrold tap," plugged the needle-like end of a branch cable into it. (This stratagem was suggested by David Liddle, a POLOS engineer and a basketball-playing crony of Metcalfe's, whose familiarity with Jerrold taps dated from his college job as a cable TV installer.) The network proved almost infinitely expandable while remaining emphatically simple, not much more than a cable terminated at both ends that anyone could tap into as easily as a water line.

Yet the Alto's first users were disconcertingly slow to get on the Ethernet bandwagon. Because the network connection was a costly $500 budget option on the first machines, many PARC engineers chose to dispense with it altogether. This was especially true as long as the network appeared to be useful mainly for sending files between computers—a superfluous function, since the Altos were equipped with removable disks that could easily be transferred from one machine to another. "Ethernet was up against 'sneakernet' from the very start," Metcalfe recalled.

All that changed overnight in 1975 with the advent of SLOT, Starkweather's laser printer. The virtues of the combined system called "EARS"—the Ethernet, the Alto, the research character generator, and

SLOT—were too powerful to ignore. One could now write a memo, letter, article, or dissertation and with the push of a button see it printed in professional-quality type. ("Before that, you had to have an article accepted for publication to see your words rendered so beautifully," Liddle mordantly observed much later. "Now it could be complete rubbish, and still look beautiful.")

Metcalfe himself did not realize the extent to which his offspring had become a indispensable part of PARC's lifestyle until one day shortly after EARS was launched. After accidentally disabling the ether by removing a piece of hardware he noticed "one after another of my colleagues popping up, wondering why the network was down." Sneakernet, obviously, was dead.

Two more important events happened that same year. On March 31 Metcalfe filed for a patent on Ethernet in his own name and those of Boggs, Thacker, and Lampson, each of whom had contributed a critical element of the technology. It was awarded (and assigned to Xerox) two years later.

Second, he resigned. Metcalfe had worked at PARC for three years, about as long as he had expected to. Industry headhunters were calling. "I was contemplating moving on and I was also contemplating staying," he recalled. Before deciding he sat down with his immediate boss, Jerry Elkind.

"What would make you stay?" Elkind asked.

"I said, 'Well, Jerry, if I did stay, how long would it take me to get your job?'" Metcalfe recollected. "Elkind thought about it. He said, 'Well, gee, you're a member of the research staff, and then you'll be a senior member of the research staff, and then you'll become a consulting member of the research staff'. . . And basically Jerry Elkind, who was twenty years older than me, said it would take me about twenty years to get his job. I told him that wasn't what I had in mind."

Anyway, the decision had already been forced upon him. His wife of seven years asked for a divorce. Simultaneously he was offered a job in Los Angeles by Citibank, which was planning to redeploy its aging electronic fund transfer system onto new computers. "So here's this job at Citibank where I'm to get a thirty percent raise and an office with a view of Catalina Island and a chance to live in L.A., which was appealing at the time. So I bolted."

Metcalfe's departure rattled the PARC staff like a tremor on the San Andreas fault. This was not only because he was the first top computer scientist to quit PARC since its founding five years earlier. More important, his resignation provided the first hint that while they had buried themselves in their research Camelot, a whole new world had sprung up outside—and that it would welcome them and their knowledge.

What they could not know was that in a very short time Metcalfe would be back.

CHAPTER 14

What You See Is What You Get

This is the story of how three sheets of lined yellow paper and three misfits spawned an industry.

The industry is desktop publishing, which today allows millions of ordinary persons to turn out newsletters, magazines, and books as though they were professionals; and allows millions of professionals—writers, editors, and publishers—to do their even more sophisticated work faster and easier.

The three sheets of yellow paper belonged to Butler Lampson. Covered with functions and algorithms written in his neat, angular hand, they represented his first pass at designing a text editor—a word processing program, if you will—for the Alto, which at that point did not have one.

The three misfits were Charles Simonyi, who one day happened upon Lampson's scribbles and asked what they meant; and Larry Tesler and Tim Mott, who had been assigned to help Xerox's textbook subsidiary find a way to make the editing and rewriting of manuscripts somewhat less tedious and time-consuming than the laying of bricks.

Together they achieved what Lampson later termed "one of the most successful collaborations in the history of PARC" (and that is a history rife with spectacular partnerships). The trio gave the Alto its "killer app"—the application that burned its unique virtues indelibly into people's minds—as well as the program that first showed professionals outside PARC how the personal computer might improve their lives.

These programs were called Bravo and Gypsy. Their development consumed more than three years, starting with the moment when Simonyi reached out his hand for Lampson's three yellow pages and said, "Can I take a look?"

With his mop of straight brown hair and his deep-set blue eyes, Simonyi might have stepped directly out of a Jacques-Louis David portrait of the young Napoleon. The similarity did not end there. Like Napoleon, Simonyi was a young man who rarely lacked the self-assurance to tell his elders where they were wrong and he was right. They also both came to prominence as outsiders: As Napoleon had come to the French revolutionary army from the rugged Mediterranean island of Corsica, Simonyi had crossed to the United States from the socialist hell of 1960s Hungary.

The elder son of a Budapest professor of electrical engineering, Simonyi had first encountered a computer at the age of fifteen. This was a Soviet-made contraption called the Ural II. The Ural was one of five computers in the whole country and a time machine of a unique variety. "All the action on this computer was directed through the console—it was truly a hands-on, one-on-one experience," Simonyi recalled. "It was exactly like the personal computer of fifteen years later, because it was just you and the machine and no one else."

The Ural could have been the model for the computer in every science fiction film of the 1950s and 1960s. The size of a large room, it was driven by thousands of vacuum tubes glowing with an eerie orange light. The operator's console was like the keyboard of an old-fashioned cash register—six columns of numbered switches and an ENTER key on the right, all operated by a mechanism with substantial Soviet heft. "All this was very exhilarating because there was a lot of noise associated with it," Simonyi recalled. "Every time I hit the switch it clicked very firmly. Whenever I cleared it, all the keys released at once with a great 'Thunk!'"

Housed at a Budapest engineering institute, the Ural bedeviled its operators by blowing out at least one tube every time it was switched on. The only remedy was never to turn it off, which meant hiring someone to babysit the behemoth all night after everyone went home. Through his father, Simonyi wangled the job for himself. With the help of a mentor on the university faculty and the endless, empty nights available for full-time experimentation, he soon taught himself all there was to know about programming in Octal, the base–8 system on which the Ural was programmed. His first programs were designed to fill in "magic squares," giant grids of numbers in which all the columns and rows add up to the same sum. Years later he could still remember how he would spend hours punching buttons on the machine to create magic squares eighty cells wide by eighty cells deep, then arrive home in the morning "with an incredible headache and giant rolls of paper printouts."

After about a year a Danish computer technician he met at a Budapest trade fair offered him a job. Simonyi was sixteen. All that prevented him from leaving the country on a temporary pass was the Hungarian military's craving for draftees. "The way I went around them was that I was underage, so they couldn't draft me, and if you were in college you got a deferment. So I got myself admitted to the university and told them if you don't let me go to Denmark I'll go to university and you won't get me. If you let me go, I'm coming back in one year, and *then* you'll have me."

Of course there was no question of his going back. This was 1966. Everywhere in Hungary memories of the aborted revolution of 1956 were still painfully fresh. "One thing that shocked me when I got to Denmark," he recollected, "was that the houses didn't have bullet holes in them." Back home his father lost his job in retaliation for his son's defection. "But he had a lot of political problems anyway, so this was just on top of it. Plus it was calculated in—either that I would have an unhappy life or he would have one more political problem. My parents agreed. My dad was practically pushing me to go."

About a year and a half later Simonyi left Denmark for the United States. Because his situation at home was deemed not to have been perilous enough to warrant political status, he arrived on a student visa, which prohibited employment. "So I told the authorities that due to extraordinary circumstances I had to take up work. The extraordinary circumstances were that I was running out of money." The job he found was at Berkeley Computer, where he encountered the troika of Thacker, Lampson, and Taylor and survived the one and only corporate bankruptcy of his life.

Following BCC's collapse, Simonyi had tagged along with Mel Pirtle to his next job, which was to supervise the building of the Illiac IV on an ARPA contract at Ames Research Center, a NASA facility just south of Palo Alto. Illiac was a vast, overdesigned attempt at a large-scale system that some called the first supercomputer and others called computing's Vietnam. (It never became fully functional, despite the expenditure of millions of dollars.) Simonyi tended toward the latter view, which is not to say he found the program entirely worthless. Aside from what it taught him about computer architecture, as a government program Illiac at one point saved him from being permanently evicted from the United States. This occurred when he left the country for a couple of days one January to visit West Germany—his first chance in seven or eight years to see his father, who was giving a lecture in Hamburg. In his excitement he overlooked not only his overcoat but the rule that once the holder of a student visa leaves the country he must reapply for permission to come back.

"So Friday evening at four o'clock I went to the embassy to say, 'Hey, my plane's leaving in one hour, would you please give me a visa.' They took one look at me and said no. I called Pirtle right away and the wheels started to turn. They opened the embassy on Saturday, just to give me the visa stamp."

Ever since his first labor-intensive experience with the Ural, Simonyi had been fascinated by the art of programming. By 1972, when he rejoined his BCC mates at PARC, he had come up with a less trying methodology, which he labeled "meta-programming" and made the topic of his Stanford doctoral thesis. Meta-programming involved a team leader's drafting a detailed blueprint for a program using a highly abstract language, and handing this over to assistants for the actual coding of the software. The idea, as Simonyi described it with his characteristic bluntness, was to improve everybody's productivity by giving the smartest programmer the freedom to think in broad strokes while a couple of overworked assistants reduced his ideas to code that the machine could understand. In essence, Simonyi was programming the programmers.

His first experiment in the process, which involved hiring two undergraduates from Stanford as these intellectual menials, he called Alpha. Around the time he was ready to conduct a second experiment, he found himself in Lampson's office, studying the three canary-colored pages.

"What is this?" he asked.

"We need a text editor for the Alto," Lampson replied. "Nobody's working on it, so I thought I'd start."

Lampson was being slightly disingenuous. The Alto did not just need a text editor—it needed *everything*. The machine had been around for nearly a year and, quite clearly, the novelty of Cookie Monster had begun to wear off. "Some people didn't really see the potential of Alto," Lampson recalled later. "We were trying to draw more people into it, because obviously the thing is useless without software. For the first year or so after it existed it wasn't very interesting because it didn't have very interesting software." The yellow sheets were Lampson's way of jump-starting the process.

Highly intrigued, Simonyi ran his eyes over Lampson's formulas. He fancied himself a great programmer, which he was, having learned the art on one of the most recalcitrant computers ever built. But he was also aware, as he said later, that "it's not enough to be a great programmer; you have to find a great problem."

This looked like such a problem. Editing text on a graphical screen seemed easy at first glance, but it was rife with hidden difficulties and unexplored potential.

"I thought we were on the cusp of a paradigm shift," he said later. "I could see books in their entirety flowing in front of you, virtual books and everything. In retrospect it seems so obvious. Uh-uh, it wasn't obvious to anyone. This stuff was in the future then. But it was suddenly clear to me that with the combination of Xerox and this machine, word processing was going to be a key application. I took it and decided to make it happen, because it looked very sweet." Since it would be the second experiment undertaken for his doctorate Simonyi moved one step down in the alphabet, and called it Bravo.

Beyond supplying his three yellow sheets, Lampson's contribution to the making of Bravo exemplified his way of casting his influential net over dozens of PARC projects simultaneously. Having outlined the program's basic building blocks for a like-minded collaborator, he let Simonyi do most of the heavy work, but stuck around to be his guide, mentor, and sounding board—as though implementing his own even more elevated form of meta-programming.

"What Butler contributed was the will," Simonyi said later, "and what I contributed was that I agreed with him. I certainly discussed everything with him. I was the active person driving it and I drove it by asking him questions."

Among Lampson's fundamental ideas was a critical algorithm for holding an entire document efficiently in memory through the use of "piece tables." These had been first developed by a programmer named Jay Moore. Instead of treating each letter or character in a text as an individual bit in memory, the piece table algorithm viewed a document as an arrangement of text blocks (or "pieces"). Inserting a sentence in the middle of a document converted the file from one piece to three—call them A, B, and C, corresponding to the insert and the blocks preceding and following it. These did not have to be contiguous in memory, as they were on the screen; it was only necessary for the computer to memorize a map—the piece table—that would allow it to find all the pieces in data storage and assemble them in the proper order for display or printing.

It is self-evidently easier to handle a document file divided into a few large pieces than one in which every character has to be manipulated individually, just as it is easier to carry a dozen eggs home in one box than to cradle them individually in one's arms. The result was a tremendous savings in computing resources. Even if the writer wanted to do something drastic like transpose the end and beginning of the document, the pieces stayed where they were. Only the piece table changed, so the system would know that the pieces henceforth had to be read not as A-B-C, but as C-B-A.

Minimizing the movement of bits within memory allowed users to create more complex documents—as long as a piece would be stationary, why not make it heavier, so to speak? As he refined and enhanced Bravo, Simonyi figured out how to encode such characteristics as fancy typefaces, odd margins, and page numbers. Eventually he had Bravo polished to the point that it could reproduce a document on the Alto's bitmapped screen almost exactly as it would appear printed out. The user could see displayed underlining, boldface, italics, and fonts of various styles and sizes—a capability that became known by the signature phrase of the comedian Flip Wilson's sassy character Geraldine: "What You See Is What You Get," or WYSIWYG, pronounced "wizzy-wig."

Simonyi was right in predicting that nothing would underscore the Alto's unique virtues like a powerful and flexible word processing program. Bravo was the all-purpose answer to the question of what a personal computer did: It magnified the productivity and creativity of every user.

"It was the killer app, no question," Simonyi recalled. "People would come into PARC at night to write all kinds of stuff, sending letters, doing all personal correspondence, PTA reports, silly little newsletters, anything. If you went around and looked at what the Altos were doing, they were all in Bravo." PARC personnel with access to the Altos found their popularity soaring on the outside. Friends writing Ph.D. theses would beg for permission to come in and type their work into the system. Then they would hit a button and get a gorgeously printed copy from the lasers.

But Bravo still had serious shortcomings. It looked every inch like a program written by engineers for engineers: The commands were complicated, difficult to learn, and prone to being misapplied. The marvels of WYSIWYG notwithstanding, the screen image appeared flat and uninviting to the ordinary user. Critics derided the display as little more than a "glass teletype" that failed to take advantage of the Alto's brilliant graphical capabilities. If Bravo were truly to be embraced by users outside PARC and the confraternity of research scientists, it would need a more creative and accessible user interface, a screen format that would render the program and its daunting menu of commands and capabilities intelligible to the average person.

It was not by accident that Lampson and Simonyi had given the interface short shrift. They figured they would have their hands full getting the program to work, much less making it look pretty. "When we built Bravo," Lampson recalled, "we made an explicit decision that we would not work on the user interface. We said, that's going to be too hard and we don't have the resources."

Fortunately, down the hall in the Systems Science Lab the two other misfits of this story had been approaching the issue of text editing from the opposite direction. Larry Tesler and Tim Mott were deeply involved in the design of just such a user interface. What they did not have, but CSL now did, was a decent word processing program to hang it on.

Almost from the moment Larry Tesler joined PARC as a recruit from the Stanford Artificial Intelligence Lab, he felt out of place. His main job was to write software for POLOS, the "PARC On-Line Office System," which was Bill English's scheme to reengineer Doug Engelbart's interactive multimedia system using the superior resources that Xerox money could buy. The work was being handled by a group of engineers English had raided from Engelbart, and they went at it with all the quasi-religious enthusiasm they had once felt working for the great man himself.

What made Tesler feel like a stranger was a rather fundamental disagreement he had with his colleagues: He thought POLOS was ridiculous.

Larry Tesler had never worked for Doug Engelbart. Not having partaken of the master's heady wine, he was troubled by POLOS's complexity. As imported from Engelbart's lab, the system required users to learn a dizzying array of commands and key sequences involving the mouse, keyboard, and—especially frustrating—a bizarre device known as the "keyset." This was a pad with five unlabeled levers, resembling the steno machines one saw in courtrooms. Pressing the keys in various combinations could give you any letter of the alphabet and a wide range of specialized commands—impressive enough as an engineering achievement. But Tesler could not imagine why anyone would want to use such an esoteric gadget.

Two other features of POLOS also offended him. The first was its time-sharing heritage. POLOS was based on the ancient principle that computers were so expensive they had to be shared. The system was designed as essentially a pool of Nova minicomputers linked by cable to video terminals in every office. A user logging in at any screen would automatically be assigned an idle Nova out of the pool, which would serve as his or her "personal" computer until the required task—typing a letter, parsing fields in a database, or performing an engineering study—was done. But no one would "own" an individual machine, nor would there be any guarantee that in periods of high demand one would not have to wait for a Nova to get free.

Tesler hated the very idea of sharing computing cycles, an emotion that dated from an incident that happened when he was a fifteen-year-old senior at New York City's elite Bronx High School of Science. In short, he had gotten banished from a university computer center for throwing the wrong switch.

The year was 1960. Tesler had acquired permission, somewhat illicitly, to use an IBM 650 at Columbia University during unbooked slots on weekends. The 650 was about the size of three tall armoires standing back to back. Among its more curious features was its memory apparatus, a magnetic drum driven by an endless rotating belt like the fan belt of a car. The computer's operators were indoctrinated with the stringent rule that if power to the system ever failed they were to wait a minimum of fifteen minutes before turning it back on, to make sure the drum could first come to a complete stop.

Left alone in the center one day, Tesler hit the wrong switch and inadvertently turned off the machine. "Instinctively I flipped it back on again—and the moment I did I went, 'Oh, shit!'"

The belt instantly snapped with a report like a pistol shot. The harvest was a maintenance call to IBM, considerable expense to the computer center, and for Tesler a summons to the director's office.

"He told me I could never use their computer again," Tesler recalled. "That day I resolved that someday I was going to have my own computer, because I didn't want anybody to ever do that to me again. And from then on many of my decisions about my life were weighed against the question: 'Does this help me get my own computer?'"

Tesler's second objection to POLOS was the hopeless inscrutability of its user interface. This violated another personal credo, that the programmer's primary duty was to render the computer intelligible to the layman. By the time he reached PARC he had already written several programs aimed at turning computers into handy tools for average users, including one to print and format simple documents which he called "Pub" and sold commercially by mail-order.

Tesler had assumed that at PARC, the world capital of the interactive imagination, he would find everyone working toward this same goal. Instead he had been thrown among the POLOS team, which seemed bent on making things even harder for the user. He could not resist mocking the system and its silly theology. Every chance he could, he tried to show his smitten colleagues that Engelbart's dazzling system was so complicated that it created more work for the user rather than less, like a telescope viewed through the wrong end.

"They had to justify the fact that it took people weeks to memorize the keyset and months to become proficient," he recalled. "So they came up with this whole mystique about 'augmenting intellect' and how in order to become literate with a computer people would need six months of training. Basically, I showed that this stuff that took six months really only had to take a week, with the right system."

Rather than heed his words, they shunned him like a parson at the orgy. "They were fed up with me and decided I was more of a pain than anything else," Tesler recalled. "I was the naysayer. I was bringing down the morale."

Finally Bill English summoned him to his office. "Larry," he said, "we've found you a new assignment."

While Tesler had been crabbing about POLOS from the inside, the system had been getting the once-over from a perceptive visitor from the outside. Timothy Mott had been dispatched to PARC as an emissary by the head of Ginn & Co., a Xerox subsidiary that published textbooks out of an office in Boston.

For a sixty-year-old publisher, this man, the provocatively named Darwin M. Newton, was an uncommonly enterprising individual. Sometime earlier he had discovered that Xerox was charging Ginn a portion of its annual revenues to cover "corporate research." As far as he could tell, this tax had never purchased Ginn a dime's worth of knowledge or technology, a deficit he resolved to correct. His inquiries led him to PARC, where he had received a short demo of the latest work on office systems—that is, POLOS. Newton returned home thinking that something like POLOS might help relieve the tedium of editing manuscripts and laying out pages, and in the process help Ginn turn out better books.

But the question of how to actually determine if his suspicions were right had him stymied. He knew everything about editing but nothing about computers. Then one day Tim Mott showed up for a job interview.

Mott was a displaced Briton with a computer science degree from Manchester University. This was a place with a much older claim to computing distinction than Palo Alto's, for it was at Manchester that the world's first electronic stored-program computer, based on the concepts of Alan Turing, had been built in 1948. After completing his studies Mott had relocated from Manchester to Oberlin College in Ohio, where he had spent a couple of years teaching math and helping the school set up its computer department. He then moved to Boston to enroll in business school. What brought him to Newton's office was a tip that Ginn had a part-time opening that might tide him over until the school year started.

Once Newton learned that the man seated before him was a certified computer scientist, he jumped at the chance to explore how to apply the intriguing system he had seen in a real world production line. The part-time job suddenly disappeared. Instead, Mott found himself shipped out to Palo Alto with instructions to bring back POLOS as an editing system.

As a Briton, a stranger, and an ambassador from the far reaches of Xerox land, Mott spent his first few days on the West Coast with his head spinning.

"I had heard of PARC, though probably only through the stuff Stewart Brand had written. I didn't think of myself as being in the mainstream of computer science research," he recalled. What he found at PARC "from the standpoint of personal computing as opposed to either batch processing or time-sharing was really fascinating. And I got the joke about the price of the technology and where it was going and the fact that what was being worked on there was really going to be commercially viable, in time."

But he also saw where the research train was going off the rails. On the POLOS team, he found, "there wasn't a lot of time spent looking at what mere mortals would be able to do with the system." Instead they had produced a system bewilderingly technical and counterintuitive. English and his software chief, Bill Duvall, had faithfully reproduced Engelbart's system of "structured text" in which every line and paragraph of a file incorporated reference pointers to other pertinent text, allowing users to follow a sort of subterranean intellectual path through a document. Mott regarded it as a fascinating model for analyzing computer programs or navigating through information space. "But it wasn't a particularly good model for editing manuscripts, let alone doing page layout of text and graphics." Like Tesler, he shuddered at the thought of training a typical Ginn editor or secretary, or any ordinary user, to utilize POLOS's baroque routines.

POLOS's inadequacies in the real world posed a real dilemma for Mott. Since his charge was to study and adapt POLOS for Ginn, after six weeks in Palo Alto he had essentially studied himself out of a job. "My report back to Ginn was basically a letter of resignation, saying this isn't technology you can use," he recalled.

Fortunately, before sending it he happened to spend a few moments in Bob Taylor's office, outlining his misgivings.

Taylor puffed at his pipe. "You're not going to just go away, are you?" he asked.

"What choice do I have? This isn't a system suitable for a publishing application."

"So stick around and help us figure out what *will* work for Ginn. That's why we're here."

Taylor's proposal to Mott was not an entirely disinterested one. At that moment POLOS and the Alto were moving along parallel paths toward the same goal—delivering computing cycles interactively to users. Taylor figured the two programs were almost certain to end up vying for money and staff in a zero-sum game. He was not alone: Even observers with little stake in the success of either system realized that when the smoke cleared only one would be left standing. No one could be surprised that Taylor would do anything to ensure the Alto was the one that would prevail.

By 1974, when his conversation with Mott took place, this rivalry was already creating tension between the Computer Science and Systems Science labs. Lampson and his colleagues were convinced the POLOS architecture was obsolete. It was true that scrapping the traditional heavy-duty mainframe in favor of the Nova pool relieved the system of the memory management and job scheduling that made time-sharing so burdensome and complex. But since one or two Novas had to be reserved for specialized tasks such as scheduling print jobs and coordinated with the users of the pooled machines, the complexity got added right back in.

"It was actually worse than trying to do it on a classical time-sharing system," Lampson explained later. "You had to keep all these balls in the air to keep everything working, which we're not that good at today. And we certainly weren't very good at it then."

The CSL staff campaigned to undermine POLOS. If Taylor's recruits from Berkeley Computer felt at all abashed about torpedoing the prize project of his recruits from Engelbart's lab, they did not show it; this was a question of engineering, in which personal feelings were not a factor. In any case, English and his people now belonged to a different lab. In staff meetings and hallway bull sessions the Computer Science Lab never let slip a chance to make its views known, as though following the habit Bob Taylor had learned in his early itinerant years among the dusty little towns of rural Texas. They were making sure the Alto's superior position in the hierarchy was established and rendered unassailable.

"We were saying our way is the right way," Lampson recalled. "We openly articulated our feelings. We really thought they were doing the wrong thing and any resources poured into it were going to be wasted, as indeed they were."

The POLOS defenders were equally spirited, arguing that CSL's plan to distribute $20,000 machines to everyone in the building would be a ludicrous waste of resources, like giving every secretary her own printing press when all she needed was a typewriter. Not to mention that such a system would present a massive maintenance headache, especially compared to one where the most complicated machines were kept conveniently in one spot and the only distributed elements were essentially cheap, low-maintenance TV sets.

What may not have been clear at the moment was that POLOS was already in trouble—and for exactly the reasons Lampson cited. The system was too complicated and inherently inefficient to survive. The POLOS team's inability to get the elaborate network operating consistently eventually became too obvious for even its staunchest advocates to ignore.

"We didn't know how to deal with a system so complicated," acknowledged Smokey Wallace, another ex-Engelbart engineer working on the project. In contrast to a modular system like Alto-Ethernet, where the whole system would keep functioning regardless of any one component's failure, POLOS was so organically integrated that the crash of any one part would knock the entire assemblage out of commission, sometimes inexplicably. "It would run for three months straight and then fall apart for half a day," Wallace recalled, "and we wouldn't know why."

Still, for more than a year after the Cookie Monster first munched its way across Chuck Thacker's display screen, it was impossible to say which system would eventually prevail. POLOS still had a lot to offer, including the spectacular multimedia capabilities of Doug Engelbart's NLS, reimplemented and in many respects improved upon. Meanwhile, the Alto was still looking for a rationale.

Taylor jumped at the chance to put Tim Mott to work. He knew Mott needed an alternative to POLOS. Clearly the answer would have to be the Alto. When he asked over at the Systems Science Lab if they had anyone with expertise in publication systems to work with Mott, Bill English suddenly recalled that Larry Tesler had done that "Pub" thing. Without hesitating, he called Tesler in to tell him about his new job.

"What is it?" Tesler asked.

"You're going to do a publication system for Ginn," English said.

By the time Mott and Tesler started working together, several prototype word processing programs had already been written at PARC.

Almost none of them functioned very well on the Alto, however—they were too slow, or too elementary, or too complicated. The exception was Bravo, which was fast, rich in features, and well-tuned to the Alto's capabilities.

Mott and Tesler, however, were among those who believed that Bravo, for all its marvelous endowments, harbored some major flaws. As with POLOS, most of these had to do with the user interface—the keystrokes, commands, and visual cues through which user and program communicated with each other.

For one thing, Bravo's interface was heavily moded, meaning that the result of typing a key would differ depending on whether the program was in "command" or "text" mode. The operator always had to keep in mind which of these states the system was in, lest disaster ensue. In "text" mode, for instance, the system functioned like a typewriter: Pressing the "D" key gave you the letter D. In "command" mode, however, the keys produced not text characters but commands—pressing a D, for example, instructed the program to *delete* a selected block of text.

Modes were such notorious pitfalls in interface design that they had spawned a standard cautionary joke. This involved a user who inattentively typed the word "edit" while in command rather than text mode: Typing "e" selected the entire document, "d" deleted the selection, and "i" instructed the machine to insert in its stead the next character to be typed . . . at which point the user discovered that his entire document had been inalterably replaced by the letter "t."

For the sake of the layman, Tesler and Mott believed, modes had to be exterminated. They thought Bravo's interface represented a vast improvement over POLOS's thicket of perverse and counterintuitive commands, but that it had not gone far enough. Its modes were simplified, but they were still modes, making it "still a very dangerous editor to use," as Tesler recalled.

Moreover, like all CSL programs, Bravo was exceedingly ugly in appearance. For all CSL's delight at its WYSIWYG capabilities, the program made scant use of the bitmapped screen's graphical power. Even the variable fonts were still displayed as bare text on a blank screen. This reflected a deliberate choice by the CSL designers, who avoided elaborate graphics because they slowed down the system. But because the Systems Science Lab engineers were mostly interested in making the computer intelligible to the average user, they loaded up their programs with graphical gewgaws of all kinds, figuring that within a generation or two the machine's speed would eventually catch up.

Tesler and Mott therefore set out to create a modeless graphical interface to make Bravo simple to use. Inspired by the costume Mott's stepdaughter was wearing for Halloween that year, 1974, they called their new program "Gypsy."

Their first step was to do something PARC had never tried before: They analyzed how non-engineers would actually use a computer.

This survey was conducted back at Ginn, to which Mott returned with an Alto display, keyboard, and mouse. He installed them as a sort of dummy setup (the machine was nonfunctional) and invited editors to seat themselves in front of the equipment, imagine they were editing on-line, and describe what they expected it to do.

"They were a little skeptical," he recalled. "But—surprise, surprise— what you got was them wanting the machine to mimic what they would do on paper." They even described the processes in terms of the tools they had always used. That is why to this day every conventional word processor's commands for deleting a block of text and placing it elsewhere in a file are called "cut" and "paste"—because Ginn's editors, the first non-engineers ever to use such a system, were thinking about the scissors and paste pots they used to rearrange manuscripts on paper.

While Mott was back in Boston studying the human factors, Tesler worked on the visual representation of the interface. His ambition was to build it around icons and menus—thumbnail-sized illustrations that would perform discrete functions when clicked with the mouse, and lists of commands that could be executed at any given time. For a while he almost started sympathizing with CSL's view of how heavy graphics burdened the underpowered Altos: His first graphical interfaces worked so slowly that to demonstrate his scheme he had to record it on videotape at one-ninth normal speed so it would appear natural when played back in real time.

In 1975, after a year of work, Gypsy was ready for launch. Mott brought a couple of Altos and a high-speed Dover laser printer back to Ginn and wired them to a phototypesetter that would output camera-ready text. For the first time on such a large scale, professional editors manipulated text on a screen and stored it on magnetic disks rather than cutting, pasting, and marking a typed manuscript with progressively illegible changes.

"Initially the reaction to the concept was, 'You're going to have to drag me kicking and screaming,'" Mott recalled. "But everyone who sat in front of that system and used it, to a person, was a convert within an hour."

In every way possible, Gypsy mimicked Ginn's customary routines. The system retained multiple versions and drafts of every file and displayed them as a list. An editor could use the mouse to scroll down the list and click on the desired version to open it. (This was the first time the mouse was used as it is today, to execute point-and-click operations; Engelbart's system and Bravo both used it simply to position the cursor within a block of text.)

Mott's diligence in drawing the Ginn editors into the design phase paid off. Instead of an editing process "so laborious that there was a point at which you threw up your hands and said, 'I just don't want to do this anymore,'" he recalled, the Ginn staff "found the ability to edit on the screen and always have a clean copy improved the quality of the editing itself. They could do a lot more of it before it became frustrating."

Within PARC, Bravo and Gypsy decisively tipped the balance in favor of the Alto over POLOS. Simonyi, Tesler, and Mott had shown that the Alto could support an interactive office system that worked fast enough to enhance—call it "augment"—the professional office worker's intelligence. Since POLOS was slipping even further behind schedule, the success of the Ginn experiment sealed its doom. "The only real question," remarked Ted Kaehler, one of Kay's engineers, "was whether POLOS would be obsolete before it was even operational." In the end, it was.

CHAPTER 15

On the Lunatic Fringe

For all their coolness as killer apps, Bravo and Gypsy only scratched the surface of the Alto's vast capabilities. Although it was not the first machine small enough to be used by an individual—the LINC had been there before—the Alto was the first one deliberately designed as a general-purpose "personal" appliance: individualistic and infinitely customizable. The computer was no longer a machine to which man had to adapt, but one endlessly adaptable to every user's needs.

The Alto's mystique worked potently on its new owners, who anthropomorphized their machines like drivers of Volkswagen Beetles, painting them in bright colors and christening them with considerable ceremony. Kay named his first so-called interim Dynabook "Bilbo," after J. R. R. Tolkien's heroic Hobbit. John Ellenby, a Briton who was placed in charge of readying the Alto design for large-scale production, called his the "Gzunda" ("because it 'gzunda' the desk"). The graphics researcher Dick Shoup connected his to a color video terminal, creating the first color computer monitor, and Taylor got his rigged to beep out the opening bars of "The Eyes of Texas Are Upon You" whenever he received an e-mail message.

Linked by Ethernet to each other, to printers, and to a host of other devices such as video displays and organ keyboards, the Altos lit PARC's creative fuse. Thacker had designed the first custom application, a program called "SIL" (for "Simple Illustrator") that automated the process of laying out computer circuits and allowed schematics to be translated directly into printed boards. But scores more were right behind.

There were "Draw" by Patrick Beaudelaire and "Markup" by William Newman, which picked up where Ivan Sutherland's "Sketchpad" left off by giving users the power to place freehand drawings directly onto the bitmapped screen. (Of course, where Sutherland's program worked only on the lone TX–2 at MIT, these would run on any Alto.) There were programs to compose music and animation, to format text documents, and to assist the writing of more programs, and dozens of programs in Smalltalk.

Meanwhile the all-pervading Ethernet encouraged the spread of e-mail and consequently the development of "Laurel," a program to simplify composing, reading, and filing e-mail messages. (A later version was dubbed "Hardy.") This was a huge leap toward Taylor's grail of the computer as communications device. "Computers didn't communicate with each other then," Thacker recalled. "Except at PARC."

And there they communicated almost nonstop, a digital chatter that would be the envy of today's Internet junkies. On the Alto network Xerox employees started the first on-line clubs, played the first networked computer games, even completed the first joint research projects without ever meeting their partners face to face. "At PARC I received my first electronic junk mail, my first electronic job acceptance, and first electronic obituary," recalled one lab supervisor. Warren Teitelman once returned from a week out of town to find his electronic mailbox crammed with 600 messages.

All this activity plainly pointed to a future in which the computer's functions would no longer be dictated by hardware, but software: standardized, commercialized, and boundlessly adaptable. Butler Lampson was one of the first to divine the possibilities. In 1972, even before the Alto took form and more than ten years before the advent of the IBM Personal Computer and the software and hardware industries it spawned, he set forth in a professional publication his "rather phantas-magoric" vision of a Utopian computer-enhanced destiny:

> Millions of people will write non-trivial programs, and hundreds of thousands will try to sell them. Of course, the market will be much larger and very much more diverse than it is now, just as paper is more widespread and is used in many more ways than are adding machines. Almost everyone who uses a pencil will use a computer, and although most people will not do any serious programming, almost everyone will be a potential customer for serious programs of some kind. . . . Such a mass market will require mass distribution. Analogues of bookstores, newsstands and magazine subscriptions seem plausible, as well as the kind of mail-order and home improvement marketing patterns we have now.

Raised on time-sharing, most of PARC's computer scientists had trouble getting acclimated to the experience of having computer cycles at their personal disposal. A few even felt a twinge of guilt the first time they turned their backs on an idle Alto, as though they were leaving food on the table while others starved. But for the first time in the history of computing, resources were abundant enough to waste.

Few people at PARC were as devoted to the machine as Alan Kay. It was as though this was what he had been waiting for all his life—indeed, it had virtually been built to his personal specifications. And when it appeared, he was fully prepared to take advantage of it.

Among the Tom Sawyers Kay was known for wielding the most beguiling paintbrush in the building. No one evangelized more convincingly on behalf of ideas he found compelling, whether they were his own or belonged to others. Kay proselytized out of necessity. The experience of emerging from grad school with a four-hundred-page thesis describing a machine that could not be physically realized had sent him into a psychological tailspin. An old tendency toward depression, spurred by his inability to execute, reasserted itself.

"Right about that first year at PARC, under psychotherapy, I discovered I was confusing my talent with my temperament," he said. "I didn't have the temperament of a programmer. I realized I needed a group."

This epiphany resembled that of a poet suddenly finding his voice. Like all the self-educated, having once grasped an idea Kay was impatient to move onto the next. He was a man of bifurcated nature, simultaneously a peerless formulator of theory and an instinctive craftsman with a short attention span. Having spent decades as an intellectual lone wolf, Kay redirected his gift for communicating enthusiasm toward the goal of attracting followers, often at the university lectures for which he was much in demand. It helped that he could size up a potential disciple in a split second, and that technical aptitude was not a prerequisite.

"After I would give a talk there would always be a fair number of people who would come up at the end with special stars in their eyes. At that stage nobody really knew how to do this stuff anyway, so I tended to hire people who could buy into the romance of the whole thing, because you could go a really good distance on romance."

Inside the building it was impossible to pass within a few yards of Kay's door without sensing a gravitational tug. Perhaps his most important recruit was swept into his orbit that way, never to leave. Dan Ingalls had come to PARC on a temporary contract to help George White set up the SDS Sigma 3 he had acquired for his work in speech recognition.

"My office ended up across the hall from Alan's," Ingalls said. "I kept noticing that I was more interested in what I was hearing across the hall than in the speech work I was hired to do. These conversations I was eavesdropping on were all about open-ended computer science stuff, which I was interested in. One day I walked over and said, 'Hey, what are you up to?' And that led to his talking about his whole picture of personal computing and how one might make a simple job of a lot of the important things through some new language."

Alan Kay on a tear through Ideaspace was a very formidable force. Ingalls hastened to finish his job for White, then cadged himself a full-time appointment across the hall. Kay had not been daydreaming when he told Ingalls about his plans for a new computer language. What he had in mind would become perhaps the first project in his life he would see through to fruition. Dan Ingalls, it turned out, was the person he needed to make it happen.

By mid–1973 Kay's so-called "Learning Research Group" numbered eight. They were so miscellaneous in their skills and credentials that Bob Taylor took to calling them, not entirely facetiously, "the lunatic fringe."

Ingalls brought along his friend Ted Kaehler, who had also come to help George White with his speech recognition project but found Ideaspace more interesting. Diana Merry's route was even more random. A transplanted Iowan with little programming training, she got a job as secretary to Gerald Lucovsky and John Urbach, managers in the General Sciences Lab.

From the first, however, Merry was entranced by Taylor's work and the other mysterious goings-on "down the hall among the computer folks" where she spent most of her free hours, as she recalled later. Eventually Taylor managed to get her transferred to a job as Jerry Elkind's assistant.

One of the office machines there was an elaborate electric typewriter that could do minimal text formatting through the application of a complicated sequence of keystrokes. No one ever utilized the beastly device's capability except Merry, who was caught at it one day by Alan Kay.

"You're a programmer!" he exclaimed.

"No kidding," she said.

Impressed by the natural skills of this secretary smuggled over from the physics lab, Kay gave her a few hours of rudimentary training. After that it was a relatively simple matter to get her assigned to his group.

Then there was Adele Goldberg, an educational technology specialist from the universities of Michigan and Chicago with fiery red hair and a turbocharged thought process ("Adele we described as speaking at nine-tenths of a Lampson," Merry recalled). Kay filled out the team with, among others, people like Tesler, whom he shared on a roughly fifty–fifty basis with Bill English until after Gypsy was finished, when he joined LRG full-time; Chris Jeffers, the childhood friend and "chief of staff"; and interns and summer students who strayed into his orbit with that telltale shimmer in their eyes.

Kay reveled in his people's eclectic backgrounds, which did not always include work toward a doctorate. "A doctoral thesis is anything you can get three faculty members to sign," he would say in their defense (quoting Ivan Sutherland, who had been a signer of his). Or: "Point of view is worth eighty IQ points." He did not care if his recruits had doctorates—although he certainly employed a high percentage of academically gifted scientists and engineers—but he monitored their points of view meticulously.

Like Taylor, he believed strongly that a lab's success depended on a shared vision. But he was determined to avoid Taylor's tendency toward militaristic discipline. The Learning Research Group's dogma sprung from Alan Kay's mind as surely as CSL's did from Taylor's or Lampson's, but the lab's ambiance was less like an Army barracks than a bohemian party where the guests all happened to concur in their host's choice of wine.

No corner of PARC generated anything like the Kay group's free-wheeling mania. "It was an amazingly seductive environment," recalled Merry. "I was there late at night all the time. People were so full of ideas and excitement, and of course everybody knew more than anybody else about how the world was supposed to be."

Socially the Learning Research Group was also PARC's most cohesive unit. "There was just a wonderful, personal feel to the group that spoke really of caring about one another and supporting one another," Merry said. Kay strived to build collegiality by sponsoring annual team "offsites" at a favorite retreat, the seaside resort of Pajaro Dunes located south of Santa Cruz, a couple of hours by car from Palo Alto. Here they could spend three or four days together on unstructured tours of Ideaspace, the pressures of work carefully relegated to the background. Later in time and inspired by Kay and Jeffers, the more musically inclined group members took to engaging in ragged lunchtime jam sessions ("We played poorly but with great zest," recalled Goldberg, the house clarinetist)—including Ingalls on flute and Merry trying to keep up on a trumpet she had rarely touched since high school. "There used to be an old joke that we really didn't care whether a new recruit could do any computer science, what we really needed was a bass fiddle," she said.

Even back home, Kay recalled, the group spent much of the daytime "outside of PARC, playing tennis, bike-riding, drinking beer, eating Chinese food, and constantly talking about the Dynabook and its potential to amplify human reach and bring new ways of thinking to a faltering civilization that desperately needed it (that kind of goal was common in California in the aftermath of the Sixties)."

Loose as the group's structure was, everyone understood where the intellectual power lay. It was in the combination of Alan Kay and Dan Ingalls. They were yet another PARC partnership, like Metcalfe/Boggs and Lampson/Deutsch, that was unlikely, implausible, and uncannily powerful. Ingalls filled a role in Kay's professional life no one else had seemed willing or able to undertake. He was Alan's reality filter. It was no secret that Kay's ideas tended to embrace about 200 percent of what was technically practical. But there were few people around willing to sift through the whole sandbox to identify the pragmatic parts. As Lampson recalled, "Alan would come around and say, I want to do x and y. You would ask him four questions about how this is actually going to work and you'd discover that it isn't actually going to work. So at CSL we'd say, 'No, we don't want to build that.'"

But Ingalls was an instinctive master at picking out the subset of Ideaspace that was actually doable, and doing it. Even before the first Altos were designed and built, Ingalls had started working on one such subset. By the time the machines were finished, his efforts had yielded the masterpiece of computer science called Smalltalk.

Smalltalk would make Kay's reputation more than Ingalls's, but Kay never forgot who transformed it from idea to reality.

"Nobody would ever have heard of me," he said later, "if it wasn't for Dan Ingalls."

Kay always claimed to get his best ideas in the shower. Conveniently, Building 34 had a shower in the basement. More expediently, it was never in use during his most productive time of the day—from four in the morning, when he typically came to work, until about eight, when the rest of his team would start drifting in.

Emerging from the basement one morning, he came upon Kaehler and Ingalls in a hallway bull session about "how large a programming language would have to be to have great power," as he recalled the scene. In a flash Kay posed a dare almost as audacious as the one Thacker had accepted from Bill Vitek.

"With as much panache as I could muster, I asserted that you could define the most powerful language in the world in a page of code. They said, 'Put up or shut up.'"

Kay's challenge was grounded in his convictions about what a programming language should accomplish. Languages are much more than mere programs: They are blueprints for the thought process itself, software for the computer *and* its programmer. Almost from the moment he had encountered his first computer, Kay understood that the hallmark of a great system must be its simplicity. Only then can one be certain it has been fully distilled down to its essentials.

For him, writing a program tight enough to fit on a page had two chief virtues. It forced him to pare it to the bone, and it suited his sense of mental geography. By allowing the structure of the language to be absorbed in a single eyeful, he could show how all its individual components were interrelated pieces of the whole.

Over the previous few years this striving for simplicity had led him to reexamine all the ideas about programming and computer architectures he had absorbed during his *ad hoc* studies in the Air Force and at Utah. The challenge from Kaehler and Ingalls provoked him to sit down and arrange his thoughts on paper.

Traditional programming languages make a distinction between data and the procedures acting on them: The programmer defines a set of data variables as, say, the integers 3 and 4, then operates on them with the procedure "+" to produce the result "7."

Simple enough on its face. What dissatisfied Kay about this sort of structure was that as the data got more complex and the operations proliferated, the program's complexity quickly got out of hand—even if the desired answer was still the single integer 7.

Using a traditional language to send Seymour Papert's display turtle along a random path would require a programmer to summon all his or her knowledge of the convoluted routes by which data wend their way through the computer, get crunched, translated, and rearranged, and lay them out on paper—just to get a simple picture on a screen!

These systems also ran into trouble when the variables defined something other than numbers—the names "John" and "Mary," say. If one sent "+" to operate on *them*, the computer would almost certainly crash out of pure confusion. (How does one "add" words?) You would actually need to define John and Mary as some form of number that told the system how to "+" one to the other so the desired answer would result—"John, Mary," perhaps.

Kay's goal was to create a language that enabled the programmer to arrive at a simple result by a simple path, regardless of the complex operations taking place beneath the surface. He called this "hiding the details." After all, one does not need to know how a television works to be able to switch it on and find one's favorite show—why should it be necessary to know all the details of data and procedure to map a simple image to a computer screen?

His solution was to invent an entirely new syntax of computer programming based not on data and procedures, but discrete modules of programming code called "objects." Objects can be thought of as black boxes, like the television set. They combine data *and* the procedures that will work on them, and are manipulated by sending them "messages." Just as clicking the "on" button of a remote control sends the TV a "message" to turn itself on, in Kay's system one sends the object "3" the message "+ 4." The object knows to interpret that as a simple addition, and returns 7.

This may seem complex at first. But in contrast to traditional languages, object-oriented programming becomes relatively simpler as the data and operations become more complex. The reason is that the underlying calculations always remain hidden within the object, never needing to be explicitly invoked by the programmer. The object "John," for example, needs only to be sent the message "+ Mary" to know that "+" in this context can mean only one thing: to append "Mary" to itself after a comma.

Although Kay drew the principles of what became known as "object-oriented programming" from several well-known languages and computer systems, his system left many traditionally trained programmers befuddled from the start. It was as if one tried to invent a new literary language using conventional English words but devising radically new rules of meaning. The individual words would look familiar, but the way in which they related to each other in a sentence would seem impenetrable—until the reader decoded the new rules, that is.

The CSL programmer Warren Teitelman, a world master of the language Lisp—a key source of Kay's ideas—was one who found Smalltalk perplexing at first. "People were used to thinking about programs in terms of instructions and imperatives. If you thought in those terms you had a lot of difficulty with Smalltalk. When you looked at it, your first reaction was, OK, I sort of understand it, but where does the work get done?"

Having been challenged by his teammates to define a language on a page, Kay emerged after eight days of 4 A.M. to 8 A.M. struggle with a blueprint in hand for this new language with an unassuming name. Smalltalk was compact enough to define itself in a page of code (although as it grew more comprehensive, the pages got bigger and Kay's handwriting more minute). It was slow, because it placed an unusual workload on the computer. But it was astonishingly flexible.

Because anything could be an "object," whether numeral, word, list, or picture, Smalltalk lent itself especially well to representing graphic images on a computer display. That became evident even in the days before the Alto was ready. The Learning Research Group tested their embryonic system on Novas equipped with their big, lumbering character generators and turned out new typefaces and half-tone bitmaps by the score. Once the Alto came along, this process picked up speed as Kay's group enhanced Smalltalk with graphical capabilities that exceeded anything else being developed at PARC.

In fact, Kay was so impatient to get his hands on the Alto that he did not even wait for the first fully engineered models with printed circuit boards to come off the production line set up in El Segundo, like the rest of the labs. Instead he requisitioned six machines to be built with the same clumsy and unreliable wire-wrapped circuitry used in the original two prototypes, which he proceeded to install in the basement of Building 34.

The idea was that he could get them cheaper and faster, even if they turned out to be flaky in operation and hard to maintain. He also ordered these first Altos with the low-end option of only 96,000 bytes of memory, rather than the maximum 128,000 bytes. The first machines also came with a 2.5-million byte, or 2.5-megabyte, storage disk. (By comparison, today's household and office PCs often come with at least 32 or 64 *million* bytes of memory and four to eight *billion* byte storage disks.)

Under this miserly configuration Smalltalk ran painfully slowly, in part because the full-screen display alone consumed 64,000 bytes, leaving almost nothing for the program kernel. By the time Kay recognized that he had engaged in a false economy and tried to scrounge a few high-performance models out of turn, the machines were such a sought-after sensation that no one would let him cut in. "Forget it, Alan," admonished an amused Ed McCreight. "You're the one who screwed up."

But once Kay finally got all his machines retrofitted with adequate memory, Smalltalk fulfilled all its developers' expectations. While the CSL engineers busied themselves with programs to format the same dull text-heavy documents as fast as they could make the Altos run, the lunatic fringe worked the machines' graphical capabilities to the bone. A typical Learning Research Group program was no blob of black-on-white text but a carnival of drawings, half-tone photographs, even animated pictures. "Objects mean multimedia documents," Kay would say. "You almost get them for free."

As a result, the group's programs tended to favor the artist over the scientist. An LRG engineer named Bob Shur had programmed, with Thacker's help, a musical synthesizer capability into the Alto that allowed the machine to output twelve real-time voices at once, an astonishing capability for a machine of the Alto's scale.

Then, in the fall of 1975, Ted Kaehler, although no musician himself, developed a program called "Twang." This was a visual interface to a number of music synthesizer programs that could capture, compose, edit, and replay music on the Alto. Twang used a nontraditional notation, black bars of differing lengths and locations to indicate differing tonic and rhythmic values, that deliberately resembled the perforations on a player piano roll. Twang was unusual in that it worked virtually in real time. All previous computer music programs, including the pioneering "FM" developed by John Chowning at Stanford, had to be compiled, meaning that several hours of programming and debugging were necessary to produce a five-minute riff. That was unnecessary with Twang, with which one could compose and program a polyphonic passage with as many as eight voices almost as fast as one could hit the keys on an attached piano keyboard.

While Merry, Ingalls, Kaehler, Tesler, and others engaged in the grown-up activity of implementing serious Smalltalk tools on the Alto, Kay decided to make good on his original claim that Smalltalk would be a language simple enough for children to use. In the summer of 1973 he and Adele Goldberg assembled a group of eager preadolescents and started teaching them how to program. The effort would shortly lead to another of Kay's painful run-ins with PARC management.

These were not average youngsters. Goldberg started with an advanced class of seventh-graders at Palo Alto's Jordan Road Middle School, which served an upper-middle-class neighborhood a mile or so from the Stanford campus. Once or twice a week the kids came up the hill by bus or bicycle to Building 34, to be escorted to a roomful of Kay's original wire-wrapped Altos down in the basement.

Goldberg loaded these with an inspired Smalltalk program she called "A Box Named Joe." Joe, an outlined square, was a direct descendant of Seymour Papert's LOGO turtle. With a series of one-line commands the seventh-graders could make it appear on the screen, turn on its side, grow larger or smaller, or disappear. By arraying the commands in a sequence, they achieved rudimentary animation.

The encounter was mutually enlightening. Although these youngsters had for the most part grown up in privileged and brainy homes, they were surprised to come across grownups so guilelessly interested in their burgeoning intellects.

"When you're a kid, adults either don't want you around, or when you ask a question they give you a lecture," recalled Marian Goldeen, then twelve, the daughter of a Palo Alto piano teacher and a businessman.

"But they weren't like that. Adele was pregnant, but she looked a lot younger than someone I thought would be working with computers."

The scientists, some with young families of their own but few with teenagers around the house, found it eye-opening to deal with twelve- and thirteen-year-olds who grasped the basics of programming instinctively. One weekend Goldeen, who was an honor student in mathematics but had never programmed a computer, went home armed with a few pointers from Goldberg and coolly returned with a full-blown paint program, complete with a menu of varied shapes from which the user could select a custom "brush." Two older students contrived programs that wrote out musical scores or drew circuit diagrams, junior versions of Twang and SIL.

A few semesters later Kay attempted with characteristic audacity to broaden his experiment. The program coordinator at Jordan Road Middle School had arranged to make a room available to the PARC researchers, and Kay decided to furnish it with a working Alto. Unhappily, spiriting an Alto off the PARC premises was an outrageous violation of Xerox rules. Kay dealt with the implications by the simple stratagem of keeping management uninformed. Late one night he and Adele Goldberg drove up to the loading dock of Building 34 in her station wagon, the only vehicle anyone owned large enough to carry the cargo.

"Isn't this illegal?" she asked nervously. Stop worrying, Kay replied. He would take the heat.

Of course, it was impossible to keep the Alto's presence at a Palo Alto public school secret. Inevitably, news of the escapade reached a furious George Pake.

Painfully aware of Kay's value to the research center, Pake had always treated him tolerantly, if condescendingly. "Alan's irrepressible," he would say. "You can't keep him under control." Even Xerox's post-"Spacewar" strictures on unauthorized press statements had not stopped Kay from granting a steady stream of illicit demonstrations and brazen interviews, of which some of the latter provoked outrage back in Stamford. The California magazine *New West* once quoted him as saying that Xerox "doesn't understand" computers and its executives "really don't have any idea what I'm doing here," forcing Jack Goldman to reassure his fellow Xerox executives in writing that "Dr. Alan Kay is a recognized outstanding scientist in his field, albeit somewhat native and unorthodox in his dealings with the press." ("The article is a piece of undistinguished journalism and the author apparently enjoys sniping at large establishments," he added.) Kay complained his quotes were fabricated.

Pake had once hoped that appointing Harold Hall as SSL chief might help rein in Kay; after all, Hall had raised five kids, four of them boys. "I thought, he's a father figure and he can help to bring Alan up," Pake said later. But Hall's discipline did not take. It was shortly after he was succeeded as SSL director in 1975 by the somewhat more accommodating Bert Sutherland that the Jordan scandal erupted, with Kay once again involved in a first-class transgression.

Goldman happened to be on the scene to deliver the obligatory dressing-down. As Pake looked on, he berated Kay and Jeffers for violating Xerox security and exposing a proprietary program to the world.

"The shit really hit the fan," Kay remembered. "Goldman tore a strip off me and Chris." But once Goldman had contented himself with playing the bad cop, he let the experiment go on. As Kay recalled later, he turned to Pake and curtly commanded, "Let them do it!"*

Through 1973 and 1974 the Alto's remarkable power and potential made LRG's creative environment "a computer hacker's dream come true," as Ingalls recalled. "We'd go out for lunch and beer and say, 'Wouldn't it be great if you could do this or that?' Then we'd come back to PARC and in an hour or two do the thing we'd said would be so neat. And then we'd give a demo and show it off to our compadres in the CSL."

The partnership was a complementary one, largely because Kay's lunatic fringe always approached the Alto's capabilities along completely different lines from the Computer Science Lab. For CSL the issue was

---

*Neither Goldman nor Pake recalls Goldman's concluding remark as Kay tells the story. But the Altos were permitted to remain at Jordan, on the condition that they were first carted back to PARC to be formally "checked out."

how rapidly they could move data through the machine, whether it was Bravo text or Thacker's design schematics. For LRG it was how to display the same data in the most mind-blowing, dynamic way.

"Our mission was to really make this hardware do what it was supposed to do," recalled Kaehler. "Make it suitable for kids, flashy and wonderful, really responsive. And CSL was more concerned with hard-core computer science issues. They wound up not making that many innovations in the interface. We knew we couldn't design hardware like them, but we could make the interface much more interactive."

They worked like orchestra members composing and rehearsing a symphony at the same time. The day might start with Kay bursting in on Merry and Kaehler, interrupting their hard work on some module of code. He would scrawl some new idea across the lab's ubiquitous whiteboards until they were covered with boxes filled with other boxes and arrows pointing to yet more boxes with pointers across to new boxes and so on. Kay was determined above all to squeeze every ounce of functionality out of the Alto bitmap. The display screen, he proclaimed, was small only in terms of its physical dimension. In terms of its graphic flexibility, it was colossal. From that standpoint, why should the user be prevented from, say, drawing a picture on the screen using a mouse and a paint program while simultaneously drafting a memo describing the procedure?

The answer, unfortunately, was that the Alto's 8½-by-11-inch screen encompassed just so much physical real estate—the space of a single sheet of writing paper. That limitation, as it happened, led directly to one of their most important contributions to the look of the computer screen—the concept of overlapping windows.

The idea began by thinking of the screen in terms of a physical desktop. People in offices got around the same problem of too much paper and not enough room, Kay reasoned, by piling pages on top of one another. The analogous procedure would be to pile up small images on the screen—perhaps in some way that allowed the user to keep track of how many sheets, or projects, or windows, were open at once and to summon the most important one instantly to the top of the pile.

As usual, Kay was formulating a concept in Ideaspace and asking his team to implement it in reality. Although they knew how to tile the screen with multiple boxes, even overlapping ones, moving these boxes around or shifting one or another to the top placed enormous demand on the processor. The Alto complained in the only way it knew how, by performing the procedure at a glacial crawl.

For several weeks Kaehler worked principally on the overlapping-windows puzzle. The team had a system for showing when one of them had hit the wall on a coding problem and needed to hand it off. This was the "hot potato": One of them would walk into another's office with the figurative object held gingerly in cupped hands, then drop it into the next one's lap. Kaehler, having hit the wall on overlapping windows, dropped the hot potato into Ingalls's lap one day in the fall of 1974, and he solved it.

The solution came in the form of a brilliant feat of coding Ingalls called "BitBlt," an abbreviation of the term "bit boundary block transfer" that was pronounced "bitblit." BitBlt was a way to shift whole rectangles, or blocks, of the bitmap from one location to another in a single operation. It enabled the system to bypass the tedium of delving into memory, locating all the components of the rectangular image, and changing them one by one; and thus cut out most of the computation that had made full-bitmap procedures so slow. Suddenly graphical changes on the display were faster, more direct, and in computing terms vastly cheaper.

Like the wheel or the gothic arch, BitBlt was one of those discoveries that was nonintuitive in advance, obvious in retrospect, and ultimately adaptable to an infinity of uses. For the first time text could scroll up or down—or across the screen—at lightning-fast speed. You could draw a square and fill it with a hound's-tooth pattern, then push it across the screen until it disappeared off the side. Or make a copy of some part of the screen, save it, and display a new image in its place. This was the key to overlapping windows, for a part of the screen that was temporarily hidden (one window beneath another, for example) could now be called swiftly back into view, as though a page hidden halfway down a stack of papers was pulled out and transferred to the top. "You now had the illusion of a separate layer of screen display, which people weren't doing before," Ingalls said.

Kay's group labored to make this striking new capability more than merely an intriguing oddity. They worked BitBlt operations into their developing user interface until the actions of creating and manipulating multiple windows, each one running a different program, seemed exactly as effortless as shuffling papers on a desk. Then, in February 1975, they let CSL know there were a few things they wanted to show them.

The team prepared for the demo like actors auditioning for a shot at Broadway. Taylor's engineers could be a harsh audience, scornful of programs that placed glitz above speed and efficiency. That was why CSL's ideal was still Bravo, which responded to commands instantaneously and was as exciting to look at as a page from the phone book.

When the moment arrived Ingalls seated himself at an Alto in the beanbag room. Lampson, Thacker, Deutsch, and most of the rest of CSL were there, along with a few engineers from the other labs. Ingalls started by creating a few windows and loading them with various programs: One held a drawing, another a block of Smalltalk code, the third a lengthy block of text. His cursor wandered over the metaphorical desktop with fluid ease, pausing to draw a line here, add a word or phrase there. As his audience watched in rapt fascination at a display that had become as supple as a living creature, Ingalls almost forgot himself. "We were just going along, giving our demo, not thinking about the fact that we were doing something nobody had ever seen before." He was deep into a routine cut-and-paste editing task when he heard a voice shout, "Hey!"

Ingalls paused. Peter Deutsch was on his feet, pointing at the screen. "Did you just do what I thought you did?" he said.

Only then did Ingalls realize what had happened. In the midst of the edit he had instinctively pressed the middle button of his mouse. As if from nowhere, a small rectangle had appeared on the screen listing several commands. Ingalls had selected "cut" and released the button, whereupon the tiny rectangle instantly disappeared (along with the selected text to be deleted). It was something they called the "pop-up menu," the forerunner of a device common to almost every Windows or Macintosh program today. "It flashed and disappeared," he recalled. "That was really a wonderful moment, and it was all done in a half a second."

In the instant it took for the menu to pop onto the screen and off again, the entire audience comprehended not only the power of BitBlt but its practical application in a world of average users. "Everyone in that room walked out in a daze," recalled Smokey Wallace, who had been hired from Englebart's lab to help design a commercial office system using PARC technology. He recognized immediately that what he had just seen would be an indispensable element of anything he could put on the market. The very next day he showed up in Ingalls's office. "Tell me all about BitBlt," he said.

The PARC user interface, with its overlapping windows, mouse clicks, and pop-up menus, had entered computing history. More than twenty-five years and many engineering generations later, it remains the indisputable parent of the desktop metaphor guiding the users of millions of home and office computers. "From that moment on," Wallace said, "nobody ever looked back."

CHAPTER 16

The Pariahs

Dick Shoup had it down to a routine. He would pedal his bicycle up the tree-lined hill to the front of Building 34, lever open the door of the main entrance with his foot and pedal through without disembarking, then proceed straight down a narrow hallway, the tires of his bike whishing softly on the worn carpeting like wind through a sparse wood. Finally he would roll to a stop next to the graphics lab.

If only his work inside that room could proceed with as few impediments. But no: Dick Shoup had invented a technology that would stand the science of video on its ear, and he was close to getting fired for it.

The machine was called Superpaint. It deserves a place in history as the only invention too farsighted even for PARC's Computer Science Lab. And all because it thought in color.

The notion that an excess of ambition could make a talented inventor into a pariah at CSL sounds preposterous on its face—more like something that would happen to a Gary Starkweather in a place like Webster, and the very antithesis of what should have happened at PARC. Yet every organization of human beings eventually comes to cherish its own orthodoxies, and PARC was no different. When a group pursues a goal with the single-minded tenacity the Computer Science Lab possessed under Bob Taylor, the potential for intolerance is even greater.

"It was hard to be a renegade in that lab," Shoup said years later with a regretful sigh. "You could be a maverick, but only a maverick of a certain kind. And I guess I was just the wrong kind."

He had not started as an outsider. Quite the contrary. One could scarcely imagine a more lace-curtain computer science pedigree than Dick Shoup's: Ph.D. from Carnegie-Mellon and employment after graduation at Berkeley Computer Corporation, followed by selection by Bob Taylor as one of the elite six to join PARC upon BCC's demise. In the small society of the Computer Science Lab, this was the closest thing to coming over on the *Mayflower*.

You would have to know Shoup very well before discerning the heretic's soul underlying those sterling academic bloodlines. One clue was his interest in things that struck even some of PARC's free thinkers as a little *outré*, like his Transcendental Meditation group, which gathered every morning in a PARC commons room to do its thing to the voice of the Maharishi Mahesh Yogi on mail order tapes.

"Dick was a little different from everybody else," related his friend Alvy Ray Smith. "He's sort of a crusty guy, and he's not political, and he's very stubborn, and I think this is why he's as good as he is."

Had he known *how* stubborn, Bob Taylor might not have given Dick Shoup such a long leash at the very outset of his PARC career. Shortly after Shoup got to CSL Taylor welcomed him into his office to discuss what he wanted to do. Shoup did not have the clear-eyed convictions of his colleagues Lampson, Deutsch, and Thacker. Instead he saw so many fascinating paths laid out before him that he was stymied by the need to pick only one. Finally Taylor drawled: "Why don't you take a year to figure out what you want to do?"

With Taylor this offer was never as open-ended as it might seem at first glance. He figured that great computer scientists left to their own devices (and subtly guided by the Impresario's hand) would invariably find their way to the grail of interactive distributed computing. But Shoup took his new boss at his word. Within a month or so he had decided to pursue a course of research in video computer graphics.

On the surface his choice sat squarely within the mainstream of Taylor's vision. After all, Taylor had underwritten through ARPA the first computer graphics "center of excellence" at Utah and hired two of its graduates, Bob Flegal and Jim Curry, as his very first recruits to CSL. Nor was it entirely random on Shoup's part. His interest in video went all the way back to his high school days in western Pennsylvania, when he spent weekends repairing TV sets for his small-town neighbors.

Adapting video raster displays to interactive computers, he knew, raised a host of intriguing technical issues crying out for further study, especially if one desired to do interesting things with the image. One would need a way to store a whole frame's worth of digital data in memory at a time, for example. The technology to do so was known as the frame buffer. What Shoup proposed was nothing less than the biggest and most flexible frame buffer anyone had ever seen.

Simply defined, a frame buffer is a box holding a hell of a lot of memory. More precisely, it is a grid in which the memory is arrayed to correspond with a video frame, so that one or more bits of memory account for every "pixel," or "picture element," on the display. Activate the bits of a frame buffer in any given pattern and the exact same pattern should appear on the screen. Connect the buffer to a computer and you can rearrange those same bits—and the corresponding image—according to any algorithm you can devise, the way you might rearrange colored marbles in a partitioned box.

With the assistance of Flegal, Curry, and a French graphics expert named Patrick Beaudelaire, Shoup spent more than a year devising and assembling his memory giant. The first prototype of Superpaint went operational in Building 34 on April 10, 1973, just a few days after the Alto, which was being built in a basement room directly under his ground-floor video lab.

While Cookie Monster was marching across the Alto screen to the delighted gasps of the PARC faithful and their visitors, Dick Shoup was seated alone before a black-and-white video camera, holding up an index card on which he had scrawled, "It works, sort of." The system recorded the image of his face and the card in buffer memory in accurate detail—save for the bright red-orange of his droopy mustache and collar-length hair—and stored it on a conventional computer disk as a pattern of bits. ("It survives to this day," he said in 1998.)

Within a few months he had added a kaleidoscopic variety of video inputs, including live television, videotape, and videodisc, as well as hardware and software to allow him to alter the images he grabbed from the screen. The finished product was the first fully video-compatible frame buffer ever built. It was also a vector apart from the computer his colleagues had assembled in the basement. Where the Alto fit under a desk, Superpaint occupied two cabinets, each standing five feet tall and holding thirty-three memory cards. Its nearly two and a half million memory bits (in semiconductor chips worth about $100,000) meant that each pixel in a video frame with a resolution of 486 by 640 pixels could be addressed by eight bits. The system required two separate display monitors, one to show the image to be manipulated and the second a menu of electronic "paintbrushes" with which it could be altered in color or pattern. "No question about it, this was a big chunk of hardware," Shoup recalled fondly.

Superpaint was a uniquely agile and adaptable graphical tool. One could "grab" a frame from a videotape, disc, or directly off a television screen and manhandle it by changing its colors, flipping or reversing the image, bleeding it across the screen, even animating it. The key was the ratio of eight bits per pixel, which allowed the user to tune every dot to any one of 256 color values. You could freeze a random frame from a taped episode of, say, *Star Trek*, overlay it on the buffer as if you were tracing a line drawing on a blank canvas, and recolor Spock's hair green by assigning new values to the appropriate pixels.

Yet Shoup's fascination with color and video drew him away from what Taylor viewed as the Computer Science Lab's principal mandate. Shoup had participated in the MAXC project like any obedient member of the CSL team; but by the time the rest of the lab shifted its attention to the Alto he had withdrawn into his personal world. Taylor was distinctly displeased at the course things were taking.

"Bob felt the whole lab needed to be working in one direction," Shoup recalled. It was not simply that he was working on his own; more critically, it was felt that the basic premise of Superpaint would never fit in with CSL's goal to build the "office of the future." It was one thing to study how digital bits could be manipulated to create an image—the direction CSL had taken since the day they mapped Cookie Monster's face to the Alto screen. To his colleagues Shoup was working backwards, starting with video images and reducing them to their digital components: What could an office system ever do with *that*?

"Everyone on that side of the house was interested in documents," Shoup recalled. "Documents are pretty much black marks on white paper. Color meant TV, and that was some other world."

The tension between Shoup and the rest of the lab intensified through the end of the year and into early 1974, as pressure mounted on CSL scientists to focus their efforts almost entirely on Alto-related projects. It seemed that the only thing keeping the simmering disagreement from turning into a full-scale break was the absence of a catalyst. Then, as if on schedule, a man arrived at PARC who really did seem to come from some other world.

Alvy Ray Smith was the quintessential 1970s dropout. A native of New Mexico, he had been a New York University computer professor until abandoning his promising academic career to drive a white Ford Torino cross-country in pursuit of the muse of abstract art. He and Shoup had first encountered each other several years earlier when Smith, an expert in the arcane mathematics of massively parallel computers, was putting together a conference panel on modular computers and someone recommended he contact Shoup, whose dissertation at CMU had covered the same territory.

They embarked on a lifelong friendship, based in part on their shared fascination with the unconventional. "Dick was always willing to talk about all kinds of other things than science," Smith recalled. "Music, art, parapsychology, out-on-the-edge stuff." When Smith abruptly quit his professorship in 1974 and headed for California to paint, it seemed only natural that he would surface at the home of his old friend Dick, looking for a place to spend the night.

PARC then was at a peak of creative ferment. Every day some new feat of engineering appeared, virtually demanding to be shown off to anyone with a free moment. And here was Alvy Ray Smith, curious as a cat, at large with time to spare. Shoup fairly tingled with anticipation as he drove to the research center the next morning. Seated next to him was the one man he knew possessed the temperament to "get" Superpaint. Sure enough, the machine hit Smith like a lightning bolt between the eyes.

"He came in the door and got completely entranced," Shoup remembered. "He just deep-ended right into it." For the next several days and nights the bewitched artist scarcely left the lab for more than an hour or two at a time. "I realized this was what I had come to California for," Smith recalled. "You could just see it was the future."

The time-honored technique of daubing paint on canvas suddenly seemed hopelessly antiquated. Smith's new obsession was to get his hands on Shoup's machine and never let go. Shoup favored the idea, figuring he needed someone like Smith on the premises to make up for his own lack of artistic skill ("I was a visual thinker, but never much of a visual artist," he said). Attempting to secure Smith a place on PARC's permanent staff, Shoup argued that Smith's artistic talent and solid scientific credentials uniquely qualified him to help develop Superpaint's full potential, like a test pilot pushing a new fighter plane to the edge of the envelope.

Among the higher-ups with their hands on the budget, this was a no sale. No one had thought to provide in PARC's head count for an artist in residence, much less a rootless hippie like Alvy Ray Smith. Still, one thing you could say about PARC was that its rank and file was infinitely resourceful at finding ways to stretch the rules. After the personnel office refused to hire Smith as a temp or a contractor, Alan Kay came up with the idea of getting him into the building virtually as a piece of furniture—executing a purchase order for his services for a couple of thousand dollars. "I didn't care how they did it," Smith said. "I didn't want a title or salary or anything. I just wanted access to the equipment."

In no time he became a fixture in Building 34. If Dick Shoup was a maverick who blended in, Alvy Ray Smith was one who was hard to miss. Big and broad-shouldered, given to loud shirts, with a luxuriant mane of jet-black hair and a flowing hippie beard, he proclaimed the genius of Superpaint in a booming voice to anyone who was willing to listen and many who were not.

Taylor, ominously, viewed him skeptically from the start. Perhaps it was his claim to superior farsightedness, which Taylor took as a personal affront. Or perhaps the reason was that Smith seemed to have a singular talent for pressing his buttons, as he demonstrated on his very first day at PARC.

Smith was in the video lab, tinkering with Superpaint, when Taylor came up behind him, evidently intent on making sure the newcomer understood that this machine was considered to be out of the main-stream. He watched silently as Smith laboriously tuned the color settings, then asked, "Don't you find this too hard to use?"

Smith wheeled on him, shocked at the very idea. One might just as well ask a painter if he found it too hard to wield his brush. "No, I don't find it too hard," was his impatient rejoinder. "Don't you get it? This machine is revolutionary!"

Taylor walked off with a grunt, unhappy at being lectured in his own lab about what was and was not revolutionary. He had never before been reproached as a reactionary, and it stuck in his craw.

Nor was the significance of the exchange lost on Smith. "From that day on," he said, "I realized my friend Dick was in an unfriendly envi-ronment."

Taylor and Smith, of course, had been speaking at cross-purposes. The Computer Science Lab was a collection of engineers who weighed every-thing pitilessly against the question: How will this get us closer to our goal? They had committed themselves to developing Xerox's office of the future, and anything that diverted their attention or served an alternative goal had to be discarded or obliterated. To them the glorification of fluke and luck so cherished by the creative artist seemed intolerably wasteful of time and effort. Even Alan Kay tested their patience with his penchant for drifting haphazardly through Ideaspace; but compared to Alvy Ray Smith, Alan Kay was as sober as a Presbyterian elder.

Smith soon rewarded Shoup's faith that someone rooted in both art and science would make a powerful contribution to Superpaint's evolution. His most important refinement had to do with the way users adjusted colors on the screen. As an engineer, Shoup had built a system with elements only another engineer could love: The controls were a set of "sliding levers" that could adjust only an image's red, green, and blue values. The process lacked a certain necessary delicacy, almost like forcing composers to do without sharps or flats.

"Artists don't think that way," Smith informed him.

As he explained later, "Dick could get any color he wanted, but he had to think in terms of how you might get pink out of red, green, and blue." (How tricky this is can be imagined by anyone who has tried to adjust the flesh tones on an old color TV using only the three primary color dials.) Making the system intuitively useful for artists, Smith recognized, required an additional set of controls. "If I gave you controls for hue, lightness, and darkness, you would know you could take red and make it lighter: That's pink." He called the new categories "hue, saturation, and value" and labeled the system the "HSV transform." (Smith's additional categories, or similar ones, survive in most video animation systems to this day.)

But Smith's devotion to Superpaint hastened Shoup's estrangement from his CSL comrades by making his machine seem little more than a toy for longhairs. Smith monopolized the device for hours at a stretch, twisting video images into intricate abstract forms. He would take a color test pattern and step it through a programmed sequence of the 256 color values so it resembled the skin of a chameleon placed against a kaleidoscopic background, or bleed the pattern across the screen in a psychedelic wash. "I took a girlfriend's face and did some tricks with it, halved it down the middle and reflected it and halved that again so it was a four-way reflected face that's hardly recognizable anymore, but still has something organic about it."

Today such manipulation is commonplace to the point of triteness, the stuff of TV special effects. But in 1974 no one had ever seen anything like it. Soon Smith was inviting friends from San Francisco's creative demimonde down for demos that turned into all-night Superpaint "jam sessions." One graphics artist, an Iowan named Fritz Fisher, had been invited out to PARC by Shoup and Smith to give a talk about his work. He took one look at Superpaint and returned home only long enough to pack his bags. Back in Palo Alto he enrolled at Stanford and got a job as night watchman at CSL. For the next few years he would attend class in the daytime and tend the lab all night. "We'd come in the next morning and there'd be these elaborate designs on the machine," Shoup said, "and we'd know Fritz had been at it."

Among PARC scientists, however, the reaction was much less fervent, except among a handful of empathetic staff members who joined Smith in the wee hours, some displaying the furtive signs of experimental drug use. ("That was one of the dividing lines," Smith later remarked jocularly: "You'd just look at people and know if they were dopers or not. If they worked all night and had a lot of fun, they were probably doing dope.") Smith kept careful note of everyone's reaction to Superpaint from his vantage point in the color graphics lab, which occupied a long narrow room strategically situated at the nexus of Building 34's traffic flow— since seven doors opened into it, the passage of personnel rarely ceased.

"Here's our stuff on the screen, mind-blowing stuff," he remembered. "Most people would stop and look. Then there were other people who would walk right by and never look. And I'd always wonder, what's with those guys?"

Inside CSL, the person who set the standard of indifference to Superpaint was, unsurprisingly, Butler Lampson. Lampson's visionary temperament was grounded in a unique pragmatism. He was determined to reach the unseen horizon not by great blind leaps—they posed the unacceptable risk of leading one into a dead end—but by a series of small, measured steps. Big leaps required faith; measured steps required only science and a ruler.

"I remember once having a very illuminating discussion with Butler about my dreams for artificial intelligence," said Dan Bobrow, the brilliant specialist in computer languages who had been brought to CSL by Jerry Elkind. "He said, 'Danny, how can you work on something where there's a goal farther out than two years away?' Butler's vision of how you choose projects was to choose those that would tell you in two years if you'd succeeded or failed. He always chose incremental things. I can't recall him ever having what I think of as a long-term vision. But with his smarts and his good taste he was able to do important next steps in computing and defend them."

Among Lampson's objections to color graphics was that it was not by anyone's definition an incremental thing. "We couldn't afford color at the time because we couldn't afford the memory to drive a color frame buffer," he was still insisting many years later. "I felt you shouldn't go for it until it's quite easy, because otherwise it's going to be a huge distraction."[*]

Sure, Shoup acknowledged, color was expensive now, but it would be cheap in five or ten years, just like memory. Why not think of it as just another feature of the Time Machine?

Here entered Lampson's other important objection to Superpaint: He was constitutionally unable to imagine color contributing anything other than window-dressing to the office of the future. Something so trivial, he argued, might just as well be ignored until it was not merely cheap, but free.

Shoup's rejoinder was that Superpaint would do much more than enhance the office of the future. "I was looking at a bigger picture: pixel-based imaging in general," he recalled later. The essential struggle was to get the rest of CSL to see video, color, and animation as not just the technologies behind Saturday morning cartoons and Disney films, but as the foundations of a new type of computer graphics.

Given Lampson's influence over Taylor and the rest of the Computer Science Lab, this was destined to be a futile mission. Yet the more Shoup sensed himself becoming marginalized, the more he insisted on going his own way. "We attempted to bring Dick into the mainstream, but Dick knew what he wanted to do, and it wasn't that," Lampson recalled. As for Taylor, he already considered Shoup an unacceptably reclusive member of a lab he had assembled to serve a shared vision. Instead of joining in the Alto project, Shoup had turned his back. While his own lab colleagues found it hard to work with him, Taylor

---

[*]"I feel the same way today about 3-D, which is that for most applications of computing it's quite marginal," he added. (This conversation took place in December 1997.)

complained, he constantly gave demos of Superpaint to outsiders—and "non-technical" outsiders to boot, like Smith's circle of artists and hippies.

As Shoup understood, once you fell out of favor with Bob Taylor there was no coming back. Taylor's shit list was a cold, forbidding place. He made a few half-hearted attempts rebuild his burned bridges. After the Alto was up and running, he rigged one with a color display. But it was the only color Alto ever seen at PARC and remained forever an object of indifference to most of the engineers in CSL. (Kay's Learning Research Group, always more highly attuned to the content rather than the process of graphical displays, eventually made excellent use of it.) With every year that passed, Shoup's performance appraisals sounded more sinister. "Dick," one read, "is going to have to find a new home."

One day Taylor walked into the video lab to find Shoup's equipment festooned with handwritten signs warning: "DO NOT TOUCH WITHOUT MY PERMISSION." To a manager whose most profound conviction was that his people were all building components of a single common system, this was anathema. He became determined to show Dick Shoup who really owned his precious equipment. One day in late 1974, while Shoup was out of town, he fired the first shot.

The occasion was the broadcast of a television program about the artistic avant-garde entitled *Supervisions*, which was produced by the Los Angeles public television station KCET. Smith's and Shoup's work on Superpaint had started to win wide notice outside PARC, thanks in part to a tape called "Vidbits" which Smith had compiled from clips of his best work for playing to artists' gatherings all around California. After one such showing, KCET commissioned the two of them to supply some brief color-cycling effects for *Supervisions*. They had scrupulously insisted that the producers give Xerox screen credit, assuming that the parent company would appreciate the honor.

Instead, Taylor marched into the video lab a day or two after the broadcast and buttonholed Smith. "Xerox wants their logo off every piece of tape," he said. "Right now."

He ordered Smith to screen for him every snippet of videotape in the lab—miles of tape. While Taylor sat next to him for an entire afternoon,

Smith laboriously ran every reel, including every copy of his own "Vidbits," punching the ERASE button to excise any frame bearing Xerox's name or trademark. When Shoup returned home he and Smith managed a nervous chuckle over the sheer absurdity of the incident. But in their hearts they knew it presaged worse trouble to come.

Sure enough, a few weeks later, Smith was dismissed—or more precisely, his purchase order was canceled. The word came from Jerry Elkind, who was nominally Smith's boss but had never even spoken to him before. "We've decided to go with black and white," he said. "This project is over."

Smith was stunned. "You're crazy!" he blurted. "It's going to be all color from here on out, and you guys can own it all! I can't believe you're shutting it down."

"Well," Elkind replied evenly, "it's a corporate decision."

Smith had no choice but to leave. With a fellow artist and Superpaint fanatic, David DiFrancesco, he drove off toward Utah in quest of permission to continue his work on a frame buffer installed at the university there. He failed to get it, but instead received an invitation to set up a video program at the private New York Institute of Technology. The department later transferred *en masse* to George Lucas's Lucasfilm and even later was spun off as Pixar, the studio that produced the hit computer-generated movies *Toy Story* and *A Bug's Life*.

Meanwhile, at PARC Shoup now stood as a solitary pariah. One morning on his way into the lab he was stopped by a sympathetic colleague, who told him: "You know, there's a meeting going on about you."

Shoup burst into Taylor's office, interrupting a discussion about dismantling and redistributing his video equipment to other projects. The group fell sheepishly silent until, clearly unwelcome, "I went down to my lab and waited," he recalled. A short while later the verdict arrived: His lab space was to be taken away. He was to pack up his taping and recording equipment and turn it over to the PARC audiovisual crew, which would use it to compile a taped archive of administrative meetings.

Shoup's eviction from CSL was answered by a rescue effort by the Systems Science Lab, which secured him a transfer into Kay's group and permission to reassemble most of his equipment.

But the computer side of PARC never really embraced color as an integral part of its mission. Within a couple of years, when it became clear that Xerox would not support his work on another generation of video graphics, Shoup left PARC. Forming his own company, Aurora Systems, he developed a commercial system that produced the first animated TV weather maps and video logos.

The final irony came in 1983, when the National Academy of Television Arts and Sciences awarded a technical Emmy jointly to Dick Shoup and Xerox Corporation in recognition of Superpaint's role as a pioneering technology of video animation. Shoup went to the ceremony in New York, where he sat at the honorees' table with his invited guest Alvy Ray Smith and a nameless functionary dispatched by headquarters to accept the award on the company's behalf. The television academy had the foresight to prepare two Emmy statuettes. Shoup took his home. After spending a cordial evening with Shoup, the staff man took the other with him back to Stamford, where it vanished into the corporate archives. "I never did find out what they did with it," Shoup said.

CHAPTER 17

The Big Machine

T he one thing I've learned is you don't ever go into a completely new situation like this one alone," Harold Hall told David Liddle one day early in 1975. "I need someone to watch my back. So why don't you come with me?"

Despite Hall's melodramatic come-on, David Liddle did not need to be asked twice, not when the pitch was to join a newly created division to turn PARC technology into actual Xerox products. Of course he knew that Hall, who had been appointed its boss, was right to be wary. There was precious little evidence that headquarters understood the scale of the undertaking it had asked this new division to assume, and no guarantee it ever would. Who knew what enemies might lurk in the woods?

But the pluses tipped the balance. Liddle and Hall enjoyed a close and mutually respectful working relationship. And the opportunity was spectacular. Hall needed him not merely to help merchandise PARC's technology, but to assemble its disparate pieces into a coherent whole—to create an entirely new product line out of a magnificent jumble.

"That was it," Liddle recalled. "I looked at all this cool stuff getting done and I did not see how it was going to get to market. There was so much great raw material just piled up there. My idea was to sit down and think through an architecture—because of course these things were all done somewhat independently and ad hoc at PARC, as you always want to do in a research setting. Also, I frankly felt that if I didn't go and do it they'd probably assign some inappropriate person who wouldn't really *get* PARC and what we were trying to do."

More than five years would pass before this fledgling division would bring its first major product to market. As Hall had feared, he did not survive the first purge. But Liddle did. When the Systems Development Division completed its arduous work and introduced the legendary Xerox Star to the world, Liddle would be the man in charge.

The Systems Development Division had its genesis in Xerox's drive to expand its brand name beyond copiers and into new kinds of office equipment. This market, like the one for mainframe computers, was dominated by IBM, if not quite as unassailably. Xerox actually was beginning to make serious headway against Big Blue with a product line of word processors, fax machines, and electronic printers bearing its well-respected nameplate. But these devices were at best state-of-the-art, not ahead of the art.

In 1974 a headquarters task force concluded there might be more opportunities yet in manufacturing more advanced office "systems" for sale to large corporate customers with extensive and far-flung operations. The committee recommended the formation of a new division to serve this market. George Pake and Jack Goldman, understanding that this was their best chance to get PARC's technology into the commercial marketplace, maneuvered to place the unit under someone with a working knowledge of the territory.

In this they succeeded, up to a point. The new Systems Development Division, or SDD, was to report not to Goldman but to another transplanted Ford finance man, Donald Lennox, who supervised Xerox product development out of an office in Webster. But on January 1, 1975, Harold Hall, whose entire Xerox career had been spent at PARC, was named to run it.

Hall had trained before the war as a nuclear physicist, but it had been many decades since he had plied that trade. Instead he had fashioned a long career as a professional research manager, touching down at places like the Livermore Weapons Laboratory (under Edward Teller), ARPA, the Aeronutronics division of Ford, and a high-tech division of Singer before landing at PARC in 1972. As he put it later with characteristic self-effacement, after so many years working among exceptionally brilliant scientists "I had developed and honed the skill of making myself useful to people whose intellectual gifts dwarfed my own."

A native South Dakotan, he had emerged from grinding poverty on a Depression-era farm to become an exemplary corporate bureaucrat with a charming personality and a store of fascinating yarns about his work on the nuclear weapons program during and after the war. When in 1971 he got nudged out of his Singer vice presidency by someone else's power play, he had called upon his old Ford colleague Jack Goldman for a job. Goldman sent him to PARC because he considered him the perfect foil for George Pake, who he would serve almost continuously as a loyal lieutenant for the next decade.

Pake initially assigned Hall to take over the Systems Science Lab from Bill Gunning, who yearned to get back to hands-on research. True to his instincts, as SSL chief Hall familiarized himself with the work being done in his lab just enough to be genially manipulated by Alan Kay and Adele Goldberg. "I knew better than to pretend knowledge I lacked, the surest way to be rejected by PARC," he said, joking that the job seemed to consist chiefly of affixing his signature to Alan Kay's expense reports.

Athletic, silver-haired, and free-thinking, Hall led a contented life raising his five accomplished children in the intellectually stimulating atmosphere of Palo Alto, displaying such neatly constrained ambitions that he could hardly pose a threat to anyone above him in the Xerox organizational chart. What he found particularly gratifying about his new assignment was that it came with a vice presidency—the one corporate title he had aspired to since the day he lost his last one at Singer.

Hall found, however, that he and his new boss were on entirely different wavelengths in terms of how they viewed SDD's mission. Don Lennox was another ex-McNamara whiz kid—one of the troupe of young and brilliant technocrats who had helped Robert McNamara remake Ford management (and would attempt the same at the Pentagon, with less distinguished results, when their boss became J.F.K.'s Defense Secretary). He was a "friendly, direct, and well-meaning" financial expert, but profoundly at sea with the complexities of advanced product development. Where Hall anticipated that SDD would design and market an entirely new generation of office information systems, Lennox appeared to think the task involved nothing more than mixing and matching a few off-the-shelf components. The disparity between their visions became clear the day Hall reported to Webster for his first meeting with Lennox. Fully expecting to be granted a staff of 100 persons or more, he learned instead that he had been assigned a rump platoon of six ex-SDS engineers in El Segundo, along with four open positions to fill as he pleased.

Hiding his dismay, he returned to Palo Alto to get on as best he could. His first call was to Dave Liddle. "Come with me," he said, "and you can pull together an architecture out of all the good work you guys have done at PARC."

For Liddle, Hall's invitation was an act of deliverance. Xerox had recently asked him to head up a research project on display devices in Webster. Even though this would be a promotion, he found the offer unenchanting. For one thing, he hated the thought of moving back East. Plus he thought of himself as a computer scientist, and the people at Webster were anything but. Finally, he was bored with display technology, which had been his field of study since his days at the University of Michigan.

The SDD job answered all those concerns. So while Hall filled out his meager roster by recruiting Ron Rider, Charles Simonyi, and Chuck Thacker to his last three open slots, Liddle dove into the task of drafting a technical road map to guide the new division.

"Harold was a smart guy, so he had some sense of which technologies were most appropriate to use," Liddle recalled. "But it was really up to me to assess them. And I got lots of opinions, talked to lots of people at PARC, and had different folks look it over."

The "Office Information Systems Architecture" as he called the document, formally set down all the elements of an integrated office information system as he and his PARC colleagues envisioned them. There would be personal workstations for every individual (fronted by high-quality bitmapped display screens) as well as communal machines, or servers, for printing and file storage. All were to be linked to each other by Ethernet with a capacity of ten megabits per second—more than three times the power of PARC's Ethernet—and powered by industrial-strength versions of PARC's most advanced operating systems and application software. It was the work of PARC's magnificent first five years transformed into a commercial product. In short, as Liddle said, "It was son of Alto."

From that moment through to the public introduction in April 1981 of the Xerox 8010 office system, the "Star," this basic outline would never change. The Star would emerge as a superb feat of engineering and perhaps the most perfectly integrated office computer system of all time. Liddle planned on the development phase taking five years, but he also anticipated that the system's architecture would set a standard in the industry for at least another ten.

The vision animating the Star's designers, however, was one of the few things about SDD that would remain stable through the coming years. Five months after launching SDD, Don Lennox was reassigned. His replacement was Bob Sparacino, an executive with solid engineering credentials Xerox had imported from General Motors. Sparacino took an instant dislike to Hall and a month later Hall, astonished at how swiftly his paranoia had been fulfilled, was dumped. (He returned to Pake's staff.) Over the next three and one-half years SDD had three chiefs, none of them lasting more than a matter of months, until finally, in 1978, the top job devolved to Liddle, who somehow had managed to keep his head down amid all the turmoil. As Metcalfe later joked: "For a while the most dangerous job to have at Xerox was to be David Liddle's boss."[*]

SDD, meanwhile, soon burst the restraints Lennox had placed on its size. The organization that presented the Star to the world in 1981—and

---

[*]On the day of Liddle's appointment Hall wrote him to observe that his three predecessors had lasted exactly six, twelve, and twenty-four months in the job. Accordingly, he predicted that Liddle would serve forty-eight. Four years later almost to the day, Liddle mailed him a copy of the note, clipped to an announcement of his resignation. "Harold," he wrote, "you were exactly right."

developed a basic system technology for a wide range of Xerox products—was no ten-person shop but a colossus employing 180 engineers in Palo Alto and another 100 in El Segundo. As the designated commercial outlet for PARC technology, the division also acquired an exalted sense of its stature as a flag-bearer for Xerox. This partially accounted for the Star's deliberately stately design. Its target users were not secretaries and clerks but their bosses, who were executives and professionals—an ambition that inspired skepticism among marketing experts of the time but accurately foretold the later evolution of the personal computer as an office device. (This ambition also drove the Star's architects to make the user interface as mouse-oriented as possible. A Xerox promotional brochure would state in 1981 that the Star was "designed specifically for professional business people with little or no typing skills.")

SDD's chiefs correctly understood that Xerox headquarters expected a product development program to possess a certain minimum heft. "Xerox had a hard time understanding anything that wouldn't be a $100-million business," observed one technology manager. Others feared, however, that in waiting for the division to unveil its fully featured product, Xerox might inadvertently miss out on myriad smaller, but still promising, opportunities.

SDD management accordingly made earnest, if infrequent, efforts to interest headquarters in staging less ambitious market probes. As head of the division in 1976, for instance, the former SDS executive Robert Spinrad attempted to persuade Jim O'Neill, the head of technology, to introduce a downscaled low-cost Alto for the office clerical market.

O'Neill responded that Xerox was uninterested in taking what he saw as a remote beachhead. It would be safer, he argued, to let others establish positions in the technical vanguard. Xerox would bide its time and overrun them later with a massive, concentrated attack. "If we put it out right now we'll tip our hand," he told Spinrad. "While we'll have an early success, others will look at us and come in with a well-engineered product that can be maintained better in the field. We'll just lose the big battle."

"My notion," Spinrad recalled, "was that we could build small and develop up. But I lost every one of those fights. There was no way the

Xerox Corporation of that era was going to do anything but full-scale product development."

About a year and a half after SDD's founding, Dave Liddle tempted Bob Metcalfe back to Palo Alto. He did not find it a difficult sale, for Metcalfe had grown disaffected with his new employer, a subsidiary of Citibank that handled the giant bank's electronic fund transfers out of a computer center in Los Angeles.

After seven months he had succeeded in weaning the operation from its aging custom-built card readers and onto Digital PDP–11s running interactive software. Unfortunately, he found his human colleagues less tractable than the machines. "I'd been promised that I would be made a vice president after six months," he recalled. But when he demanded that the company make good on its offer, his boss reneged on the grounds that he was not yet thirty. "He said, 'I can't do that, you're just too young. It would really upset the applecart. It's no big deal.' I said, 'It's a big deal to me.'"

The friendship between Liddle and Metcalfe was anchored by a multitude of common traits. They were both tall, solid men with built-in swaggers, unashamed to throw their weight around. As ex-college jocks they worked out their frustrations on the field of play, often on each other. Metcalfe could regularly beat Liddle at tennis, his game; but Liddle, who had briefly played varsity basketball at the University of Michigan in the mid–1960s, could whomp him decisively under the boards.

One time his varsity background enabled Liddle to score a decisive victory off Metcalfe. The latter, living high off the hog as a newly divorced bachelor in Los Angeles, had secured a pair of floor seats to the L.A. Lakers games, close enough to the action for the toes of his shoes to nuzzle the side line. He invited Liddle, who had long bragged of having played ball at Michigan with Lakers guard Cazzie Russell.

"We'd all say, yeah, yeah, you were at Michigan and Cazzie Russell was there too, yeah, sure," Metcalfe recalled. On this occasion, he and Liddle took their seats on the floor of the Los Angeles Forum just as the Lakers came out for their warmup. As Metcalfe watched in mute astonishment, Cazzie Russell made a beeline for Dave Liddle. "He came over and said something to the effect of, 'How you doin', Liddle, my man, it's been a long time,' then he brought over another famous guy like Kareem Abdul-Jabbar and it's, 'Meet my friend David I've been telling you about . . .' Well, thereinafter I believed Dave Liddle could never lie, because he had obviously not been exaggerating in the slightest about his relationship with Cazzie Russell."

When Metcalfe quit Citicorp in a huff over his withheld vice presidency, Liddle was ready to grab him on the rebound. Metcalfe, who had inspired awe at PARC by becoming the first well-known researcher to leave, now became the first to return (although technically he was returning to SDD, rather than PARC). The difference between his final PARC salary and his new wage of $37,000 amounted to the biggest raise anyone in the building had ever received. The strategy of extracting a raise from Xerox by working somewhere else for a spell was known ever after as the "Metcalfe promotion," a term that further gratified its honoree.

"I got twenty to thirty percent from Citibank, then Liddle gave me another ten to fifteen percent premium to get me back," he said. "But the problem was I knew people who were making much more, and they were people I didn't think were that much smarter than me."

Metcalfe's new job was primarily to upgrade Ethernet's capacity from three to ten megabits per second to meet the demands of SDD's formidable product plan. But he was also expected to ride herd, as a sort of contract administrator, on the designer of the Star's mission-critical central processor, Chuck Thacker.

As if his historically charged relationship with Thacker were not problem enough, on assuming his new duties in June 1976 Metcalfe discovered that the entire project was careening off the tracks. Structurally speaking, SDD was a mess. The division had two headquarters, one in Palo Alto and the other in El Segundo, where it had taken over a block of manufacturing facilities vacated by SDS. This arrangement burdened Liddle and his cavalcade of immediate superiors with two mutually resentful semi-organizations located five hundred miles apart—the northern contingent thickly seeded with PARC alumni and the southern branch staffed with reassigned SDS employees nursing old grievances against the fancy Ph.D.s in Palo Alto. No volume of e-mail or networked file sharing could quench the rekindled tensions, only the personal intercession of SDD managers shuttling endlessly back and forth by air.

The geographical rift was only one of numerous headaches. The project's schedule had slipped almost from Day One. Building the ambitious Star "was taking longer than everyone thought and it was harder than everyone thought," recalled Bob Belleville, a former Engelbart engineer who helped Metcalfe supervise Thacker's work. And there lay the main predicament. Thacker's processor design, which was dubbed "Dolphin," satisfied no one. It busted its specifications in almost every measure—too big, too slow, too hot, too expensive—as if Thacker, the minimalist paragon, had unaccountably succumbed to an alarming attack of biggerism.

Most of the blame, however, belonged to the specs themselves. SDD's ambition was to bundle together two separate technologies: office automation, including programmable word processing and networking; and high-quality digital copying and printing with high-speed lasers. Designing a processor to handle either task might have been manageable, but putting them together was like squaring the circle—simple on its face and impossible in practice.

"Chuck ended up designing a machine that wasn't very good for either purpose," remarked his friend Butler Lampson. "At a very early stage they should have said, 'This is impossible, we can't meet both of these requirements.' But instead he soldiered on and designed this thing which was kind of big and clunky for the office automation application and didn't have the power that was needed for the imaging application. It was a bust."

Moreover, Thacker was fighting his battle using the weapons of the last war. Because the new system's components were exponentially bigger and faster than the Alto's—that the Ethernet had tripled in speed only hinted at the size of the problem—his design plan was to take the original Alto processor and simply scale it up. In fact, what was needed was an entirely new architecture.

"The Alto was a machine that was a happy confluence of technologies," Belleville observed. "It was built at the right time. It took a mess of ideas and made them into a machine that was for the time extraordinarily powerful and cheap. But now the display was bigger and faster, and Ethernet was bigger and faster, and the disks were bigger and faster. The complexity rose very quickly and Thacker ran into a brick wall."

The central processor's inability to keep up with its supercharged peripherals increased pressure on the rest of the system. One could never be sure the processor would be finished with one task in time to handle the next—data bits might stream in so fast from the disk, for example, that the processor, like a tennis player trying to return the volleys of a souped-up ball machine, might not be in position to receive them. In that event, the system would crash.

Thacker felt deadlocked. "You can trade off cost and performance and time to market in various ways," he explained. "But if you try to bind all three of them you may wind up in an infeasible part of the design space. That's what happened with the Dolphin. In order to cut the costs we cut the performance down quite a bit—and still couldn't meet the cost goals. It was still faster than the Alto and it had some things the Alto didn't have, like virtual memory and caches, but it was just too expensive."

Metcalfe pelted him with acerbic demands for progress while he tried to maintain a grueling schedule. The pressure brought him to the edge of burnout. "My group had about fifteen people in it and half were in Palo Alto and half in El Segundo," Thacker recalled. "And I would commute two days a week to El Segundo. That just broke me."

To a great extent, Metcalfe was only passing on the same tension he received from above. "Xerox had these staff guys who would come in from Connecticut to check up on what we were doing," he recalled. "It was my job to stand up in front of these bastards and give them these presentations. I had the *fun* job. I'd say, 'Remember last time I told you how well it was going? Well, it hasn't worked out that way. Here's the unforeseen problem . . .' And this went on forever."

SDD had few options. If Thacker could not get the job done, the entire project was in jeopardy, for he was the ace processor designer and the font of knowledge piped direct from PARC. Yet there was only so far they could push him, for he was not technically an employee of SDD—just a contractor, formally on loan.

"Dave could not simply bang on Chuck's desk and say, 'Dammit, I'll fire you!'" Belleville recalled. During one morose staff meeting, "They were all worrying about whether Chuck would be hit by a truck, because he was the one developing the hardware for SDD. Right then Metcalfe joked, 'What you guys don't realize is that I'm waiting in an alley, *driving* the truck.'"

Against these great odds, Thacker's team finally produced the Dolphin. It was as problematic as everyone feared, for the fundamental issues had not been solved. All the design compromises made had still left it too big, too slow, too expensive. Weary and demoralized, Thacker returned to CSL, where he could work once again sheltered from the merciless pressure of commercial deadlines. As though in exchange, CSL provided one more favor for Liddle's division. This was the intercession, like the *deus ex machina* in a Greek tragedy, of Butler Lampson.

Lampson had become aware while Thacker was still struggling with the Dolphin design that SDD's hardware effort was hitting the wall. Thacker, Metcalfe, and Liddle were his friends and he could almost smell their panic. "I kibitzed with them quite a bit and I noticed at some point that the Dolphin wasn't going to be satisfactory. But they were in denial. I decided myself to go back to the roots of the Alto and give it another spin." This was classic PARC (and classic Lampson)—an unsolicited answer to an unasked question dropped casually over the transom.

For him the task of designing a substitute processor resembled a jazzman's noodling on a handy sax. The raw materials were his ability to take a fresh look at the problem, and the appearance of a new integrated circuit that had been announced by National Semiconductor Corporation. Because the chip was actually not yet in production, he based his work entirely on its written specifications. But the flash of insight that enabled him to overcome the obstacles that had stymied Thacker came when he realized that the Dolphin processor—like the Alto's—did not keep time with its own internal clock.

This so-called "asynchronous" architecture had never before been a problem, which is why Thacker had reimplemented it for the new machine. In simple terms, the Dolphin and Alto varied the number of instructions they performed each clock cycle according to the procedure they were executing. More complicated procedures required more instructions (and more time) than easy ones. Therefore the system could only guess when the processor would be available to service the next needy peripheral, whether that was the Ethernet transceiver or the disk controller. Since the processor speed of the Alto was more than fast enough to handle all these functions together, nothing ever went awry. Given the stepped-up demands of the Dolphin machine, however, such an informal arrangement would not do.

Lampson's "synchronous" design differed by feeding a fixed number of instructions through the processor and memory per clock cycle, which enabled him to synchronize all the peripheral devices to the processor and eliminate the guesswork about when an incoming bit could be processed. With everything ticking along according to the same clock, a much smaller volume of data had to be held in buffers—which relieved the design of the Dolphin's hardware bloat.

Belleville and the others saw instantly that the design Lampson had sketched out on seven sheets of lined yellow paper would run faster, more efficiently, and cooler than the Dolphin. After making a few minor changes, they renamed it "Dandelion" (most of the machines being turned out by Xerox's Palo Alto engineers in this period got names starting with "D" for "Digital" and became known collectively as the "D machines") and installed it in the Dolphin's place as the heart of the Star. A major hurdle had finally been cleared.

But the Star was still more than two years from its launch—and that would make all the difference in its future. For while the Star was designed to be the office professional's personal nirvana, meticulously assembled from the finest technological components money could buy, it was destined to get blindsided in the marketplace by a new species of machine that was quite explicitly less than nirvana, assembled quick and dirty from the cheapest components available, and so low-tech it bore almost the same relationship to the Star that a roller-skate does to a Mercedes-Benz.

A legend in its own time, boasting capabilities still unmatched nearly twenty years after its launch, the Star would end up as one of the most resplendently obsolescent machines ever sold.

By 1975, the fifth year of PARC's existence, George Pake's prediction had come true: The center had outgrown its original quarters, and then some. There were two hundred employees spread among three locations ranging from Porter Drive up to Hillview, where two buildings were now rented. In March Jack Goldman's original vision of a free-standing shrine to basic research was realized with the opening of PARC's ten-million-dollar permanent home at 3333 Coyote Hill Road, directly across the street from Building 34.

The new building had a difficult birth. Its groundbreaking had been delayed for more than two years, until August 1973 (Goldman and several other dignitaries took home silver-plated shovels marking the occasion), by an old land-use controversy enflamed by a local conservation group's discovery that Stanford University, the site's owner, had illegally subdivided the land. The so-called Committee for Green Foothills sued, tying up all development on the site until Xerox, desperate to get its construction project under way, brokered a settlement.

As part of the deal Xerox and Stanford agreed to stringent construction restrictions. The PARC building was to be no more than 200,000 square feet (its first phase actually came to only 120,000) and situated out of view of motorists passing on most of the major local thoroughfares. Stanford's penance was a pledge to leave several neighboring (and potentially lucrative) acres permanently undeveloped.

Designed by Gyo Obata, an architect who had made a name for himself with the arresting design of the National Air and Space Museum in Washington, D.C., PARC was a long rectilinear concrete building adorned with hanging gardens. The building cascaded down the hillside in steps, arranged like an upside-down cake so that visitors entered on the third floor, where the administrative staff was housed, and descended to the second (occupied by the computer and system science labs) and first (the general and optical science labs). There at the bottom was a staff entrance, gratifyingly outfitted with a sheltered bike rack. Responding to suggestions Rick Jones had dutifully collected from the building's future occupants, Obata generously fronted PARC's northern elevation with horizontal ribbons of glass to bathe its interior in ample sunlight, and furnished it with numerous open-air atriums ideal for the tranquil contemplation of nature, technology, and the nexus thereof.

The completion of the Coyote Hill building represented a milestone in

PARC's public profile. The local newspapers featured fulsome interviews with Pake, glimpses of the office of the future ("scientists at the Xerox Research Center in Palo Alto aren't even working with copiers . . . "), and optimistic talk about the blending of the new sciences with the old.

The contrast could not be greater with the grim saga playing itself out a few hundred miles to the south. This was the death watch over SDS.

"McColough's Folly" had been an invalid virtually since the moment it changed hands back in 1969. Periodically it would come under the microscope of one task force or another (Jerry Elkind served on one such group in 1972), but no one could ever find a way to stanch the flow of red ink. Instead, Xerox management tried to hide the losses deep within the balance sheet by reorganizing the company into three functional organizations—sales and marketing, engineering and manufacturing, and strategy and planning—and distributing pieces of the computer business among them. As part of this program, Xerox in 1972 dissolved SDS as a separate entity and fired Dan McGurk, the former Palevsky lieutenant who had been running it ever since the sale.

But this tactic could not disguise the losses in computing, any more than a farmer can obliterate the stench of manure by spreading it over more acreage. By early 1975 Xerox's poor overall performance had destroyed the last of Wall Street's confidence in its management. The stock, which had hit an all-time high of $179 a share in 1972, dropped to $50. Corporate legend has it that one day in the men's room at Stamford headquarters Archie McCardell, the company's finance-oriented president, told McColough he thought it was time to give up on the computer business altogether. In response, McColough convened his final computer task force. Its purpose was to find the best way to cut adrift what was left of SDS, which may be why it was given the Homeric code name "Odyssey."

Among Odyssey's members was Rigdon Currie, who tried to fight a rearguard action against the extinction of his old division. "I put in a pitch to cut the operation back to our original customer base in scientific and real-time computing, instead of competing with IBM in the business market," he recalled. "I got stepped on."

Odyssey's conclusion, instead, was that the computer business could be neither saved nor sold at any price. Currie was handed the disagreeable assignment of cutting the best possible deal for its remaining odds and ends with Honeywell, which had made a practice of scavenging the shards of other companies' failed ventures in computing. To cover the expense of getting out of the business, Xerox took an enormous $84.4 million writeoff. The action produced the company's first annual loss since the introduction of the Model 914 copier, fifteen years earlier.

Nothing was left of the long misadventure of SDS other than the platoon of researchers now installed in their imposing new hillside palace in Palo Alto. If Xerox was to be persuaded that digital technologies were the key to its future, it would be up to them alone to make the case.

PART III

Messengers

CHAPTER 18

Futures Day

During the course of 1977 Peter McColough began to fear that his corporation was coming apart at the seams.

The previous few years had been a skein of disappointments and embarrassments for Xerox. In 1975 had come the unraveling of the SDS purchase—"McColough's Folly"—and the resulting $84.4 million writeoff. The foreign invasion had turned into a full-scale rout, with a hundred thousand inexpensive Japanese copiers sold in a market segment for which Xerox had no competing product. Then IBM and Kodak took direct aim at the heart of Xerox's traditional customer base by introducing fast new copiers of their own. There were antitrust lawsuits and patent infringement battles. To top it all off, the U.S. economy was in terrible shape, squeezed by the pincers of high inflation and savage recession—an unprecedented combination known as "stagflation."

The Xerox chairman knew something had to be done to stem the erosion of morale or his best executives and salespersons would flee. His solution was to throw one huge, historic party.

McColough envisioned the Xerox World Conference of November 1977 as a sort of company-wide revival, a last attempt to restore the passion that had fueled its rise nearly twenty years earlier, when Joe Wilson bet the farm on an untested technology and won the world. The guest list would comprise the top 250 executives of the worldwide organization and their spouses. The setting would be Florida's exquisite Boca Raton Country Club, where the food, accommodations, and entertainment through four days of celebration, exhortation, and rebirth would be first-class all the way. In McColough's imagination, the affair would evoke the atmosphere of the previous World Conference, held in 1971 when Xerox's wealth and hubris were at their very peak.

It is not clear which individual first proposed that PARC play a major role at the World Conference. In any case, once McColough heard the idea of using Boca Raton to introduce the technologies PARC had invented to the sales force, he embraced it whole heartedly. PARC would not only get a chance to show off; McColough decreed that one entire day of the four in Boca Raton would be devoted to PARC alone.

One morning that summer, the SSL's director, Bert Sutherland invited John Ellenby into his office. Ellenby had worked in the Computer Science Lab for three years, during which time he had gained a well-deserved reputation as a man who Got Things Done—schematics realized, prototypes built, projects completed—not at all an easy proposition amid the clash of egos and the religious wars raging unceasingly over engineering and design at PARC.

"If you had a free hand, John, what would you do to show off our work?" Sutherland began. "You see, there's this big conference coming up for managers from all over the world, and we've been invited."

Ellenby thought for a moment, then asked, "Just what do you mean by a free hand?"

John Ellenby was a slender, pale Briton with a fringe of brown hair crowning his high forehead. His unusually varied education and work experience had included the study of economic geography at the University of London, a teaching post at the London School of Economics, and, following a course in systems engineering from IBM, a dual appointment as a lecturer in computer science at the University of Edinburgh and consultant in computer architecture and graphics to Ferranti Ltd., the pioneering British computer maker. His first encounter with PARC had occurred back in 1971 thanks to Dan Bobrow, who was passing through Edinburgh on a fellowship. Bobrow described PARC to Ellenby and, when he returned stateside, described Ellenby to PARC. Not long after that Ellenby happened to be passing through the Bay Area; an invitation was issued for him to address a Dealer, and in September 1974 he was hired by Jerry Elkind, who no doubt saw in Ellenby's ability to shuttle so easily between academia and industry a reflection of his own skill in balancing good science and solid pragmatic judgment.

The terms of Ellenby's employment amounted to a pay cut. Owing to the good salaries he pulled down from two full-time jobs, he lived in relative luxury in a large old stone house in Edinburgh with his sculptress wife, Gillian, and two young sons. "But that was immaterial," he said later. "The chance was to work at PARC, which was absolutely the top-notch computer sciences lab in the world. So I joined, and we all moved."

He had worldliness enough to discern at a single glance the dividing line separating PARC's virtues from its flaws. The former included the work that had produced the Alto and the Ethernet, which impressed him as marvels of elegant design and superb feats of engineering. The latter included Taylor's dogmatism, which Ellenby believed discouraged thoughtful dissent in the Computer Science Lab. He was dismayed to find genuinely farsighted projects such as Shoup's Superpaint and Bobrow's work in artificial intelligence, both of which challenged CSL orthodoxy, hanging on by their fingernails.

"Computer architecture in those days was a major battleground for religious wars," he recalled, "and Xerox had them big-time." His first assignment would have him interceding between two of its contending armies.

The task was somehow to get the Alto manufacturing process jumpstarted. The machine had been designed and prototyped but as yet there were only five in existence. The construction program, it seemed, had mysteriously stalled somewhere between Palo Alto and El Segundo.

As it happened, Ellenby had distinguished himself as an industrial consultant in Great Britain by transforming dysfunctional programs into operational ones. Turning his experienced eye to the Alto, he recognized instantly that the machines were indeed hostages of a religious war—this one between the Computer Science Lab, which designed them, and

SDS, whose downtrodden factory staff was tasked with building them to PARC specifications in El Segundo, five hundred miles away.

"El Segundo was a product organization with a lot of pride," Ellenby recalled. "It had a lot of good guys from the days when they had built a lot of quite impressive machines. And now they were getting fucked over by this copier company that knew how to put powdered coal onto drums that went whistling around and transferred it to paper but didn't know shit about electronics. So there was a religious problem right there. Then there was this funny group of weird Northern Californians they had to deal with while they were trying to solve their other problems. Meanwhile there was not a lot of respect at PARC for SDS. And nobody was really assigned at PARC to make it all happen. The Alto was kind of a baby looking for its mother."

Ellenby stepped in to referee. His first achievement was getting El Segundo to complete twenty Altos stuck in the pipeline. Then he took a radical step. Organizing a small cadre of product engineers into an integrated engineering and manufacturing unit he called the Special Programs Group, he arranged for Chuck Thacker's time machine to be reengineered into an object that could be efficiently mass-produced. The Special Programs Group replaced all the Thackeresque shortcuts, which looked like virtues when the goal was hastily to turn out a serviceable machine with spare parts, but were now merely the sources of annoying glitches.

"No fault of Chuck's, but the machine was just flaky," Ellenby said. "I had come from a pretty rigorous background because the machine for which I had been consulting designer at Ferranti, the Argus 700, was designed for very high-reliability process and communications control. I thought that somehow or other a machine that stops for no reason was not a good machine."

Ellenby's group added a memory error-correction system similar to the one Thacker had designed for MAXC (but had left off the Alto). This substantially cut the manufacturing cost of the machine by allowing the SPG to use more error-prone, but cheaper, memory chips without compromising the machine's reliability. The original Alto was almost unmaintainable ("In order to get to something you had to take a lot of other stuff out," Ellenby recalled); he ordered the innards redesigned so every component would be easily accessible just by opening the cover, as in today's desktop PCs. The so-called Alto II was both durable and easy to manufacture on a small production line. "We just popped 'em out," Ellenby said proudly. This was the machine that proliferated throughout PARC as a springboard for some of the most striking technological innovations the world has ever seen.

Soon after the new machines started rolling off the fabrication line in early 1976, however, Ellenby came face to face with the realities of technology politics at Xerox. Heady from the triumph of the Alto II, he forged ahead with a plan to design and manufacture an Alto III. This would be the Holy Grail: a mass-marketable, programmable computer that would exploit the snowballing manifestations of Moore's Law (such as faster and cheaper memory chips) by offering user-friendly word processing, professional database programs, and more. The goal was for the Special Programs Group to design the machine for manufacture by Xerox's Office Systems Division, a Dallas-based unit that turned out electric typewriters and other non-copier office machines under the leadership of a former Webster lab chief named Robert Potter.

That July, Xerox's Display Word Processing Task Force endorsed the plan. For a few short, glorious weeks, official Xerox policy was to service the growing market for electronic word processing with the Alto III, a programmable personal computer that would bear the same relationship to the competition's glorified typewriters as a Harley does to a tricycle. Ellenby's group was on target to engineer an inexpensive computer-cum-word processor and printing system for shipment to customers by mid–1978. Had it done so, Xerox would have beaten the IBM PC to market by three years—with an infinitely more sophisticated machine.

But it was not to happen. Bob Potter was not on board and never would be. Potter had visited PARC in 1973, shortly after taking over the Dallas division. But he and the CSL engineers communicated like creatures of different species. "I went out there and I sat in their beanbags, but I just couldn't get anything out of them," he groused later. "They were only interested in their own thing. They thought they were four feet above everybody else."

PARC's people returned the sentiment, dismissing Potter rudely as a hopeless technical illiterate whose exalted position owed less to managerial aptitude than to having the ear of Archie McCardell, Xerox's new president, a "bean-counter" with scarcely any instinct for marketing.[*]

Potter's group had brought out a low-performance word processor in 1974 that failed in the marketplace. But instead of accepting the office task force's recommendation that Xerox throw its weight behind the Alto III, he pushed his own new machine, another nonprogrammable word processor called the Xerox 850—essentially a typewriter with enough memory in it to hold a few pages of a business letter long enough to be proofread.

For the rest of the summer Potter's and Ellenby's planners staged a battle of numbers, producing contradictory analyses of the Alto's manufacturing costs to bolster their arguments—Ellenby trying to prove that the Alto could be mass-produced for less than the five-thousand-dollar manufacturing cost of the 850, and Potter that it could never meet its claimed price target.

Ellenby even enlisted the support of Xerox's most respected manufacturing engineers, experts from the product cost estimation division in Rochester. "The dispute was over screws and things, all the minor stuff," he recalled. "And they were the experts in that. As engineers they were most extraordinarily anal—in the right sense. They actually went through and asked me what would be the finish on the screws. Would I be using beryllium plate? Then they'd look it up and tell me how many cents that would cost. They did a very thorough job verifying that our costs were right . . . And Dallas still didn't believe it."

But as Ellenby gradually realized, the numbers were merely cannon fodder in a battle that was political to the core. It was Xerox's organizational structure, not cost estimates or technological visions, that was driving the two sides apart. The Dallas group knew that if they were forced

---

[*]McCardell's intoxication with figures would weigh on the company until his departure in 1977. He was named chief executive of International Harvester, over whose drift into bankruptcy and near extinction he presided, joined by Potter.

to add an entirely new product to their customary line of office machines, any hope of meeting their near-term sales and financial quotas for the year would be demolished.

"They had to sandbag the Alto III, because with it they wouldn't make their numbers and therefore wouldn't get their bonuses," Ellenby concluded. "In fact, it would have been an absolutely impossible burden on them to be successful in making typewriters and also introduce the world's first personal computer. And they should never have been asked to do it that way. So it was shot down like most things that have to do with numbers, based on rumor and wrong data."

With the power of tradition behind them, Potter and his political allies prevailed. On August 18 the word processing task force, reversing itself under pressure from McCardell and others, declared the 850 the official Xerox word processor. As a Xerox product, the Alto III was dead.

The news landed with a hard thud at PARC. Even Alan Kay, who had always proclaimed the Alto an "interim" machine (he once advised Pake to think of them like Kleenex, to be used briefly and discarded as soon as the next big thing came along), took the decision as a "huge blow." It was clearer than ever that PARC lacked the necessary juice to seize and hold the attention of anyone who mattered at headquarters. The researchers watched helplessly as Bob Potter and his product development group in Dallas continued to manufacture clunky and obsolescent electromechanical typewriting machines as though PARC had never existed—and got thrashed by the market into the bargain. In its three years of operation, the Dallas division had never had a profitable quarter.

Ellenby spent the next year trying to quell his disappointment by burying himself in another can-do project. This involved reengineering Starkweather's printer so the laser device could reliably keep pace with Xerox's fastest copiers, a problem harder to solve than anyone had expected. Thanks to a program called Orbit, a cunning shortcut developed jointly by Bob Sproull, a young graphics researcher, and Severo Ornstein, a journeyman engineer whose distinguished record included working on the LINC with Wes Clark and on Bolt, Beranek & Newman's original ARPANET proposal with Jerry Elkind, Ellenby produced a machine known as the "Dover" in mid-summer 1977.

He was still waiting for his next assignment when, a few weeks later, Bert Sutherland dragged him into his office and told him about an unprecedented event scheduled for Boca Raton and already nicknamed "Futures Day."

It soon became clear that Ellenby's hand at the upcoming Xerox World Conference would be very free indeed. Futures Day, which was scheduled for the world conference's fourth and closing day on Thursday, November 10, was expected to be the PARC demo to end all demos, in full dress and with top-level production values. As one of his colleagues recalled, Ellenby responded by approaching the job "as though he was invading a foreign country."

The venture's scale seemed only to stoke his ambitions. He hired Hollywood producers and scriptwriters to prepare a two-hour multimedia stage show, and commandeered half of PARC's working Altos to ensure that the entire audience could have a hands-on experience; two DC–10 cargo planes were rented to transport all the equipment to Boca Raton. One day he outlined the program to Chuck Geschke, a CSL researcher who had signed on somewhat casually as logistics officer for the enterprise. Geschke sat through the meeting with a sense of impending catastrophe. "We were basically going to pick up PARC and put it all on an airplane and fly it across the country," he recalled. "I was thinking, 'Oh, my God, and we've got only two months left?'" Geschke was aware that the group would be fighting not only the calendar, but less than uniform support from their own colleagues. "The range of opinion at PARC," he recalled, "went all the way from 'This is the greatest thing we could possibly do,' to 'What an incredible waste of time' and 'You'll never pull it off.'"

Fortunately, Geschke himself decided to join the enthusiasts' camp. For too long, he thought, the prevailing attitude at PARC had been that it was a higher calling for a scientist or engineer to stay in research rather than to follow an idea through to the delivery of product. He concluded that this was no way to build anything people would buy. Hadn't they learned anything from the scorn of hidebound managers like Bob Potter?

"On the few occasions when we'd have McColough come by it was like getting a state visit," he said. "You'd get your fifteen minutes to pitch but there'd be no follow-through, no delegation to anyone who could actually understand what we were saying. We just weren't communicating." The more he thought about it, the more he was convinced that Futures Day would be PARC's best chance—or only chance—to break down the walls hiding its inventions from the world.

To make Futures Day happen, Ellenby had his pick of PARC's top engineers. In addition to Geschke as logistics officer, he recruited Tim Mott to supervise the marketing production and Dave Boggs to oversee the installation of equipment, and sent John Shoch to Stamford to work as on-site liaison with headquarters. Dick Shoup and Bob Sproull rounded out the platoon, along with product and manufacturing engineers from El Segundo whose resourceful scrounging had impressed Ellenby during the Alto II and Dover programs. The team grew steadily until it numbered sixty-five persons, all working frenetically against the looming deadline.

By late October they had assembled a dramatic presentation on a Paramount Pictures sound stage in Hollywood and buffed it to a high gloss, right down to an original orchestral score shamelessly evoking the soundtrack of *Star Wars*. Mott occasionally had to struggle to familiarize his freelance stage producers with a future that was more than a façade and flashing lights, but that actually *worked*. "Their bread and butter had been multimedia shows for corporate meetings, things like that," he remembered. "What was unusual for them, as it would have been for anyone, was the level of technology involved as well as the degree of vision that was to be communicated."

Peter McColough, who viewed PARC as his legacy and the World Conference as his party, took an intense personal interest in all the planning. He insisted that Ellenby deliver regular progress reports and in late October even attended a dress rehearsal at Paramount. From these encounters Ellenby took away an impression of a deeply burdened corporate chairman. McColough had lost the confident bright-eyed glow visible at the PARC dedication seven years earlier. In its stead he displayed the profound weariness of a captain steering a balky ship through a merciless storm.

One afternoon, treated to a private lunch with the chairman at the

Stanford Club in Palo Alto, Ellenby took the opportunity to regale him with the full story of the aborted productization of the Alto III. The war over word processing had been waged deep within the corporation at the level of task forces and middle management. The chairman listened raptly, evidently hearing it all for the first time. Then, warming to his subject, Ellenby went too far. He capped the story with an amusing anecdote—at least he *thought* it was amusing—illustrating the cynicism about Xerox's costly and fruitless product planning that afflicted the company's own staff.

One day during the Alto III campaign, he said, he had a conversation with a friend from the corporate office. "John," the friend said, "you really think you've got a product program there, don't you?"

"Well," Ellenby said, "I think it certainly could be."

"You're wrong," came the rejoinder. "I'll tell you when you'll know you've got a product program at Xerox Corporation. You'll start seeing people turn up and make a couple of big bottomless pits outside your lab. Then trucks will drive up night and day loaded with hundred-dollar bills, and just pour them into those pits. Your only job, John, will be traffic control—and *that's* how you'll know you've got a product program at Xerox."

Instead of appreciating the wry yarn, McColough suddenly looked stricken. He changed the subject and brought the encounter to a close without giving Ellenby any clue to what had gone wrong.

He soon found out. McColough had recently been wrestling with the dire harvest of that same dysfunctional process. For the previous five years, 1,000 Xerox engineers and technicians had been working on a project code-named Moses, which aimed to develop the company's next great copier. Moses would be the vanguard of the Xerox counterattack against Kodak and its other big rivals. Fast and innovative, it was to offer such pioneering features as a high-speed document handler that could copy multiple pages by cycling them through the machine, wedged between two layers of clear plastic.

But by 1977, after the expenditure of $90 million—more than Boeing Corporation had spent in designing the 747—Xerox had not yet produced a machine that could credibly compete in the marketplace. Worse,

Kodak had just introduced a superior product, with a document handler so fast that the Moses version still on the drawing board was already obsolete. Only a few days after his lunch with Ellenby, on the very eve of the World Conference, McColough made one of the most painful decisions of his career: He killed Moses outright.

The edict sent a shock wave through the entire company—not only because of the horrific financial toll, but also because it meant Xerox would have nothing but aging, derivative products in the market for at least the next two years. "Moses was supposed to lead us into the promised land," said one executive. "Instead the Red Sea came crashing down on us."

Back at PARC, Ellenby recognized that McColough had been girding himself to make the Moses decision at the very moment he was telling his tactless joke. "He made a very tough call," he recalled later. "And that was bloody stupid of me."

With the Moses debacle still painfully fresh, the Xerox World Conference convened on November 7 at the Boca Raton Country Club. As McColough hoped, the gaiety of the affair helped at least temporarily to dispel the gloom. The company spared no expense to keep its 500 guests entertained. There was deep-sea fishing and lavish dining. At one formal luncheon the keynote speaker was Henry Kissinger, only lately retired as secretary of state. A circus-sized tent was erected on the club grounds for a casino night at which everyone received an allotment of scrip, which winners could redeem for a motor scooter and other fancy prizes.

Meanwhile, Ellenby's team worked like fiends to prepare for the final day, which PARC would have all to itself. Willing to brook no hindrance from Xerox policy or personnel, Ellenby kept in his possession a signed letter from McColough ordering the organization to provide anything he required in the event he found himself thwarted by a recalcitrant bureaucrat. He never had to use it, which is not to say he did not on occasion sail rather close to the wind.

"We broke Xerox rules when we needed to get things done," Ellenby recalled. "Certain things were expensed that probably never should have been." And not, to be truthful, only for conventional business. "Some of the guys decided I needed to have an alligator in my bathtub. So they went off in one of these airboats to where the pilot said he'd show them some alligators. Two very hefty engineers jumped in and wrestled this alligator into the boat, tied it up much against the protests of the pilot, brought it back, and stuck it in my bathtub. I expensed the floatplane for them, as 'special transportation' or some such thing."

The group's exuberance reached its climax on the conference's final night, when Ellenby threw a party for the entire Futures Day team, from engineers to truck drivers, at the Blue Bayou, a somewhat less than four-star Boca restaurant. The event was so festive it even attracted a few senior executives from the more demure official dinner a few blocks away—one of whom chose to drive his rented Lincoln Continental from the restaurant back to the country club by the shortest possible route, leaving tire marks all the way across the golf course.

Despite their week of conviviality, Xerox's guests might have been forgiven if they greeted the dawn of November 10 thirsting for good news. McColough's opening speech Monday morning had painted a dark picture of the company's performance. "We are being out-marketed, out-engineered, outwitted in major segments of our market," he lectured. "We simply have not been prepared for this . . . We are now faced with the urgent need for change within this company!" McCardell and David Kearns, an up-and-coming ex-IBMer who would shortly succeed McCardell as Xerox President, had followed over the next two days with downbeat assessments of their own.

Finally, on the last day, Peter McColough again took to the podium, this time in an attempt to revive the optimism with which he had tried to lead his company into the digital age. His instrument was the same vacuous phrase which had caused so much confusion from the start, but now it carried much more urgency.

" 'The architecture of information,' " he proclaimed, "is still the basic purpose of Xerox, except that it's no longer just a concept."

PARC's turn had finally come.

The Futures Day presentation that morning was like Doug Engelbart's famous San Francisco demo on steroids. The club's vast ballroom boomed with portentous music. "The problem is paper," intoned a professional narrator, while actors and PARC engineers piled onstage to demonstrate Altos, the Ethernet, even a prototypical color printer, all working in perfect harmony to establish Xerox's rightful place atop the world of office automation.

The audience watched people send and receive real e-mail, collaborate on joint projects, write memos in Japanese characters, and conjure up engineering schematics on the Alto's arresting black-on-white display—all live. Secretaries typed letters and shot them over the network to a laser printer, while engineers designed buildings on a video screen and software developers debugged code. If there had been any doubt that PARC could develop a marketable product, it was dispelled by the debut of the Xerox 9700—a two-page-per-second laser printer based on Starkweather's machine that would anchor the company's lucrative franchise in that developing market for years to come. But even the 9700 was trumped by the Pimlico, a prototype color laser printer built by Sproull and Ron Rider as a rush job for the Boca demo.

Adding to the thrill was the element of pure surprise. Determined to keep the demo shrouded not only from the prying eyes of IBM, which maintained a research lab nearby in Boca Raton, but from Xerox's own executives, Ellenby had taken the precaution of hiring his own security force (provided by a company conveniently owned by the Dade County sheriff's son-in-law).

"So Futures Day came as a complete shock," Ellenby recalled. "Not only the breadth and comprehensiveness of the products but that they all worked flawlessly was quite astonishing to the senior management."

Finally the wowed audience trooped off to a catered lunch while a platoon of forklift trucks moved the equipment off the stage and into a capacious demonstration room, where they would be accessible for hands-on demos for the rest of the day. Unbeknownst to the guests, this part of the demonstration almost failed before it started, for Florida's humidity and the club's meager air conditioning made the room so hot it threatened to blow the computers' delicate circuits. (The Altos always behaved flakily in hot weather, even at home in Palo Alto.) Ellenby averted catastrophe by renting one of the refrigeration trucks Eastern Airlines employed to keep its planes cool on the ground at the Miami airport. Since the vehicle was not licensed to drive on public thoroughfares, it was provided with a state police escort to Boca Raton, where Boggs and Sproull managed to run a ventilation pipe through the kitchen and into the meeting center.

"All the computers were happy and everyone could walk around in their suits—this was Xerox, after all," Ellenby recalled. (After the show was over Boggs and Sproull tried to see if they could use the truck to produce snow in the ballroom. They turned it up until one of the compressors blew out, ending their experiment. "That was another expense we had to slide through the system as something else," Ellenby recalled. "Fairly expensive, too.")

Disaster averted, the executives and their wives were encouraged to spend as much time as they wished familiarizing themselves with the Altos. They could type and draw on the bitmapped screens, meet a remarkable pointing device called a "mouse," send their handiwork off to the networked printers, and store it in electronic file cabinets known as "file servers." They could prepare documents on computer and send them by fax anywhere in the world—without generating a single sheet of printed paper.

The demo room with its thirty Altos stayed open until late in the evening. "Lots of people came by and they all said how fantastic it was," Ellenby remembered. Most of the PARC scientists on the scene seized the opportunity to witness for the first time how nonengineers would react to their fabulous technology. The results were mixed. On the one hand, it was clear they were "very impressed that the stuff all worked, because they'd heard PARC was sort of a flaky place," Ellenby recalled. "There was sort of a feeling around that PARC was a luxury, so it was a relief for them to see some real value and even some things they might want." Yet clearly they were also perplexed and mistrustful about the effect these mysteriously overeducated contraptions might have on their careers.

Xerox's top executives were for the most part salesmen of copy machines. From these leased behemoths the revenue stream was as tangible as the "click" of the meters counting off copies, for which the customer paid Xerox so many cents per page (and from which Xerox paid its salespersons their commissions). Noticing their eyes narrow, Ellenby could almost hear them thinking: "If there is no paper to be copied, where's the 'click'?" In other words: "How will I get paid?"

For Geschke, the most discomfiting revelation was the contrast between the executives' reactions and those of their wives. "The typical posture and demeanor of the Xerox executives, and all of them were men, was this"—arms folded sternly across the chest. "But their wives would immediately walk up to the machines and say, 'Could I try that mouse thing?' That's because many of them had been secretaries—users of the equipment. These guys, maybe they punched a button on a copier one time in their lives, but they had someone else do their typing and their filing. So we were trying to sell to people who really had no concept of the work this equipment was actually accomplishing.

"It didn't register in my mind at that event, but that was the loudest and clearest signal we ever got of how much of a problem we were going to have getting Xerox to understand what we had."

There was at least one other harbinger of the coming letdown. Toward the end of the evening McColough, Kearns, and a few of the executive staff materialized in the demo room. Their appearance had been prearranged. "They were there to have an opportunity to say, 'Well, now we're going to do something, guys,'" Ellenby recalled. "But they didn't take that opportunity. They just said, 'Thank you.'

"I was expecting a bit more than that," he said. "We'd developed a camaraderie that was quite unusual. My people felt pumped up and hyped, like a sporting team. Instead what we got was, 'Thanks, boys, the war is over, and you can take your horses back.'"

Thus did the doubts surface almost before the euphoria of a flawless demonstration had a chance to run its course. Despite McColough's ringing re-endorsement of "the architecture of information," his and Kearns's equivocal farewell told Ellenby and his team that they were naïve to think Xerox would exploit this technology anytime soon.

And in this beleaguered and distracted corporation, Ellenby knew, time was the enemy.

CHAPTER 19

Future Plus One

Not all the signals PARC received from headquarters after Futures Day were as deflating as the initial one. In fact, the event did have two promising offshoots.

The first was an unusual visit to Coyote Hill Road the following January by Peter McColough and his nine top subordinates, including Archie McCardell, David Kearns, and Jack Goldman. Their purpose was to attend a two-day crash course in the art and science of software—the brainchild of Bob Taylor, who managed to get it sold to the executives while they still felt some gratitude, however begrudging, for PARC's bravura performance in Boca Raton.

Taylor believed that the unique success of the 914 copier had inculcated Xerox management with the doctrine that good things derived only from hardware. He was determined to show them that this idea was obsolete. As PARC envisioned the office of the future, a single piece of equipment could be made to serve multiple uses simply by changes in its software. As long as the brass found this idea an alien one—and it was revolutionary to most people in 1977—they would remain blind to the superiority of programmable Altos over narrow-minded electromechanical word processors like the 850.

Taylor asked Alan Kay to help him break up what might otherwise be two days of lectures in the nasal drone of Computer Science Lab engineers by designing a hands-on software demo for the visiting brass. "You can have them for one and a half hours each day," he said. "See what you can do."

Kay delegated the task in turn to his educational expert, Adele Goldberg. The deadline was about the same as Ellenby had faced for Futures Day, nine weeks. But the challenge was possibly even more daunting: Bring ten stuffy male executives face to face with the unfamiliar rigors of computer programming, and make it fun. The strangeness of the experience for these men could not be underestimated. Even Jack Goldman, the *paterfamilias* who battled so tirelessly to get PARC's technology into the Xerox product stream, would be doing serious work on a computer for the first time in his life.

Goldberg figured the attention span of top corporate officers with much on their minds would be about the same as that of a classroom of fidgety adolescents. To hold their attention, she developed a demonstration program called "SimKit" and loaded it with plenty of animation and music (one tune sounded automatically when class time was over). But underlying the bells and whistles would be a sophisticated system able to simulate situations the executives would recognize from the real world. Its basic format was a generic workplace scene populated by workers and customers. This could be altered to suggest the copy center of a large office, or a mechanized production line, a payroll department—whatever setting the executive-pupil might find comfortable and familiar.

"We really were teaching them that while there are independent pieces in a program you can build something out of, there's also a context in which different kinds of objects are interacting," Goldberg recalled. "They'd have stations with workers they could select and specialize to do one function or another. The animation would let them actually see the customers come in and queue up and get service. We gave them the ability to draw in their own workers and say what they looked like: This one's frowning, that one's smiling. And we had it all structured so they would never touch the keyboard. It was all mouse-pointing and mouse-clicking, because we knew these guys wouldn't type. In those days, that wasn't macho."

As the event approached a few glitches cropped up, including one that no one on the youthful LRG team could have anticipated. During a dry run staged with ten middle-aged secretaries from the third-floor administration offices, it developed that none of their subjects could read the Alto typefaces. "The small fonts our thirtysomething eyes were used to didn't work for those in their fifties," Kay recalled. Goldberg made a virtue out of necessity by rewriting the curriculum so each student's first task would be to select a custom typeface and font size to use for the two-day session. This enhancement had the dual merits of instantly acclimating the executives to the mouse and impressing them (it was hoped) with the unprecedented flexibility of the Smalltalk interface.

A more harrowing crisis arose the week before D-Day.

This was a glitch in "Ooze," Smalltalk's intricate memory management system, which had been designed by Ted Kaehler. Ooze worked by rapidly shuttling data and objects between the Alto's scanty main memory and its spacious hard disk, based on an algorithm that made the disk seem merely an extension of the memory. Nowadays this stratagem of fooling the computer into thinking it has more memory than really exists is a standard feature of desktop computers known as "virtual memory"; in 1978 implementing the system on such a small computer was a great programming feat. Ooze had its limits, however. Goldberg had loaded the system with so much new material that Ooze's capacity was strained to the breaking point. With five short days left before the seminar, Kaehler delivered the bad news.

"Adele, the Ooze design is wrong," he said. "We didn't plan for all these subclasses."

"Yeah?" she replied warily. "What does that mean?"

"It's not clear it'll hold up during the seminar. And if it crashes, we're in trouble."

"Well, what's the alternative? Should I simplify the curriculum?"

Kaehler had nothing so modest in mind. "It seemed obvious to me," he said later, "that I should just fix the problem in Ooze."

Goldberg grew fidgety at the very notion. This was no mere bug, she figured, but a major design change. "Ted," she said, "something tells me this is *not* a good idea."

He waved his hand. The fix involved rewriting code in about seven places in the program to double its capacity. Easy enough in principle, he recalled later—assuming he could be sure of finding every place that needed fixing. In any event, he figured the team would have five days for testing. To Goldberg he said, "Don't worry about it."

Easier said than done. Nervous about his tinkering with such an important component of the system so close to its make-or-break audition, Goldberg and the other team members put Kaehler on a short leash. "Adele, Alan, Dan Ingalls, and Larry Tesler each sat down with me separately to hear what the fix was and impress on me that it had to work," he recalled. "That was fairly intimidating." Goldberg told him that if it worked the first time, she would use it. Otherwise, they would restore the original Ooze and she would pare down her lesson plan.

Kaehler finished his reworking in one evening and demonstrated the fix to his colleagues. To Goldberg's relief and amazement, it worked perfectly. "It was like you're building the Taj Mahal," she said later, "and just as you're about to put the final cap on it you decide that the foundation brick isn't right and you need to replace it. Just jack it all up, replace it, and put it back down again. That's what he did. Pretty remarkable stuff, and also a remarkable guy who could do that."

The executive hands-on, as Kay recalled, proved "a howling success." To ensure victory, each corporate officer was assigned an LRG tutor to sit by his side during Goldberg's simulation exercise. Nine out of ten finished their programs before the bell rang. One, who was in charge of a large Xerox manufacturing arm, even uncovered a flaw in his own real-life production line by plugging actual figures he carried around in his head into his computerized model.

But whether the executives took away impressions of lasting value is another question. Diana Merry, who served as a tutor, doubted they had a very good idea of what they were looking at—that is, the remarkable engineering achievement underlying the simple and intuitive animations playing over the Alto screen.

Some may have been struck more by PARC's unstuffy ambiance. At one point Jack Goldman barged into an office on the first floor and almost tripped over Adele Goldberg, nursing her infant daughter inside. In 1978 such informality was unheard-of in a corporate setting and entirely unexpected. Goldman backed away, embarrassed, never to forget the moment. Goldberg's reaction was sharper: "It served him right. The door was closed and he shouldn't have walked in without knocking."

As for David Kearns, Xerox's future chairman and chief executive officer, his most vivid impression was of PARC's unkempt and self-indulgent culture, perpetuated by its isolated and tranquil campus. "The place," he said later, "just sort of drifted along on its own course." This impression would not work to PARC's advantage when Kearns's help and understanding would be needed in a crisis.

The second important consequence of Futures Day was, oddly enough, the creation of a formal program to commercialize the Alto. Led by Jerry Elkind, who chose John Ellenby as one of his top lieutenants, the new venture was empowered to dribble Altos into the marketplace by offering them to select customers on stringent terms.

As crafted by Jack Goldman, the charter of the Advanced Systems Division, or ASD, would be the mirror image of that of the SDD unit building the Star. Where David Liddle's team was assembling an arsenal of maximum firepower to deploy in the market only after everything was in place—quite similar to the bottomless money pit Ellenby had so tactlessly described to Peter McColough—ASD could weave and dart like a PT boat, using whatever ammunition it found handy to keep a few key buyers intrigued. Ellenby liked to compare the arrangement to the Normandy invasion, with Liddle as a General Eisenhower tolerating an experimental foray or two to reconnoiter the beaches. Liddle implicitly acknowledged the metaphor: "We were very deliberately strategic," he said. "ASD was tactical."

The new division solved two of PARC's most pressing problems. First, it indulged the veterans of Futures Day by giving them a chance to prove the Alto's commercial viability. Perhaps more important, it gave Jerry Elkind a place to go.

Elkind had only recently returned to PARC from a temporary assignment to the corporate engineering staff. It was not a joyful homecoming. His absence had not only distanced him further from the daily routine of the computer science lab, but also underscored the gulf between his management style and Taylor's.

For a long time it had been evident he could not hope to compete with Taylor for the affection of most of the lab personnel. One problem was that he comported himself as their equal in technical ability, something which Taylor would never presume and which was bound to annoy the egotistical staff even if it were true. Moreover, he continually reminded the Computer Science Lab that for all its independence and arrogance, it belonged to a larger organization, PARC, which was in turn beholden to yet a greater entity, Xerox. Taylor, by comparison, behaved as though CSL was the sun around which PARC, Xerox, and indeed all known computer science revolved.

"I took a much less aggressive stance with respect to the resource issues, and I would hope a less antagonizing stance, than Bob did," Elkind said later. "In times when you're competing for resources I always had to make the argument with Bob that there *was* such a thing as a fair share."

Perhaps the greatest friction point was Elkind's frequently blunt and condescending temperament. One could argue that in this he scarcely differed from Butler Lampson or, indeed, Taylor himself. But as long as Elkind lacked the former's intellectual charisma and the latter's sympathetic paternalism, many at PARC would not consider him authoritative, just officious.

"Jerry had a shorthand in his management style I never could appreciate," said Ed McCreight, as mild and complaisant a person as anyone who ever walked CSL's hallways. "He'd come into my office and say, in effect, 'I don't think you're doing anything important.' It was his way of saying, 'Explain how this fits into the grander scheme,' but it made you get down on yourself."

Some of McCreight's colleagues like Jim Mitchell did not feel demeaned, just infuriated. "Jerry would always say, 'Let me play devil's advocate,'" he said. "But that was all he goddam did! Every time you went to him he was always telling you what was wrong with your ideas, so most of us stopped going to him. I told him once, 'Jerry, when that's all you do it's kind of a downer. You need to be going "rah, rah" sometimes, too, not just being a devil's advocate.' He was technical but he wasn't as smart as any of us, and we knew it. He should have, too."

Elkind's manner would not have polarized the lab as much if he had not had his fans, too. Several CSL staff members were quite comfortable with Elkind's style. This group included Dan Bobrow and Warren Teitelman, both recruits from Elkind's old firm, Bolt, Beranek & Newman, as well as Peter Deutsch and Bob Metcalfe, the last of whom had known Elkind at MIT and considered him "a fine man, a gentleman, and an intellectual."

But they were a minority. Considered strictly as the laboratory's chief, Jerry Elkind was an increasingly isolated figure. While he was away for an extended assignment to a corporate task force in 1977, the notion arose that the lab might function just as well without him. One day after Taylor had been running CSL unhampered for several months, McCreight remembered, Bob Sproull walked into his office.

"Ed, have you noticed anything different in the atmosphere recently?" he asked.

"You know," McCreight replied, "I sort of enjoy having Bob run the place."

"You're not the only one who feels that way."

As Mitchell recalled, "Every one of us noticed the difference in feeling in the lab. We all felt more productive, and we sure as hell liked the atmosphere a lot better."

With the end of Elkind's assignment nearing, several CSL engineers visited Pake to ask him to find Elkind a new home. Taylor, wisely, laid low. But Pake was convinced he knew who was behind the move. "While Jerry was gone, Taylor really did settle in," he recalled. "And he did definitely consolidate his position."

The situation confronted Pake with an unappetizing prospect. He had come to rely on Elkind as a buffer between Taylor and the other lab chiefs. Sure enough, during Elkind's absence the tensions between the physicists and computer scientists had increased, aggravated by Taylor's oft-expressed view that only the computer labs (and specifically CSL) did any work worth financing at PARC. The surge of petty antagonism had all but destroyed Pake's dream of a multidisciplinary utopia on Coyote Hill.

(The CSL engineer Jim Morris recalled being cornered at a party in town one night by a GSL physicist. "How does it feel to be working for a boss who doesn't have a Ph.D.?" the physicist gibed. "At the time I thought that was an asinine remark to make," Morris said, "but it did reflect the interdisciplinary pissing match that was going on at PARC.")

Pake himself had reached the point where he could barely stand the sight of Taylor, much less engage him in conversation. He disliked Taylor's individualistic management technique and was even more appalled by the feral dynamics of Dealer. On the whole, he was unpersuaded by the argument that good researchers should be able to take criticism in the same spirit in which they dished it out. The white-suited physicists and optical scientists on the ground floor of the building—his people—were every bit as uncompromising in their scientific standards as Taylor's, but *they* did not feel constrained to abandon all civility as CSL did.

The thought of dealing directly with Taylor as one of his laboratory directors made him blanch. Yet inserting someone new as Elkind's replacement as CSL chief might be taken as an intolerable insult by Taylor's coterie. Pake chose to buy time by sticking to the status quo, informing the lab that he had promised Elkind his old job back and owed it to the man to be true to his word.

Meanwhile the anti-Elkind talk left loyalists like Dan Bobrow deeply perturbed. Thoughtful, a bit naïve, but optimistic that by bringing well-meaning people together in good faith he could find a middle ground satisfying everyone, Bobrow arranged for a group of CSL engineers to pay a formal visit to Elkind's task force quarters a short distance down the hill from PARC.

"I was trying to smooth things out," he recalled. "To me, Jerry was a superb manager who always asked good hard questions and was very supportive. I didn't see why he couldn't continue in his role, and Bob in his. I didn't realize how much of a power struggle there was behind the scenes or how deep the division was, in the sense that some people thought Bob was a listener and a pusher of their vision and that Jerry had his own views."

He was about to find out. Most of the other participants viewed the meeting not as an effort at reconciliation, but as the vehicle for an ouster.

The meeting opened in a strained atmosphere. Elkind was facing the most powerful members of his laboratory, including Lampson, Thacker, Mitchell, McCreight, Chuck Geschke, and Severo Ornstein. Their message, as McCreight recalled, was: "How about finding something else to do?"

"I'm pretty sure he'd been warned about why we were there to see him," Mitchell recalled. "I don't think this was completely out of the blue. He tried his best to be very calm. He didn't get mad and rail at us or anything. He tried to start it off with some bonhomie, trying to say, 'Gee, I'm glad to see you,' and everything. But man, you could see him shaking in his boots just under the surface, because he was being rejected. It was very hard for him."

Elkind listened, but did not capitulate. As the meeting broke up, he said: "It's up to George Pake to decide what should be done, and he invited me to come back to CSL."

Taylor's role in this challenge to Elkind's authority is hard to establish. He has always contended he had nothing to do with dispatching the delegation, and Elkind declines to hazard an opinion. "I don't have any idea whether Taylor encouraged those people to come," he said. On the other hand, Lampson, Thacker, McCreight, Geschke, and Ornstein were all among Taylor's "Greybeards," a sort of kitchen cabinet he relied on for technical and administrative advice. And it is far from implausible that after seven years as associate director—especially following Elkind's yearlong absence—Taylor might think he deserved to be *de jure*, not *de facto*, director of CSL.

Bobrow speculates that Taylor had finally recognized the limitations of being the power behind the throne. "When Jerry went off for a year," he said, "Bob got a sense of what it meant to actually have a throne."

In any case, Elkind did return to CSL as its director for a brief, uneasy period. "It was apparent that Bob had won the battle," Bobrow recalled.

All that remained was to find Elkind some face-saving retreat. Finally, when Jack Goldman parlayed the success of Futures Day into a chance to deploy the Alto as a "market probe" of the commercial acceptability of small computers, the path was clear. With Jerry Elkind appointed as its chief, the new Advanced Systems Division was authorized to put the Alto out into the world.

Elkind's transformation from the skeptic who vetoed Alan Kay's proposal for a small computer into proselytizer-in-chief of the Alto actually dated back to the first time he had seen Bravo running on an Alto screen, long before ASD's creation in January 1978. "I thought to myself, seeing the machines work and seeing the Bravo stuff, that it was just smashing."

The Taylor group's distaste for his management style notwithstanding, he had turned into one of the machine's hardiest champions. Now his enthusiasm was fired even more by the computer's commercial potential. Like Ellenby, Elkind was a bruised veteran of the 1976 battle between the Alto III and the Dallas-built 850 word processor. "A lot of us were feeling very frustrated," he said. "Like everyone, I was very anxious to get this stuff out."

The group he attracted to his new venture was a remarkable collection of talented malcontents. There were Ellenby and Tim Mott, who had felt the sting of headquarters indifference after Futures Day as well as the taste of power that comes from pulling off a hit performance on a lavish $1-million-plus budget. Another recruit was Charles Simonyi, who had made himself an undesirable at SDD by openly denigrating the biggerism of the Star. At ASD he found an entirely different culture and worked with renewed vigor, incorporating the Gypsy interface in a rewritten Bravo specifically tailored for the commercial Altos and known as BravoX.

Elkind took seriously ASD's mandate to develop outside markets by selective sales and leases of "pre-products." Taking over Ellenby's El Segundo–based Special Programs Group, he commandeered several projects they had already started, including one to produce word processors for Sweden's government-owned telephone company. The Swedes got Altos instead.

So, too, did the Carter White House, which awarded ASD a contract to create a document and file system for its information office. Altos running BravoX were installed in 1978, giving the otherwise ineffectual Carter Administration the distinction of being the first in history to use personal computers for word processing. The Senate and House of Representatives followed suit. "It turned out that if the White House was going to do it, then the House of Representatives and the Senate had to do it," Elkind remembered. "That was politics: As long as they all did it, they could all get the funding. If the White House tried to do it without the House and Senate, then they wouldn't get the money."

Other customers included the Atlantic Richfield Company in Los Angeles and the Seattle headquarters of Boeing Corporation. More machines went to Xerox divisions outside PARC, where demand was so fierce that Elkind, Pake, and a research executive from Rochester sat as a committee of three to allocate the scarce machines to employees of their own corporation.

For a short time Elkind's people reveled in the thrill of actually getting PARC technology out to the marketplace. "After we sold, like, twenty machines, we had this wonderful dinner in Palo Alto," Simonyi recalled. "I made this wonderful speech about how today it's ten machines, and next year it will be one hundred, and then ten thousand. Everybody was laughing from sheer hubris."

The inevitable crash landing awaited just over the horizon. As ASD placed more Altos out in the world, John Ellenby was receiving the all-too-familiar impression that he was hitting a brick wall. Rather than absorb the lesson that these were marketable products, Xerox management seemed largely to view ASD as a sort of stalking horse for the Star.

"It was a sacrificial thing," Ellenby said. "It was, 'Let's show some customers we're coming'—but it pissed off the customers that we didn't follow through with it." He compared himself more and more to a member of Eisenhower's expendable vanguard, like the decimated Canadians at Dieppe in 1944: "Market probes were good if they got follow-up. But you don't just go and land troops on a beachhead without a means of getting further inland or pulling them out."

Adding to his frustration were the mounting signs that SDD was faltering. The Star's launch date was now off into the next decade, and not a sure thing even then. Ellenby saw a unique opportunity for Xerox to offer a computer product with proven market acceptance that could be ready in a matter of months. "Basically, I said if you really want to get some products out there quickly, then we can do it. We know people are willing to pay for these things because that has come out in the probes. We do need to perform the engineering that makes them high-quality, and we need to put in place the manufacturing. But we know how to do all that."

In late 1978 he consigned to paper a plan to manufacture an updated Alto out of electronic components available off the shelf, to be bundled with BravoX and a suite of SSL-developed office systems software known as OfficeTalk, as well as a black-and-white laser printer called the Penguin. The result was an inch-thick document whose title, "Capability Investment Proposal," aimed to stress the point that Xerox should implement the Alto program on a small scale, but with serious follow-through.

Drafting the proposal was only part of the battle, however, and a small part at that. Quite justifiably, Ellenby had doubts about how long it would take his report to wend its way up the Xerox chain of command. As it happened, the issue got taken out of his hands by a legendary corporate figure named Shelby H. Carter.

Then Xerox's national sales manager, Shelby Carter was the type of person who could not but bridle at Xerox's torpid decision-making. A Texan ex-Marine fighter pilot who pursued his quarry with the implacable force of a tornado and fashioned himself one of the greatest salesmen of all time (few customers dared disagree), Carter was a throwback to the old Xerox of relentless sales targets and blood-in-the-shoes pounding of pavement. Every bit as instinctive an inspirer of men as Bob Taylor, he preferred to work his magic among bigger crowds.

"He used to conduct what were known as Jet Squad Meetings," recalled David Kearns. "Carter would hop into the corporate jet and fly to two or three cities a day and stir up the troops. In New York City they might gather at Shea Stadium. Carter would stand on the pitcher's mound and deliver his spiel, and the salesmen in attendance would be spellbound. Then they would go out and sell copiers with an almost crazed intensity." On sales reps who met his exacting standards Carter would bestow the treasured memento of a Bowie knife mounted on a plaque. For many of them it meant more than a cash bonus.

By the late 1970s, however, Carter's influence within the corporation was distinctly on the wane. With the possible exception of David Kearns, he could no longer command a rapt audience in the executive suite. The genetic code of the place had changed. "The hip-shooting Shelby Carters weren't listened to as much at meetings anymore," Kearns observed. "Carter would say, 'I have a hunch about this,' and everyone would respond, 'No way. We don't act on hunches.'"

One of Carter's hunches concerned the Alto. Convinced that a properly motivated sales force could sell the machine, big-time, he had placed a trusted lieutenant named Frank Sauer inside ASD to keep him up to date on the marketing program and to involve Xerox's Santa Clara sales office in the planning. One day Sauer slipped him a copy of Ellenby's proposal. Carter, who had been deeply involved in the Futures Day planning and appreciated Ellenby's talents as a result, "took a look and got pretty excited," Ellenby recalled. "He was a great believer in making things happen. So one day he happened to be sitting next to David Kearns at a New York Mets game and said, 'Hey, John's team is really up to something exciting. Don't forget these are the guys who did Boca Raton for you.' And Kearns said, 'Get me a copy right away.'"

The proposal thus skipped over several levels of management on its way to the top. This was a dangerous move. As much as senior executives liked to talk about tearing down the bureaucratic walls to get Xerox moving again, they remained very fussy about protocol. When word filtered down that the proposal had somehow reached Kearns, Ellenby was assumed to have deliberately leaked it to the chief executive—understandably, since his can-do style at Boca Raton had earned him the reputation of "a hot shot who got the job done regardless of other people's organizational feelings," as he put it himself. An "extremely pissed off" Elkind even threatened to fire him, Ellenby recalled.

Ellenby denied having had anything to do with sending the report upstream. But now that it was done, he remained unrepentant. He was fed up with Xerox and considered the proposal his last crack at achieving his goals within the organization. If it did not fly, he was ready to go off and start his own company. He also felt that the proposal would never have made it to top management any other way.

"Elkind would not have passed it to his boss, who would not have passed it to his boss," he said. "Xerox did not work that way."

He was right. Elkind said later he did not think Ellenby's program could ever succeed within Xerox, even absent "the disruption of bouncing it several steps up the management chain"—especially with the Star still holding pride of place as the corporation's designated spearhead in office systems. Carter's impertinence had earned the Alto no friends. As Elkind predicted, the proposal met with nothing but resistance and hostility all the way along the management line.

Still, it might have succeeded had Kearns thrown some real weight behind it. This he was unwilling to do. Having reached down to grab the proposal as though to demonstrate he could be as entrepreneurial and spontaneous as the next man, he turned it over to a deputy for a routine appraisal.

The deputy, Robert Wenrik, tested it against the judgments of the usual suspects, including SDD and Bob Potter. Both found plenty to carp at, including the perennial issue of cost. In the end Wenrik shot down Ellenby's work with a bureaucratically vacuous rejection letter. "We have concluded that Xerox will not adopt the proposal you have prescribed," it read; "however, we appreciate the thought you have given to the many issues covered in your proposal . . ."

"I kept a copy," Ellenby said one day many years later, withdrawing it from his files. "It's pretty interesting what he did say here, like *'Some of the challenges which you clearly identified are being pursued through the normal management channels, and should be resolved over the next few weeks . . .'* Which was not the case, because they never were. And *'Your proposal assisted us in dealing with the problem more expeditiously than we normally might have . . .'* I don't think that's true, I think actually the proposal delayed things, it was like throwing a wrench into the works.

"Then he goes on to say, *'I'm confident that you will continue your support to the challenges we face in Jerry Elkind's probe activity . . .'* Knowing full well that Jerry wanted to fire me."

In January 1980, about one year after receiving Wenrik's letter, Ellenby quit Xerox. Partially with the money he had earned in his corporate profit-sharing plan by staying the extra year, he founded a company called Grid Systems, which manufactured the world's first laptop computers. The product line derived not from any work he had done at Xerox, whose lawyers had cautioned him sternly against recruiting any of his team members to his new company, but from flat-panel display and micro-processor technology he had learned from Ferranti. The dream of transferring PARC's technology to the outside would have to wait. Ellenby, like so many others, had found it impossible to accomplish this as an employee of a company that treated his brand of aggressive advocacy purely as a threat.

"Dave Kearns took it upon himself to come out to PARC and spend a bit of time discussing my capability proposal after he saw it," Ellenby recalled. "He said, 'What will you do if I decide not to do this?'

"I said, 'I'll make sure my folks are well set and happy within their corporation because they like this corporation. But I'm going to have to leave, David, because I've burned too many bridges.'"

CHAPTER 20

The Worm That Ate the Ethernet

O ne morning in 1978 dozens of PARC scientists arrived at work to discover their Altos were dead. At first this did not raise any alarm. The crash of an Alto was a common enough phenomenon and easily remedied: One simply reached over and pressed a reset switch Thacker had obligingly provided on the console. The machine then rebooted from a spare disk coded with a copy of the operating system or, if one was not available, remotely by Ethernet.

For the first hour or so no one even suspected that the crashes might be part of a more general crisis. But it soon became obvious that the Altos had been infected by an entirely new quirk. They booted up fine, but step away from your machine for even a few minutes—and it crashed again. Reboot again, fine. Leave it idle . . . and death. Soon the first and second floors of 3333 Coyote Hill Road were fairly echoing with voices raised in apprehension and protest.

Hey, what's the matter with my Alto? . . . Something go wrong with yours, too? Mine was dead when I came in! . . . Mine too! . . . And mine! . . . What's going on? There must have been a hundred machines crashed when we came in this morning!

At length someone in CSL put two and two together. "You know, Shoch and Boggs were here all night."

"Working on what?"

"Something to do with the Ethernet. . . ."

And so the summons went out. John Shoch, who had indeed been working all night on a network diagnostic program with Dave Boggs, had scarcely dropped off to sleep when he was jarred awake by the fire call from PARC. Machines were dead all over the building. Did he happen to know anything about it?

Uh-oh, he thought to himself. *Something must have gone wrong with the Worm.*

By the late 1970s much of the work in PARC's two computing labs entailed elaborating on the inventions produced during its first few glorious years. Inventing the Alto and Ethernet was like seeding a field. Now it was time to harvest the crops—in other words, to look more closely into how these systems worked in the real world and in concert.

John Shoch decided to tug on one of these threads for his Stanford doctoral thesis. His plan was to study how a network behaved under various message loads and traffic patterns. But it would not be enough to watch it operate under normal conditions. The really interesting thing would be to see what happened if you really pounded on the system, loading it to the absolute limit to see if it blew a gasket.

He knew he had a major advantage over other students of network theory. He had daily access to the Ethernet, then the world's largest and busiest computer network. The only question was whether Xerox would let him publish what he learned.

This was not an idle consideration. Xerox was acutely aware that its wealth flowed from secrets and property rights. Behind its domination of the copier market—which was waning but still strong—were a handful of ferociously defended patents, as well as other inventions so critical they had never been exposed to the public scrutiny of a patent application. Instead they were locked in a vault as secure as the one that safeguarded the recipe for Coca-Cola. By 1973 the company had assigned a corporate patent lawyer to PARC full-time and decreed that even technical papers were to be vetted by counsel and cleansed of any inadvertent proprietary disclosures before they could be submitted to professional journals.

On rare occasions PARC issued technical papers on its own. These were known as "blue books" from the color of the horizontal stripes across the covers. But for the most part the legal department controlled the publication of research with an iron hand. So much creative talent went into the building on Coyote Hill Road and so little information came out that PARC, recalled one former manager, was sometimes called "the black hole of computer science."

PARC researchers participating in conferences and other public events had to carefully comply with the company's paranoid rules. They did not always avoid embarrassment. One of the more delicate situations involved the Ethernet team of Shoch, Bob Metcalfe, and several other engineers. As an ARPANET host location PARC was honor-bound to help address any technical problems cropping up during construction of the nationwide system. Unfortunately, Xerox's lawyers had given the Ethernet engineers strict orders to keep to themselves everything they knew.

This quandary first surfaced in 1973, when Metcalfe attended an ARPANET conference at Stanford. One issue under discussion arose from the proliferation of independent "local area networks," or LANs, similar to the Ethernet at PARC. These networks' technical standards, or protocols, were often incompatible with each other and with the ARPANET itself. The question was how to coordinate them so data could smoothly pass from one to another via the ARPANET backbone—a critical step toward ARPA's goal of expanding its network into a larger and more comprehensive system linking computers everywhere—transforming it, in other words, into an "internet."

For the ARPANET's technical honchos this question was still largely hypothetical. So far there were only a few operating LANs sophisticated enough to tap into the main network. For PARC, however, it was already a pressing issue. At Stanford Metcalfe held his tongue, but he returned to his office convinced he could not wait for ARPA to solve the problem. Xerox was already planning to use the Ethernet to link corporate locations all over the country—indeed, the globe. Data packets would have to traverse outside systems on their way from one local Xerox loop to another, like trucks hopping on the interstate en route from California factories to New York retail shops.

"We have a more immediate problem than they do," Metcalfe confided to Shoch, "because we have more networks than they do. We're going to have to build an internet protocol ourselves."

Working with Boggs and Ed Taft, a mathematician from Harvard, Metcalfe and Shoch came up with a solution they called the PARC Universal Packet, or "Pup." The basic idea was to enclose a data packet in a sort of electronic envelope consistent with the protocol of the transporting network—rather like a child's birthday present wrapped and tagged with a Federal Express airbill for transport by its planes and trucks. As the packet moved from network to network, it could be further wrapped in any number of network-specific capsules. By the time it reached its destination the various envelopes would have been stripped away, leaving the original message to be read.

In the year they spent developing and testing Pup over dozens of variant networks, the PARC engineers moved well ahead of the ARPANET team in their technical expertise. This was unsurprising. Their sandbox, comprising nearly 500 host computers scattered around the country, was already much bigger and busier than the ARPANET.° Moreover, PARC was immune to the ARPANET's lumbering bureaucracy.

"We had the great advantage of getting paid to do this full-time for a living," Shoch recalled. "The ARPANET guys were working under government funding and university contracts. They had contract administrators and students working for them and all that slow, lugubrious behavior to contend with. We had a lot of resources and a lot of machines and we didn't have much else going on. We were evolving ahead."

°It would be several years before overall activity on the ARPANET significantly surpassed what PARC generated within its own building. As late as 1979 the average daily traffic on the PARC Ethernet, which linked 120 Altos and Dorados, came to fully half what was carried nationwide on the entire ARPANET.

But when ARPA invited them to a technical meeting to work out the very same issues they had already solved, they faced a painful dilemma. Xerox's lawyers, still deliberating whether to patent Ethernet or market it as a proprietary product, placed the PARC team on a short leash. "We were told to participate in the meetings," Shoch said. "But we were ordered *not* to describe what we were doing."

Nevertheless, they felt a powerful urge to impart their wisdom to their friends at ARPA. Thanks to the legal beagles' strictures, they were reduced to getting their points across by a weird pantomime of asking inscrutable but cunningly pointed questions. "Somebody would be talking about the design for some element and we'd drop all these hints," Shoch recalled. "We'd say, 'You know, that's interesting, but what happens if this error message comes back, and what happens if that's followed by a delayed duplicate that was slowed down in its response from a distant gateway when the flow control wouldn't take it but it worked its way back and got here late? What do you do then?' There would be this pause and they'd say, 'You've *tried* this!' And we'd reply, 'Hey, we never said that!'"

Eventually they managed to communicate enough of Pup's architecture for it to become a crucial part of the ARPANET standard known as TCP/IP, which to this date is what enables data packets to pass gracefully across the global data network known as the Internet—with a capital "I." PARC's contribution is mostly unsung; one recent history of the Internet acknowledges only that PUP "inspired" TCP/IP. Metcalfe, Shoch, and the others have gotten used to their contribution being minimized unfairly. "The TCP/IP guys will never tell you they did this because of Xerox, because they don't remember it that way," Shoch said. "But we would sit there explaining the problems and trying to coach them along. We had all this shit up and running, and we couldn't tell them."

Despite the lawyers' strictures on cooperating with ARPA and others on the outside, Shoch figured he should be allowed to play in his own sandbox. What was the point of having access to the Ethernet if you could not even use it to finish a paltry doctorate? He carefully assembled a stack of provisional clearances and approvals and made sure the

Xerox bureaucracy knew that more was at stake for him than a ten-page paper in a scientific journal. Finally, confident that he would be able to publish what he learned, he set out to pound on the Ethernet like a kid beating a drum.

To begin with, he wrote a program that would spew message bits onto the Ethernet for a ten-minute period without interruption, starting at the stroke of midnight. He and a colleague named Jon Hupp spent hours laboriously loading the software into 100 idle Altos after dark, when the rest of the lab had gone home. Then they waited for 12:10 A.M. and repeated the circuit, this time collecting each machine's data on how many of its packets got through to their destination, compared to how many got tied up in the system by gridlock. Before this ordeal had run its course, Shoch realized he had committed himself and his friend to the dreariest and stupidest exercise known to man.

Doctorate or not, he was damned if he was going to go through that again. Somehow he had to figure out how to make the machines do the bleak scutwork. It should not be an insurmountable task, he figured—just a simple matter of getting the machines to tell him they were idle, then distributing by Ethernet the very same program that he had hauled around to a hundred offices on that first night. In principle this was not much different from booting up or sending files over the net, something that happened at PARC dozens of times a day.

Within a few days Shoch had written a new program that would instruct one Alto to ask the others if they were free. The only complication was that unoccupied Altos at PARC were never entirely idle. After their owners departed they remained on, spending the night running a diagnostic program that continually tested the memory chips—those old buggy Intel 1103s—for incipient failures. The test program, which kicked in automatically whenever the machine remained inactive for a certain number of minutes (just like today's automatic screen savers), would prevent the Altos from responding affirmatively to his query.

Shoch strolled down the hall to David Boggs, who had written the diagnostic. "Could you just add this thing to the program so the machine will answer mine and tell me he's free?" he asked.

Boggs shrugged. Helping a colleague like this was coin of the realm at PARC. "No problem," he said. "I can do that."

"And while you're at it, can you make sure that if I send him this kind of packet he'll reboot with my software?"

"I can do that."

"So all of a sudden," Shoch recalled later, "you could send out a 'Hello' to any free machine and say, 'I'm going to load this program on you through the net, and when I say *"Go"* you're to start generating bits onto the network. Then I'm going to poll you all remotely one by one and take back all the data and make a printout. And then I'm going to produce this chart and get my Ph.D.'"

Inducing fifty or a hundred Altos to answer a summons dispatched by the press of a button gave him a giddy feeling of power. "It was like sitting at the helm of the Starship *Enterprise,*" he said, "in control."

Perhaps that was why his thoughts soon turned from communicating directly with each machine to instructing them to talk to each other. What if, rather than loading the same program onto fifty machines from one central point, he gave each one the ability to seek out the others?

"Instead of my having to find fifty machines, maybe I just find two, and tell each of them to find fifty more. Then each of *those* machines is told to find twenty-five more." And on and on—the possibilities were infinite. "It's the kind of thing you think about late at night," he laughed—but it was not the first time something of the sort had occurred to the human mind. As he explained the concept one day to a group of colleagues, he was interrupted by a Stanford intern named Steve Weyer.

"That's the tapeworm!" Weyer said.

"The what?"

"The tapeworm, from *The Shockwave Rider*. I'll give you a copy."

The Shockwave Rider was a recent novel by the British science fiction writer John Brunner. In the course of the story its hero unleashes an invulnerable self-perpetuating virus—perhaps the first computer virus of fact or fiction—to destroy a sinister global network. (*"It can't be killed. Not short of demolishing the net!"*) Paging through Weyer's copy of the book, Shoch thought the similarities between his device and Brunner's were mostly metaphorical. "It wasn't quite what we were doing, although it did evoke the right images," he recalled. He appropriated the name anyway, slightly truncated, and from that moment on Shoch's Ethernet-polling program was known around the building as "the worm."

Rather than destroy the network like Brunner's hero, Shoch aimed to enhance it by allowing PARC's distributed machines to perform computations in concert. Theoretically, the worm could be programmed to start out in one machine and reach out to others as its computing needs expanded. "In the middle of the night, such a program could mobilize hundreds of machines in one building," he wrote later. Before morning, as users arrived to reclaim their machines, the worm would retreat. After hibernating in a machine or two during daylight, it would reemerge the next evening—an image that led one of Shoch's colleagues to liken it less to a worm than to a vampire.

The point was to convert 200 Altos, each with the power of a single processor, into one distributed, interlinked machine with the exponential power of 200! Shoch's brainstorm hinted at a method of compounding processor power that would one day find wide application in the field of supercomputers. (The IBM machine "Deep Blue" employed a distantly related architecture when it instantaneously mustered billions of calculations to defeat chess grandmaster Gary Kasparov in 1997.)

Shoch was well aware that the privilege of taking over scores of idle computers in their owners' absence meant he would have to govern his program stringently. He invested his worm with the ability to seek out idle Altos, boot up a host machine through the network, and replicate itself by sending copies of itself from machine to machine. But he strictly forbade it access any Alto's disk drive—a necessary precaution lest it inadvertently overwrite someone's work, which he knew would be viewed as "a profoundly antisocial act."

Even within those limits he reveled in finding new ways to extend and elaborate the worm. In time he improved the program to the point where it could remain in constant communication with its dispersed offspring, so it would know how many segments were out and what they were doing. The mother worm could even sense if an Alto had crashed with an active segment inside, a signal that she would need to colonize another host.

But in imagining a world with a tapeworm gone amok, John Brunner had not underestimated the obstinacy of a runaway program. Eventually the moment arrived for Shoch and his colleagues to discover just how stubborn and dangerous one could be. The worm was about to commit an "antisocial" act beyond anything they could have foreseen.

One night they set a small worm loose to test a control function. Confident they had loaded a perfectly innocuous program into a modest number of Altos, they left it running and went home. At some point—they never figured out exactly when and why—one piece of the program became corrupted so badly that it crashed its host computer. Sensing it had lost a segment, the control worm sent out a tendril to another idle Alto. That host crashed, and the next, and the next. The program was now probing insatiably for new hosts and "killing" every one it touched. For hours the silent carnage spread through the building until scores of machines were disabled. Then morning came.

Ted Kaehler was one of those who got to his office to find his machine in a state of catatonia. Without thinking twice, he rebooted. But it soon seemed that the entire building had been taken over by a malevolent spirit. Whenever a machine went idle, instead of slipping routinely into the memory diagnostic it would suffer this bizarre seizure and die. "We couldn't get rid of it," he recalled.

Finally the alarm reached the worm researchers. It was still early in the morning when Boggs and Shoch responded, barely able to wipe the sleep from their eyes. They began disassembling the network and probing its recesses, like exterminators pursuing rats through a sewer line. Even after they were sure they had eradicated the program from every Alto, machines continued to crash bizarrely. Exhausted from the ordeal, Shoch found himself reimagining scenes from *The Shockwave Rider*—"workers running around the building, fruitlessly trying to chase the worm and stop it before it moves somewhere else."

The building had to be harboring a reservoir of diseased worms still seeking hosts. Finally they realized where the nest was located. More than a dozen Altos were up on the third floor, the administrative quarters. No one up there had arrived for work yet, and the offices were all locked.

That left them no choice but to unleash their neutron bomb. Thanks to a lucky precognition, Shoch had equipped the worm with a self-destruct mechanism, like a spymaster providing his agent with a suicide capsule as insurance against some unpredictable disaster. He injected a specially coded packet into the Ethernet that instructed every worm to instantly stop whatever it was doing. For a few nerve-racking seconds he waited. Then he checked the system.

To his relief, all the worm activity had ceased. That was the good news. The bad news was that the entire Ethernet had been figuratively reduced to a smoking ruin. Scattered around the building were 100 dead Altos. "The embarrassing results," he said, "were left for all to see."

With that lone exception, the worm ranked as a welcome addition to the PARC programming arsenal. Shoch came to calling the plain-vanilla version the "existential" worm—it simply reached out for hosts, copied itself, and self-destructed after a programmed interval. But there were dozens of other applications. The Billboard worm, for example, snaked through the system depositing on every machine a bitmapped image, such as a "cartoon of the day" to greet workers in the morning. The Alarm Clock worm maintained a table of wakeup calls, and at the pertinent time accessed PARC's telephone directory and placed a call to the user's phone. The Peeker logged the results of each night's memory tests and notified PARC technicians which machines might need a new chip.

Shoch always thought of these applications as "toy programs." In his view the worm's real value lay in tying widely distributed computers into multi-machine units of exceptional power. Yet the potential of parallel computing would not become evident to the outside world for a long time. Silicon microprocessors would soon become powerful enough to handle complex calculations without help. Only years later would scientists again need to harness the power of multiple processors at once, when massively parallel processing would become an integral part of supercomputing.

Years later, too, the genealogy of Shoch's worm would come full circle. Soon after he published a paper about the worm citing *The Shockwave Rider*, he received a letter from John Brunner himself. It seemed that most science fiction writers harbored an unspoken ambition to write a book that actually predicted the future. Their model was Arthur C. Clarke, the prolific author of *2001: A Space Odyssey*, who had become world-famous for forecasting the invention of the geosynchronous communications satellite in an earlier short story.

"Apparently they're all jealous of Arthur Clarke," Shoch reflected. "Brunner wrote that his editor had sent him my paper. He said he was 'really delighted to learn, that like Arthur C. Clarke, I predicted an event of the future.'" Shoch briefly considered replying that he had only borrowed the tapeworm's name but that the concept was his own and that, unfortunately, Brunner did not really invent the worm.

But he let it pass.

CHAPTER 21

The Silicon Revolution

Years later Lynn Conway could still remember the moment she first laid eyes on the chip that would launch a new science. It was a week or two after Christmas 1979. She was seated before her second-floor window at PARC, which looked down on a lovely expanse of valley in its coat of lush winter green, sloping down toward Page Mill Road just out of view to the south. But her eyes were fixed on a wafer of silicon that had just come back from a commercial fabrication shop.

There were dozens of chip designs on the wafer, mostly student efforts from a Stanford course being taught under PARC's technical supervision. They all strived toward an intricate machine elegance, comprising as they did tens of thousands of microscopic transistors packed into rectangular spaces the size of a cuticle, all arranged on a wafer that could fit comfortably in the palm of one's hand. A few years earlier the same computing power could not have fit on an acre of real estate.

One design stood out, and not only because it bore along its edge the assertive hand-etched legend: "Geometry Engine © 1979 James Clark." Where the others looked to be simple arrays of devices that formed simple digital clocks and arithmetic search engines and the like, Clark's was obviously something more—larger, deeper, more complex than the others, even when viewed with the naked eye.

Clark's got something really amazing going on in there, Conway thought to herself. *But who knows what?*

What Clark had going on, as it would turn out, was the cornerstone of an entirely original technology. The "Geometry Engine," which he designed with the help of several of his Stanford students, was unique in compressing into a single integrated circuit the huge computing resources needed to render three-dimensional images in real time. After the appearance of Clark's chip, the art and science of computer graphics would never be the same: The computer-aided design of cars and aircraft, the "virtual reality" toys and games of the modern midway, the lumbering dinosaurs of the movie *Jurassic Park*—they all sprang from the tiny chip Lynn Conway held by its edges that winter day.

With the Geometry Engine as its kernel, Clark founded Silicon Graphics Incorporated and developed it into the multibillion-dollar company it is today. But without Lynn Conway and PARC, he could not have built the Geometry Engine. The irony is that when Conway first proposed that PARC step into the vanguard of the science of designing such extraordinarily complex integrated circuits, many of her colleagues doubted it was worth doing at all.

Conway's program would never even have gotten started had not Bert Sutherland decided that PARC needed a shot of "havoc."

Sutherland had taken over management of the Systems Science Lab in 1975 after leaving Bolt, Beranek & Newman, the Boston consulting firm that had earlier given PARC Jerry Elkind, Bob Metcalfe, Dan Bobrow, and Warren Teitelman. Like them, he held strong views about research methods which did not always conform to PARC orthodoxy, especially as it was practiced in Bob Taylor's Computer Science Lab. Sutherland believed that research conducted in a closed environment was doomed to suffocate, like an animal trapped in an airtight cage. He admired the Computer Science Lab's work but regarded Taylor and some of his engineers as overly prone to facile prejudices and snap judgments—conditions, he thought, that deprived CSL of the necessary aeration. The harvest was its self-destructive elitism.

"They were the best and the brightest," he said later. "That was the good news. The bad news was that they knew it."

Sutherland did not allow SSL to become so sequestered. His policy was to keep its atmosphere enriched via continual contact with the outside world. One of his first acts upon succeeding Hall, for example, had been to send the engineers Tim Mott and Bill Newman on an "archeological dig" to Xerox's copier sales office in Santa Clara, a few miles south of Palo Alto. The idea was for them to study how real office workers performed their daily routines, the better to design the equipment they would use in the future. This effort yielded OfficeTalk, a sophisticated and integrated system of office automation that heavily influenced the later design of the Star. Sutherland also recruited to SSL experts in cognitive science such as Stuart Card, Tom Moran, and John Seely Brown, whose research into how real people actually used computers, step by step and motion by motion, led to groundbreaking insights into man-machine ergonomics—insights that not even J. C. R. Licklider had anticipated when he wrote his own pioneering treatise on the subject in 1962.

At CSL, unsurprisingly, Sutherland's democratic instincts provoked grumbling—wasting precious resources on anthropology, of all things!—even before he brought Carver Mead into the SSL tent. Then all hell broke loose.

Mead was one of the most popular and influential professors in the computer science department at California Institute of Technology, where Sutherland's brother Ivan had recently become department chairman. Mead instantly struck him as the right person "to wander in and create some havoc" within PARC's insulating walls. For sheer intellectual brio, Sutherland knew, Carver Mead could stand toe to toe with Butler Lampson and the rest of Taylor's gunslingers any day. A compact, energetic man with a black mustache and goatee and lively, searching eyes, Mead possessed a confident mastery of electrical engineering, particularly at the extremes of the infinitely complex and the infinitesimally small—regions where ordinary engineers hesitated to venture but which he considered his personal preserve. He filled out that expertise with a breadth of interests that encompassed subjects as diverse as walnut farming and particle physics.

At the time of his first visit to PARC, he and Ivan Sutherland were deeply engaged in studying what happened to electronic systems at the edges of the physical scale—in other words, how minuscule a transistor could be without its becoming nonfunctional, and how large and complex a system one could build without its becoming unmanageable. At their core these questions were identical, for as transistors got smaller and more densely crowded on the silicon surface of an integrated circuit, the chip became more complex. The implications of this dual phenomenon were only just becoming understood when Bert Sutherland invited Mead to give a technical address at the Systems Science Lab in 1976. Mead's formal topic was the design of silicon-based integrated circuits, but his real purpose was to propose a new way of thinking about computer design—one that threatened to make much of PARC's work obsolete.

As Moore's Law predicted, the technology of integrated circuits had been surging ahead ever since Intel—the company Moore co-founded—introduced its first microprocessor in 1971. The 4004 chip was fundamentally an arrangement of microscopic transistors that packed into the space of a matchbook cover the computing power of a mainframe—circa 1946. That was hardly an achievement to prompt a major reconsideration of computer architectures; but a year later came the 8008, which had twice the power, and in 1974 another doubling again.

There was no reason to think the trend would not continue well into the next millennium. From his academic aerie on Caltech's Pasadena campus, Mead imagined the curve of shrinking transistor size and mushrooming density extending almost limitlessly into the distance. He believed that the traditional principles of computer design, of which MAXC and the Alto represented the intellectual pinnacle, were fated to fall off this curve well before it disappeared over the horizon. Both machines employed integrated circuits to help control their slowest peripheral devices, like the keyboard and mouse, but even those chips were of the passing generation known as MSI, or "medium-scale integration." Mead had pioneered research into the next step—LSI, or "large-scale integration"—and he was still thinking ahead. In partnership with Ivan Sutherland, he began exploring the difficulties and possibilities presented by the coming quantum leap in miniaturization, which would bring them to VLSI, or "very large-scale integration." This was the gospel he came to preach at PARC.

Traditional computer design, he reminded his listeners, was essentially a mathematical exercise. One chose from the standard inventory of Boolean logic gates—ORs, ANDs, NORs, and so on—and arranged them to operate sequentially on a stream of bits. This worked fine as long as the logic elements (mostly transistors) were slow and expensive and the wires connecting them were relatively fast and cheap, as had been true throughout the history of digital computing. But it also meant that the blinding speed of digital computation was something of an illusion. The logic elements were such data bottlenecks that when you really examined what was happening inside the system, you could see that computers were still constrained "to perform individual steps on individual items of data"—that is, to do only one thing at a time.

The new technology would turn that architecture inside out. As silicon-based chips got smaller and denser, the microscopic transistors that were packed on them to make up the logic became faster and cheaper than the wires linking them. The *wires* became the bottlenecks. Soon the most important factor limiting the computer's efficiency would not be the sequence of gates, but their geometric arrangement on a flake of silicon and the rising relative cost of transporting electrons over the minuscule pathways linking one to another. Computers were about to cease doing one thing at a time, in favor of doing many things simultaneously. Consequently, their architects would have to abandon the old methods of designing them simply as linear sequences of logical functions. They would have to also consider how to get bits from one logical function to another along the shortest path.

Traditional digital technology required designers to think like factory planners figuring out how to get raw materials in one end of a building and finished product out the other. Silicon, however, "forced you to think like an urban planner," Conway said later. "You had to think hard about where the roads go." Just as cities reaching a certain size suddenly find themselves threatened by highway gridlock, she observed, in VLSI, "if you weren't careful you could end up having nothing but roads going nowhere." Fortunately VLSI also offered a way out of that quandary: Because the logic gates and other devices were now so cheap, "it didn't cost you anything to have more of them, if that paid you back by having less highway."

For engineers who had reached the top of their game the old way, VLSI was full of murky ideas. Many doubted it was physically possible even to fabricate functioning devices as tiny as the ones Mead prophesied. Even those who thought VLSI an interesting idea with great potential questioned whether it would ever supplant the tried-and-true architectural structures that had brought them this far. In CSL the general opinion was that VLSI was more than they needed to have on their plates. "We didn't have to be able to design chips," Lampson said—not while the industrial designers at Intel and other chip companies were already hard at work on it.

In any case, PARC could hardly hope to contribute much to this nebulous science. At CSL "they were already out front in their own revolution," one researcher later remarked. "To them VLSI was not really mainline, it was just this weird sort of thing happening somewhere else."

But for two of Sutherland's laboratory scientists, Lynn Conway and Douglas Fairbairn, Mead's talk scored a direct hit.

Conway was a rarity at PARC—an accomplished designer of advanced mainframes who chose to give the hardware gurus of the Computer Science Lab a wide berth. She ranked among PARC's senior veterans, having joined in 1972 from IBM, where she had helped design a supercomputer at the Yorktown Heights lab, and Memorex, where she had worked as an architect of minicomputers. But at PARC she had played no role in developing the Alto or MAXC. On the contrary, something about the intellectual gunplay of CSL alarmed her, as did the intimidating presence of Butler Lampson.

"I always had a hard time dealing with Butler," she recalled. "He had this complete photographic memory of all theory that ever existed about anything, but sometimes that can be kind of a mental block to being creative. You can be so confrontational and challenging about how smart you are that you can't always see that somebody else has got this cool idea."

Like Kay, Tesler, and Shoup, Conway found the ambiance more obliging among the Systems Science Lab's lunatic fringe. "Taylor was someone who could manage the 'neats' and Bert could manage the 'scruffies,'" she remarked. "In SSL I could survive. I could get all excited about an idea that was half-formed and go tell Bert about it, and he'd get all excited about it, maybe tell me somebody I should talk to about it. In CSL I'd be really afraid to present anything until it was perfect, and it would probably get immediately shot down anyway."

Her inaugural assignment at PARC had been something of an acid test in the implementation of half-formed ideas. The job was to design and build a combination fax and optical scanning system known as Sierra, the aim of which was to transmit pages of mixed text and graphics at high speed via the trick of stripping off the text and sending it in compressed digital form, leaving only the graphics to be conveyed by conventional (and slower) fax. The entire page, it was hoped, would therefore transmit much faster than if faxed as a single coherent image.

Thanks to her big-iron training at IBM and hands-on experience at Memorex Conway was able to get the machine built in eighteen months, to everyone's candid surprise. To their disappointment, it emerged as two gargantuan racks of special-purpose hardware that devoured so much power one could heat a building with it.

"You could make it, but you wouldn't make any money off it," she recalled wistfully. "It was such a giant, kludged-up thing with so many exotic little systems that all it demonstrated was that architects could envision and build useful systems that would take too much circuitry to be financially viable."

Sierra would never be feasible as long as it came in such an unwieldy package. Intel's new 4004, which packed thousands of transistors onto one chip—a full circuit board's worth of her hard-wired machine reduced to something you could hold between thumb and index finger—provided Conway with the first hint of how the circuitry might eventually be reimplemented in a manageable package. The hint of a new class of architectures was somewhere inside there, whispering to her. "The itch," she said, "was trying to be scratched."

Doug Fairbairn, Mead's second true believer, had arrived at PARC by way of the Stanford artificial intelligence lab, where he had worked with Kay and Tesler. "After getting my master's at Stanford I'd gone to Europe," he recalled. "After six months I came back. I wasn't very driven to start a career but was thinking, what's my next job? Then I heard about Xerox and thought, 'If Alan Kay's there, I bet I won't have to wear a tie to the interview.' And I didn't."

The interview was with Bill English. As usual, English was in desperate search of engineers to help him and Bill Duvall complete POLOS. Fairbairn spent three years entangled in POLOS hardware implementing the terminal system, which meant bringing together the TV display, keyboard, and mouse. (The ergonomic design of the latter consumed him for weeks. "I spent a lot of time on the cord. A normal cord would cause the mouse to move if you took your hand off. Then I found a wound cord that stayed put, but constantly unraveled. We ended up spending an incredible number of hours looking for the right insulated cord.")

Bert Sutherland, who was more willing than Taylor to tolerate independent projects in his lab, but wielded an even more ruthless hatchet when they did not work out, canceled Sierra and POLOS within weeks of each other in 1975—the former because of its impracticality, the latter because it was finally and unmistakably overtaken by the Alto. His two ace hardware designers were still looking for their next projects when Mead showed up a few months later. Whether it was their enforced idleness or their experience in building systems whose sheer size had gotten out of hand, both were captivated by his discussions of how to handle machine complexity.

"Lynn Conway and I," Fairbairn remembered, "were the ones who said, 'This VLSI is hot shit.'" They immersed themselves in the new technology, Fairbairn commuting weekly from Palo Alto to his parents' home in Los Angeles so he could sit in on Mead's classes at Caltech.

Mead was similarly seduced by PARC's atmosphere of pure invention. Having spent years on campus and also been involved in commercial startups, he viewed PARC as a unique hybrid of both without the downside of either. "There was a lot more teamwork than in academia," he said. "It was about getting things done, not about publishing papers."

Nor was there the agitation to get product out the door he had observed at hard-charging enterprises like Intel. Instead he found himself surrounded by the enthusiasm for learning as an end in itself that drives people to come early to their labs and stay late into the night. Mead considered himself a pathologically early riser, but he could never remember a morning at PARC on which he was the first one in the building. "I'd get in at six in the morning," he said, "and Alan Kay would already be there."

He was even more profoundly impressed by the power of the integrated computing environment they had invented. "It was really obvious to me that this whole thing with the network and Altos and the file and printer servers was dynamite, and that it was going to be the way computing got done."

For the next year Caltech and PARC educated each other. Mead transferred his theories about microelectronics and computer science, and Conway and Fairbairn paid him back by developing design methods and tools giving engineers the ability to create integrated circuits of unprecedented complexity on Alto-sized workstations. The science of VLSI was developing exactly as Mead had predicted. Systems that previously could be realized only as shaggy mats of diodes and wire strung on six-foot metal racks were getting reduced to filigreed etchings on the silvery surface of a silicon wafer—and they worked. They were approaching the goal of modularity, in which circuits that once required a square yard of schematic diagram could be reduced to a single compact chip for a computer designer to plug into a machine, like a simple building block from which a child can build a model skyscraper.

"This headed us in the direction of designing and building bigger, better, more elegant things," Conway said. "Everybody's ambition was cranking up month by month."

They were a noisy group, given to loud and sometimes angry debates in the hallways that reminded people of a Dealer in full cry. Conway and Mead made for prickly teammates, sometimes collaborating, sometimes quarreling openly about how to organize and explain a technology moving ahead at breakneck speed. "Carver and I were both highly crazed by all this," Conway recalled. "We'd compete and conflict with each other and there was so much noise around the project that it didn't seem completely sane."

VLSI also left some of their colleagues behind. The Computer Science Lab still held to the party line that VLSI was an untested technology and would remain so until there was proof the chips could be manufactured and exploited on a commercial scale. Mead was accustomed to such skepticism and on the whole untroubled by it. "At the time, the common wisdom was that if you make these things smaller and faster they'll just melt," he recalled. As early as 1971 he had written a paper predicting that the tiny chips would soon be part of every telephone, washing machine, and car. Nothing he had yet seen on the technical landscape suggested he should revise his opinion.

But Conway and Fairbairn were more sensitive to how their work was viewed by others at PARC. She felt CSL was not giving them the benefit of the doubt. "They didn't seem to recognize that we were principled scientists who had our own self-check on things."

She was right: CSL was profoundly dubious. "I didn't like what Lynn Conway's group was doing and I didn't think it was very productive," Lampson complained, troubled to see valuable PARC resources draining down a speculative rathole. Adding to the pain, Xerox was again tightening up the budget just as CSL was hoping to launch a few new initiatives.

"There was a zero-sum game in PARC resources and we thought there were all kinds of great opportunities for things we might do," he recalled. "We wanted to get into databases and things like spreadsheets which we had completely ignored in the past. We wanted to do a lot of work on user interfaces and programming environments, all sorts of things. We did what we could, but it seemed clear that with more resources we could do a lot more."

Conway started to feel that something had to be done to fight off CSL's criticisms. Sutherland was a strong defender of her work, but by nature he was not a confrontational individual. If the computer lab—particularly Lampson, who commanded management's respect—continued to carp at the money being spent on the hazy potential of VLSI, who knew how long she could survive at PARC? Especially since the power of the technology did not leap out at first glance. Compared to commercial integrated circuits, the schematics of VLSI looked simple and amateurish on the surface, because they employed novel, unfamiliar design techniques that had never been employed in building earlier generations of integrated circuits.

While discussing this one day with Mead and Fairbairn she realized the problem was not just scientific, but cultural. VLSI had not been around long enough even to generate textbooks and college courses—the paraphernalia of sound science that, she was convinced, would force everyone else to take it seriously.

"We should write the book," she told Mead. "A book that communicates the simplest, most elegant rules and methods for VLSI design would make it look like a mature, proven science, like anything does if it's been around for the ten or fifteen years you normally have behind a textbook."

Mead was skeptical. They had no publisher and, given that they normally worked in two locations five hundred miles apart, no easy way of collaborating.

That's where you're wrong, she replied. What was the aim of all the technology that surrounded them at PARC, if not to facilitate just the project she was proposing? They had Altos running Bravo, a network to link long-distance collaborators, and high-speed laser-driven Dover printers to produce professional-looking manuscripts.

"With all that," she said, "we can do it, and get it out there fast, and it'll *look* just like a regular textbook."

Their collaboration that summer on what became the seminal text of the new technology was only one of Conway's efforts to distill and spread the VLSI gospel. The same year she agreed to teach a guest course at MIT (using the first few chapters of the still-maturing textbook), then printed up her lecture notes for instructors at an ever-enlarging circle of interested universities. By mid–1979 she was able to offer an additional incentive to a dozen schools: If they would transmit student designs to

PARC over the ARPANET, PARC would arrange to have the chips built, packaged, and returned to the students for testing.

That summer her offer came to the attention of Jim Clark, then an untenured associate professor of electrical engineering at Stanford.

Clark had no prior expertise in integrated circuit design. "He'd never even worked in silicon before," Conway recalled. But his expertise in computer graphics came from well within PARC's universe: He had received his doctorate at the University of Utah, where his thesis advisor was Ivan Sutherland and his research funding had come from ARPA.

At Utah and later at Stanford, Clark was driven by the impulse to push the technology of graphics beyond the limits of existing hardware. As one of his Stanford students later recalled of a meeting in 1979, "The first day I went to speak to Jim, he pointed to a picture of an airplane he had up on the wall. 'I'm going to make this move,' he said."

Like no one PARC had seen since Bob Metcalfe, he was also driven to explore all the commercial possibilities of his work, academia be damned. ("I love the metric of business," he told an interviewer in 1994. "It's money. It's real simple. You either make money or you don't. The metric of the university is politics.")

Clark understood at once that the computing efficiency VLSI offered was the key to expanding the potential of computer graphics. That summer he essentially relocated to PARC, taking over a vacant office next door to Conway's and steeping himself in VLSI lore. Within four months he had finished the Geometry Engine chip, the product of that summer's total immersion.

Perhaps more than any other project, Clark's chip fulfilled Conway's quest to give VLSI credibility. Not only did it launch computer graphics as a profitable segment of high-powered computing, it showed that the unprecedentedly complex circuits could be designed rapidly, and then manufactured in huge quantities that would work flawlessly in an industrial context. The technology eventually matured into today's generation of Motorola and Intel microprocessors, which run most of the world's desktop computers, as well as a wide range of special-purpose circuits. Carver Mead's prediction did come true. VLSI did turn every telephone, washing machine, and car—and thousands of other workaday appliances as well—into tiny computers. (Clark's expectations were fulfilled too: Silicon Graphics Inc. made him a multi-millionaire.)

Carver Mead performed one more service for PARC after completing of the VLSI text with Lynn Conway. This was a visit he paid to Stamford to warn Xerox of the dangers of squelching the inventiveness at PARC.

The mission grew out of a conversation he had one day with Pake and Bert Sutherland. "I told them Xerox has got to get itself together," he recalled, "because there's no way a big company can take advantage of things moving this fast. People will get frustrated and start their own companies. Pake said, 'You should talk to the people at corporate headquarters.'"

Mead's familiarity with new-technology companies such as Intel won him a respectful audience from McColough and Kearns. "I spent a delightful morning with those guys," he said. "I told them, 'You'll never have a better shot. If people leave because they don't see anything happening, that'll be like a bomb going off inside PARC. The only question is whether you participate and enable it, or let it happen for someone else.'"

"What do you suggest?" Kearns asked.

"Set up a venture capital arm," Mead advised. "Smell out the technology, find it, incubate it. Take an equity position in things as they happen, otherwise it'll all be gone and you won't have any part of it."

What he proposed would become standard operating procedure in American business twenty years later under the label "intrapreneuring"—a way to nurture innovation outside the dead hand of a corporation's entrenched bureaucracy. In 1979, however, Xerox management regarded the concept as too elaborate to take seriously. That day over lunch Kearns confided to Mead that tradition's hold on Xerox was almost too powerful even for him, its president and heir apparent to the chairmanship.

"Let me tell you a story about big companies," Kearns said. Xerox employed a group of engineers to tear apart every new machine coming off the production line. Their goal was to figure out the most likely problems that would crop up under the stress and strain of daily operation, develop routines to fix them, and warn the design engineers of their mistakes. Yet every new model incorporated the same design blunders as the last. Finally the service engineers took matters into their own hands by designing their own machine. This was the Model 3100, a proposed desktop copier which, with its high reliability and decent resolution, was the closest thing Xerox could offer to compete with the Japanese models devouring its customer base. Yet instead of winning praise and rewards from the company, the bootlegging research engineers were widely vilified for interfering in the design process.

"You know what?" Kearns told Mead. "I spend most of my time trying to keep the rest of the company from killing those guys."

Mead shook his head. No company so riven by tribal conflicts would ever bring itself to welcome the exceptional gifts of PARC. He returned to California with a mixed message, if a prescient one, about the likely fate of the powerful technologies he had himself used to such wonderful effect. He was sure they would sooner or later be developed and marketed for the world. But he was almost equally sure that when this happened, Xerox Corporation would be standing glumly on the sidelines.

CHAPTER 22

The Crisis of Biggerism

One day Alan Kay sat alone in the conference room of the Systems Science Lab, feeling a powerful urge to trash Smalltalk and start over from scratch.

For some time he had watched uneasily as his own group succumbed to the software equivalent of biggerism. With every iteration of Smalltalk—they were now on the fourth version, Smalltalk–76—he felt the language had become more elaborate, more sophisticated—and farther removed from his original vision of a system easy enough for children to learn.

But Smalltalk–76 was only the latest blow to Kay's dream of a transparently simple programming language. The first, sadly, had been delivered by the children themselves. They had stopped learning.

The flush of triumph Kay and Adele Goldberg felt from teaching the Jordan kids how to program had barely worn off before they realized they had accomplished far less than they thought. While ten or a dozen kids had shown genuine aptitude and creativity in programming, these turned out to be the cream of an exceptional subset, pupils from the gifted track of one of the best school systems in the country. Most of the Jordan kids still struggled with the most rudimentary concepts as though they were programming in Greek.

Kay realized he had expected too much from the start. No matter how lucid the software interface or natural the commands, programming still presented difficulties to children—not to mention to many of the non-professional adults at PARC he had tried teaching as well—that could only be surmounted in one of two ways: by intuition (a gift granted to a precious few), or by being told the answer. He finally capitulated to reality that day in the SSL conference room, as he sat pondering a white-board on which he had scribbled out the code for a simple problem that had left his subjects confounded. With a shock he realized it was full of ideas obvious only to those who were, like himself, already steeped in the techniques and culture of computing. "I counted the number of nonob-vious ideas in this little program. They came to 17," he recollected. "And some of them were like the concept of the arch in building design: very hard to discover, if you don't already know them."

He was disheartened to discover that what had seemed at first to be a spectacular breakthrough with a group of preadolescents was nothing more than the "hacker phenomenon" at work: "For any given pursuit, a particular five percent of the population will jump into it naturally, while the eighty percent or so who can learn it in time do not find it at all nat-ural." It was also painfully evident that maintaining the learning curve of even the most talented kids demanded a tremendous effort by teacher and student—even here in Palo Alto, an ideal setting that would be impossible to reproduce on a large scale.

Perhaps the instinctively understandable programming system he sought was a chimera after all. As Adele kept reminding him, "It's hard to claim success if only *some* of the children are successful."

He was forced to wonder whether his very approach had been mis-guided. He had been convinced that teaching kids to program at an early age would permanently shape their thought processes. His real ambition had been to provide them with a singular window on human enlightenment. Yet his experiments led him to a contradictory conclu-sion. Programming did not teach people how to think—he realized he knew too many narrow-minded programmers for that to be so, now that he considered the question in depth. The truth was the converse: Every individual's ingrained way of thinking affected how he or she programmed.

And was it not the same in every other field of human creativity? "A remarkable number of artists, scientists, philosophers are quite dull outside of their specialty (and one suspects within it as well)," he said later. "The first siren's song we need to be wary of is the one that promises a connection between an interesting pursuit and interesting thoughts. The music is not in the piano, and it is possible to graduate Juilliard without finding or feeling it."

Suddenly he felt a powerful desire to throw out all the old tools and start afresh. Scarcely four years after he had first outlined his ideas to the Learning Research Group, he was ready to make another run at the grail of simplicity. Drawn toward a new vision of Ideaspace, he brought the entire group to Pajaro Dunes for a three-day offsite in January 1976 to chart the new journey. Reinfused with enthusiasm, he even gave the retreat a theme—"Let's burn our disk packs," an allusion to the big yellow Alto storage disks on which they kept Smalltalk's master code.

Then he discovered that they were no longer willing to follow him blindly.

The revelation was staggering. He spent most of the retreat trying to inveigle them into a fresh start on a hardware and software system radically different from Alto/Smalltalk. "No biological organism can live in its own waste products," he exclaimed one evening. In earlier days that would have started them off on a thematic tour of Ideaspace and an exploration of the multifarious purposes of death and renewal. This time they took it as a threat to their own investment in a growing body of work, and turned him down.

"When Alan said to burn our disk packs it was Dan Ingalls who would have had to do it," recalled Diana Merry. "And Dan couldn't do it. There were too many bits on those disks he would have to recreate again, which made it very, very hard to let go. We lost the will to break it all apart. Alan finally had to realize it wasn't going to happen."

Smalltalk was no longer his system. He had started it, but once he turned it over to the "completers" like Ingalls and Adele Goldberg it had morphed into their own property. Ingalls was particularly determined to transform Smalltalk into a full-service programming language, the last thing Kay desired. Were it anyone else, he might have been able to keep control of the effort. But he could not fight Dan Ingalls, one of the few people in the world whose skill in his chosen field awed even Alan Kay. He had to let it go and admire the system for what it was, not what he wished it to be.

"Pajaro led to Smalltalk–76, which was two hundred times faster than Smalltalk–72," Kay said later, unable to avoid expressing admiration for Ingalls's finely crafted code, no matter how far it departed from his own goal. "But," he added wistfully, "no kid ever wrote any code for Smalltalk–76."

The 1976 offsite permanently changed the human ecology of Kay's group. It was not a disaster, exactly, as he acknowledged later. There were no shouting matches or overt recriminations. They returned to PARC still friends and colleagues. "But the absolute cohesiveness of the first four years never rejelled," he recalled. There might still be bicycle runs to Rosati's in town for beer and brainstorming, but the thrill of biking back to PARC and implementing some unprecedented new idea on the spot had evaporated. To Kay the team had lost its balance. The idea of a Dynabook for Children had "dimmed out," overwhelmed by everyone's professional imperatives and their desire to elaborate on what were now, to him, old ideas.

Kay remained preoccupied with a lesson he had assimilated from Marshall McLuhan: Once humans shape their tools, they turn around and "reshape us." That was fine if the tools were the right ones, but he was unconvinced that Smalltalk fell into that category any longer. Within a few weeks of the Pajaro Dunes offsite he enticed Adele Goldberg and Larry Tesler, two who were still willing to follow him off on a tangent, into joining his quest to regain the simplicity initiative.

The result was the Notetaker.

As Kay first sketched it out early in 1976, the Notetaker would be compact enough to perch on the user's lap. Although a direct descendant of the Alto in its basic concept, it would jettison the Alto's hard-wiring-and-microcode architecture in favor of one using microprocessors, the new family of silicon-based integrated circuits being developed by Intel and others. In his first sketches Kay incorporated a number of innovative technologies that had not yet appeared in the marketplace—but nothing, he insisted, that would not be available within a few years.

One thing that shortly became clear was that in building the Note-taker, Kay's group would be on its own. The days of turning to CSL for hardware help were past. Lampson, whose word on technical issues was paramount in that lab, regarded Kay's new project with icy disdain.

"Sometimes Alan isn't really in touch with reality," he said later. The Notetaker offended Lampson's doctrine of research priorities, which stated that one needed to look ahead of the curve, but not too far ahead. As a Time Machine the Notetaker was pitched so far into the future that Lampson could not believe it would teach PARC anything useful. Given the limitations of the new chips, the machine was shaping up to be smaller, slower, and dumber than anything they had ever built.

"I told them that within the limitations of the technology of today you will not be able to build anything interesting," Lampson recalled. "You'll be able to build a gadget that will work and it will be possible to program it. But you won't be able to make it do anything interesting because the technology's just too limiting. And that turned out to be absolutely correct."

To Kay, Goldberg, and Tesler this was just Butler being exceedingly subtle. Who was he to say what was "interesting"? If they could build a truly portable machine that had, say, fifty percent of the Alto's functional-ity, or thirty percent, or ten, would that not be "interesting"? In any case, he had made the same arguments about Dick Shoup's Superpaint being too far ahead of the curve. Well, the Systems Science Lab had given Shoup a refuge from CSL's cold contempt. If necessary they would steam ahead with the Notetaker by themselves.

But there was more to Lampson's dismissal of the Notetaker than his doubts about the design. At about the time Kay first broached his idea for a compact portable machine, CSL had come under the spell of an idea that amounted to its polar antithesis. While Kay was scorning biggerism, the Computer Science Lab was embracing it, in the form of a dream computer they called the Dorado.

Like the Notetaker, the Dorado claimed the Alto as its direct forebear. But the resemblance ended there. The Dorado was to be the most ambitious computer PARC ever built. Where the Notetaker was to be deliberately modest and compact, Dorado would be fast, powerful, big, and noisy. Where the Notetaker turned out small enough to fit inside a suitcase, the Dorado was the size of an industrial refrigerator, with five fans for heat dispersion that roared like "a 747 taking off."

That the Dorado was the product of rampant biggerism is evident from the way Thacker, its principal designer, described his earliest ambitions: "The original idea was that it would continue in the simple tradition of the Alto. I described it as sort of a 40-nanosecond Nova (that is, a Nova with a much faster clock)."°

His plan was simply to build a machine that would enable him to test a new generation of chips that promised to be faster and more reliable than those he had used in MAXC and the Alto. But by 1976, when the project finally got under way, those modest goals were overwhelmed by the vaulting ambitions of his colleagues. When Thacker laid out the Dorado's preliminary schematic on an Alto running SIL, his program for automated circuit design, there was scarcely anything available to run on the Alto *except* SIL. By the time the first Dorado circuit boards came off a manufacturing line to be fitted into a seven-foot cabinet, the flowering of PARC technology had produced Mesa, a programming system so big it could burst the seams of any Alto in the building.

"The Dorado certainly got more complex than I had planned on," Thacker said ruefully years later. "I do think it was the second-system syndrome at work. You're successful and you say, 'I'll build something that's a little bit better.' Dorado may have been better, but it was cer-

---

°This 40-nanosecond clock cycle translates to a processor speed of about 25 megahertz (i.e. 25 million processor cycles per second). Compare this to today's desktop computers, which range in speed from about 133 to as much as 450 MHz.

tainly a lot more complicated. It took five years to get working and there were several false starts."

The first of these occurred while he was still assigned to the Systems Development Division in the old Building 34 across the street from Coyote Hill. By then the Dorado had been designated to be the heart of a digital copier SDD was planning to build. The flaw in this plan, it quickly emerged, was that the new chips Thacker had been so eager to fit in his new design were a major headache to use. Employing a technology known as ECL, for "emitter-coupled logic," they were indeed much faster and less buggy than the TTL—"transistor-transistor logic"—chips they had used in the Alto. But they were also terrible power hogs and threw off huge volumes of heat, which required patching in an additional power source to drive a fan. By the time Thacker finished his first-cut design of the Dorado processor, he knew he could never make it cheap enough for SDD to ship as a commercial product.

The labs regrouped. Thacker started over on a processor for the Star that would use the buggy old (but familiar) TTL chips. This evolved into the ill-fated Dolphin. Meanwhile, the Dorado program returned to the Computer Science Lab, which was immune to the ferocious pressures of shipment deadlines and commercial price points afflicting SDD. Everyone at CSL knew from the start, Lampson recalled later, that the Dorado would be "entirely impractical as a product." But if the commercial marketplace was not prepared to spend the money to get one, they certainly were. The Dorado would be the biggest and best Time Machine ever.

The man assigned to oversee what was sure to be a record-breaking engineering project was Severo Ornstein. A solemn and intense individual whose professional resume included critical roles in the development of the LINC with Wes Clark and the construction of the first IMPs for the ARPANET at Bolt, Beranek & Newman, Ornstein's black beard and beetling eyebrows gave him the stern mien of a biblical prophet but masked an artist's temperament beneath. He was the son of professional musicians—as a Harvard undergraduate he had briefly dallied with the idea of taking a music degree before settling instead on geology. In any case, his prickly temperament fit well into CSL's unforgiving environment, where his barked *"Nonsense!"* became as familiar a hunting call as Chuck Thacker's *"Bullshit!"* Although he had been recruited to CSL by Elkind, his stubborn and rigorous mind rapidly won over Bob Taylor, who soon invited him into his inner circle, the Greybeards.

Ornstein's long experience with quixotic hardware projects made him a natural to head up the Dorado effort, even if his tough-minded assessment of the job made his colleagues uneasy about the scale of the undertaking. "I said it would take two years and ten people," he recalled. "That was twice what anyone else was talking about."

One day Lampson took him aside for an attempt at jawboning. "Look, Severo, I know you're right," he said. "But if you tell people how long it'll take they'll never start it. You have to lie to them." One could almost imagine Ornstein's eruptive reply: *"Nonsense!"* In the event, his estimate was right on the money.

Building the Dorado presented new logistical issues compared with MAXC, which was physically a bigger machine but was not expected to be mass-produced, or the Alto, which was mass-produced but small. Since there was no room for an assembly line on Coyote Hill, Ornstein rented another building about a mile away on Hanover Street, which became known as the "Garage."

The CSL engineers' fixation on building the Dorado helped fuel the Notetaker team's inclination to go in the opposite direction. Given CSL's determination to pervert the Dynabook concept by building a machine *bigger* than the Alto, "it'll be a long time before we have the Dynabook," Goldberg said one day. "Let's do something that's between the Alto and the Dynabook."

In time she came to think of the Notetaker as an electronic notebook for kids to use in school. The idea was doubly ingenious: It not only gave them a paradigm to shoot for, but also established the machine's physical dimensions. "That told us it had to be light enough to carry around so the kids could use it to take notes in class, then bring it home and back to school," Tesler observed.

"Adele had in mind the eMate," he added, referring to a small school-oriented laptop Apple Computer manufactured years later which bore a striking resemblance to Kay's original Dynabook sketches.* "She knew it had to be somewhat heavier than the eMate, though she was hoping it wouldn't turn out to be what it did, which was forty-five pounds, heavier than the kid."

Between 1976 and 1978 the Dorado and the Notetaker projects proceeded along parallel but antithetical courses. The Dorado was so huge in scale that its sheer physical power sometimes overwhelmed the Garage's efforts at quality control.

Recalled one technician, "It was easy to set a circuit board on fire because you had this unlimited amount of current. We saw several just literally burn up. The fans were so powerful you couldn't see where the smoke was coming out. You could smell it, and you knew that there was something seriously wrong, but you couldn't tell. So you had to shut the machine off and pull the boards to find out."

One day, working with a partner, he spotted a wisp of smoke coming off a board and leaned into the machine to pinpoint its source. Suddenly a dozen little capacitors went off like incendiary bombs. The technicians hit the floor. When the devices ceased ricocheting off the walls, they got to their feet and gingerly eyeballed the errant board. The capacitors, they realized, had been installed backwards. They had been ticking away like tiny time bombs until the powerful current finally blew them and the board to pieces.

Kay's group, meanwhile, focused not on how to pump an incendiary current through their machine, but how to make it run adequately on an electrical trickle and with the smallest and lightest components available.

Doug Fairbairn, who had joined the effort as chief hardware designer, was aware that Intel, which had long provided PARC with memory chips, had just introduced a processor-on-a-chip, the 8086. (This was the precursor of Intel's x86/Pentium line of microprocessors, which today power most

---

*The eMate was a hit in the education market but a failure in the general market. Apple discontinued the model during its financial retrenchment in 1998.

personal computers.) With Tesler's help, he worked out a design in which three 8086's would serve as the brains of the entire machine. They ordered the first chips Intel produced off the production line and promptly discovered a bug in the product, much to the manufacturer's dismay.

"They said, 'We just gave you the 8086 last week! How could you report a bug already?' " Tesler recalled. But Intel had not reckoned with PARC's do-it-yourself mentality. Years earlier the lab had purchased a rare million-dollar machine known as a Stitchweld, which could turn out printed circuit boards overnight from a digital schematic prepared on Thacker's SIL program. "It turned out that no one else using the 8086 had Stitchwelds. Everyone else was going through complicated board designs, so they wouldn't know for months if there was a bug. But at Xerox we gave them that feedback in a few days."

Cramming everything inside a portable case remained their biggest challenge, for they did not intend to skimp on any of the technical features that made PARC machines distinctive. The Notetaker was to have a custom-built display with a seven-inch diagonal measurement and a touch-sensitive screen (to substitute for the mouse); stereo audio speakers and a built-in microphone; 128,000 bytes of main memory; a rechargeable battery; and an Ethernet port.

The latter, in fact, proved to be a particular headache. There was no question of going without it, of course—PARC could no more turn out a non-networked computer than it could go back to using electric typewriters. But fitting a standard Ethernet board—now boasting more than eighty chips—into the Notetaker's cramped interior was equally out of the question.

One day Tesler crossed the street to SDD's quarters in Building 34 and laid the dilemma before Ethernet's inventor, Bob Metcalfe.

"Why does it take so many chips?" he asked.

Metcalfe patiently explained the function of every chip on the standard Ethernet board and why each was indispensable. Tesler countered that plenty of the circuitry could be discarded without undermining Ethernet's basic operability. While everybody at PARC had their heads stuck in their high-performance systems, he told Metcalfe, a new world of computer design was taking shape on the outside. PARC was going to have to adjust.

Tesler's views on the matter approached the heretical. He was referring to the hobbyist market, which was indeed exploding. The first annual West Coast Computer Faire, held in April 1977, had attracted thousands of young fanatics from all over the Bay Area. These were serious amateurs who built computers named Altair and PET out of kits ordered by mail, and gathered every weekend to swap shortcuts and software at gatherings like the Homebrew Computer Club.

They were enchanted with computing's gadgetry as an end in itself, just as a previous generation had been with their ham radio sets. For many years yet their mindset would remain alien to those who had learned their computing at PARC. But Tesler, one of the few PARC engineers familiar with this niche, already saw they knew plenty that PARC would need to learn. They had found new ways to move functions out of hardware into software and to cut corners to save money and space. It wouldn't do to dismiss them as kids playing with toys: Their computers *worked*.

"I don't think the chips are all necessary on the Ethernet board," he told Metcalfe. "These PC guys make their computers so cheap because they go through all these tricks. We ought to start doing the same."

"That's them," Metcalfe replied. "Our boards have to work perfectly."

"Maybe so, but our computers are worth ten to twenty thousand dollars in parts alone and they *sell* theirs for a hundred bucks. We're trying to do a cheap portable computer and we only have room for twenty-five chips on each board."

"Then you'll never do Ethernet," Metcalfe replied. "You'll have to wait for the Ethernet integrated circuit, which is at least five years away."

"We can't wait," Tesler replied.

Then he recrossed the street and set about proving Metcalfe wrong. Tesler and Fairbairn compressed the Ethernet design as you might wring out a damp sponge, working it down to twenty-four chips by shunting more of the work to software than Metcalfe thought possible. The result was a board that just barely kept up with the three-megabit-per-second PARC Ethernet—but that did fit inside the Notetaker. ("Metcalfe loved it," Tesler recalled. "But he was already working on the ten-megabit Ethernet for SDD, so it wasn't relevant to anything he was doing.")

* * *

The Garage rolled out the first Dorados in 1978 to conspicuous acclaim. "The Dorado was the only really great computer that PARC built," judged Ed Fiala, who had played a role in every previous CSL hardware project. Where the Alto had been slow even for its time, the Dorado was a speed demon by any contemporary standard. "All the funky old Alto software ran on the Dorado so fast I got headaches from not waiting," Jim Morris recalled. "Suddenly I realized that for the first time, *I'm* the bottleneck."

For a Time Machine, the Dorado was also relatively inexpensive. Moore's Law was beginning to make its power known in earnest: The machine cost only about $50,000 in parts while delivering the computing resources of three powerful Digital Equipment Corporation VAX–11/780 workstations, which sold for $500,000 each in 1980.

The machine's power almost shook its creators' faith that they were building something for individuals to use. "It was difficult to think of the Dorado as a personal machine, since it consumed 2,500 watts of power, was the size of a refrigerator, and required 2,000 cubic feet of cooling air per minute," Thacker said later. Yet that, after all, was the essence of the Time Machine. Potent as the Dorado was, he was still confident that something on the same scale would be available on a desktop to the individual user within five or ten years, and he was right.

Meanwhile the CSL's programmers plunged into work that had been stymied by the Alto's limitations of speed and memory. Deutsch, Teitelman, and several others had already compiled a "wish list" of desirable features of an ideal programming system. To their delight, Dorado was powerful enough to incorporate them all into a system they called "Cedar."

Cedar combined the best features of Mesa and Smalltalk. It offered the former's industrial strength and clarity, which allowed programs written by one person to be understood and elaborated on by others, without giving up the latter's graphical flexibility or its nifty features such as "garbage collection"—a sort of housekeeping function that used memory more efficiently by automatically clearing memory space occupied by data a program no longer needed.

For all its performance enhancements, the Dorado did have a few significant flaws. For one thing, it could not coexist in an office with a human being. The machine's voracious appetite for electricity made it radiate heat like a barbecue pit, while the fans created an unimaginable din. In an attempt to make the machine quiet enough for an office, the designer tried housing it in a case so bulky it was nicknamed the "armored personnel carrier." But the sound-insulating material stuffed inside only made the system run hotter, which made the fans work harder, which created more noise and heat in an endless, vicious circle.

"They were such an efficient heater in the office that the guy just about had to work in his underwear," recalled Charles Sosinski, a PARC technician. Eventually they hit upon the solution of removing the Dorados from the offices altogether, stowing twenty machines together in a single, *very* well air-conditioned room from which they were linked by cable to the terminals, keyboards, and mice in individual offices.

But these technical problems never quelled the furious demand for the swift and robust machines.

"People would say, 'I could get my work done in an hour, and it would take me all day on an Alto,'" Sosinski remembered. For the first time since a couple of prototypical Altos nicknamed Bilbo and Gandalf emerged from CSL's basement shop, there were not enough computers at PARC to go around. Even after full-scale production began, the Garage was able to turn out no more than ten or fifteen Dorados a year; in 1982 there were still only thirty in existence. Some junior scientists, especially those outside the favored halls of CSL, were reduced to reliving the bad old days of time-sharing. "It was very hard to get Dorados for quite a long time," recalled Diana Merry. "When we were writing Smalltalk–80 I would have to come in late at night, because that was the only way to get one to work on."

Almost simultaneously with the Dorado, the first Notetaker prototype was completed. Kay immediately termed it a triumph. What it lacked in the Dorado's overwhelming power it made up for with a sort of bantam-scale élan.

The Notetaker ran a compact version of Smalltalk–76 and boasted an ingenious physical design that would be shamelessly mimicked by the first generation of so-called "luggable" computers six years later. When closed the computer looked like a plump plastic attaché case. One opened it cross-sectionally, like a cracked-open egg, by flipping two latches. The screen and disk drive were set in the larger piece, facing the user when the box was laid flat on a table. The keyboard was part of the second, smaller section, connected to the first by a flexible cable.

Bolted back into one piece, the Notetaker could be carried, albeit with great effort. Lifting it by the built-in handle strained the plastic case until it warped. "We used to say it ran at five herniations per block," Kay joked. To avoid rupturing the case and dumping ten thousand dollars' worth of components on the ground like groceries out of a wet paper bag, Tesler and Fairbairn built a rolling cart that also allowed them to slide it, just barely, under the seat of an airliner. One day Fairbairn, bringing the prototype to Rochester for a show-and-tell, fired it up on its batteries in mid-flight, therefore becoming the very first person to operate a personal computer on an airplane—the first of a legion of electronic road warriors wired to their work at 35,000 feet.

The Dorado and the Notetaker shared one other distinction. They were the last major projects undertaken at PARC by the scientists of its first generation. Between 1978 and 1982 the Dorado almost entirely replaced the Alto as the computer of choice inside PARC, and elicited numerous expressions of interest from customers on the outside. But no assembly line other than the low-volume Garage was ever approved by Xerox. Come 1983, a series of dramatic events would strip the Dorado of its design team and render it a technological orphan.

The Learning Research Group manufactured ten Notetakers and tried in vain, as usual, to interest Xerox in the product. Tesler spent the better part of a year flying around the country displaying the prototype to division executives. But whatever influence PARC ever had in Stamford or Rochester had visibly drained away. "Xerox executives made all sorts of promises," Tesler said. " 'We'll buy 20,000, just talk to this executive in Virginia, then talk to this executive in Connecticut.' After a year I was ready to give up."

Soon after the last Notetaker was built, Alan Kay announced that he was taking a long-promised sabbatical. For Kay the project's exhilaration had already yielded to his familiar feelings of despair. The Notetaker was enticingly similar to the old cardboard model he had once used to illustrate the Dynabook. But his unquiet nature was to focus not on how close it came but on where it fell short. His outward glee at creating a new machine masked his real disappointment at how its compromises on weight and size had once again "squeezed out the end-users for whom it was originally aimed"—that is, the children.

Southern California beckoned. He had a new girlfriend, Bonnie MacBird, who he had met while she was researching a screenplay about computer wizards and who lived in Los Angeles. (After endless tinkerings by Hollywood executives this screenplay became the movie *Tron*, which came out in 1982, two years after Kay and MacBird were married. "We like to say the marriage turned out a lot better than the movie," he said.) He announced he was temporarily relocating to L.A. to take organ lessons. He never returned to PARC.

Adele Goldberg took over the group after his departure. She was the logical choice, like Ingalls a champion implementer, as she proved by shepherding the next version of Smalltalk to completion—Smalltalk–80. A few years later with Dave Robson, another team member, she wrote the definitive Smalltalk textbook.

But the Learning Research Group was a very different place without Kay, its font of ideas. "It was like getting our heart cut out when he left," Merry recalled. "It wasn't too long after he left that we had another Pajaro Dunes offsite. I remember that being very sad, the first Pajaro Dunes when Alan wasn't there. We missed him very badly. It really was in many ways the end of a lot of the good stuff."

The rest of them hung on for another couple of years, finishing old projects. Some started looking for new challenges. Larry Tesler, fed up by his fruitless quest to interest Xerox in the Notetaker, was awaiting only a sign of when and where he should go.

That sign appeared one day in 1979, when a Silicon Valley legend in the making walked through PARC's front door.

CHAPTER 23

Steve Jobs Gets
His Show and Tell

hus we come to Steven P. Jobs.

The Apple Computer co-founder's visit to PARC, from which he reputedly spirited off the ideas that later made the Apple Macintosh famous, is one of the foundation legends of personal computing, as replete with drama and consequence as the story of David and Goliath or the fable of the mouse and the lion with an injured paw. It holds enough material to serve the mythmaking of not one corporation but two, Xerox and Apple. If one seeks proof of its importance, one need look no further than the fact that to this date no two people involved in the episode recollect it quite the same way.

For a chronicler of PARC this presents a unique difficulty. No anecdote from PARC's history is burdened by so much contradictory testimony. The collective memory of the Jobs visit and of its aftermath is so vivid that some former PARC scientists are no longer sure whether they were there themselves, or just heard about it later. PARC engineers and their guests from Apple disagree with each other (and among themselves) about who delivered which portions of the demonstration; on how many demos there were and when they took place; whether Jobs and his people saw an Alto or a Dorado; and whether Steve Jobs was desperate to get a look at PARC's technology, or so dubious about anything produced by a big corporation that he had to be wheedled into going in the first place.

Some of these discrepancies result from the demo's patchwork nature. "Nobody knows everything that happened, because there's nobody that was there all the time," says Larry Tesler, who was present for more of it than most.

Nobody, that is, except Adele Goldberg, who nevertheless agrees with Tesler that it is difficult for almost anyone to have a lock on the demo's ultimate truth. She thinks of the Jobs demo in terms of the story about the eight blind men and the elephant, each one stroking a different part of the same animal: "It's unbelievable to me the number of eyes on this elephant in people's memories. It just astounds me. Sometimes I just have to go, 'I'm right! Because I was the only one there all the time!'"

Some inconsistencies are the product of Apple's mythmaking rather than PARC's. The idea that Steve Jobs and his troops saw in PARC a priceless, squandered gem aims to say as much about Jobs's peerless perspicacity as Xerox's obtuseness. The author who wrote, "You can have your Lufthansa Heist, your Great Train Robbery . . . the slickest trick of all was Apple's daylight raid on the Xerox Palo Alto Research Center" perhaps desired more to promote a heroic vision of Apple than to get at what really happened.

Yet it is possible to resolve all these accounts and reconstruct a story that has never before been told in its entirety. To take the most obvious questions first: There were two separate demonstrations, not one, and the second covered all the most secret material. They occurred in December 1979. The computer was almost surely an Alto and the principal demonstrators were Goldberg, Tesler, Dan Ingalls, and Diana Merry. Steve Jobs was initially skeptical of what PARC might have to offer but allowed his engineers to convince him otherwise. As for Jobs's acuity, he later admitted that he was shown three mind-bending innovations at PARC, but the first one was so dazzling it blinded him to the significance of the second and third.

Perhaps most important, the Steve Jobs demo was not a random event or a stroke of luck for Apple, as it has sometimes been portrayed. Apple's engineers knew what they were after. They had taken great pains to plan for the moment, and they arrived at PARC fully prepared to ask the right questions and interpret the answers. The seed of the famous Jobs demo, in fact, had been carefully planted eight months earlier.

The occasion was a meeting on April 2, 1979, in an office building at 9200 Sunset Boulevard in West Hollywood. The host was Xerox Development Corporation, a unique little fiefdom that operated with great independence from the headquarters in Stamford.

Steve Jobs, the quintessential countercultural entrepreneur, was there to offer the corporate behemoth of Xerox a deal. He knew Xerox desired to invest in Apple, which would soon go public in one of the most eagerly anticipated stock offerings of the era. Jobs was willing to let the company in on the ground floor in return for access to Xerox technology—just what technology, he was not yet quite sure—and to Xerox's marketing knowledge.

This was the sort of pitch the principals of Xerox Development Corporation were used to hearing. Formed for the purpose of making strategic investments in small technology companies, XDC existed as a sort of personal playground for a brilliant but rather irksome executive named Abraham Zarem. Xerox had acquired Dr. Abe Zarem the same way it got Max Palevsky: by purchasing his company. In his case it was Pasadena-based Electro-Optical Systems, which, as its name implied, did research in leading-edge optical technologies, including lasers. When Xerox bought EOS in 1962, Joe Wilson predicted that within a decade most of the corporation's profits would come from such new technologies. That never happened, but the acquisition did turn Zarem into Xerox's single largest shareholder, a distinction he held until dislodged by Palevsky seven years later. By then Xerox, disenchanted with Zarem's costly and fruitless attempts to transform EOS into a major government contractor, was searching for a way to keep him happy but distracted. The answer was to create a venture unit and place him in charge. Thus was XDC born.

For all his faults, Zarem was an experienced hand at the difficult process of moving technology from the laboratory to the commercial marketplace; that was how he had made EOS into an attractive acquisition target in the first place. By 1979, seeing that the same familiar issues had sprung up around PARC's work, he resolved to stick his nose in. His idea was to turn the technology over to a young, hungry company with a modest cost structure—one that would not dither endlessly about whether a promising innovation would fit into its tradition-encrusted product line but would simply march ahead (while paying Xerox royalties). A company, say, like Apple.

The idea was not wholly implausible. Apple was coming on strong. Started in the proverbial Silicon Valley garage by Jobs and his high school classmate Steve Wozniak, Apple had successfully negotiated the transition in its product line from kit versions of Woz's little personal computer to a more versatile version, the Apple II. This machine was unique in the hobbyist market. It came already assembled, with a keyboard (although it required a separate monitor). Shortly after Jobs's appearance before Zarem's group, Apple started bundling it with VisiCalc, a unique software program known as a financial spreadsheet—a "killer app" that would single-handedly turn the Apple II into a popular businessman's tool.

With fewer than forty employees in 1978, Apple was already one of the most sought-after investments among the small community of speculative private investors known as venture capitalists. When the company raised $7 million in "mezzanine" financing during the summer of 1979, traditionally one of the last private offerings before a company sells stock to the public, the sixteen buyers included some of the most prominent institutional investors in the country. Xerox would almost surely have been shut out, had not one of Jobs's advisors finally won a long-standing argument.

The advisor was Jef Raskin, a talented computer engineer and artist who had joined Apple to help design the Apple II. Raskin knew that the Apple founders' low opinion of big business was the product of Wozniak's experience as an engineer at Hewlett-Packard, where his proposal for a personal computer project had been rebuffed by his bosses. The incident "ever after remained part of their psychological motivation," Raskin recalled. "Jobs repeatedly told me (and anybody else he could get hold of) that a large corporation like Xerox couldn't do anything interesting."

But Raskin had friends working at PARC. At their invitation, he had watched dazzling new technologies take shape on Coyote Hill Road.

Around the time the mezzanine financing was being assembled, he won Jobs over. When Xerox asked to be included in the deal, Jobs made his pitch: In exchange for an invitation to PARC, he would sell the corporation 100,000 private shares at $10.50 each. XDC agreed to fork over the $1.05 million, and one of the unlikeliest—if shortest-lived—alliances in high technology history was forged.

If Steve Jobs harbored an enduring mistrust of big companies, Apple Computer was scarcely a blip on the radar screen of most PARC engineers. They were Ph.D.s who had worked on some of the biggest computing projects the world had ever seen; Apple was a bunch of tinkers. The "personal computers" of the day were hobbyists' kits, contraptions with names like the Altair and the Commodore PET that arrived in pieces for sixteen-year-olds to drip solder on until something started to work, usually to their own amazement, so they could spend hours staring at the blinking red lights that served as output displays. What a joke! Blinking lights had gone out with the Whirlwind computer in the 1950s; they were as relevant to PARC's definition of computing—Altos with graphics programs and bitmapped displays—as were relics of the Flint Age. The general opinion on Coyote Hill was that Apple's customers were a waste of time. They were not very sharp, they were self-taught, and their machines were toys.

Such, at least, was the reaction of people who had never met Steve Jobs. Those who had made his acquaintance came away with a stronger, and often less favorable, impression.

The Jobs of this period—call it the "pre-Armani era"—wore scruffy like a badge of honor. He was perpetually clad in blue jeans, with a black beard that never seemed to grow in. His thin lips seemed locked in a knowing smirk. Ever since he was twenty years old and worth zero on paper he had worn his pride and contempt nakedly. Thwart him, and it scarcely mattered whether you were an eighth-grade dropout or a Ph.D. in electrical engineering; he would trash your arguments like they were so much chaff in the blades of a thresher.

Jobs's associates had a label for his unyielding confidence in his own vision and judgment. They called it his "reality distortion field." He lived securely within his worldview and seemed to exist chiefly for the purpose of imposing it on others. He had a way of seeming at once intolerably brash and older than his years. Those were the qualities that enabled him to hold the experienced investors of XDC rapt by relating the story of how he had founded Apple. Those, and the fact that at the age of twenty-four he was the chairman of a company already worth $70 million.

A small handful of PARC engineers, like Larry Tesler, had not allowed their preconceptions about Apple's customers or Jobs's personality to cloud their perception of where these little computers might lead. Rather than shun the growing underground of youthful hackers, Tesler dove in. For a year or two he had been attending such cultural events as meetings of the Homebrew Computer Club, where young Altair and Commodore users met to trade their tiny software programs and swap lore. He was no stranger to Apple, having gone out with a woman who worked for the company. "I'd been to an Apple picnic as her date in 1978, when there were thirty employees," Tesler recalled. "It was at Marineworld in Redwood City and the entire staff, with kids, fit around four picnic tables."

Tesler thought PARC orthodoxy had blinded it to this alternative culture. He also thought he understood why. PETs and Apples were not the pedigreed offspring of the academic time-sharing tradition like the Alto and almost every other machine PARC had built. They had sprouted from an entirely different technology, that of the silicon microprocessor, the so-called "computer-on-a-chip" developed by Intel and Motorola (Apple would long be designed around the Motorola chip, while IBM-compatible PCs, which came later, would be based on the Intel version). As he had lectured Bob Metcalfe during the Notetaker's design phase, he believed PARC could learn from the kids. In fact, *had* to. If PARC did not change its attitude, he felt, it was going to look back one of these days and discover it had been passed by.

Tesler's opinion was well enough known on Coyote Hill that one day in late 1979 Harold Hall summoned him to a secret meeting in his office. Tesler arrived to find himself part of a tidy little gathering that included Bill Gunning and Roy Lahr, a Xerox functionary who had been dispatched by Abe Zarem to keep a solicitous eye on Jobs. They explained that they were seeking advice on how to manage an entry into the personal computer market and had heard Tesler might be an ideal source.

"You see," Lahr revealed, "we've invested in Apple."

"I said, 'That's great,'" Tesler recalled. "Lahr and Gunning explained that Xerox couldn't build computers cheaply enough to compete because its cost structures were very high. 'If we built a paper clip it would cost three thousand bucks,' they complained. I agreed."

Then they informed Tesler that their scheme was to get Apple to build computers for Xerox.

"Under what kind of arrangement?" he asked.

"We don't know yet," Lahr replied. "But they took our money on condition they could see what was going on at Xerox PARC. They didn't really need the money because everyone wanted in on Apple. But they let us invest."

Tesler's enthusiasm for giving Apple a look inside PARC placed him in a distinct minority on Coyote Hill, especially within the Systems Science Lab, where much of the Smalltalk software was still officially closely guarded.

The lab fragmented into opposite camps, their membership largely based on how one assessed the chances that Xerox might eventually get around to bringing out the technology on its own. Tesler, who had all but given up, saw no reason not to show Apple everything they had. Adele Goldberg, who still cherished the hope that they might yet bring Smalltalk to market under the Xerox banner—or at least that Xerox might let them keep some control over the work they had slaved over for so many years—had a different view. She felt adamantly that disclosing PARC's intellectual property to a team of engineers capable of understanding it and, worse, exploiting it commercially would be a mortal error. "I wanted a deal to happen," Tesler observed. "Adele was trying to kill one."*

---

*Goldberg maintains that Tesler is incorrect in portraying her as specifically opposing a Xerox deal with Apple, as she was unaware of any arrangement between the two companies until the day of the second Jobs demo. (Goldberg, personal communication.)

It was not that Tesler wanted Smalltalk to be widely published and Goldberg wished it kept secret. The issue was the more complex one of who should see the technology and under what circumstances. Goldberg, for example, was happy to demonstrate Smalltalk to legitimate corporate clients who were prepared to help support the group's research by paying for further development.

That had been the case about a year earlier, when she and Tesler ended up in opposing camps over a demo to another enterprise that expressed interest in Smalltalk. This was the Central Intelligence Agency. The CIA had sent a team of engineers to PARC under the auspices of Xerox's Special Information Systems division, which sold customized systems to the federal government.

Goldberg was gratified by the CIA's interest in her work. She viewed the agency as a traditional Xerox paying customer of the sort that routinely got Smalltalk demos over the years, and one whose representatives further seemed "remarkably interesting and innovative." The agency's manifest curiosity about Smalltalk and the Dynabook could not help but give those technologies and their inventors added credibility within Xerox, she figured—and at the very least, she said later, the CIA people touring PARC had needs that fit perfectly with the Dynabook's capabilities for ordering and communicating information.

By contrast, the liberal-minded Tesler treated the CIA visit as a chance for Berkeley-style agitprop. The day of the agency demo he came to work wearing a trenchcoat, dark glasses, and a fedora pulled down over his brow. Then he spent the day hanging around the PARC commissary and conference rooms glowering at the visitors, much to the amusement of his own co-workers.

Tesler thought Apple was different because it was unlikely to put Smalltalk to nefarious use; Goldberg thought it was different because it was likely to become a Xerox competitor rather than a customer. In any case, one thing that became clear early in the debate was that the decision of what and how much to show Jobs's team did not rest with PARC. The engineers could decide how to stage the demo, but Xerox headquarters had decreed that one way or another, it was going happen.

Jobs later maintained that he harbored few expectations about what he would be shown at PARC when he arrived with his team one day early in December. "I thought it would be an interesting afternoon," he said. "But I had no real concept of what I'd see."

What he did see was as bowdlerized a show-and-tell as the Learning Research Group knew how to deliver. Jobs saw the Alto, mouse, Bravo, and several other CSL technologies, as well as a limited number of innocuous graphical applications in Smalltalk.

"It was very much a here's-a-word-processor-there's-a-drawing-tool demo of what was working at the time," Goldberg recalled years later. "No harm done, no problem. What they saw, everyone had seen. The conversation they had with us, everyone had. There was no reason not to do it, it was fine."

Jobs left, apparently content with his sanitized tour. He quickly discovered, however, how much information had been denied him. Two days later he and his entourage returned, primed for a second demonstration. Bemused, Hall ushered them into a conference room to get a better idea of what they hoped to learn. Goldberg had not yet arrived for work, so Tesler and Diana Merry from the Learning Research Group sat in. The parley was a rocky one. Jobs sat fidgeting while Apple's hard-nosed president, Mike Scott, engaged in a round of executive-speak with Hall.

"We were having this very beat-around-the-bush conversation that went on for about four or five minutes, which for Steve Jobs is like seven eternities," Tesler recalled. Suddenly the hyperactive Jobs blew his top.

"Let's stop this bullshit!" he cried, leaping from his chair. "There's no point trying to keep all these secrets. We'll never accomplish anything if we don't talk to each other." Turning to Scott, he ordered, "Scotty, tell them what we want!"

Scott gave an exasperated gesture, as if he knew that any attempt now to settle Jobs down would be pointless. He took a deep breath, but before he could get a word out Jobs interrupted, "We need to tell them about the Lisa!"

The Apple group looked stricken. "Well, tell me why we can't!" Jobs exclaimed. "These guys think we're going to make the Xerox computer, which would cost ten thousand bucks to build. But we all know we want them to help us with the Lisa!"

The PARC team listened in astonishment. Lisa was a name that had never come up before. Even Lahr seemed perplexed. Finally someone asked, "What's Lisa?"

After an uncomfortable silence, an Apple engineer explained with resignation, "Lisa is an office computer we've designed with a bitmapped screen and a simple user interface. We think some of your technology would be useful in helping make the machine easier to use."

Tesler was fascinated, and not only because his own daughter's name was Lisa. Apple had obviously developed this project in great secrecy—so great that it had come as a bolt from the blue to its own babysitter, Roy Lahr. "It completely threw in the air Lahr's idea of what this meeting was all about," he recalled with great amusement. Tesler also knew the Apple team was correct: The Smalltalk interface, parts of which they had not yet seen, *would* make computers easier to use. He was even a little pleased that Apple had now forced the issue. Why not show them Smalltalk? If Xerox was not going to market a personal computer, why should all the Learning Research Group's work simply go to waste?

While this drama was still playing out, Adele Goldberg arrived for work, only to learn that Steve Jobs was back on the premises. She was neither amused nor intrigued, but incensed.

"I come in to work and there was Steve Jobs and the entire Lisa programming team, ten of them or so, in the conference room. No warning. Two days later. Then Harold Hall came out in the hallway with Roy Lahr to explain to me that I'm supposed to give them a second demo."

"Look, Adele, it's no sweat," Hall said. He reminded her that PARC could show Jobs more than he had already seen without necessarily showing him everything. There were two grades of Smalltalk demo at PARC—classified (for corporate bigwigs and other specially cleared VIPs) and unclassified. "Tell Tesler to just give Jobs the regular unclassified briefing," Hall said. "It'll dazzle him and he'll never know he didn't get the confidential disclosure."

Goldberg was mollified, but just barely. Begrudgingly, she admitted that if the demo kept to Hall's specifications, there would be little harm done—*if*. But who knew what else the savvy Apple engineers might pick up during another hour or two on the premises, and how much more they might insist on being shown? Deep down she was frustrated that Apple had been permitted to wheedle its way into the building in the first place. She blamed Hall and Lahr equally for lacking the technical savvy to understand the risks of showing Apple—especially its professional programmers—anything at all.

"We had never, ever given a private programming lesson to another company's engineering team," she said later. "And no one informed me of any reason to do so."

As she feared, however, the unclassified demo was still not enough. Almost as soon as Hall returned to his office, his phone rang. On the line directly from Stamford was a livid Bill Souders, the head of Xerox's business planning group. Souders informed Hall bluntly that Jobs was to be shown whatever he wanted to see, up to and including all of Smalltalk. "You *will* give Mr. Jobs the confidential briefing!" he barked.

Hall was mystified. Bill Souders, who knew even less than he did about software and programming environments, could not possibly understand the importance of PARC's proprietary technology. Hall could only assume that Jobs had somehow discovered on the spot that he had been conned—possibly Tesler or someone else on the team had unwisely let drop that he was receiving another subpar briefing—and taken a piece out of Roy Lahr. Lahr presumably blitzed his complaint directly to Abe Zarem, who fired up the big guns in Connecticut to shell PARC into capitulation. Whatever the process, it had occurred with lightning speed. Hall marveled at how high up in the Xerox hierarchy Apple's influence seemed to reach.

Still, Hall was nothing if not a faithful follower of the corporate chain of command, no matter how many of the links were time-servers and idiots. The important thing, he recalled, was that Souders's "authority was unmistakable and he used the military imperative language. It was exactly as in 1943 in basic training when I was told, 'You *will* pick up that cigarette butt!'"

Obligingly, he passed word to the demo team that they were to give

Jobs and his engineers the full-dress treatment. Goldberg was stunned. Her worst nightmare was unfolding: The hard-won understanding about what Apple could and could not see was about to be breached. Turning red and teary with rage, she told Hall, "That's nuts! It's the stupidest thing I've ever heard."

That was for starters. Hall and Lahr escorted her into Hall's office to try to calm her down. It was an uphill struggle that lasted, by her estimation, about three hours.

"I finally said to Harold, 'You are making a really big mistake,'" she recalled. "'You are throwing away something that this company itself hasn't had a chance to even consider using. And you'll have to order me to do it, because I'm not walking in there voluntarily.'

"And that's what he did."

Merry and Tesler had spent the intervening time trying to keep Steve Jobs distracted with more of the plain-vanilla demonstration. They had just about had it with his constant wheedling when, suddenly, Adele Goldberg arrived back on the scene. "I can still see her," Merry recalled. "She was in pigtails and her face was red as a beet. And she was holding one of our yellow disk packs with Smalltalk on it."

The demo began. A full-dress Smalltalk show-and-tell was a sight to behold. There were educational applications Goldberg had written and software development tools by Tesler. Merry demonstrated her galley editor, a nifty program with animation capabilities built in so that a user could incorporate text and pictures into a single document. Almost every program had capabilities that had never been seen in a research prototype anywhere, much less in a commercial system. "There was lots to Smalltalk," Tesler remembered. "You could see it thirty times and see something new every time."

What was interesting—or to Goldberg, ominous—was the intensity with which the Apple engineers paid attention. Bill Atkinson, a brilliant programmer who would later put his distinctive stamp on the Macintosh, kept his eyes on the screen as though they were fixed there by a magnetic field. He was standing so close that as Tesler conducted his assigned portion of the demo he could feel Atkinson's breath on the back of his neck.

Atkinson had clearly come prepared. "He was asking extremely intelligent questions that he couldn't have thought of just by watching the screen," Tesler recalled. "It turned out later that they had read every paper we'd published, and the demo was just reminding them of things they wanted to ask us. But I was very impressed. They asked all the right questions and understood all the answers. It was clear to me that they understood what we had a lot better than Xerox did."

Given this rare psychic encouragement, the Learning Research Group warmed to their subject. They even indulged in some of their favorite legerdemain. At one point Jobs, watching some text scroll up the screen line by line in its normal fashion, remarked, "It would be nice if it moved smoothly, pixel by pixel, like paper."

With Ingalls at the keyboard, that was like asking a New Orleans jazz band to play "Limehouse Blues." He clicked the mouse on a window displaying several lines of Smalltalk code, made a minor edit, and returned to the text. *Presto!* The scrolling was now continuous.

The Apple engineers' eyes bulged in astonishment. In any other system the programmer would have had to rewrite the code and recompile a huge block of the program, maybe even all of it. The process might take hours. Thanks to its object-oriented modularity, in Smalltalk such a modest change never required the recompiling of more than ten or twenty lines, which could be done in a second or two. "It was essentially instantaneous," Ingalls recalled. Of course, it helped that as one of Smalltalk's creators he was able to make the change as though by instinct. "We were ringers," he confessed. "We knew that system from top to bottom."

"They were totally blown away," Tesler confirmed. "Jobs was waving his arms around, saying, 'Why hasn't this company brought this to market? What's going on here? I don't get it!' Meantime the other guys were trying to ignore the shouting. They had to concentrate and learn as much as they could in the hour they were going to be there."

The creation myth of the Lisa and Macintosh holds that Steve Jobs, in the grip of an epiphany brought on by PARC's dazzling technology, headed straight back to Apple headquarters and ripped up a year's worth of planning for the Lisa user interface. Jobs himself recalled how he returned to his office that afternoon "a raving maniac," insisting the Lisa be reconfigured to replicate the Alto's dynamic display. "It was one of those apocalyptic moments," he said. "I remember within ten minutes of seeing the graphical user interface stuff, just knowing that every computer would work this way some day. It was so obvious."

Something of the sort did happen, but without quite so much *sturm und drang*. The essential appearance and functionality of the Smalltalk interface—its "look and feel," so to speak—did become reflected in that of the Lisa and Macintosh.

Lisa's architects, many of them transplants from the staid purlieus of Hewlett-Packard, had already designed a graphical user interface, but their version was far more static than the Alto's. Theirs lacked Smalltalk's dynamic overlapping windows, for example, but rather displayed one active application at a time, taking up the whole screen.

Nor did the Lisa originally place as much reliance on the mouse. This was the subject of heated disagreement within Apple. The main pointing device of the original Lisa interface was something called a "softkey," which appeared on the screen as a sort of menu listing the command options for the user at any given moment: If the active application was a text editor, for example, it might offer the choices of *insert* and *delete*. The user selected a softkey by using keyboard keys to move an arrow on the screens, then executed the command by striking "enter." The mouse was available, but it was scantily used and entirely optional.

Bill Atkinson, whose intense concentration during the demo left such a strong impression on Tesler, had spent months trying to design a more dynamic interface. But he had been unable to solve several programming problems, including how to write text into an irregularly shaped region of the screen—for example, the corner of one window peeking out from beneath another. This, of course, was a problem Dan Ingalls had long since solved via BitBlt (but had never published). Atkinson later maintained that seeing the overlapping windows on the Alto screen was for him more a confidence-builder than a solution to his quandary. He subsequently solved the same problem in his own way but, as he later remarked, "That whirlwind tour left an impression on me. Knowing it could be done empowered me to invent a way it could be done."

The demo also gave him the necessary ammunition to win the battle over the mouse. Atkinson thought the device needed to be standard equipment on every Lisa, rather than an option; only then would Apple be sure that software developers would always deploy it as an integral part of the system. After PARC he no longer got an argument from Steve Jobs, or anyone else.[°]

On the other hand, Atkinson discerned in Smalltalk numerous short-comings he resolved to correct. For one thing, it was painfully slow, an artifact of the Alto's lightweight memory and the language's "inter-preted" structure, which loaded the central processing unit with more work than it could comfortably handle. "The system was crippled by a factor of ten, and it showed," he recalled. "It wasn't fast enough for a commercial application. You would watch characters appear on the screen one by one, like on a agonizingly slow modem."

As for Jobs, he was so "saturated" by the power of the user interface he had seen that he ignored the other two phenomena he was being shown: object-oriented programming, which was the essence of Smalltalk, and networking. The fact that PARC had some 200 Altos connected to the Ethernet at the time of the Jobs demo made no impression on the Apple team. Neither the Lisa nor the first versions of the Macintosh were equipped with network ports. (A famous story had Jobs answering a question about how to network the Mac by flinging a floppy disk at the questioner and barking, "There's my fucking network!")

It may be that PARC's most important influence on the Lisa and Mac-intosh was a spiritual one. A design manifesto the Lisa designers pro-duced with a month or so of their visit could have sprung full-blown from the mind of Alan Kay or Larry Tesler. "Lisa must be fun to use," it com-manded. "It will not be a system that is used by someone 'because it is part of the job' or 'because the boss told them to.' Special attention must be paid to the friendliness of the user interaction and the subtleties that make using the Lisa rewarding and job-enriching."

[°]Atkinson has long resented the importance others have attached to his visit to PARC. "In hindsight I would rather we'd never have gone," he said. "Those one and a half hours tainted everything we did, and so much of what we did was original research."

And for all the impact that the PARC had on Apple, over the long run Apple's impact on the PARC scientists themselves may have been more pronounced. They had started out disparaging Jobs and his customers, but his fanatic enthusiasm for their work hit them like a lightning bolt. It was a powerful sign that the outside world would welcome all they had achieved within their moated palace while toiling for an indifferent Xerox. Steve Jobs did more than open the floodgates of ideas out of PARC. He started the exodus of human beings.

Among the first to go was Larry Tesler. During the summer preceding Jobs's visit, Tesler had traveled around Europe. In a rural French village he stopped to have his tarot read by a fortune teller. "She was just an interesting old French lady who made a bunch of predictions, all of which came true. Maybe they were self-fulfilling prophecies. She told me I'd leave my job within a year, and I left eleven months later. I couldn't believe her at the time. I said, 'But I have the very best job . . .' But maybe I was ready."

Early in 1980 Jobs asked Xerox for a license to use Smalltalk in the Lisa. In an unexpected burst of proprietary pride, Xerox turned him down. (The company had already divested its equity in Apple, thus missing out on the computer company's extraordinary run-up in value at the time of its 1980 initial public stock offering.) Steve Jobs made his offer instead to Tesler, one of Smalltalk's developers.

Heeding the mysterious tarot, Tesler accepted the job that April. He would go on to head the Lisa user interface team and to help design the Macintosh, eventually rising to the position of Apple's chief scientist. The sign he was waiting for had come. PARC's elitism had begun to seem threadbare, and even a little reactionary.

"I remember once I said to Bob Taylor, 'You know, I've been going to these Homebrew computer meetings and I've been talking to people at Apple and hanging out in the personal computer scene. There's a lot of smart people out there who are going to run way ahead of PARC in PCs. Xerox will never catch up, even with better stuff.'

"And Taylor smoked his pipe and said, 'No, that's not going to happen, because we have the smartest people here. I believe if you have the smartest people you'll end up ahead.'

"I said, 'Bob, I've met people outside. They're very smart in this place, no question about it, but there are smart people who don't work for PARC. They do exist, and there are enough of them out there that they can do just fine.'

"He said, 'If you find someone as smart as the people here, just tell me who they are and we'll hire them!'

"I just told him, 'It's not going to work like that.'"

CHAPTER 24

Supernova

E ven before Steve Jobs's arrival on the scene PARC had been facing the prospect of wrenching change. The first sign that trouble lay ahead came in May 1978, just after that year's annual corporate meeting in San Francisco. That Friday, when the Xerox contingent had already returned back East, George Pake got a phone call from Jack Goldman.

In terms of both men's careers, it was almost as momentous a call as the one eight years earlier when Goldman had offered Pake the chance to manage a unique new research center. But this was a different Jack Goldman. Pake's old mentor, far from being at the top of his game with all the resources of a powerful industrial machine at his command, sounded frightened and querulous.

"George," he said, "you gotta be here in Connecticut on Monday. I gotta talk to you. They're taking the research labs away from me."

As long as Jack Goldman had toiled under the protective shade of Peter McColough he tended to win a fair share of his battles with Xerox culture and bureaucracy, especially the early crucial skirmishes over the consolidation of all Xerox research in his own hands and the establishment of

PARC. But as the lost decade of the 1970s wore on and Xerox sank deeper into its slough, Goldman's distance from the chairman's ear lengthened and his influence waned. Just as McColough had recruited Goldman from Ford to reanimate Xerox research, he had imported a group of outside finance experts to modernize the company's ailing revenue and expense structures. More and more, they were in charge.

They proved to be a stultifying and self-perpetuating cadre. Company President Archie McCardell, whose passion for figures rivaled that of the ancient numerologists, came from Ford, whence he recruited Jim O'Neill, who had once been his superior, to head the Information Technology Group. Soon they were joined by three other Ford men, clustered in the highest stratum of Xerox management. By the start of 1978 Goldman was still a member of Xerox's board of directors, but no longer reported directly to Peter McColough. Instead he was sequestered three rungs down in the organizational ladder and outnumbered by the newcomers.

He did not take well to the *de facto* demotion, nor to the alien management culture that McCardell and O'Neill had brought with them. As he witnessed the new men's ineffectual struggle to stem Xerox's decline from a vantage point hopelessly remote from the seat of power, he became more irascible. Jack Goldman's aura was beginning to fade, one loyalist recalled, "accelerated by his indubitably abrasive manner in the presence of incompetence, which was abundant at the higher levels of Xerox."

This was a somewhat unfair assessment of the new executives. Many were simply in the wrong place in the wrong company. Xerox needed to embrace radical new technologies to resuscitate its product lines. But they were trying to squeeze the last drops of blood from the same tired copiers by applying snazzy new management theories and pinching pennies. Had the crisis been rooted solely in Xerox's complacency or a bad economy, their reorganizations and cost-cutting strategies might have borne fruit. But the affliction ran much deeper.

Perhaps the best illustration of the conflict between the new technologists and the financial engineers was the short, bitter career of Myron Tribus, who was hired on Goldman's recommendation as senior vice president for research and engineering in 1972 and got driven out by O'Neill before the close of 1974. Crusty and temperamental, Tribus was a former Commerce Department official and dean of engineering at Dartmouth. He was also, as Goldman attested, "one of the most brilliant engineers in this country. A difficult guy to deal with, as is often the case when you're dealing with geniuses, but an absolutely brilliant engineer."

Tribus realized within a few weeks of his arrival in Rochester that Xerox executives did not define their business as making copiers, but rather as making money. The products generating the revenues were almost irrelevant; for them the issues of management would have been no different had they been turning out cars, or raw steel, or shoes. "They saw Xerox as a money pump and they organized it around that concept," Tribus said. "The people at the top of Xerox were not really interested in technology."

As a result, Xerox technology and engineering had turned distinctly slovenly. Customer complaints battered against the company walls like a storm surge, but no system existed to convert reports from the field into product improvements. Tribus imposed a rigorous order on this haphazard environment. He demanded that every part going into a Xerox copier, down to the smallest spring, be documented like a component in a jet engine so that repairmen and engineers needed only to flip open a book to locate the trouble spots. "I realized," he said, "we had to get reliability."

Almost alone among the top executives, Tribus was enchanted with PARC. He visited Palo Alto regularly and, back home, pressured O'Neill to market the laser printer as an alternative to the slow and noisy IBM machines whose hideous output then passed for high-tech computer printing. After Tribus's secretary was awarded an Alto out of the corporate consignment he studied the change in her work habits with frank fascination. "When they took it away to check on its wear and tear she cried, really cried," he said. "I thought to myself, 'This is something really big.'"

Unfortunately, one skill Tribus had not learned during his long career in government and academia was how to survive in a corporate executive suite. He was constitutionally unable to coddle underlings or suffer fools gladly; nor was he alert to the necessity of protecting his flank. Even subordinates who admired his brains hated his brusque and doctrinaire manner. As for his peers in management, who resented the blunt delight with which he rubbed their noses in his superior technical judgment, they smelled his lack of corporate savvy like lions circling a lame wildebeest.

Eventually he ended up sandwiched in the pecking order between O'Neill and an engineering manager named Robert J. Sparacino. Sparacino had honed his corporate infighting skills at that war college of internal competition, General Motors, where an executive at Pontiac would win as much praise for outsmarting his compeers at Buick as for beating Chrysler. O'Neill at first assigned him to be Tribus's subordinate, but over a period of months arranged to give the junior man more responsibilities at Tribus's expense.

"They connived to get rid of me," Tribus recalled. "I had never been in a corporation. I found myself in an alien land, and working at the top I saw a lot of things going on that I thought were just plain stupid. But the other guys had MBAs and I did not, and they talked a common language and I was clearly an outsider. I fought that system tooth and nail until some of my good friends came to me and said, 'Myron, you look like hell, working from seven in the morning till seven at night surrounded by guys who just want to do you in. You've got to get out of there or you'll be dead in a year.'"

Tribus's resignation in 1974 to accept a teaching post at MIT deprived Goldman of a soulmate and an ally. He was left to fight the Ford finance clique as a minority of one. What he lacked in manpower he made up for in vituperation. The carping within the executive suite grew intolerable. While Goldman sniped at the very idea of having "the engineering division headed up by an accountant who just didn't understand things like Moore's Law or the role of software," O'Neill and Sparacino nagged him about the half-baked and unmarketable prototypes coming out of PARC. Sparacino at one point was heard to remark that "office systems will never amount to diddly-squat at Xerox," a prophecy many thought he worked to make self-fulfilling.

But Goldman did not always have realism on his side. Even his closest allies recognized that he had little conception of the economics of product development—the indispensable second half of "R&D."

"Jack did not understand what you had to do with bright ideas from bright people to make them into real products that could go into a real market," acknowledged George White, a member of his research management staff. And with O'Neill and Sparacino continuing to control all marketing and engineering, Goldman had less clout than ever to force research-driven products into the marketplace even as market probes. It was his old problem at Ford ("Not much of your stuff gets on a car, does it, Jack?"), exacerbated by vicious personal animosities. He could only watch powerlessly as his most cherished ventures—the laser printer sale to Lawrence Livermore, the marketing of the Alto III—became the victims of political spats.

After Archie McCardell, O'Neill's chief sponsor, resigned the Xerox presidency in 1977 to become chief executive of International Harvester, Goldman apparently believed he might yet gain the upper hand over his adversaries. Instead the conflict only became more disruptive. The backdoor sniping was bad enough, but when Goldman and O'Neill were face to face, as at executive conferences or board meetings, they treated each other with such an excess of gritted-teeth deference that the tension in the room was palpable. McColough and David Kearns, who had been appointed McCardell's successor as president, "were kind of embarrassed by the feuding, which went on even in public," George Pake recalled. "The corporation got pretty impatient with that."

The 1978 annual shareholders meeting in San Francisco was another glittering showcase for Goldman, who invited his fellow board members down to Palo Alto for a beguiling tour of his citadel on Coyote Hill. But it was his last hurrah. On their first day back in Stamford he received a summons from David Kearns. The new president informed him that research needed to be yoked more closely to engineering and manufacturing. Therefore, he said, he was reorganizing it from a corporate-level function to a subdivision of engineering—that is, under Jim O'Neill and Bob Sparacino. Kearns, to be fair, may not have fully understood the historic message he was thereby sending: Since the days of Chester Carlson and John Dessauer, research had never been ranked so low in the organizational charts at Xerox.

Goldman's initial reaction was outrage. He viewed the new president as a novice—"my junior on the board of directors," he fumed—floundering in the murk of a corporate reorganization without understanding the importance of technology or that top researchers were mobile assets who could vote with their feet. He stormed directly into McColough's office and threatened to resign on the spot. "I pounded on his desk," he recalled, "and said, 'You can't do this shitty thing!' "

Summoning all his powers of appeasement, McColough managed to get Goldman calmed down, but he did not rescind Kearns's order. Regaining his composure and examining the situation pragmatically, Goldman realized he was overmatched. The forces arrayed against him extended well beyond David Kearns, and the battle was more than merely personal. A political drama was unfolding at Xerox, with technology and research the pawns.

He now had a new goal: to keep his beloved research labs—his legacy—out of his enemies' clutches. "The independence of the research organization is what enables you to attract the kind of people you attract," he explained later. "And certainly putting it under an O'Neill type of guy would kill it from Day One." He understood that to stop this from happening he would have to fall on his sword. When he called George Pake in Palo Alto that Friday, it was to ask him to pick up the mantle of research as it fell from his own hands—by stepping in as research chief.

Pake felt deeply for his boss. "If I'd have been Jack I'd have been totally shocked that with no warning at all they would just yank the three research centers away from me," he said later. (Goldman's jurisdiction covered PARC, Webster, and a third lab outside of Toronto.) At Goldman's urging he flew to Connecticut that weekend. "We had breakfast together on Monday and he said, 'George, this is a play by the engineers in Rochester to gain control of the digital technology at PARC.' He was indicating that he had lost that round. And he told me the only way to keep the first-rate science we had in research was for me to agree to take the job of overseeing the three labs."

Pake detected a few flaws in the scheme. The job had not been offered to him and he had no knowledge that it would be. Second, he could not see himself functioning any more cozily under O'Neill and Sparacino than Goldman had. Finally, he was concerned about his health. Back in

1974 he had accepted a one-year staff appointment at headquarters and relocated to Stamford, leaving Hall behind as acting PARC director. The stress of corporate politics had driven his fragile blood pressure sky high and brought him to the verge of a stroke, forcing him to return home before the full year was up. He was not sure he wanted Goldman's job under any circumstances, and certainly not if it meant working in Stamford again.

Goldman bulled through all Pake's objections by invoking the threat to Xerox research. He ushered him in to meet with Kearns, to whom Pake dutifully delivered Goldman's dire message. "I told David, 'Jack feels and I feel that the research scientists will just abandon this sinking ship if you put O'Neill and Sparacino in charge of the labs. We worked so hard to build this research enterprise that that would be a terrible tragedy.'" He offered to take over as head of research—on condition he could do the job from Palo Alto. "I'll just agree that whenever you want me here I'll get on a plane and come," he said. ("Many hundred airplane trips later I kind of regretted that," he remarked later.)

Kearns said he would think it over and let Pake know. Pake left Kearns's office in the same frame of mind in which Bob Taylor had left his own in 1970, convinced the deal was dead. Instead, his offer evoked widespread approval in Stamford, where Pake was viewed fondly as a high-caliber scientist and a consummate gentleman. He defended his positions but never turned them into personal crusades like Jack Goldman. Furthermore, Pake had always been content with the opportunity to create good science and technology at PARC. "He never had a focused ambition to turn the world or Xerox on its ear like Jack did," George White observed. "He didn't challenge these other 'experts' in their own fields, like marketing and finance. In short, he wasn't uppity."

Two weeks later Kearns called to welcome him back onto the corporate staff.

Even though he was staying in Palo Alto, Pake's new responsibilities ruled out any possibility he could remain PARC's director. Of the candidates to replace him, one stood out. He was Bob Spinrad, the genial New York-born electrical engineer who had risen from a post at Max

Palevsky's Scientific Data Systems to a corporate staff job under Goldman. He was now head of the Systems Development Division, which was building the Star.

Spinrad seemed to have all the qualities Pake valued most in a research manager. His scientific and research credentials had been earned at Columbia, MIT, and Brookhaven National Laboratory, a government nuclear research center. He was an old hand at navigating the shoals of digital computing, having served as SDS's software chief and managed the large-scale engineering team at SDD.

Best of all, Spinrad was popular on both coasts. He had served with dozens of PARC and SDS people on corporate task forces (including Odyssey, which put Xerox's computer business out of its misery), and frequently dealt face to face with Jim O'Neill. "Goldman used to send me to talk to him when he couldn't because they were fighting," he recalled.

What no one could have predicted was that Spinrad's biggest problem would not be Jim O'Neill, but George Pake.

About a year after his accession as director July 1, 1978, PARC's internal battle over research resources took a turn for the worse. The catalyst, ironically, was the corporation's consent to the most significant expansion of the research center since its founding. This was the establishment of a program in the new technology of silicon-based integrated circuits. Taking the science of VLSI a few steps beyond the work Lynn Conway and Doug Fairbairn were doing with Carver Mead, the new lab would actually manufacture devices on an experimental fabrication line. This was not a trivial commitment. It meant millions of dollars in capital expenditures and the recruitment of an entirely new professional staff. But it was a particularly gratifying victory for Pake, for whom it meant that PARC would be doing cutting-edge research in his own academic specialty, solid-state physics.

The IC lab, however, was far from universally popular on Coyote Hill, where it was viewed as a carpetbagging rival for money and head count. CSL trotted out the same arguments used against the VLSI program— that it was unnecessarily duplicative of work done by other companies that were in the *business* of making integrated circuits.

"Xerox didn't have any strategic need for integrated circuits research,"

Butler Lampson argued. "You could buy it perfectly well: That was the crux of the argument against it. There would be a very good chance that spending all this money would not only lead to no substantial payoff but would actually hurt you, because you would be attempting to do things internally that were better to do externally, and you'd end up with worse components. Meanwhile it seemed obvious to me that if we took that money and spent it on hiring more computing researchers we'd get a lot more mileage out of it."

The IC lab added a difficult new factor to Spinrad's struggle with the eternal question of how best to balance the resources of PARC. Almost from the start he found Taylor in his face, entreating his new boss as only he knew how. Taylor recalled: "I was making sure Spinrad was briefed and encouraged him to get briefed by others to decide how to allocate PARC's resources. I'd say to him, 'Do you think PARC's resources are allocated to the best benefit of the corporation?' He'd say, 'No,' and I'd say, 'I think you're right.'"

Spinrad did agree that computer science gave Xerox the best bang for the buck at PARC. But he disagreed that CSL should receive the lion's share of the budget at the expense of the Systems Science Lab, for he was quite taken by some of programs Sutherland had undertaken as head of SSL. "Some of those projects were beginning to probe the edges of important things about user interfaces and social systems," Spinrad recalled. "Studies of the applications of the systems in offices. The ethics and etiquette of e-mail. Some didn't work out and some did, but I felt it was important. Taylor's lab was narrowly hard sciences and unambiguous results and measurable performance and communications reliability, and it didn't get into what clearly was the important area: How the hell are you going to use this stuff?"

Nevertheless, he did share Taylor's general opinion that the physics labs had been overfunded. Perhaps failing to recognize that virtually since the day of PARC's opening the physics lab had played the role in Pake's mind of a political counterweight to Bob Taylor, Spinrad in March 1980 took a step that forever marked him, unfairly or not, as Taylor's cat's-paw. This was his preparation for Pake of a five-year plan in which he proposed reallocating PARC's budget in favor of the computer labs (including SSL) and reducing the money spent on the General Science Lab.

"I figured if I had a zero-sum game"—that is, if PARC's budget were to remain static overall—"I was going to have to cut back slowly in some areas," he recalled. "It would not be sudden, but some people's oxen were going to get gored more than others. I was going to change the status quo."

Spinrad's plan violated PARC and Xerox orthodoxy in at least one important respect. Xerox's corporate culture always treated budget cuts as burdens to be shared equally by every cell of the organism. If a 10 percent cut was indicated, every division and branch office took a 10 percent cut whether it was a marginal contributor to the company or an indispensable cog in the machine. "I was probably the first one not to be egalitarian about cuts," Spinrad recalled. "I had prejudices, and I thought one of the few roles management has is to make choices and judgments."

But inside PARC many people found it hard to distinguish Spinrad's prejudices from Bob Taylor's. "Spinrad succumbed to Taylor's unrelenting pressure," was Harold Hall's judgment. Pake agreed. "My perception was that Taylor, being in complete ascendancy in the political jockeying between the two labs, enlisted Spinrad." That the reallocation plan took direct aim at the physicists in Pake's pet laboratory—and Taylor's *bête noire*—only reinforced that impression. Pake had spent ten years defending the General Science Lab from Taylor's carping. He was not about to sit by and let it be gutted now.

Pake viewed the situation even more urgently because he harbored growing doubts about Spinrad's overall performance. For several months he had been fielding complaints from within the research center about Taylor's ambitions—complaints that would never have reached him if Spinrad had kept Taylor on a properly short leash. Moreover, he believed Spinrad had deliberately dragged his feet in recruiting a director for the new integrated circuits lab, which consequently had not yet gotten off the ground.

On March 21 Pake summoned Hall to his office and, clearly anguished, outlined his concerns along with what he called a "really zany solution."

"Maybe I can split the center in two parts," he told Hall. "That might solve the problem."

Specifically, he would divide PARC into two independent research centers, manifestly configured to keep Taylor isolated. One, the "Science Center," would comprise SSL, GSL, and the new IC lab and be headed by Hall. Spinrad would retain jurisdiction over the "System Center," which was limited to CSL and the Optical Science Lab.

Hall assented to return to line management. Within hours after Pake first broached it, the change was official. "I suppose if I had been a scientist when this was happening I wouldn't have known what was going on," Pake acknowledged later, "because all of a sudden everyone gets this memo through the internal mail saying PARC is now two PARCs."

In truth, everyone at PARC regarded the arrangement of two research centers sharing the same building—and in some cases the same floor— as unsustainable over the long term. But Pake could see no other solution to the dual problems of Taylor's imperialism and the stalled progress on the IC lab. Spinrad, philosophical as ever, accepted the rebuff complaisantly. But he was clearly chastened, and within a year accepted a reassignment back to the corporate staff.

Meanwhile Hall assumed responsibility for recruiting a chief for the integrated circuits lab. After several months he was convinced he finally had his man: a physicist from the University of Kansas named William J. Spencer.

The physically imposing Spencer's academic credentials were less than sterling—before taking his Ph.D. from Kansas he had gotten his bachelor's degree in physical education—but at the age of fifty-six his professional career was distinguished by management posts at Bell Labs and the Sandia and Lawrence Livermore national laboratories. Although Spencer had been Hall's third choice for the job (the two other candidates had turned him down), he felt better about his find as time went on. Heading the IC lab, he thought, would only be the start of things for Bill Spencer. As he reported to Pake, "When he's ready for the big job I'll let you know, but I can't help thinking that I've hired not only my successor, but yours."

Meanwhile, the pressure of the outside world was being felt more and more inside PARC. "The only problem with PARC was a law of physics," Charles Simonyi observed. "A star that bright eventually has to blow up."

Simonyi began to sense the impending supernova in 1980. One day that fall he found himself wandering the hallways of Xerox headquarters in Stamford, having his lowest expectations confirmed. The disparity between the opulence of his surroundings and the paltriness of the brain-power housed therein beggared the imagination. He felt wholly irrele-vant, like a wayward tourist rather than an employee being interviewed for a corporate staff position.

Simonyi had been inveigled into making this trip by Jerry Elkind, who sensed that the Advanced Systems Division was losing its charm for his young subordinate. He was right. The excitement Simonyi had savored in getting Altos out to the world had worn thin. With BravoX nearing com-pletion he was unsure of his next step, especially given the absence of any sign that Xerox meant to follow up ASD's market probes with a full-scale merchandising program.

He had only grown more restive when a friend showed him an Apple II running VisiCalc. The spreadsheet program was new to him but daz-zling in its power. One typed numbers or formulas into the cells of a grid and linked them, so the answer from one cell could be part of the formula of another. This allowed anyone to tabulate data in an infinite number of permutations. It was particularly valuable for businessmen and engi-neers, who could perform "what-if" analyses simply by altering a figure here or there and letting the grid automatically calculate the myriad ram-ifications of the change. Sure enough, within months VisiCalc had trans-formed the Apple II into a commercial sensation.

By contrast, at PARC, where funds had flowed so limitlessly that no one ever felt the urge to run "what-if" budget scenarios, the spreadsheet idea had not even occurred to the greatest software engineers in the world. What Simonyi found even more depressing was that VisiCalc was simple, intuitive, and fast—all the qualities he and his colleagues had strived for in their work over the past decade.

"That alarmed me a lot, how good it was," he remembered. "They were using even fewer cycles than the Alto to run it on the Apple II, way fewer."

Like Larry Tesler, Simonyi had discovered the power of low-end computing. Until the day he saw VisiCalc on the Apple II he too had dismissed the hobbyist machines as a joke, as absurd in their triviality as the Star was in its bloat. Now he recognized in them a future that PARC had missed.

As a guide to the new world Simonyi turned to his former SDD boss, Bob Metcalfe, who was heading his own startup, an Ethernet equipment maker named 3Com Corporation headquartered in Santa Clara, a few miles south of Palo Alto.

Metcalfe rather relished the role of trailblazer for his old PARC and SDD colleagues ("I was the one who had gone out into the world and didn't die," he observed). He invited Simonyi to lunch, and over appetizers handed him a list of ten young entrepreneurs who he thought had a chance of propelling the computer industry toward its exciting future and who might make good use of Simonyi's talents. The first name on the list was someone Metcalfe described as "a crazy guy," which in Simonyi's eyes bathed him with a perverse appeal. His name was Bill Gates. Simonyi would never meet any of the others.

A few weeks following that lunch, Simonyi happened to be overseeing the installation of an Alto at the Seattle headquarters of Boeing, one of the VIP customers granted a shipment of ASD machines. On his last afternoon in town he dropped in on Gates's little company. Microsoft's thirty or so employees occupied half of the eighth floor of the Old National Bank building in Bellevue, just across Lake Washington from the city of Seattle.

Carrying a portfolio of his work, Simonyi entered Suite 819 relaxed and confident, thanks to his mistaken impression that Metcalfe had already called to smooth the way. In fact, he was an unexpected visitor. Bill Gates being tied up at the moment with a delegation from a Japanese manufacturing company, Simonyi was escorted instead into the office of Steve Ballmer, a friend of Gates's from Harvard. Unlike Gates, Ballmer had stayed at Harvard to graduate, after which he signed on to be Microsoft's maniacal chief salesman and hyper-motivational troop leader.

"I projected supreme confidence and everything," Simonyi recalled. "I had a great portfolio and so Ballmer was incredibly impressed." This was an understatement. After a few minutes Ballmer bounced out of his chair, exclaiming, "Bill has to see this!" He dragged Gates out of his meeting and badgered him into thumbing through the portfolio until it was time for Simonyi to catch his flight home. Gates offered him a ride back to the airport.

"We were going in the car and walking up to the gate together," Simonyi said, "and then and there pretty much decided our whole futures. It was amazing. Bill was like twenty-two, looking seventeen. I was thirty-two. The bandwidth we had and the energy just flowing from him was incredible. In a five-minute conversation we could see twenty years into the future."

First, however, he had to resolve the issue of the corporate job in Stamford. Simonyi agreed to make the exploratory trip back East more as a courtesy to Elkind than any other reason. His one visit to Bellevue had already told him that there was infinitely more opportunity outside Xerox than in some "technology staff puke job" in Stamford, Connecticut. "I wasn't unhappy to go. I thought it would be a nice trip. Though I knew there wasn't a chance in hell."

Had he been wavering, his interviews with the staff planning executives would have decided the issue. "Here's Stamford, they had a wing of the building just for these six executives and they're sitting like a Politburo behind two layers of secretaries in their chairs. You could see the bandwidth was minuscule. I was talking to my prospective employer and the guy didn't know what the hell he was talking about and he didn't even know that he didn't know. He knew he wanted some advice on technology and he pretty much knew what he wanted to hear and his questions didn't make sense. It's not that I didn't have the answers, it's that he didn't know enough to ask the right questions."

The contrast with Microsoft was sobering. "We are talking about a sunset industry and a sunrise industry. It was like going into the graveyard or retirement home before going into the maternity ward. I could smell it and feel it. You could see that Microsoft could do things one hundred times faster, literally, I'm not kidding. Six years from that point we overtook Xerox in market valuation."

Simonyi paid two more visits to Bellevue before the end of the year and brought Gates down to PARC once to show him the Alto. Since Gates had expressed an interest in Microsoft's entering the applications business, Simonyi obliged him by charting out a strategy to exploit every market: word processors, spreadsheets, e-mail, even voice recognition— everything PARC had worked on and several things it had not. Helpfully he prepared the document on BravoX and printed it on the SLOT. Form followed function: Gates could read the program and simultaneously absorb its tremendous graphic potential, laid out in a dizzying variety of typefaces and formats. As Simonyi said later, this was his way of becoming "the messenger RNA of the PARC virus."

On Christmas Eve Gates sent Simonyi a job offer by Federal Express. By February he was in place as Microsoft's director of advanced product development. Shortly thereafter Gates asked him, "Have you seen the Chess machine?"

Simonyi waved him off. "Bill, I'm really disappointed. I want to be in serious business. These chess computers are just a vogue. There's no money in them. We should be doing applications, serious stuff."

Gates shook his head. "Charles, you don't understand." He led Simonyi down a hallway toward a small enclosure and opened the door on two engineers working on a machine that in a few short months would alter the office computing market forever and show Xerox the path it had missed.

"Here it is," Gates said. "IBM is making a personal computer. Its code name is Chess."

CHAPTER 25

Blindsided

T hat the Systems Development Department (it was no longer simply a "division") was finally able to bring any product to market, much less the triumph of integrated system design known as the Star, must have struck some of its own employees as nothing short of miraculous.

The Star program's duration and complexity, the personal tensions within SDD, Xerox's ceaseless vacillation, and numerous other agonies had driven many engineers off the project long before it reached the promised land. Thacker abandoned ship to return to PARC. Simonyi left to sell Altos with Jerry Elkind. Bob Metcalfe quit in 1979 in search of the entrepreneurial main chance.

Even the machine's code name demonstrated SDD's need to clamor for Xerox management's attention. It had been coined by Bob Spinrad in the hope of lending the project some luster in the eyes of Dave Culbertson, a group executive to whom SDD then reported.

"Culbertson was a sailing enthusiast," David Liddle recalled, "so Spinrad decided to name it after a one-design sailing class." After considering "Lightning" and "Sunfish" they settled on "Star," which, as Liddle observed, "was a decent sailboat and a tolerable name for an office appliance."

Engineers both inside and outside SDD expressed frequent doubts about the department's course. At PARC, many computer engineers viewed the Star as Xerox's attempt to yoke their inventions to its fading office monopoly, to the former's disadvantage. Around mid-1980 Butler Lampson predicted to his SDD friends that they would never ship a product. "They had a system with a million lines of code in it built by a team of people hired off the street," he said. "The whole thing took four years, and in my experience any project that had those properties had another property, which is it wouldn't work. I predicted it wouldn't work and they wouldn't be able to ship it."

He was wrong. On April 27, 1981, at the National Computer Conference trade show in Chicago, SDD formally unveiled the Star as the Xerox 8010 Information System.

With its unique seventeen-inch bitmapped screen and graphical interface, the product was an instant sensation. Its full-dress demos every hour on the hour "had people overflowing into the aisles," recalled Charles Irby, a former Engelbart engineer who had been one of SDD's first recruits from outside PARC.

Irby was particularly amused to notice among the repeat visitors Larry Tesler, then at Apple, and his Lisa design team. "They'd watch every demo, then go off into a corner and talk about what they had seen," he recalled.

The Star's success attested to the pertinacity of David Liddle, who had managed to keep his mind and his organization focused through years of indifferent and even hostile treatment from the Stamford headquarters. Year by year SDD got kicked around the corporate organizational chart—now under the Information Technology Group, now under Xerox Business Systems—until, as Bob Belleville recalled, "We just stopped paying any attention to where we were."

In 1979 the division finally fetched up like a beached whale at the doors of the Office Products Division. This was the Dallas operation originally managed by the detested Bob Potter. But after Potter had moved to International Harvester with his patron, Archie McCardell, the division had come under the charge of an entrepreneurial firebrand.

Don Massaro had joined Xerox when it purchased Shugart Associates, a disk drive company he had co-founded. Brash, risk-oriented, abrasive, and persuasive, he seemed a throwback to the glory days of Shelby Carter. For his divisional symbol he chose the Road Runner from the Warner Brothers cartoons, the better to taunt the Xerox "coyotes" he maintained were constantly out for his tail. "I had not spent twenty years of my life climbing the Xerox ladder rung by rung, playing according to the rules," he told an interviewer. "I was prepared to fail." When Dave Liddle flew down to Dallas to show him the Star software, he was jazzed. "I said, 'Fuck it! This is incredible technology and we're going to bring it to the marketplace!"

Talk like that was just what the weary engineers of SDD needed to shake off their torpor. Massaro was the first Xerox executive they had met who displayed any business acumen at all. He made snap decisions, moved fast, and had more confidence in his own judgment than the rest of the executive roster put together. Rallying behind his drumbeat—"I think we have another 914 on our hands," he crowed to *Business Week*—they redoubled their efforts to get the Star out the door.

Massaro also contributed some desperately needed rationality to Xerox's treatment of PARC technology, much of which had been kept under wraps as though by reflex without any consideration given to how best to exploit it. For example, the company had long insisted that Ethernet be kept secret in case it chose someday to market the network as a proprietary product.

"But how would the Xerox Corporation make any money by proprietarily pulling coaxial cable?" as Liddle asked rhetorically. He, Massaro, and Metcalfe proposed an alternative. If other electronics companies could be persuaded to adopt Ethernet as an industry standard, Xerox could profit from what was sure to be an exploding market for the peripherals that were already part of its product line, like laser printers. This would also break IBM's stranglehold on the networkable equipment market, which it maintained by promoting its inferior "token ring" network—a system that, once installed, compelled users to buy only IBM-made peripherals.

This argument finally prevailed in Stamford, which in 1979 granted

Massaro and Liddle approval to make Ethernet public by enlisting Intel and Digital Equipment Corporation in the effort to turn it from an experimental system into one of commercially viable robustness. The new industrial-strength specifications were published in 1980 as the joint Xerox-Intel-DEC Ethernet standard. Xerox's liberal licensing rules, which allowed any company to manufacture Ethernet cards, cables, transceivers, and peripherals after paying of a one-time $1,000 license fee pledging to support the standard as written, turned Ethernet into the most widely used local networking technology in the world.

Don Massaro's enthusiasm for the work of SDD was requited by the ultimate product. The Star workstation he shepherded to launch was an amazing accomplishment. Enclosed in a squat beige-colored box which, like its ancestral Alto, slid on casters under a desk, the machine came packed with features no one had ever seen before and few envisioned in a commercial office machine. These included a bitmapped screen (in "muted blue," as Xerox promotional literature described it at the time), a mouse ("an electronic pointing device"), windowed displays, and "What You See Is What You Get" document preparation. The bundled functions included text processing, a drawing program, the first integrated "help" program, and electronic mail.

By far the system's most striking feature was its graphical user interface, the stylized display that communicated with the user via the bitmapped screen. This arrangement of icons and folders built around what the Star designers called the "desktop metaphor" is so familiar today that it seems to have been a part of computing forever. But its pioneering implementation on the Star included some capabilities that had yet to resurface on the market nearly two decades later. Text, formulas, and graphics could all be edited in the same document. (Compare today's "integrated" software, in which a drawing imported into a text document can no longer be altered, but must be changed in the original graphics program and reintroduced into the text document.) Out of the box the Star was multilingual, offering typefaces and keyboard configurations that could be implemented in the blink of an eye for writing in Russian, French, Spanish, and Swedish through the use of "virtual keyboards"—graphic representations of keyboards that appeared on screen to show the user where to find the unique characters in whatever language he or she was using. In 1982 an internal library of 6,000 Japanese *kanji* characters was added; eventually Star users were able to draft documents in almost every modern language, from Arabic and Bengali to Amharic and Cambodian.

As the term implied, the user's view of the screen resembled the surface of a desk. Thumbnail-sized icons representing documents were lined up on one side of the screen and those representing peripheral devices—printers, file servers, e-mail boxes—on the other. The display image could be infinitely personalized to be tidy or cluttered, obsessively organized or hopelessly confused, alphabetized or random, as dictated by the user's personality and taste. The icons themselves had been painstakingly drafted and redrafted so they would be instantaneously recognized by the user as document pages (with a distinctive dog-eared upper right corner), file folders, in and out baskets, a clock, and a wastebasket. Thanks to the system's object-oriented software, the Star's user could launch any application simply by clicking on the pertinent icon; the machine automatically "knew" that a text document required it to launch a text editor or a drawing to launch a graphics program. No system has ever equaled the consistency of the Star's set of generic commands, in which "move," "copy," and "delete" performed similar operations across the entire spectrum of software applications.

The Star was the epitome of PARC's user-friendly machine. No secretary had to learn about programming or code to use the machine, any more than she had to understand the servomechanism driving the dancing golf ball to type on an IBM Selectric typewriter. Changing a font, or a margin, or the space between typed lines in most cases required a keystroke or two or a couple of intuitive mouse clicks. The user understood what was happening entirely from watching the icons or documents move or change on the screen. This was no accident: "When everything in a computer system is visible on the screen," wrote David Smith, a designer of the Star interface, "the display becomes reality. Objects and actions can be understood purely in terms of their effects on the display."

What was even more remarkable was that much of this was accomplished over the objections of Xerox marketing experts, whose kibitzing about even trivial matters slowed the development process by months. Irby recalled a particularly trying confrontation over the mouse with a marketing man from the Dallas division named Ron Johnson.

"The first time he'd ever used a mouse he'd had a bad experience— apparently he'd used a dirty one that didn't track right," Irby said. "So for two years he was against our using it, while we spent all our time on user studies and tests to show him it was the right thing. We spent at least $1 million of Xerox resources proving that it was better than a cursor button or touch screen, which is what he wanted. Finally we presented all these findings to him at a meeting—and he still wouldn't go for it!

"That was one of the very few times when I totally exploded. I got out of my chair and towered over him and yelled about what an idiot he was being. I screamed, 'We're going to use the mouse, goddamn it!' and walked out. We never got a complaint from him again."

Had the Star performed up to the level of its dazzling first impression, Xerox might have been able to to establish and hold that beachhead in office computing craved by dozens of executives ranging from Jim O'Neill to David Liddle.

But the glow faded fast.

The first shortcoming users noticed was its speed. The elaborate system ran, as one of its designers acknowledged, "like molasses." While the Dandelion processor was a marked improvement over Thacker's Dolphin, it was still overwhelmed by the pure tonnage of a million lines of heavy-duty Mesa code running under the surface. "The Star software was built to consume all available computing resources in the universe," cracked Smokey Wallace, an SDD engineer.

Another hurdle was its cost. The Star workstation reached the market at a retail price of $16,595. This might have made sense for equipment aimed at a high-performance engineering market. But it was far more than most commercial businesses would spend to furnish a secretary or clerical worker with capital equipment. Furthermore, nobody could buy just one Star workstation any more than one can eat just one potato chip. A meaningful installation required two to ten workstations, plus a high-speed laser printer and Ethernet to link it all together. That raised the per-user cost to at least $30,000 and the price of the whole integrated system to a quarter of a million dollars or more. Some experts forecast that the Star would not sell until Xerox reeducated its customers to use it properly and made it cheaper. "It's a good product," one said, "for the second half of the 1980s."

Within a few months of its launch the Star began to look like an egregious marketing blunder. It was the old story of engineers building a system that only engineers could love—except that instead of building one too complicated for average users, SDD had built one too big.

It seemed as though SDD as an organization had been driven by designers lacking any counterweight of sales and marketing professionals. As Lampson observed later, "It was kind of amazing that this company whose biggest single strength was marketing set up an organization composed entirely of engineers to get them into a whole new line of business."

In truth, SDD did have marketing advice. The problem was that, possibly for the first time in Xerox history, the marketing experts were so overawed by the system they were examining that they were themselves swept up in the engineers' enthusiasm.

The upshot was a series of surveys known internally as the "Wave" studies, on which the company spent hundreds of thousands of dollars to analyze its customer base. Undertaken during Spinrad's stewardship of SDD, well before the division priced and launched the Star, the Wave studies compiled data from telephone and face-to-face interviews with decision-makers at nearly 100 companies, as well as on-site surveys at another fifteen businesses that lasted several weeks each, into a shelf full of thick loose-leaf binders.

Wave concluded that the Star was so good and latent demand so strong that customers would clamor for the technology regardless of price. To the monopoly-minded executives of Xerox, this was familiar and gratifying territory. A machine that could be sold or leased for any price—it was the 914 all over again!

The SDD engineers therefore considered themselves free to create absolutely the best office system they could imagine. Blinded by the almost religious fervor that seizes software and hardware developers set loose in a boundless design space, they shoveled every sophisticated function they could contrive into the Star without giving a moment's thought to the one real-world player whose opinion was critical: the buyer.

"The techies were given their head to make the best system they could," Spinrad lamented years later. "There were no constraints of any substance put on us as to the cost of the product, as far as I remember. But what the Wave studies missed was that there were other things coming along they didn't recognize."

This was an understatement. In 1975, or even 1979, one might have argued that the Star's technology would place it in a class by itself, that it would blow away every other office machine on the market on its way to becoming an instant *de facto* standard. In 1981 the same argument was dangerously presumptuous. For at a secret skunk works in Boca Raton, a couple of miles from where Xerox had held its spectacular company picnic, an IBM team had slapped together a machine that would annihilate the market for big, integrated office systems.

IBM launched its Chess machine, renamed simply the Personal Computer, in August 1981, a scant four months after the Star. Judged against the technology PARC had brought forth, it was a homely and feeble creature. Rather than bitmapped graphics and variable typefaces, its screen displayed only ASCII characters, glowing a hideous monochromatic green against a black background. Instead of a mouse, the PC had four arrow keys on the keyboard that laboriously moved the cursor, character by character and line by line. No icons, no desktop metaphor, no multitasking windows, no e-mail, no Ethernet. Forswearing the Star's intuitive point-and-click operability, IBM forced its customers to master an abstruse lexicon of typed commands and cryptic responses developed by Microsoft, its software partner. Where the Star was a masterpiece of integrated reliability, the PC had a perverse tendency to crash at random (a character flaw it bequeathed to many subsequent generations of Microsoft Windows-driven machines).

But where the Star sold for $16,595-plus, the IBM PC sold for less than $5,000, all-inclusive. Where the Star's operating system was closed, accessible for enhancement only to those to whom Xerox granted a coded key, the PC's circuitry and microcode were wide open to anyone willing to hack a program for it—just like the Alto's.

And it sold in the millions.

The introduction of the IBM PC changed the business computer market the way Hiroshima changed the world's conception of battlefield weaponry. The PC demonstrated that the business user would gladly forego graphical bells and whistles and seamless system integration and would tolerate a large dose of flakiness in order to save on price. IBM proved correct everyone who had warned that the Star was too big, too complicated, too expensive—too good.

How serious a blow the IBM PC represented to large-scale systems like the Star would become increasingly evident over the next year, as the Star's sales lagged behind Xerox's projections and the PC's surpassed IBM's.

The Star was to enjoy just one more moment of triumph. In December 1981 the Japanese version was introduced at the Tokyo Data Show by Fuji Xerox, the company's Japanese partner, with Liddle in attendance along with Bill English and his engineering partner Joe Becker, who had created the Japanese display system. The price was 4 million yen per workstation, or about $16,000. The acclaim was even greater than its domestic cousin had received in Chicago eight months earlier.

"The presentation aimed at the most dramatic effect; it seemed to disembowel the other exhibitors," wrote the correspondent of the Japanese computer journal *ASCII*. "Comparing Star with Japanese computer makers' office computers in the 4-million-yen class, their capabilities are as different as clouds from mud."

Clouds from mud? Upon hearing the phrase from a Japanese interpreter reading the review aloud, Dave Liddle burst out with a delighted laugh. "Boy," he said, "you can't do any better than that!"

The exodus from SDD picked up steam after the Star introduction. One day Bob Belleville got a call from Steve Jobs, who badgered him into quitting by yelling, "Everything you've ever done in your life is terrible, so why don't you come work for me?" Massaro and Liddle left in 1982 to found Metaphor Computer. Metaphor soon brought out a workstation that resembled the Star on the surface, but ran on a lightning-fast Motorola 68000 microprocessor, the same one that would soon turn up as the heart and brain of the Apple Macintosh. A dimly remembered name now, Metaphor experienced great success for more than five years, until it was bought out and its nameplate retired—by IBM.

As for the Star, it lived on for many years as the crowning glory of a niche market, a specialty product and a legend, somewhat like the fancy futuristic cars—time machines, so to speak—which Detroit auto makers manufacture for the big car shows but seldom actually get on the road. Instead of sales in the hundreds of thousands, as Xerox once dared anticipate, only about 30,000 Stars were ever ordered.

By 1989 the architecture that Liddle once foresaw lasting ten years was already a relic. That year *Computer* magazine published an article by several of the machine's original designers entitled, "The Xerox Star: A Retrospective." Among its features was a roll call of lessons the team had learned from bitter experience: "Pay attention to industry trends. . . . Pay attention to what customers want . . . Know your competition."

Blinded by their own technology, the Star's designers had been almost entirely unaware of the coming revolution of cheap PCs—the equivalent of scaled-down Altos, as opposed to the scaled-up Star. They did not see it coming until the moment IBM announced its blockbuster. At that point it was too late.

"It was a disaster beyond words," Belleville said later, "because the world was already different."

CHAPTER 26

Exit the Impresario

Bill Spencer's introduction to PARC was jolly enough. On the day he assumed leadership of the Integrated Circuits Lab, his new colleagues welcomed him with a green cake: It was St. Patrick's Day 1981.

But the charm rapidly paled. As he got to know the place better, he grew appalled at the working atmosphere at 3333 Coyote Hill Road. The lab that a few short years before had been the most exciting research venue in the country, if not the world, now appeared to be in the grip of some malignant virus. Whole departments shunned each other, except to fight over resources and belittle each other's work. Everywhere you looked you found people harboring mysterious grudges and grotesque suspicions.

The most routine personal transactions were like minefields. Not long after his arrival Spencer, believing that he ought to be in touch with his "customers"—that is, the other labs at PARC that would be using his chips—sent out an e-mail message inviting several lab chiefs to a friendly meeting to toss around ideas. Everyone accepted.

A few days later Bob Taylor graciously offered the Computer Science Lab commons as a venue for the get-together. A gratified

Spencer sent out another round of messages informing his guests of the new location. The next few hours brought a cascade of cancellations.

Bewildered, he picked up the phone and dialed Lynn Conway, the first respondent.

"What's going on?" he asked. "Why aren't you coming?"

"It's CSL," she responded. "I'd be physically assaulted if I went in there."

"That's ridiculous!"

"Think what you want," she replied simply. "But I won't set foot in that lab." The meeting never took place.

The more Spencer investigated, the grimmer he found the situation. Pake's strategy of isolating Taylor by sundering PARC in two had exacerbated the schism, not resolved it. "At every staff meeting power grabs and disputes over resources dominated the discussion," he observed. "Computer resources, office space, budget—you name it, they fought over it. It was so acrimonious and divisive that the center had ground to a halt while people spent all their time defending their turf."

The contention was general, but Taylor appeared to stand at its center. His claims on PARC's resources, based on his presumption that any work done outside his lab was scarcely worth doing at all, forced the others to dig in against any change that threatened even tangentially to shift the balance of power. Further roiling the atmosphere were rumors that he was shopping the Computer Science Lab as a wholesale package to a Xerox competitor (speculation focused on Hewlett-Packard, which was building a research center on a Palo Alto hillside just over the ridge from Coyote Hill). Taylor always steadfastly denied the story, but the suspicion never entirely waned.

Yet to blame Taylor entirely for the dysfunctional atmosphere would be unjust. To a certain extent the internal conflicts grew out of the ineluctable life cycle of a creative institution. In one form or another the same tension had been present almost since PARC's founding; for most of the first decade it simply had been channeled more fruitfully.

"Up until 1977 or so the lab conflicts seemed more dynamic and actually productive in stimulating healthy competitiveness and innovation," Lynn Conway observed. As projects matured, people moved on, and outside organizations assumed the exciting work of bringing PARC's innovations to market, there was less of substance to fight about within the walls. And as is known to veterans of all intramural politics—whether they take place on a university campus or inside a corporation—the less at stake, the more vicious the battle.

At PARC the excitement had faded but the pressure cooker remained. The internecine competition took on a reflexive quality, as though people were going through the motions. Severo Ornstein recalled a telling incident soon after CSL spun off its graphics programs into a separate lab under Chuck Geschke and John Warnock. "These were guys we had worked very cohesively with," Ornstein recalled. "But not two weeks later I heard someone in the hallway refer to them as 'they.' Chuckling, I thought, 'This is how wars start.'"

Xerox's indifference to PARC's work also deserves some of the blame for nursing these unproductive conflicts. Futures Day had underscored how divergent were the vectors between parent and offspring. More depressing miscues followed, such as the clash of expectations over "Interpress."

Interpress was a programming system that aimed to reconcile the different image resolutions of computer screens and laser printers. This difference often resulted in documents that looked perfect on an Alto display, but emerged as gibberish on the higher-resolution printers—which of course made a mockery of Bravo's WYSIWYG feature. After years of painstaking work and several intermediate versions, Geschke, Warnock, Bob Sproull, Lampson, and others had at last invented a so-called page description language allowing printers of any type to output a document that accurately reproduced its on-screen representation, regardless of the incompatibilities between display and laser. But the difficulty of persuading Xerox to integrate Interpress into its laser printers and other typographical products made the process of actual invention look like a cakewalk.

"We spent months traveling around to all the divisions within Xerox and back to corporate selling this idea," Warnock recalled. The program was extensively rewritten to meet objections by the various divisions.

Finally, in 1982, the company agreed to make Interpress a standard component of its entire program line—but refused to announce or release it until every product could be reengineered to take advantage of it. The upshot would be an unendurable delay.

"I knew that would take at least five to ten years, and really it was just never going to happen," Warnock recalled. "Chuck Geschke and I had a conversation in his office and said, 'You know, we need to go do something else, because we've spent two years of our lives trying to sell this thing and they're going to put it under a black shroud for another five.' You were seeing PCs get announced, and Apples, and you kept asking yourself, 'When is all this great stuff going to see the light of day?' And you'd think about the Xerox infrastructure and the process it would have to go through to get into products, and it became sort of depressing."

A short time later he and Geschke resigned to start their own company, Adobe Systems. After a couple of false starts they settled on a business plan that would ultimately turn Adobe into a $1-billion-a-year enterprise: the refining and marketing of a new "typesetting," or page description, language, along the lines initially developed in Interpress. This language was Postscript, a typesetting system first bundled with Apple printers. Postscript allowed computer-generated documents to be printed on laser printers, linotype machines, and virtually everything in between. In its later versions it proved able to handle graphics and color with amazing fidelity. Within a few short years it became the *de facto* standard of computerized typesetting, and a dominating rival of Interpress itself—yet another technology that broke free from cloistered PARC to flourish on the outside.

Thus conflicts that might have been channeled into helping a new product reach market got turned inward instead. But Spencer, who arrived at a point when PARC's most impressive achievements were already behind it, had not lived through these battles with the corporate mindset. He found it difficult to view the internecine tensions as anything other than childish squabbling. In any case, none of the quarreling had been resolved by late 1982, when George Pake asked him to succeed Hall as head of the half-PARC "Science Center."

To Pake's surprise, Spencer turned him down. The bifurcation of PARC was untenable, he said, and he would not be interested in managing one half of a house divided against itself. He did, however, offer to step in as PARC director—if and when Pake saw fit to reunite the two halves.

Pake agreed without hesitation, even with relief. He had found it painful to watch the bickering continue even after the partition. Moreover, he admired Spencer not only for his skills as a technical administrator but for his apparent ability to co-exist with Bob Taylor. Spencer and Taylor played tennis together every Saturday, their wives and children were friendly, yet Pake could see no sign that Spencer had bought into the CSL orthodoxy. He dared hope that after more than ten years he had finally found the one man on Earth who could keep Taylor in his place.

There was much about Taylor that Bill Spencer respected. In all his years in research he had met few managers so adept at running small or medium-sized teams. Taylor's method of forging personal bonds and keeping up a jealous defense of his own role as laboratory autocrat was one Spencer thought would fail miserably in a large lab. But there was no denying it worked marvelously inside CSL.

"He never traveled," Spencer recalled. "He would come in every day at ten in the morning, park his BMW in the same space every day, and pick up his badge from the security guard. He would go in his office, break out a Dr Pepper, and for the next eight to ten hours individually touch every member of his lab. As a consensus manager he was extraordinary."

Professional problems, personal crises, interpersonal spats—whatever the issue—Taylor's people came to Taylor. "Bob's office was like the hub of a wheel. Through the day each of them would come in there. The question could be anything. 'Can I go to the bathroom?' 'Is it time for me to go to lunch?'"

One day Spencer witnessed an incident that seemed to sum it all up. He was sitting and chatting in Taylor's office when a member of the CSL staff poked his head in to mention that he was going out for a game of tennis. As Spencer recalled, "Taylor said, 'I see you've got a new can of balls there. You're not good enough yet to play with new balls. Here's a can of old ones. Use these, they'll be better for you.'

"Now, here's a thirty-five or forty-year-old man, a Ph.D., and he needs Bob Taylor to tell him how he's going to play tennis!"

After Spencer became PARC director the troublesome consequences of Taylor's all-encompassing paternalism got driven home. One of the most serious problems he faced was CSL's inability to resolve its members' disputes with the other labs, no matter how trivial. As he settled into his new office, Spencer started to bridle at the amount of time he spent mediating quarrels that should have been settled further down the line. "Whenever a CSL guy had a problem with anyone else there was no one he could take it to but Taylor, and Taylor would never deal with it. So every time there was a problem it ended up in my office. And I said, 'This is not a workable situation. I will not solve the problems of fifty individuals in that lab.'"

He also recognized more strongly than ever the other deficiencies in Taylor's management style. Taylor's vaunted "flat" management structure, which meant that every researcher in the Computer Science Lab reported to him rather than to an intermediate level of management, had outlived its usefulness. In the old days it had served the purpose of ensuring that all the researchers pulled together in pursuit of a coherent vision (with the exception of renegades like Shoup and Bobrow). But it had also stifled creativity and—more important from the point of view of PARC management—prevented the center from spotting and nurturing management talent among the CSL staff. If any of the researchers possessed the skills to be the next Bob Taylor, no one would ever find out.

Meanwhile Taylor, still viewing Spencer as a potential ally, strived to draw him into his own vision of PARC, which was as a research center devoted entirely to personal computing, free of the dead weight of a physics lab. Shortly after Spencer's promotion to head of PARC, Taylor asked him along to CSL's annual Greybeard offsite at the Bear Hollow resort north of San Francisco.

"We invited Spencer so we could tell him how the resource allocation should be reorganized," Taylor said—in other words, to repeat the case he had made to the ill-fated Bob Spinrad. "Everybody there complained to him about the investment imbalance." The wary Spencer, however, thought the plan sounded like a blueprint for giving Taylor control of both CSL and SSL, something he was not about to do. He sat through the discussion noncommittally. Later, after they had all returned home, Taylor talked as though he thought the group had made its case to the new director. Ed McCreight disabused him of the notion at once. "Spencer listened," he cautioned, "but don't get it into your head that he agreed."

On the contrary, relations between these two strong-willed individuals were destined to build rapidly toward a crisis.

Twenty years of experience as a laboratory manager had given Spencer very firm ideas about the obligation of researchers to help their employers turn their work into product—"technology transfer," as it was known in industry. On this task he judged that much of PARC, and particularly CSL, deserved a failing grade. Henceforth, he decreed, fifty percent of the lab bosses' annual evaluations would be based on how well they worked with their "customers"—i.e., the development and manufacturing units of Xerox.

Taylor's response was, perversely, to step up his demand for new resources. If Spencer wanted this sort of additional contribution out of CSL, he said, he would need more "billets"—in other words, more staff openings. Spencer was astonished. The issue of staffing and budgets was exceptionally sensitive at Xerox, given that the company's financially desperate situation had already led to layoffs in its 125,000-strong workforce. "The fact that the research budgets weren't *cut* was amazing," Spencer said. "In 1981 Xerox hit a wall and by 1982 it was in serious trouble. That year there was no profit-sharing for employees for the first time in company history. The place was being torn apart."

In contrast to Pake, who dealt with Taylor largely through avoidance, Spencer was not one to suffer defiance mutely or let an affront go unremarked. He liked to give as good as he got: Upon his departure from one job his peers had presented him with a giant mock hypodermic, a testament to his penchant for "needling" others. When Taylor pushed, Spencer pushed back harder, dictating more and more explicitly how he expected Taylor to manage his lab. Taylor, the old expert at defining his role in the hierarchy, had finally met someone insistent on defining his role for him.

"Taylor is spiraling out of control," Harold Hall observed to his diary on June 28 from the secure perch of a corporate staff job. The CSL staff watched apprehensively as the initial friendliness between Taylor and Spencer deteriorated into outright animosity—the tennis Saturdays were a thing of the past. Butler Lampson, who had become one of the world's first networked "telecommuters" by moving to Philadelphia, where his wife was working as an immunologist, viewed the situation gravely enough to fly to Palo Alto to beg Pake to avert the impending cataclysm. But Pake, toughened perhaps by having Spencer around as spear carrier, proved unexpectedly determined.

"His position boiled down to that Taylor was too much a pain in the butt," Lampson recalled. "And it's true that Bob was a pain in the butt, absolutely no question about it. But he wasn't actually causing George that much trouble. It's ridiculous to say the functioning of the whole research center was being disrupted. What was really happening was these guys just got on some kind of power trip. They had to have control over Bob."

This is too limited a view. Pake regarded Taylor's behavior not merely as a personal tribulation, but as a roadblock preventing PARC from fulfilling its corporate destiny. As much as the laser printer represented a commercially valuable technology, Pake thought that only by persuading the company to link it with other PARC digital technologies could the lab help Xerox claim a piece of the future of digital electronic copying.

"That meant I needed to foster good relations between PARC and the development and engineering units of the copier division," he said later. "Having a group of computer scientists, including their manager, who scoffed at and derided the copier engineers in Rochester did not help PARC develop such good relations." Under Bert Sutherland the System Science Lab had forged a suitably collegial working alliance with the copier division. Pake's alarm at Spinrad's five-year plan had sprouted in part from the thought of how swiftly those friendly ties would be obliterated if Taylor were allowed to take over SSL.

Which is not to deny that Pake also had become deeply distrustful of Taylor's powerful personal influence over his researchers' souls. "I saw Taylor's relationship to his lab members as analogous to Jim Jones and the Jonestown cult," was his remarkable recollection. This impression must have been reinforced, if not inspired, by one senior researcher's explanation for why he had turned down a chance to work with Taylor's lab. "George," the researcher told Pake, "I wouldn't be willing to drink the Kool-Aid."

"We understood very well Taylor's relationship to his lab members," Pake said later. "What we did not understand was what to do about it."

Meanwhile, it fell to Spencer to get everyone on Coyote Hill working together in an atmosphere of mutual civility. That August, in a desperate attempt to ease the rancor among his lab chiefs, he convened his own offsite at Pajaro Dunes. There, in the same setting where Alan Kay's group had regularly repaired to contemplate the digital future, the senior lab managers of Xerox PARC flayed each other in an emotional showdown. Until two or three in the morning they vented their feelings like patients in gestalt therapy. "People let their hair down to talk about what really were the problems at PARC," Spencer recalled. The debate seemed honest and heartfelt. As dawn was breaking over the dunes, he allowed himself to think that Taylor—the target of most of their complaints—had finally realized the error of his ways.

"Bob said, 'I've never heard any of this before,'" Spencer said. "'Nobody's ever told me what I did wrong. I'm sorry, I didn't know that I was doing these things. I'll change and it will never happen again.' Everybody thought, 'Wow! We've solved the problem. Now we can go back and start doing research.'"

But Taylor did not come away from the retreat with the same perspective. What he had chosen to hear was not a blanket condemnation of his personal behavior, only a rehashing of a few old incidents about which no one had ever directly complained to him before. On those terms he was perfectly willing to apologize for any inadvertent misunderstandings and let bygones be bygones.

In any case, the era of good feelings did not last long. The very next day Taylor showed up in Spencer's office. As Spencer recalls this encounter, Taylor all but disavowed every promise he had made. "Don't believe anything you heard last night," he said, leaving Spencer dumbfounded. "That isn't the way it's going to be."

Taylor recalls having a distinctly different agenda. He said he was merely anxious to set Spencer straight on some incidents in which he thought he had been cast unfairly as the villain. "I certainly did not tell him, 'Hey, I was just bullshitting when I said such and such.' "

Either way, it was obvious that the Pajaro Dunes bloodletting had not produced the catharsis Spencer had hoped for. Whatever Taylor thought of the recent confrontation, clearly he was not committed to improving his intramural relationships. Spencer was fed up. He was determined to lay down the law, in writing, and give Taylor a hard deadline to alter his behavior.

A few days later he summoned Taylor to his office for a formal reading out of his alleged violations of good corporate conduct. He ordered Taylor to end any contact he had with competing companies; to reorganize his lab into sections and create an intermediate level of management to supervise them; to stop denigrating the other PARC labs and their work; and, most humiliating, to report to Spencer's office every Monday at 9 A.M. to discuss his progress toward those goals.

Failure to fulfill those terms, Spencer said stiffly, could result in Taylor's termination. Then he sent Taylor away with a written memo reflecting what he had said, along with the injunction that the document was confidential and he was not to discuss its contents with anyone.

But for Taylor to leave his own people in the dark was unthinkable. Before the end of the day he called his closest advisors, including Thacker, Mitchell, and Ornstein, to his house in Palo Alto, where he handed Spencer's memo around. He appeared stunned and dejected, as though recognizing that the final act in his Xerox career was playing out.

"I don't know what's going to happen, but the handwriting's on the wall," he told them. He seemed to take particular umbrage at the injunction to cease seeking a deal with another company, an offense of which he insisted he was innocent. "That's like telling me to stop beating my wife," he said.

Spencer's memo prompted Taylor's supporters to stage another round of appeals to Pake, this time with explicit warnings that the upshot of forcing Taylor out would be wholesale resignations from CSL. "A whole bunch of people who were in a position to know went to them and very carefully explained what was going to happen if they did this," Lampson said. "And they didn't believe us, even though it was perfectly obvious that we were the source of knowledge on this subject because we were the people who were going to leave. They didn't believe us, or they didn't care."

Taylor himself figured there was only one avenue of appeal: directly to David Kearns. Spencer had already apprised Kearns, by now the Xerox CEO, of the impending storm by sending him a copy of the memo with the notation that he expected Kearns to back him up on the conditions therein. Otherwise one of them—Spencer or Taylor—would have to go "and he could choose which one." When Taylor asked for a meeting Kearns deputed his chief technical officer, Sandy Campbell, to mediate the quarrel.

Campbell called Spencer and Taylor to Stamford for a marathon parley aimed at resolving the battle "based on the principle," as Spencer put it, "of who had the bigger bladder." Convening in Campbell's office at eight-thirty in the morning, they aired their grievances without respite, fueled only by coffee and Dr Pepper. All the old issues took their turn on the stage: Taylor's arrogance, his demand for a disproportionate share of the budget, his failure to develop managerial talent on his staff. Spencer further suggested that Taylor by his intransigence had actually impeded technology transfer at Xerox.

"My response was that there was more technology transfer from CSL to SDD than ever in the history of computing," Taylor recalled, "because every tool SDD used they got from us."

"But SDD failed," Spencer said.

"That's not my fault," Taylor snapped back. "I was hired to produce the best technology I could. If the product group was not able to take advantage of our technology a lot of people are culpable, not me."

Finally Spencer accused Taylor of making his memo public in contravention of a direct order. By then it was two in the afternoon and they had been hard at it for more than five hours.

"Did you do that?" Campbell asked Taylor.

"Sure I did," Taylor replied breezily. And why not? "Could anyone be foolish enough to think that this guy was going to tell me to change the way I operated and I'm not going to explain that to the lab?" he remarked later. "That's stupid."

On that note, Campbell broke up the meeting. Taylor and Spencer shared a corporate car to New York's Kennedy Airport without exchanging a single word during the more-than-hour-long trip. On the commercial flight home that evening they sat far apart, silently preparing for the final confrontation.

Taylor had tipped the Greybeards in advance to his agenda when he summoned his lab the following Monday morning, September 19, to the beanbag room. The rest of CSL could only guess why Taylor had called Dealer for such an unusual day and hour. They listened in mounting consternation as the only boss many of them had ever known recapitulated the high points of his career, teary-eyed and emotional. Several of his points he had earlier made in a separate memo to Spencer, who was present.

"Most people spend a lifetime without opportunities for pioneering completely new ways of thinking about large collections of ideas," he said. "I have been fortunate to have been a leader in three: time-sharing; long-distance interactive networking; and personal distributed computing."

Under Spencer's uneasy gaze, Taylor proceeded to rehash the recent sequence of meetings and confrontations. Then came the fatal words.

"I want you all to know I've handed in my resignation," he said, and walked out.

A stunned hush descended on the room. Spencer unwisely took the floor and, as one participant later remembered, "tried to continue the meeting as though what had happened was routine and it was now time to move on to new business."

Instead the room exploded in fury, all of it aimed directly at him. "I have never watched a grown man be shat upon like that by forty people at once," said Severo Ornstein. "I almost felt sorry for him—except that I was so angry at him."

The desperate Spencer tried to hold his own against an audience with all the forbearance of a lynch mob. He argued that Taylor's departure need not represent a major shift in the way the lab was run or a change in their work, that it was a temporary blip soon to be overcome. No one was buying the line. Suddenly a stentorian voice rang out.

"This is *bullshit!*"

All heads swiveled to the source of the outburst. Chuck Thacker had risen to his feet. In the most precise terms an engineer's engineer could summon to his lips at that fervid moment, he informed Spencer that he had just committed the gravest mistake of his life. His eyes swept the room. He said he hoped what he was about to do would not be taken as a model or a hint to anyone else; it was a personal statement and he wished it to be viewed that way.

Then he said, "I resign," and followed Taylor out the door.

Spencer was dumbfounded. Taylor's resignation he was prepared for; Thacker's came out of nowhere. As the meeting erupted in further recriminations he lost what remained of his grip.

"What can I do to rectify this?" he asked aloud.

A voice from the back of the room, over by the whiteboards—he never learned whose it was—called out: "You can fucking *resign!*"

His jaw set, Spencer replied, "The company made this choice, not me." Shaken and humiliated, he departed.

"Spencer fired Taylor," Butler Lampson said later. "Taylor got fired, he didn't resign, no matter what you think happened technically. They created an environment within which he had to resign. They told him, you must do the following twelve things. Basically what it came down to was going into Bill Spencer's office every Monday morning to lick his boots."

Kearns, to his credit, granted the Greybeards' subsequent request for an emergency audience. Presumably he was aware of how Taylor's ouster had played in the computer science community, because he had been inundated with telegrams and letters from dozens of top academic researchers—as though Taylor's entire ARPA army had risen in protest. Nevertheless, as the commanding officer of a company locked in apocalyptic battle with the Japanese, his sympathy for the self-indulgent eggheads of PARC was necessarily restrained. He preferred to view the flap as the unfortunate result of an executive's ordering a subordinate quite properly to get with the program. If Taylor refused, he had to go.

For their part, the Greybeards were under no great illusion that Kearns would overrule Spencer. The very episode carried within itself its own irrevocability; as Ornstein reflected, a reinstated Taylor would have been "completely unmanageable." But having flown East on the principle that silence would only be worse, they went through with it.

Thus they spent a futile morning with Kearns and McColough, who was still chairman of the board. Ornstein found himself repeating in Kearns's ear, like a mantra, "This lab will be gone inside of six months." The third time, Kearns turned to him with a steely glare and said curtly: "I heard you."

"I came away thinking, he'll back his guys," Ornstein recalled.

The exodus did occur as they predicted, although not instantaneously. While Thacker left immediately to work with a startup company marketing a paging device he had invented, many other CSL staff members deferred their resignations until after the end of the year, when their bonuses, retirement credit, stock options, and other perks would vest for 1983.

But then the floodgates opened. "During that first couple of weeks in January there were like two or three resignations a day, because people had already done their looking around," Warren Teitelman remembered. "We would stand out in the halls afraid to read our e-mail, because it would only say, well, we lost two principal scientists and three senior scientists today."

There can be little doubt that Bob Taylor's bosses underestimated—and more critically, misunderstood—his relationship with his laboratory members. On an administrative level he had ceded the job of corporate politicking to Jerry Elkind; on a technical level he was vastly overshadowed by Butler Lampson (as was almost everyone else). But his role was always more subtle, and bound to seem different depending on whether it was viewed from within the lab or without. Taylor had created the very habitat that his engineers and scientists depended on to pursue their work. He was not only the buffer between them and the mundane concerns of corporate Xerox, but the indispensable lightning rod for all the complaints about their arrogance and elitism.

"Taylor sacrificed a lot of his career at Xerox so we wouldn't see a lot of the bullshit," Alan Kay remarked later. This sentiment was widely shared. It accounted for much of their loyalty to him (even among those with whom he had clashed), and even more for their fear that things would be immeasurably different once he was gone.

His resignation marked the passing of an era at PARC that some people believed, perhaps correctly, had run out its string anyway. To Spencer and Pake, Taylor was not merely the strident exponent of CSL privilege; he was the defender of a stultified regime.

"I knew there was a high risk we would lose people," Spencer recalled. "But by 1980 the research center had really come dead in the water. So you'd had this wonderful burst of imaginative things, a great burst of energy, and by that time it was dead. I had a feeling we were going backwards. Absolutely, the place needed a change.

"If I had had my choice I would not have chosen to lose all of those computer scientists. But in retrospect, it may have been a good thing."

Taylor meanwhile found a sponsor for a new lab. It was not Hewlett-Packard, as Pake and Spencer suspected, but Digital Equipment Corp., the maker of the PDP–10 minicomputer that had caused CSL's very first flap with Xerox so many long years before. "DEC called to ask if I would consult," Taylor said. "Then three of their real estate people showed up and asked: Where should we build the lab?"

Selecting a site near downtown Palo Alto, on the far side of the Stanford campus from PARC, Taylor ultimately attracted fifteen CSL staff, among them Thacker and Lampson, to the DEC Systems Research Center, Robert W. Taylor, director. The emigration of so many top scientists to one place finally got Kearns's attention. He and his right-hand man,

Bill Glavin, flew to DEC headquarters outside Boston to implore Ken Olson, its founder and CEO, to halt the raid on PARC. They even delivered a rather fatuous warning that Xerox was a very large DEC customer . . . for the moment.

Nothing ever came of the threat. But as Kearns later recounted, a few years later Olson pulled him aside at a corporate chief executive's conference to complain about the Palo Alto SRC's independent-minded engineers.

"We're having some difficulty with the group," he griped, "now that we're trying to tie them more directly to the business strategy."

Kearns chuckled. "Ken," he said, "that's how you got them in the first place."

Spencer, meanwhile, was left with the task of restoring the morale of dozens of PARC engineers shocked and upset at Taylor's departure. Shortly after the ouster he joined the Learning Research Group at one of its last Pajaro Dunes retreats.

The atmosphere of change could not have been stronger. Kay and his fecund imagination were gone. Adele Goldberg and Dave Robson had published the first commercial guide to Smalltalk, which Xerox had officially released to the public.

PARC's original three laboratories had fissioned into six, including the Intelligent Systems Laboratory under John Seely Brown—spun off from SSL, which was recast as the System Concepts Laboratory under Goldberg. With the exception of the Optical Science Laboratory, which was still headed by John Urbach, all of the original PARC labs had new managers.

Spencer took it as his duty to communicate to Alan Kay's old group how different the world had become. The PARC of Jack Goldman and George Pake, of researchers following their instincts into a new world without the least concern for corporate imperatives, was gone. Pake's original deadline—the ten-year grace period before Xerox would see results from PARC—had passed. In that time the center had given the company the laser printer, Ethernet, and the technology of the Star, but there was more to do. Henceforth the researchers would have to play a more direct role in helping the company exploit their knowledge. People like Taylor, with his worldview of scientific research and corporate profit as two somehow antagonistic forces, were now in the way.

"I can still see myself sitting with Spencer on the steps looking out at the dunes, toward the water," recalled Diana Merry. "I was trying to get him to explain to me why he thought he had to push Taylor out.

"He said, 'Well, you know, he just wouldn't play on the team.'"

Did Xerox Blow It?

X erox could have owned the entire computer industry today. Could have been, you know, a company ten times its size. Could have been IBM—could have been the IBM of the nineties. Could have been the Microsoft of the nineties."

The speaker is Steve Jobs, interviewed for a 1996 public television documentary on the history of the personal computer. The castigation is familiar fare. Almost everyone aware of PARC's achievements also has heard the corollary that Xerox, having invented the technology underlying present-day personal computing, committed the monumental blunder of letting it slip through its fingers.

This image of Xerox as a company uniquely maladroit at exploiting a new technology offers the incontestable allure of a high-concept Hollywood melodrama, in which the protagonists are the inventors of dazzling innovations and the villain is the dead hand of corporate bureaucracy. The record is certainly damning: Xerox had the Alto; IBM launched the Personal Computer. Xerox had the graphical user interface with mouse, icons, and overlapping windows; Apple and Microsoft launched the Macintosh and Windows. Xerox invented What-You-See-Is-What-You-Get word processing; Microsoft brazenly turned it into Microsoft Word and conquered the office market. Xerox invented the Ethernet; today the battle for market share in the networking hardware industry is between Cisco Systems and 3Com. Even the laser printer is a tainted triumph. Thanks to the five years Xerox dithered in bringing it to market, IBM got there first, introducing its own model in 1975.

Nor does the saga lack aspects of comic opera. There is Bob Potter beating John Ellenby in the battle of cost analysis, then losing the battle of the marketplace with an obsolescent machine; Harold Hall launching the company's most far-reaching new product initiative with a second-hand staff of ten; Jim O'Neill vetoing the sale of five printers to Lawrence Livermore National Laboratory because it might cost Xerox $150,000 over the contract term, in a period when the company's profits ran at more than $350 million a year.

When a PARC invention survived Xerox decision-making and reached the market, the determining factor was usually a stubborn champion placing his career on the line. One thinks of the difficult gestation of the 9700 laser printer: Jack Goldman flying two executives to PARC for an eleventh-hour demonstration of its superiority over the CRT-based "Superprinter," followed by Jack Lewis's ignoring three successive directives to kill the project. The factors governing the corporation's decision-making on dozens of occasions when its future hung in the balance were not technologies and opportunities, but personalities and politics.

Yet to chalk up the mixed fate of PARC's technologies purely to Xerox's blundering, as has been done for many years, is misleading. It encourages others to believe that the commercializing of advanced new technologies is easy, provided only that one has the will to do so; and that a company's early domination of a high-tech market will reward it with an unassailable competitive advantage for decades to follow. It presupposes that a corporation should invariably be able to recoup its investment in all its basic research—a mindset bound to lead not to more effective corporate-funded basic research but simply to less of it. And it overlooks Xerox's generous funding of PARC to this day—despite the extinction of SDS, which the research center had been created to serve.

° ° °

The notion that Xerox squandered a golden opportunity to monopolize the personal computer business—that it "fumbled the future," to paraphrase the title of a 1988 case study—rests on several very questionable assumptions. One is that any company can control so polymorphous an industry for very long. The fact is, the technologies of personal computing bestow their commercial favors with great capriciousness.

One need look no further than the roster of companies that at one time or another claimed a lead in computing to see how resolutely the technology foils its tamers. The IBM Personal Computer became the industry standard almost instantly upon its introduction in 1981; yet as of this writing IBM's market share in desktop personal computers is infinitesimal. Apple Computer's Macintosh, the most successful commercial expression of PARC's design principles, was launched in 1983 and by 1985 ranked as the world's most popular personal computer; far from parlaying that advantage into a lasting franchise, Apple committed a series of management blunders that today leave its very existence in doubt. (At the very moment Steve Jobs was so self-confidently critiquing Xerox's performance for PBS, his old company was sinking toward a single-digit market share for the first time since the launch of the Macintosh. It soon breached this dubious milestone.) AT&T, Sony, even Exxon all tried to grab a share of the PC business by throwing their marketing muscle behind the packaging of cutting-edge technology, and all suffered embarrassing flops.

At this writing Microsoft remains the single most formidable force in the computer industry. This position it achieved thanks not to hardware but (as Butler Lampson, Alan Kay, and Bob Taylor predicted would happen) to the power of software. Yet Microsoft is not without challenges that may someday condemn it to the same fate as IBM, whose market position was once considered every bit as unassailable. These challenges include an antitrust attack by the government, the appearance of new technology platforms in which its dominion is less than absolute, and distracting and costly dalliances in entertainment "content" and cable television services. Tomorrow may bring new, unexpected threats. Whether Microsoft itself will be the "Microsoft of the nineties," in Steve Jobs's phrase, will not be known until well after the turn of the millennium.

Another dubious assumption is that Xerox, simply by dint of its size and marketing savvy, should have been well up to the demands of commercializing the Alto, Ethernet, and dozens of other orphaned PARC innovations. This argument is most often expressed as a question: "If little Apple could sell personal computers, why couldn't big Xerox?"

The answer, of course, is that Apple was able to market the PC not in spite of its small size, but *because* of it.

Commercializing a radical new technology often means betting the company on the outcome. In 1981 this had decidedly different meanings for Xerox and Apple. Xerox employed 125,000 workers, Apple forty. Virtually Xerox's entire workforce was focused on selling one type of product: the office copier. They represented decades of corporate investment—hundreds of millions of dollars—in embedded training, technology, and customer service.

This might not have been an impediment if the customer bases for copiers and computers were identical. But for the most part they were quite different. Through the 1980s, copiers typically were high-volume machines designed to be installed in central copy rooms inhabited by clerks and secretaries. They were ordered by the same managers who handled the purchases of typewriters and telephones. But computers were systems, designed to support corporate professionals a rung or two further up the ladder. Their purchasing came under the jurisdiction of a new category of professional information manager, a breed entirely unfamiliar to the platoons of copier salesmen on Xerox's payroll.

Apple, obviously, faced none of these issues. Young and agile, it was in a perfect position to build suitable factories and a computer-oriented sales force from the ground up—just as Xerox had been when it chose to commercialize another innovative and suspect technology, fifteen years earlier. In fact, the two companies' relationship perfectly illustrates the "creative destruction" model of industrial evolution proposed by Joseph Schumpeter in the 1930s, in which entrepreneurial opportunists snatch markets away from their anachronistic precursors.

Computers, moreover, did not lend themselves to the pricing regime that many considered Xerox's most important invention: leasing the copiers and charging customers by the page. When 250 Xerox salesmen contemplated the Alto on Futures Day and wondered, "Where's the click?" they were asking a question fundamental to the difference between the old machines and the new. To sell computers, Xerox would not only have to build a new kind of machine, but also a new system of compensating and motivating its more than 100,000 sales executives. The combined task of retooling plants, retraining factory workers and salesmen, and adjusting to the mentality of a new set of customers resembled that of turning a supertanker around in mid-ocean.

History suggests that corporations are seldom able to remake themselves as thoroughly as a Xerox trying to turn into a computer company. How many leading American corporations have survived multiple revolutions in industrial technology to stay atop the business pyramid for more than two or three decades? With the exception of perennial leaders such as General Electric and, possibly, Hewlett-Packard, the examples are scarce. The more usual pattern is that a company is granted one or two runs at the fence before it is finally overmatched by changes beyond its control—as a sort of corporate Darwinism ruthlessly ensures that openings will always exist for fresh entrepreneurial companies to arise and nurture the technologies that make every generation's future.

Even under the best circumstances, the Xerox of the 1970s and 1980s was not a promising candidate to exploit a new technology, governed as it was by the twin burdens of its culture and its business environment.

Its culture was formed by betting on a long shot and seeing it come up trumps. For Xerox the spectacular, instantaneous success of xerography has always been something of a mixed curse. While it brought the company fabulous wealth, it blinded management to the fact that sometimes the marketplace needs time to absorb new technologies.

Xerox "fundamentally was cursed by the Chester Carlson vision," contends its former chief technology officer, Paul Strassmann. "This is the immaculate conception view that all you have to do is give us the right technology and the whole world will come to us. Unfortunately, when it happens like that it's a fluke."

The first generations of post–914 executives were therefore decidedly unreceptive to a business, like computers, that might grow only slowly and for which Xerox would have to battle ferociously for every point of market share. They viewed the Star as the closest thing in computing to the sainted 914—a machine that could spring fully mature from the development pipeline, poised to sweep up the entire market and hold it against all challengers. Had the computer market remained receptive to $16,000 systems-oriented workstations, the Star might well have dominated. But the market, of course, transformed in the blink of an eye into something entirely different. Xerox had no machine to compete with stand-alone desktop workstations costing only $2,000.

Xerox's second burden, too rarely acknowledged by critics of its handling of PARC, was the merciless business environment confronting it during this period. Only a few months after Peter McColough proclaimed the company's commitment to the "architecture of information" his company was overwhelmed by war on multiple fronts—new foreign and domestic competitors, an antitrust investigation by the federal government, and a deteriorating economy. Even a management team seasoned by years of scratching and clawing in competitive markets would have found these challenges daunting; the serene monopolists of Xerox were left as disoriented as weekend sailors caught in an ocean squall.

The distractions of the "lost decade" left more by the wayside than the "architecture of information" battle cry: Although Japanese competitors materialized in force in 1975, Xerox did not introduce a low-cost machine to rival theirs until four years later. It is not surprising that Peter McColough and David Kearns, embroiled in the fight of their lives simply to protect the copier franchise, had scarcely any patience for the revolutionary solutions being floated for the tough problems of technology transfer at PARC.

In 1972, for example, Jack Goldman presented McColough with a novel plan to expedite the manufacture of laser printers by spinning off an entrepreneurial manufacturing venture. "The idea was to start a little company in the Palo Alto area," Goldman recalled. "Guys were ready to jump ship and build in garages, assuming Xerox was willing to make available the xerographic engines. They would get venture financing. One-third would go to capital, one-third to the employees, and one-third to Xerox for providing the Xerox machines.

"McColough would absolutely not hear of it at all. His attitude on such things back in the 1970s was that we could not encourage our people to go off like that when they had a good idea, otherwise we'd lose their loyalty. Of course, they all went off anyway, people like Chuck Geschke and Bob Metcalfe who went to start their own companies, not to speak of Charles Simonyi who went off to Microsoft and brought Microsoft Word with him." Today the sort of spinoffs Goldman proposed are commonplace at Xerox. But the company needed ten years—and a complete change of management—to learn that lesson.

Of the many mistakes Xerox committed in handling PARC technology, some were clearly visible in advance, others only in hindsight. Critics should never confuse the two. The former category includes such blunders as the unnecessary delay in marketing the laser printer and the repeated rejection of the Alto as an alternative to the nonprogrammable electromechanical word processors manufactured in Dallas.

In the marketing of the Star, however, many decisions that appear short-sighted or perverse in retrospect made perfect sense at the time. The Star was designed in part to serve a market many office equipment pundits of the day expected to thrive for decades: for large-scale, closed, fully integrated office systems—"turnkey" systems—that would be sold and serviced exclusively by the vendor (i.e., Xerox). That this architecture seemed inevitable is unsurprising, for it was the perfect analogue to the large-scale, closed, turnkey mainframe office data processing systems the Star would replace.

The Star's software was not designed to be accessible to outside software engineers—as would be that of the IBM PC and the Macintosh—for two reasons. One was that no independent software industry existed at the time. (It would not emerge until the mid–1980s.) The other was that software was then quite clearly deemed not to be patentable; the U.S. patent office would not even accept an application. Although it was possible to copyright particular screen displays and certain sequences of code, that was a feeble protection against theft of the intellectual ideas embodied in the system—as was shown by Apple's unsuccessful lawsuit against Microsoft for copying the "look and feel" of the Macintosh display in Windows.

For the most part, the computer scientists and engineers of PARC's early years are ambivalent about the research center's relationship with Xerox. They remember the frustrations of trying to communicate the significance of their inventions to East Coast executives who viewed them as alien technologies. Yet they cannot forget that Xerox brought them together, paid them handsomely, and allowed them with considerable forbearance to pursue their own dreams of a personal interactive computer.

Some who have gone on to chair their own corporations or research labs would not dare to grant their employees the same latitude they enjoyed themselves. Says Chuck Geschke, co-founder and chairman of Adobe Systems, "Our attitude at PARC was sort of that it was a higher calling to do pure research. But here at Adobe our advanced technology group does not just stay in advanced technology. If they put together the germ of an idea and start to get it close to prototyping and even decide to turn it into a product, we encourage them to follow it all the way through to first customer shipment. The only way I know to transfer technology is with people."

Others salute their troubled parent for tolerating them as long as it did. "When SDS crashed and burned Xerox might have decided that all this electronics stuff isn't what it's cracked up to be, in which case the whole thing would have disintegrated," observes Butler Lampson. "But in fact they stuck to their original charter with great tenacity. At least that's the way it looked to us."

Some were grateful for the opportunity to create, and rather indifferent to the issue of who eventually booked the profits. Still others are aware that PARC's staff only rarely took the lead in forcing an understanding of the technology upon their corporate bosses.

"All of us who worked there enjoyed blaming Xerox for what went wrong," observes Bob Metcalfe. "But Xerox gave us the job. Why blame them? So few of us accepted responsibility."

One last misconception about PARC—indeed, about any research center engaged in open-ended fundamental research—is that the corporation is somehow obligated to exploit every idea the lab throws off. In a sufficiently broad-based research program, some ideas will simply not fit into the corporation's business.

"One of Pake's lines was that a great research organization produces a lot of ideas that its company can't use," says John Shoch. "He was saying that you shouldn't be surprised when the business planners turn down an idea."

Yet this notion of the corporate research center as a sort of public benefit, like endowing college scholarships for the needy or underwriting opera performances on television, is the one for which Xerox is most commonly derided.

"I sometimes wonder now if Xerox isn't unduly pummeled because they failed to realize such monumental opportunities," Gary Starkweather says. "John Sculley [the former chairman of Apple, where Starkweather worked after leaving PARC] said to me once, 'I don't ever want a PARC.' I said, 'Why not?' He said, 'All the technology leaked out.' I said, 'You just want the ability to control such an institution, not to not have the institution.'"

But Sculley's view remains the prevalent one. No corporate lab exists today that resembles the PARC of the 1970s and 1980s, not even the PARC of the 1990s, where great advances are being made in physics, information science, and graphic technologies. There are several reasons for this, some having to do with the life cycle of technological change. For the science of computing is no longer at the historic inflection point it occupied at the start of the 1970s, when every step on the road of discovery was the equivalent of a giant leap into a new world.

A more important reason, however, is that the corporate landscape has changed, perhaps inalterably. No company, no matter how wealthy, dares devote even a fraction of its wealth to a search for knowledge that may not produce a return to the bottom line, as Xerox did. The utopian ideal of a corporate laboratory whose scientists are free to roam through Ideaspace draws only ridicule today. Consider Microsoft, the company that comes closest to the Xerox of 1970, at least in terms of its torrential cash flow. It is no coincidence that Microsoft Research today employs Butler

Lampson, Chuck Thacker, Charles Simonyi, Gary Starkweather, and Alvy Ray Smith. It is engaged in as explicit an attempt to replicate Xerox PARC as any company has attempted in recent years. Yet even Bill Gates, Microsoft's chairman, prefers to define Microsoft Research in terms of what PARC was not: "We didn't want a situation like Xerox, where the research was decoupled from product design. [We want] people who are supersmart but also have a desire to see their work in use."

This does not mean that great discoveries, even surprising ones, will not be made here and there by researchers working for corporations. It simply means that a certain quality once possessed by PARC in its extraordinary early years seems to have departed from the world of science and technology, perhaps forever. Call it magic.

Afterlives

Daniel G. Bobrow is a senior researcher at Xerox PARC.

David R. Boggs lives in northern California, where he designs and markets a new generation of networking circuit boards.

John Seely Brown is chief scientist of Xerox and director of PARC.

Lynn A. Conway is professor of electrical engineering and computer science at the University of Michigan.

L. Peter Deutsch lives in northern California, where he develops and markets a version of GhostScript, a page description language related to PostScript.

William Duvall, who lives in Idaho, invented Surfwatch, a program to prevent children from inadvertently encountering objectionable websites while surfing the Internet.

Jerome I. Elkind is retired and living in northern California, where he is helping develop software to help the disabled use computers.

John Ellenby founded Grid Systems to develop and market laptop computers, then sold it to Tandy Corporation, the owner of the Radio Shack retail chain. He has since founded GeoVector, which develops and markets marine navigation and communication devices.

Douglas Fairbairn is a vice president and general manager at Cadence Design Systems, a maker of VLSI design tools in San Jose, California.

Edward R. Fiala is a senior researcher at Adobe Systems in San Jose, California.

Charles M. Geschke is co-founder and co-chairman (with **John Warnock**), and president of Adobe Systems, Inc.

Adele Goldberg is a co-founder of Neometron, a Redwood City, California, company that develops learning and management tools for the Internet and other projects. Earlier she co-founded ParcPlace, a joint venture with Xerox to develop Smalltalk applications.

Jacob E. Goldman is retired and living in Connecticut, where he is a private investor.

William F. Gunning is largely retired, but still reports regularly to his Xerox office in Palo Alto.

Harold H. Hall retired to his family home in South Dakota.

Chris Jeffers is president of Teklicon, a northern California firm that provides experts on science and technology for parties involved in lawsuits and patent and insurance cases.

Richard E. Jones retired from Xerox in 1998. He lives in southern California.

Alan C. Kay is a fellow at Walt Disney Imagineering in Glendale, California, where his research group includes **Ted Kaehler** and **Daniel H. Ingalls**. He worked briefly at Atari after leaving PARC and subsequently joined Apple Computer as an Apple Fellow, leaving in 1996.

Butler W. Lampson is a fellow at Microsoft Research in Cambridge, Massachusetts, and an adjunct professor at the Massachusetts Institute of Technology.

David Liddle is chairman and chief executive officer of Interval Research Corporation, a high-technology think tank located within walking distance of PARC and funded by Microsoft co-founder Paul Allen.

Edward M. McCreight is a senior researcher at Adobe Systems in San Jose, California.

Carver A. Mead is Gordon and Betty Moore Professor of Engineering and Applied Science at the California Institute of Technology.

Diana Merry-Shapiro lives in New York City and works for J. P. Morgan & Co. as a consultant on Smalltalk-based programming systems.

Robert M. Metcalfe co-founded 3Com Corporation in 1979 and retired from the company in 1990, when its annual revenues approached one-half-billion dollars. He is vice president/technology at International Data Group, a publisher of computer industry trade journals, and a weekly columnist on networking and telecommunications issues for IDG's *InfoWorld*.

James G. Mitchell is vice president for technology and architecture for the Javasoft division of Sun Microsystems, the developer of the Java programming language.

James H. Morris is H. A. Simon Professor of Human-Computer Interaction and chairman of the department of computer science at Carnegie-Mellon University.

Timothy Mott is a venture capital investor and lives in Idaho.

Severo Ornstein is retired and living with his wife, the former PARC researcher **Laura Gould**, in northern California. In 1981, concerned about the threat of nuclear war, he co-founded Computer Professionals for Social Responsibility.

George E. Pake is retired and living in northern California.

Max Palevsky is a self-employed industrialist and private investor in Southern California.

Ron Rider is vice president of Xerox's Digital Imaging Technology Center in Palo Alto.

John F. Shoch is a venture capital investor at Asset Management Inc. in northern California.

Richard Shoup, who has been awarded an Emmy and an Oscar for his work on digital paint systems, left PARC in 1979 to co-found Aurora Systems, a developer and manufacturer of digital videographic and animation system. In 1993 he joined Interval Research Corporation.

Charles Simonyi works at Microsoft Research in Redmond, Washington, where he is developing a programming system known as "intentional programming."

Alvy Ray Smith was director of computer graphics research at Lucasfilm and a co-founder of its spinoff, Pixar. He joined Microsoft as its first graphics fellow in 1994.

William J. Spencer, who retired in 1990 as Xerox's chief technical officer, is chairman of Sematech, a joint research initiative formed by ten U.S. semiconductor companies.

Robert Spinrad retired as Xerox vice president for technology strategy in 1998. He lives in northern California.

Robert F. Sproull is a vice president of Sun Microsystems, Inc., and a fellow of Sun Laboratories, its research center.

M. Frank Squires joined Sematech in 1991 as chief administrative officer. He died in May 1998, shortly after being named managing director of the consortium's international branch.

Gary K. Starkweather, who joined Apple Computer after leaving PARC, is now a fellow at Microsoft Research in Redmond, Washington.

Paul Strassmann lives in Connecticut, where he is a private consultant on corporate information management.

William R. (Bert) Sutherland is vice president of Sun Microsystems, Inc., and director of Sun Laboratories, its research center, which he joined upon its founding in 1990.

Robert W. Taylor retired as director of Digital Equipment Corp.'s Systems Research Laboratory in 1997. He lives in northern California.

Warren Teitelman is Vice President of Research and Development at BayStone Software, a developer of integrated sales and marketing software for corporate clients.

Lawrence G. Tesler, who stayed at Apple Computer until 1998, rising to the position of chief scientist, is now president of Stagecast Inc., a developer of interactive simulation software in Palo Alto, California.

Charles P. Thacker worked for DEC until 1997, when he resigned from the Systems Research Center to join Microsoft Research in Cambridge, U.K.

David Thornburg, director of the Thornburg Center for Professional Development, is a lecturer and consultant on the uses of technology in education.

John C. Urbach is retired and living in northern California.

John Warnock is co-founder and co-chairman (with **Chuck Geschke**) and chief executive officer of Adobe Systems.

Source Notes

The bulk of the material for this book comes from hundreds of hours of interviews I conducted with the individuals whose lives and work are chronicled in the preceding pages. For the most part, the reader can assume that direct quotes of individuals in the text are drawn from those interviews. Where that is not the case or the context might invite confusion between secondary and primary source material, the origin of the quotation is identified below.

Introduction: The Time Machine
Page
xxv Bill Gates's defense: Manes & Andrews, *Gates*, p. 361.
xxvii Didn't even patent: "Xerox Won't Duplicate Past Errors," *Business Week*, 9/29/97, p. 98.
The Alto failed: Stross, Randall E., "Mr. Gates Builds His Brain Trust," *Fortune*, December 8, 1997.

Chapter 1: The Impresario
8 The notion of a human: Palfreman & Swade, *The Dream Machine*, p. 97.

9 "The Computer as a Communications Device": *Science & Technology*, April 1968.

12 That made me nervous: Licklider Oral History, Charles Babbage Institute, University of Minnesota.

12 I did not feel: Ibid.

Chapter 2: McColough's Folly

22 McColough thought: George White, 10/6/97.

24 If we're going to be big: McColough, quoted in Jacobson & Hillkirk, *Xerox: American Samurai*, p. 214.

24 Peter turned over: White.

25 He should have known: Goldman, 11/6/97.

25 The only ballgame: Jacobson & Hillkirk, p. 214.

26 determined to make a deal: Palevsky, 4/21/98.

26 very, very short: *Los Angeles Times*, 2/11/69.

29 It had been making profits: Jacobson & Hillkirk, p. 214.

29 It was a great phrase: David Liddle, 6/17/98.

30 He was talking: Richard Jones, 3/10/98.

30 He never tired: White

31 If the new research center: Goldman, *Proposal for a New Corporate Advanced Scientific & Systems Laboratory*, 6/23/69.

Chapter 3: The House on Porter Drive

41 I'm one of the oldest: Wes Clark Oral History, Charles Babbage Institute, University of Minnesota

41 That of a very large: Clark, "The LINC Was Early and Small" in Goldberg (ed.), *A History of Personal Workstations*, p. 357. (Italics in original.)

41 Time-sharers were still: Clark oral history.

41 At that time computers: Severo Ornstein Oral History, Charles Babbage Institute.

44 During his time at ARPA: Robert Taylor, J. C. R. Licklider oral histories, Charles Babbage Institute

44-45 Taylor conversation with Herzfeld: Taylor oral history; Taylor to author, 9/10/98.

45 I blackmailed: Ibid.

46 It was ridiculous: Ibid.

47 Taylor visits to Vietnam: Taylor, Wessler interviews; Taylor oral history.

47 the White House got a single report: Taylor oral history.

Chapter 4: Utopia

56 Xerox's "lost decade": Jacobson & Hillkirk, p. 69.

59–60 Goldman's meeting: Thornburg interview 9/12/97; Perry & Wallich, "Inside the PARC: The 'Information Architects,'" *IEEE Spectrum*, October 1985, p. 72.

61 PARC pay scale: Frank Squires, 1/8/98.

64 Engelbart first encountered: Engelbart, "The Augmented Knowledge Workshop," in Goldberg, p. 234.

65 No one is quite sure: Ibid., p. 196.

65 We built special electronics . . . Don't tell me!: Ibid., p. 203.

66 a prophet of biblical dimensions: Kay, *The Early History of Smalltalk*, p. 7 (in manuscript) (henceforth *Smalltalk*).

67 rats running in his maze: Smokey Wallace, 11/16/97.

Chapter 5: Berkeley's Second System

74 The second is the most dangerous: Brooks, *The Mythical Man-Month*, p. 55.

Chapter 6: "Not Your Normal Person"

80 Alan believed his role: Harrold, "The Organ at the Alan Kay & Bonnie MacBird Residence," in *The American Organ Academy Newsletter*, Winter 1996.

85 Computers' use of symbols: Kay, "Microelectronics and the Personal Computer," *Scientific American*, Sept. 1977, p. 244.

86 By the time I got to school: Shasta and Lazere, *Out of Their Minds* (1995), pp. 39–40.

89 As he toiled in Chippewa: Kay, *Smalltalk*, p. 4.

90 Take this and read it: Ibid., p. 5.

91 you had to understand that: Shasta and Lazere, p. 42.

91 like seeing a glimpse of heaven: Palfreman & Swade, p. 96.

91 Minsky's "terrific diatribe": Kay, p. 9.

92 The best outputs: Kay, "Microelectronics and the Personal Computer," p. 127.

92 If the medium: Kay and Goldberg, "Personal Dynamic Media," in Goldberg (ed.), *A History of Personal Workstations*, p. 256.

93 users found repellent: Kay quoted in Rheingold, *Tools for Thought*, Chapter 11 (Internet version, unpaged).

94 The big whammy: Kay, *The Early History of Smalltalk*, pp. 9–10.

Chapter 7: The Clone

99 I must be on every sucker list: *New York Times*, 6/26/72.

99 We sold them a dead horse: DeLamarter, *Big Blue*, p. 100.

99 He denied: Palevsky interview, 4/21/98.

100 Palevsky fantasizes about IBM: "Xerox-SDS: Marriage That Was Meant to Be?" *Los Angeles Times*, 2/11/69.

100 Telling McColough what he wanted to hear: Palevsky interview, 4/21/98.

101 IBM and competitors' financial results: Delamarter, p. 352.

110 Intel's problems with the 1103: Jackson, *Inside Intel*, p. 79.

111 Pake memo to management: Smith & Alexander, *Fumbling the Future*, pp. 145–146; Pake interview, 5/19/97.

Chapter 8: The Future Invented

118 The IMPs formed a subnetwork: Hafner & Lyon, *Where Wizards Stay Up Late*, p. 80.

118 Jerry was not universally liked: Severo Ornstein Oral History, Charles Babbage Institute, University of Minnesota.

122 Pendery really didn't understand . . . to invent it: Kay, *Smalltalk*, p. 13.

Chapter 9: The Refugee

143 A bunch of horse's asses: Perry & Wallich, p. 67.

143 It was Monday night: Goldman interview, 5/6/97.

144 Jack Lewis saving the 9700: Harold Hall, personal communication.

Chapter 10: Beating the Dealer

152 continuous form of peer review: Thacker, "The Alto and Ethernet Hardware," in Goldberg, p. 268.

Chapter 11: Spacewar

160–161 I recall almost a sadness: Perry & Wallich, p. 72; Thornburg, 9/12/97.

Chapter 12: Thacker's Bet

163 Thacker-Lampson-Kay conversation: Kay, *Smalltalk*, p. 18.

164 Origin of "Smalltalk" name: Ibid., p. 14.

164 Kay meeting with Elkind: Ibid., p. 16.

166 What's a budget: Ibid., p. 19; English, 5/21/97.

169 Chronology of the Alto design: Kay, *Smalltalk*, p. 19; Thacker, in Goldberg, p. 274.

170 Ron Rider . . . put it together himself: Perry & Wallich, p. 66. The manager quoted was Bert Sutherland.

170 *quality* of man-machine interaction: Thacker in Goldberg, p. 272.

Chapter 13: The Bobbsey Twins Build a Network

179 He padded over: Metcalfe, "How Ethernet Was Invented," in *IEEE Annals of the History of Computing*, vol. 16, no. 4, p. 84.

179 The first time I ever heard: Ted Kaehler, 4/18/97.

185 The ultimate 29-Nova: Metcalfe, p. 83.

185 too many moving parts: Ibid.

187 luminiferous aether: Ibid.

189 There was no chip . . . every piece of it: Ibid., p. 84; Metcalfe, 9/15/97.

191 Ethernet was up against: Ibid., p. 86.

192 One after another of my colleagues: Ibid., p. 87.

Chapter 14: What You See Is What You Get

195 All this was very exhilarating: Lammers, *Programmers at Work*, p. 9.

196 with an incredible headache: Ibid., p. 8.

Chapter 15: On the Lunatic Fringe

211 The graphics researcher . . . e-mail message: Perry & Wallich, p. 68.

212 Warren Teitelman once returned: Ibid., p. 68.

213 Millions of people: Lampson, guest editorial in *Software-Practice and Experience*, vol. 2, pp. 195–196.

218 With as much panache: Kay, *Smalltalk*, p. 18.

225 Article in *New West*: Johnston, "Will Your Next Home Appliance Be a Mini-Computer?" in *New West*, 3/14/1977, p. 50. Goldman's memo was dated March 1, 1977.

Chapter 16: The Pariahs

237 Here's our stuff: Perry & Wallich, p. 68; Alvy Ray Smith, 12/5/97.

Chapter 17: The Big Machine

245 friendly, direct: Hall, personal communication.

247 Its target users: "The New Lean, Mean Xerox," *Business Week*, 10/12/81, p. 129.

247 We'll just lose: Spinrad, 10/16/97.

254 Committee for Green Foothills: "Xerox Deal May Settle Dispute on Coyote Hill," *Palo Alto Times*, 9/21/72, p. 1.

255 The local newspapers: "Xerox Scientists in Palo Alto Preparing for Office of Future," *Palo Alto Times*, 1/24/75, p. 6.

255 The stock: Kearns & Nadler, *Prophets in the Dark*, p. 88.

255 Corporate legend has it: Currie, 6/2/97.

255–256 Odyssey's conclusion: Kearns, p. 87.

Chapter 18: Futures Day

263 Potter's visit to PARC: Smith and Alexander, *Fumbling the Future*, p. 168.

265 huge blow: Kay, *Smalltalk*, p. 32.

266 Ellenby responded: Geschke, 10/16/97.

269 Moses was supposed to: Jacobson & Hillkirk, p. 75.

270 We are being out-marketed . . . within this company: Smith & Alexander, p. 197; Kearns & Nadler, p. 100.

270 The architecture of information: Smith & Alexander, p. 201.

271 this part of the demonstration: Ellenby, 10/15/97.

Chapter 19: Future Plus One

276 The small fonts: Kay, *Smalltalk*, p. 35.

278 The place . . . just sort of drifted: Kearns & Nadler, p. 103.

279 He'd come into my office: McCreight, 10/7/97.

281 He chose to buy time: Smith & Alexander, p. 244.

285–286 Carter would hop . . . we don't act on hunches: Kearns & Nadler, pp. 40–41.

287 Wenrik tested it against the judgments: Smith & Alexander, p. 213.

325 It was difficult to think: Thacker in Goldberg, p. 285.

326 They were such an efficient heater: Sosinski.

327 Xerox executives made: Perry & Wallich, p. 73.

Chapter 23: Steve Jobs Gets His Show and Tell

330 You can have your Lufthansa heist: Steven Levy, *Insanely Great*, p. 78.

331 Joe Wilson had predicted: Jacobson & Hillkirk, , p. 58.

331 The answer was to create: George White, 10/6/97.

332 When the company raised $7 million: Michael Moritz, *The Little Kingdom*, p. 271.

332 Raskin recollection of Jobs and Wozniak: Raskin, "Mac and Me," in *The Analytical Engine* 2.4, November 1995 (Computer History Association of California).

Chapter 24: Supernova

346 you gotta be here in Connecticut: Pake, 5/19/97.

349 office systems will never amount: Hall, private communication.

350–351 my junior on the board: Smith & Alexander, p. 216.

358–359 I projected supreme confidence: Simonyi, 12/4/97.

359 Bill has to see this: Manes & Andrews, p. 166.

360 Gates at PARC: Ibid., p. 167.

360 Gates could read the program: Ibid., p. 167.

360 messenger RNA: Simonyi, 12/4/97.

Chapter 25: Blindsided

363 I had not spent . . . marketplace: Smith & Alexander, p. 229.

363 I think we have another 914: "The New Lean, Mean Xerox," in *Business Week*, 10/12/81, p. 132.

365 When everything in a computer system: David C. Smith in Jeff Johnson et. al., "The Xerox Star: A Retrospective," in *IEEE Computer*, September 1989, p. 15.

367 It's a good product: *Business Week*, 10/12/81, p. 132.

369–370 Everything you've ever done: Belleville in Manes & Andrews, p. 224.

Chapter 26: Exit the Impresario

381 My response . . . not me: Taylor, 5/1/98.

382 Most people spend: Smith & Alexander, p. 253.

383 You can fucking *resign!*: Sosinski & Yeary.

386 Olson conversation with Kearns: Kearns & Nadler, p. 104.

Epilogue: Did Xerox Blow It?

389 Xerox could have owned: *Triumph of the Nerds*, broadcast on PBS 6/12/96.

397 We didn't want: Stross.

Glossary of Selected Terms

ARPA: The Advanced Research Projects Agency of the Department of Defense, established after the Soviet Sputnik launch of 1957 to marshal America's scientific resources in a research counterattack. By the mid–1960s the principal source of funding for computer science in U.S. academia.

ARPANET: The Pentagon-financed system interconnecting incompatible mainframe computers at research centers and universities across the country; in time evolved into the Internet.

ASCII: The "American Standard Code for Information Interchange," a table of 128 simple letters, numerals, and other characters, each of which can be encoded in seven binary digits, or bits; until the emergence of WYSIWYG displays, ASCII text was the standard, charmless format of computer display and printing.

Bit: From "binary digit," the smallest unit of information that can be read or used by a digital computer. A bit can be set to one of two values, often signified by 0 or 1, true or false, or yes or no.

Bitmap: A display in which each dot, or pixel, on the screen corresponds to one or more bits in computer memory. Thus turning on a pattern of bits in memory can create a corresponding image on the screen. Because of the speed at which it can be altered, the bitmapped display is the essential element of graphical user interfaces like those developed at PARC.

Boolean functions: The mathematical and logical elements at the heart of digital computing. Boolean functions are based on two values, usually represented as true and false. An AND function, or AND gate in a computer's circuitry, for example, will return a "true" value only if both of its inputs are "true," and a "false" value in all other cases. The NOT function returns the converse of its input— "true" if the input is "false," and vice versa. From such trivial functions and their cousins machines can be built that add, subtract, multiply, divide, and do much more.

Byte: A string of eight bits (by current convention) large enough to encode a single character or symbol to be input to a computer or output to its display.

Central processing unit: The brains of a computer, which supervises such other parts (or "peripherals") as the disk drives and printers and controls their access to memory and display.

Internet: Capitalized, the worldwide network of research and commercial computer sites that grew out of the ARPANET. Lower case, any interconnection of discrete local networks.

Killer app: Abridgment of "killer application." Any program that so perfectly exploits its hardware that it radically speeds the hardware's adoption. Examples include the Bravo word processing program, which ran on the Alto, and VisiCalc, the digital spreadsheet that made the Apple II computer a coveted business tool.

Kludge (pronounced "klooge"): An overelaborate and frequently temperamental device or system, often one designed or built over time to serve incrementally broadened or inconsistent goals. Think Rube Goldberg.

LAN: "Local Area Network." A network of adjacent and usually compatible computers, often within a single building or a one-kilometer radius. Numerous rival LAN designs emerged during the 1970s, often promoted by individual computer companies to lock customers into using their proprietary machines (as with IBM and the "token ring"). Ethernet's standardization after 1980 made it the most common.

Moore's Law: The principle articulated by Gordon Moore in 1965 that computing power would exponentially increase in performance and diminish in cost over the years along a predictable curve, so that digital memory costing $500,000 in 1965 would come all the way down to a few hundred dollars by 1998. This is the force behind the unprecedented influence technology exerts over modern life.

Second system: From Frederick Brooks's *The Mythical Man-Month*. The often-unsuccessful sequel to a successful first project, whether this is a machine, program, novel, or building. As Brooks noted, second systems tend to incorporate all the extras that a creative team was forced by penury or haste to leave out of their first. The result is a product that is overly complicated, overly expensive, and late.

TCP/IP: "Transmission Control Protocol over Internet Protocol." The set of standardized rules for the transmission of data over networks that allows disparate computer systems to remain synchronized enough to communicate reliably with each other. The "IP" element grew out of PARC's development of the PUP, or "PARC Universal Packet," which allowed Xerox offices with incompatible computers to communicate with each other.

Time-sharing: A system allowing several users to run programs simultaneously on one computer without interfering with each other. When computers were costly and centralized machines, this was the standard means of accessing computer resources. Technologies such as the personal computer made time-sharing obsolete.

VLSI: "Very Large Scale Integration." The incorporation of millions of transistors in a single integrated circuit, or chip, to provide computing power a quantum leap beyond that previously available. VLSI's offspring include the Pentium family of chips powering many of today's personal computers and laptops. The design principles of VLSI were pioneered by researchers working at PARC and the California Institute of Technology.

WYSIWYG: "What you see is what you get." Describes a system in which the computer user interacts with the machine visually through a screen display that offers instant feedback to inputs such as mouse clicks and keystrokes. Also refers to programs whose screen images—a document page, for example—can be exactly duplicated by a printer.

Bibliography

Books

Biermann, Alan W. *Great Ideas in Computer Science*. Cambridge, Mass.: MIT Press, 1990.

Brand, Stewart. *The Media Lab*. New York: Viking, 1987.

Brooks, Frederick P., Jr. *The Mythical Man-Month* (Anniversary Edition). New York: Addison-Wesley, 1995.

Cringely, Robert X. *Accidental Empires: How the Boys of Silicon Valley Make Their Empires, Battle Foreign Competition, and Still Can't Get a Date*. Menlo Park, Calif.: Addison-Wesley, 1992.

DeLamarter, Richard Thomas. *Big Blue: IBM's Use and Abuse of Power*. New York: Dodd, Mead, 1986.

Dessauer, John H. *My Years with Xerox: The Billions Nobody Wanted*. Garden City, N.Y.: Doubleday, 1971.

Feynmann, Richard I. *The Feynmann Lectures on Computing* (Anthony J. G. Hay and Robin W. Allen, eds.). Reading, Mass.: Addison-Wesley, 1996.

Freiberger, Paul, and Michael Swaine. *Fire in the Valley: The Making of the Personal Computer.* Berkeley, Calif.: Osborne/McGraw-Hill, 1984.

Gelernter, David. *Machine Beauty: Elegance and the Heart of Technology.* New York: Basic Books, 1998.

Gleick, James. *Genius: The Life and Science of Richard I. Feynmann.* New York: Pantheon Books, 1992.

Goldberg, Adele, ed. *A History of Personal Workstations.* Reading, Mass.: ACM Press, 1988.

Hafner, Katie, and John Markoff. *Cyberpunk: Outlaws and Hackers on the Computer Frontier.* New York: Simon & Schuster, 1992.

Hafner, Katie, and Matthew Lyon. *Where Wizards Stay up Late: The Origins of the Internet.* New York: Simon & Schuster, 1996.

Hodges, Andrew. *Alan Turing: The Enigma.* New York: Simon & Schuster, 1983.

Jackson, Tim. *Inside Intel.* New York: Dutton, 1997.

Jacobson, Gary, and John Hillkirk. *Xerox: American Samurai.* New York: Macmillan, 1986.

Kearns, David T., and David A. Nadler. *Prophets in the Dark.* New York: HarperBusiness, 1992.

Kidder, Tracy. *The Soul of a New Machine.* Boston: Little, Brown, 1981.

Lammers, Susan. *Programmers at Work.* Redmond, Wash.: Microsoft Press, 1986.

Levy, Steven. *Insanely Great.* New York: Viking, 1994.

Malone, Michael S. *The Big Score: The Billion-Dollar Story of Silicon Valley.* Garden City, N.Y.: Doubleday & Co., 1985.

Manes, Stephen, and Paul Andrews. *Gates.* Garden City, N.Y.: Doubleday, 1993.

Marsh, Barbara. *A Corporate Tragedy.* Garden City, New York: Doubleday & Co., 1985.

McConnell, Steve. *Code Complete: A Practical Handbook of Software Construction.* Redmond, Wash.: Microsoft Press, 1993.

Metcalfe, Robert M. *Packet Communications.* San Jose, Calif.: Peer to Peer, 1996.

Moritz, Michael. *The Little Kingdom: The Private Story of Apple Computer*. New York: Morrow, 1984.

Palfreman, Jon, and Doron Swade. *The Dream Machine*. New York: BBC/Parkwest Publishers, 1992.

Reid, T. R. *The Chip*. New York: Simon & Schuster, 1984.

Rheingold, Howard. *Tools for Thought*. New York: Simon & Schuster, 1988.

Shasta, Dennis E., and Cathy A. Lazere. *Out of Their Minds: The Lives and Discoveries of 15 Great Computer Scientists*. New York: Dub-Copernicus, 1995.

Smith, Douglas K., and Robert C. Alexander. *Fumbling the Future*. New York: Morrow, 1988.

Strassmann, Paul A. *The Politics of Information Management*. New Canaan, Conn.: Information Economics Press, 1995.

Stross, Randall E. *Steve Jobs and the NExT Big Thing*. New York: Atheneum, 1993.

Ullmann, Ellen. *Close to the Machine: Technophilia and its Discontents*. San Francisco: City Lights Books, 1997.

Wallace, James, and Jim Erickson. *Hard Drive: Bill Gates and the Making of the Microsoft Empire*. New York: Wiley, 1992.

Oral Histories

Clark, Wesley, interview by Judy O'Neill, New York, N.Y., 3 May 1990. Charles Babbage Institute, University of Minnesota, Minneapolis, Minn.

Engelbart, Douglas C., interview by Jon Eklund, Washington, D.C., 4 May 1984. National Museum of American History, Smithsonian Institution, Washington, D.C.

Jobs, Steven P., interview by Daniel Morrow, Palo Alto, Calif., 20 April 1995. Smithsonian Institution, Washington, D.C.

Licklider, J. C. R., interview by William Aspray and Arthur L. Norberg, Cambridge, Mass., 28 October 1988. Charles Babbage Institute, University of Minnesota, Minneapolis, Minn.

Ornstein, Severo, interview by Judy O'Neill, Woodside, Cal., 6 March 1990. Charles Babbage Institute, University of Minnesota, Minneapolis, Minn.

Sutherland, Ivan, interview by William Aspray, Pittsburgh, Penn., 1 May 1989. Charles Babbage Institute, University of Minnesota, Minneapolis, Minn.

Taylor, Robert W., interview by William Aspray, Palo Alto, Calif., 28 February 1989. Charles Babbage Institute, University of Minnesota, Minneapolis, Minn.

Acknowledgments

I
n a very real sense this book was born one day in September 1996, when Steve Jobs came to lunch at the *Los Angeles Times*. As a technology reporter for the newspaper I was invited to join the select company. I vividly remember Jobs attired in an elegant black turtleneck, a pair of simple wire-rim glasses perched on his aquiline nose. I remember that he picked at his vegetarian lunch while flanked by two of his top lieutenants at Pixar Studios, which had recently scored a resounding success with the release of the movie *Toy Story* and, further, that he steadfastly turned away all questions about the burning high-tech industry issues of the day—Microsoft v. Netscape, the long decline of Apple Computer, *et cetera, et cetera.*

"That's my former life," he said when I tested him with one more query about the ailing Apple (this was well before his return to the company as interim chief executive). "The great thing about being involved with Pixar is that I don't have to think about any of that." With a satisfied grin he spread his arms to take in John Lasseter, the talented director of *Toy Story*, on his right, and Edwin Catmull, Pixar's chief technical officer, on his left.

Jobs hewed to his resolve almost to the very end of the meal. The discussion had drifted onto an oddity of computing history: that the science of computer graphics had virtually been born at the University of Utah. Catmull was an alumnus of this little-known program, as were—he rattled off a hall-of-fame roster: Jim Clark, the founder of Silicon Graphics; John Warnock, co-founder of Adobe Systems; Alan Kay, the renowned proselytizer of personal computing (then at Apple). Bob Taylor, the Pentagon grantmaker who financed the birth of the Internet, had spent a year there. Several of them, he added, went on to refine their work at Xerox PARC.

That gave me one last opening. As a technology writer I could not but have noticed the glancing references to PARC that cropped up repeatedly in newspaper and magazine articles, usually describing it as the source of technology exploited by Microsoft and Apple. I had been unable to find enough written about PARC to fully satisfy my curiosity about the place. But I had learned enough to know at least one famous story—the one about Steve Jobs and his legendary demo.

"Tell me," I said. "You saw what was happening at PARC. Why do you think Xerox never was able to exploit the technology fully?"

Suddenly *Toy Story* and Pixar were forgotten. For the next twenty minutes Jobs was an unstoppable fount of theory and speculation on the subject of PARC. When he was through one thing was clear to me: that much about this story was still waiting to be told.

As I learned over the many months of inquiry and self-education that followed, any project of this scope is necessarily a collaborative effort. My closest collaborators were the scores of scientists, engineers, and executives now or previously associated with Xerox PARC who graciously contributed their time and memories to the foregoing chronicle. Time and again I was astonished and gratified at the enthusiasm with which these busy men and women opened their minds and hearts to help a stranger reconstruct a cherished part of their own pasts. Even stronger than the mystique PARC experts on our own world is the one it exerts on the souls of those who worked there.

They welcomed me into their offices and homes, took time out from pressing business, provided me with invaluable research materials. They submitted to my often uninformed questioning, sometimes over multiple sessions lasting several hours each, followed by further queries by e-mail or telephone. Finally several consented to read drafts of portions of this book to correct stray errors, misconceptions, and injustices. Any that remain are my own.

For their time and recollections I would like to thank William Atkinson, Robert Belleville, David K. Biegelson, Daniel G. Bobrow, David R. Boggs, John Seely Brown, Stuart K. Card, Wesley A. Clark, Lynn Conway, Rigdon Currie, L. Peter Deutsch, Bill Duvall, Jerome I. Elkind, John Ellenby, William English, Douglas Fairbairn, Edward R. Fiala, Charles M. Geschke, Adele Goldberg, Marian Goldeen, Jacob E. Goldman, Laura Gould, William F. Gunning, Harold H. Hall, Daniel H. Ingalls, Charles Irby, Chris Jeffers, Richard E. Jones, Ted Kaehler, Alan C. Kay, Roy Lahr, Butler W. Lampson, Charles Lee, David Liddle, Edward M. McCreight, Carver Mead, Diana Merry-Shapiro, Robert M. Metcalfe, James G. Mitchell, James H. Morris, and Timothy Mott.

Also, Severo Ornstein, George E. Pake, Max Palevsky, Rod Perkins, Steve Purcell, Jef Raskin, Ron Rider, Jeff Rulifson, John F. Shoch, Richard Shoup, Charles Simonyi, Alvy Ray Smith, William J. Spencer, Robert Spinrad, Robert F. Sproull, M. Frank Squires, Gary K. Starkweather, Paul Strassmann, Bert Sutherland, Robert W. Taylor, Warren Teitelman, Lawrence G. Tesler, Charles P. Thacker, David Thornburg, Myron Tribus, John C. Urbach, Smokey Wallace, John Warnock, Barry Wessler, George M. White, and George R. White.

Geri Thoma, my agent at Elaine Markson Literary Agency in New York, contributed her confidence in this project before I was sure a project existed. Laureen Connelly Rowland, my editor at HarperBusiness, strengthened my resolve with her enthusiasm and refined the manuscript immeasurably with her wise and elegant pen. My friends and editors at the *Los Angeles Times* deserve my gratitude for their forbearance over the lengthy period needed to bring this work to fruition.

My wife, Deborah, was a loving and steadfast partner in this project from beginning to end, whether the demand was for the heavy labor of transcribing interviews or for the definitive and lucid insights that alone can rescue a hopelessly snarled chapter from the hell of a weary writer's bewilderment. Lastly, I owe more than I can express to my wonderful sons, Andrew and David, who will inherit the world PARC made.

Index

Artificial intelligence, 91, 98
  Bobrow and, 121, 237, 261
ASCII, 135, 139
"As We May Think" (Bush), 63
Asynchronous architecture, 252–53
Atkinson, Bill, 340, 342–43
Atlantic Richfield Company, 284
AT&T, 30, 53, 57, 391
Augmentation Research Center, 63–67
Aurora Systems, 241

Ballmer, Steve, 358–59
Bardeen, John, 57, 160
Barker, Ben, 180
Bates, Roger, 173
Bauer, Bob, 59
Beat the Dealer (Thorp), 146
Beaudelaire, Patrick, 212, 231
Becker, Joe, 369
Bell, Alexander Graham, xxiii
Belleville, Bob, 250–52, 253, 369–70
Bendix LGP30 computer, 70
Berkeley Computer Corporation, xiv,
    68–69, 73–79, 106, 107–8, 197, 230
  500 computer and, 76, 78, 109
  Genie and, 69, 70, 72–73
  1 computer and, 74–76
Biegelsen, David, 52–53, 58, 152
"Biggerism," Thacker and, xx, 75
Bilbo, 326
Billboard worm, 298
BitBlt, Ingalls and, xv, 226–28, 342
Bitmapped screen
  Alto and, 173–74, 272
  Star and, 362, 364
Blue books, 291
Bobrow, Daniel G., 261, 376, 399
  artificial intelligence and, 121, 237, 261
  Bolt, Beranek & Newman and, 121,
    280, 301
  Elkind and, 280, 281, 282

Boeing Corporation, 284
Boggs, David R., 178–79, 399
  Alto and, 294
  Ethernet and, 141, 176, 187–92
  Futures Day and, 267, 272
  Novas and, 188
  Worm and, 290–91
Bolt, Beranek & Newman, 76, 118, 119,
    120, 121, 180, 265–66, 280, 301, 320
Boolean logic, 109, 304
"Bose Conspiracy," 152–53
Box Named Joe, A, 222
Brand, Stewart
  Rolling Stone and, xv, 155–62, 204, 223
  Whole Earth Catalog and, 157
Bravo, 208–9, 210, 227, 283, 310, 373
  Lampson and, 194, 195, 198, 199, 201
  Simonyi and, xv, 194–95, 198–201
BravoX, 283–84, 285, 364
  Simonyi and, 283, 357, 360
Brittain, William, 57
Brooks, Frederick, 74, 76
Brown, John Seely, 302, 386, 399
Brunner, John, 295–96, 297, 298–99
Brushes, Alto and, 174
Building 34, 140
Burroughs, 24, 89, 101
Bush, Vannevar, 63–64, 67, 122
Buvall, Bill, 64

C++, xiv
Campbell, Sandy, 381–82
"Capability Investment Proposal"
    (Ellenby), 285, 286–87, 288
Card, Stuart, 302
Carlson, Chester, 22, 35, 130, 350, 393
Carnegie-Mellon, 43
Carter, Jimmy, 283–84
Carter, Shelby H., 285–86, 287, 363
CD-ROM, 55, 123
Cedar, 325